MW00615315

View downriver from ruins of Castle Hill, the last SS bastion in Buda. In the immediate foreground, the Elizabeth Bridge collapsed into the Danube. Farther south, the ruins of the Franz Joseph and Southern Railway Bridges.

Cecil D. Eby

HUNGARY AT WAR

Civilians and Soldiers in World War II

The Pennsylvania State University Press
University Park, Pennsylvania

Library of Congress Cataloging-in-Publication Data

Eby, Cecil D.
  Hungary at war / Cecil D. Eby.

    p.   cm.
    Includes bibliographical references and index.
    ISBN 0-271-03244-8
    1. World War, 1939–1945—Hungary.   I. Title.
  D765.56.E33   1998
  940.53'493—dc21   97-29704
                                                                             CIP

It is the policy of The Pennsylvania State University Press to use acid-free paper for
the first printing of all clothbound books. Publications on uncoated stock satisfy
the minimum requirements of American National Standard for Information
Sciences-Permanence of Paper for Printed Library Materials, ANSI Z39.48-1992.

Contents

List of Illustrations

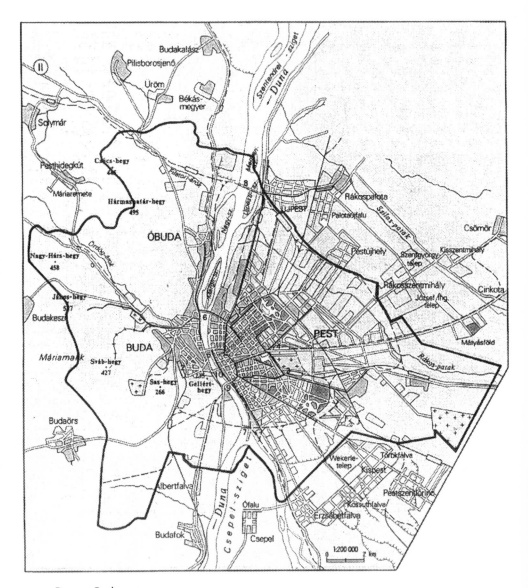

Prewar Budapest

Preface

Although other events of World War II have been chronicled many times from a variety of perspectives, historians of the West have written little about the role of Hungary during that war. The reasons for this neglect are obvious. Because the country was occupied in 1945 by the Soviet Union and was by 1948 sealed hermetically into the Communist bloc, opportunities for "objective" history (as we like to call it in the West) were confounded, both there and here. In Hungary historical reconstruction of the war years had to conform to a totalitarian ideology that rendered content secondary to intent, while in the West traditional avenues of research were closed off. Moreover, Hungary is, and has always been, a linguistic *terra incognita*, a small island in a vast Teutonic and Slavic sea. The strangeness of its agglutinative language, its aversion to loanwords, its disconnection from other Western tongues—all these have contributed to the neglect of Hungarian culture and history by mainstream Anglo-Europeans. For example, fewer than a half dozen American universities regularly offer instruction in Hungarian. Even now jokes about Budapest's being confused with Bucharest are legion. Thus it comes as no surprise to learn that at the end of the war, when Hungarian fliers stranded in Austria tried to surrender to the American army, they had to explain to MPs that the United States and Hungary had officially been at war.

Between 1988 and 1990 I spent eighteen months in Budapest and Szeged researching this book, and returned in 1993 and 1995 for further interviews. To date I have interviewed nearly one hundred men and women—many of them repeatedly—who actively participated in or merely passively endured the war in Hungary. One major handicap must be explained at the outset. I have no oral fluency in Hungarian, and only an elemental reading ability. However, I had the good fortune of having in Eleonóra Arató, a native of

Budapest who holds a doctorate in linguistics from Eötvös Loránd University, a superb translator (one of those rare interpreters who can listen to a cacophonous babel of English and Hungarian spoken at the same time yet somehow make sense of both). Further, through her connections as a teacher and administrator at both Semmelweis Medical University in Budapest and Tudományos Ismeretterjesztő Társulat (the "open" university), I was able to reach a wide variety of Hungarians, with backgrounds ranging from landed gentry to Party stalwarts. Fifty-eight of these interviews were conducted in Hungarian, twenty-seven in English. Fifty-one were with men, thirty-four with women. Although the principal value of my book resides in the materials collected from these interviews, I have backstopped these with major historical works in English treating the period between the Treaty of Trianon and the Russian occupation. Foremost among these is C. A. Macartney's two-volume masterwork, *October Fifteenth*, which has yet to be superseded, in any language, as the authoritative account of Hungarian history between 1918 and 1945. Nicolas Nagy-Talavera's *Green Shirts and Others* supplied invaluable insights into the politics of the period. The memoirs of Regent Miklós Horthy and Prime Minister Miklós Kállay were indispensable primary sources. For background on the Jews of Hungary the definitive work is Randolph Braham's two-volume *Politics of Genocide: The Holocaust in Hungary*, which builds upon Eugene Lévai's earlier *Black Book on Martyrdom of Hungarian Jewry*. Other secondary works are cited in my notes.

My objective has been to write an account of the final years of the war that would record and analyze the experiences of "ordinary" people forced to cope with extraordinary crises imposed upon them by the external forces of history. My primary focus is upon domestic, not military, history. The progression is roughly chronological and conforms to what I see as four evolving "moods" through which a majority of Hungarians passed between 1938 and 1948—from optimism to skepticism, to pessimism, to despair.

As David Henige observes in his *Oral Historiography* (1992), history is never synonymous with that elusive entity we call "the past," but rather consists only of whatever relics—whether words or artifacts—happen to survive. Oral sources share with written sources the limitation of being, as Henige puts it, "prisms on the past—not windows." For the most part, traditional historians are more comfortable with the written word than with the spoken, even though utterance precedes transcript in the majority of cases. Perhaps they prefer to believe that prismatic refraction is less when a text is pinned to a page rather than free-floating as sound. Much of this bias merely reflects the elitist culture in which we are nurtured. (Nearly all American universities require a course in writing. Speech courses that might prove more useful are usually optional.) Subliterary folk rarely build written cages for what they say or think. (By subliterary I refer not only to those unable to write but also to those without the inclination to do so.) If their history endures—other than through the dead matter of official statistics—an outsider must record it for them. Historically they are a subculture of the underprivileged and the dispossessed. In Henige's words: "Oral history is a record of the done-untos rather than the doers." Without such records time would erase the individual and collective histories of these people as thoroughly as if they had never lived.

Since the human memory is not a precision instrument, any attempt to reconstruct events half a century after the fact is subject to obvious pitfalls. It ought to go without saying that even if specific details are remembered accurately—though who really can be sure that they are?—attitudes toward them may have been modified or distorted through the passage of time. Hindsight most certainly allows an informant to claim greater knowledge of events and to achieve "wisdom" not available at a moment of crisis. Eva MacMahon makes this Heraclitean point in her *Élite Oral History* (1989): "[E]very putative re-cognition of a text is really a new and different cognition based upon changes with the interpreter." Added to these problems, which are endemic to any method of information gathering, are the political inhibitions that have plagued Hungarians since the war. For half a century most of my informants were encouraged to conceal, rather than to reveal, what had happened to them during the war and its aftermath. Their anxiety and dubiety was especially noticeable when they caught sight of my tape recorder. Many refused to allow it to be turned on, and who could blame them? How could they be sure that the information they gave to this stranger, who was protected by a passport from another country and was able to escape the ring of machine-gun-toting guards at the airport any time he chose, would not in some way circle back and damage them? Sometimes when I interviewed husband and wife, one of the partners refused to contribute but seemed poised as a silent witness, prepared to issue a warning to the spouse not to go too far. Yet this wariness often came hand in hand with an eagerness to spill it all out through what seemed to be cathartic relief that at long last their recollections might be permanently recorded somewhere. In most instances my informants had never spoken of their experiences so fully to anyone other than close friends or family members. About one in every four persons we contacted refused to be interviewed. Despite zephyrs of "liberalization" in

Hungary during 1989 and 1990, the habit of caution remained. Hungarians of that generation will carry to their graves the psychic scars inflicted by a repressive police state that warred against truth and honesty. The wonder is not that some refused to be interviewed but that so many consented.

One of the major problems encountered in writing this book was estimating how knowledgeable my projected readers would be concerning the main events of modern Hungarian history. While I could assume that most would know that Hungary fell within the Axis orbit during the war, I could not take for granted that they would know why the country made that decision or how its army and civilian populace responded to the conflict. Clearly there has always been a tendency to lump together the Axis powers and to stereotype their governments as "fascist" without carefully considering the respective political nuances at work in each country. Necessarily more exposition on my part was required than for more familiar topics falling within the "oral history" genre. (For Hungarians of that generation the genus "good war" does not exist.) It would be meaningless to record in full our conversation with a Volksdeutsche informant without telling the reader about the special tensions of German minorities before and during the war, or to record the agonizing story of a Jewish member of a labor battalion on the Stalingrad front without a discussion of the three anti-Jewish laws that put him there. While the best, and most original, materials of this saga come from personal interviews, these have been fused into my own exposition. Not all the interviews were of the same quality. Some, because of the richness of the experience or the dramatic power of the raconteur, form the basis of subchapters. Others, while confirming general attitudes and thereby contributing to a consensus, are in themselves relatively mundane and are subordinated within a collective portrait. In my view, and by my intent, this book is less "oral history" than reportage. Specialists in Hungarian history will doubtless find my exposition tedious and obvious. They might be better rewarded by riffling through those pages and moving on quickly to the individual interviews—the heart of the narrative.

All tape recordings and holograph notes of my interviews will be archived in the Labadie Collection of the Harlan Hatcher Library at the University of Michigan.

Acknowledgments

My greatest debt is owed to all those who consented to be interviewed and had to endure my questions. Conversations with these men and women constitute the bone and marrow of this book. Without their generous patience and assistance, no book would have been possible. In many cases interviews were repeated as many as five or six times.

Those interviewed in English were Per Anger, Mária Badal, Miklós Bárd, Júlia Berkes, Robert Carpenter, Zsolt Dienes, Adrienn Fiam, György Györffy, Piroska Hegedüs, Magda Kende, Béla Király, István Kós, Domokos Kosáry, Charlotte Kretzoi, Attila Makay, Gábor Merfelsz, Andrew Nagy, John [Giovanni] Nastasi, Márta Ofner, Aladár Sarbu, Mária Schreiner, Arthur Silbelka von Perleberg, Jenő Tarján, Livia Turgon, György Vágó, Béla Vanyek, Mária Winter, and Sándor Zoltán.

Those interviewed in Hungarian (with Eleonóra Arató as translator) were Ilona Almási Szabó, József Arató, Ervin Bán, József Bárdos, Antal Blumenthal, Kató Borosnyay, József Borus, Jenő Borzsák, Ilona Cser, Zoltán Falta, Gyula Farkas, László Felkai, Géza Galló, Ferenc Gegsi, Irén Gercser, Teréz Gróf, György Hahn, Irene Hasenberg, Judit Herceg, Joan Horváth, "Attila Hunfalvy," Károly Jobbágy, Ilona Joó, Gabriella Kardos, Malvina Kerner, József Kiss, Olga Koós, István Körmendi, Gabriella Kornhauser, Ilona Kriskó, Tibor Lakner, Eleonóra Majorosy, Lea Merényi, Zsuzsa Merényi, Jenő Murányi, Tibor Murányi, Erzsébet Ökeli, Károly Orbán, Andor Pál, Mariann Pertl, Gyula Pintér, Gyula Sághy, Endre Sásdi, Rudolf [Singer] Sas, Valéria Singer, Margit Szabó, János Szentiványi, Sári Szücs, Tibor Tabak, Anna Tarr, Mária Ujhelyi, Sándor Ujhelyi, Lajos Ürge, Veronika Vadas, András Vértes, Augusta Vértes, Károly Vigh, Kálmán Wittinger, Tibor Zinner, and György Zsohár.

Without question my greatest debt is to Eleonóra Arató, who arranged for me to meet nearly all of the informants and who translated not only those interviews conducted in Hungarian but also relevant Hungarian sources. Moreover, she supported and encouraged this project from beginning to end with her great reservoir of patience and her encyclopedic knowledge of Hungarian history and culture.

In Hungary József Borus guided me through the minefields of Hungarian history. Recollections of our many excursions together—"living history" at its most rewarding—I will not forget. In the United States Béla Király not only read and meticulously critiqued my manuscript but also shared with me his experiences as a young general staff lieutenant during the war and kindly gave me access to his unpublished memoir. Géza Jeszenszky, Hungarian parliamentarian and professor of history at the Economics University of Budapest, read my manuscript at an early stage and offered invaluable suggestions. Professor Robert Zaretsky of the University of Houston, my "outside" reader at Penn State Press, assisted by highlighting accounts in the text requiring amplification. Special thanks are owed Zsolt Dienes for providing entrée to former members of the Hungarian Royal Air Force, a dynamic group whom I should certainly have missed without his introductions. Krisztián Flautner served as ombudsman in all matters relating to computer malfunctions. And finally, but by no means least, I wish to thank Peter Potter of Penn State Press, for his service as my editor, and Keith Monley, whose command of the English language is awesome.

The Conference Board of Associated Research Councils assisted this project by appointing me Fulbright Lecturer in American Literature at the University of Szeged during the 1989–90 year.

Chronology

1914	July 28	Austro-Hungarian monarchy declares war on Serbia.
	August 1–4	Declarations of war between Central and Entente Powers.
1915	May 23	Italy declares war on the monarchy.
1916	August 25	Romania declares war on the monarchy.
1918	October 25	National Council assumes control of Hungarian government.
	October 30	Bourgeois revolution after riots in Budapest.
	November 3	Monarchy signs armistice with Entente at Padua.
	November 11	Germany signs armistice with Entente at Compiègne.
	November 16	Hungarian republic proclaimed.
	November 24	Communist Party of Hungary founded.
1919	January 28	Communists expelled from Workers Council.
	February 21	Communist leaders arrested.
	March 20	French army supports Romanian claim for Hungarian land.
	March 21	Hungarian Soviet Republic proclaimed under Béla Kun.
	April–May	Romanian and Czech armies attack Hungary.
	August 1	Hungarian Soviet Republic dissolves. Romanians occupy Budapest.
	August 9	In Szeged, Miklós Horthy sets up independent military command.
	November 16	Horthy enters Budapest.

1920	March 1	Horthy elected regent.
	June 4	Treaty of Trianon.
1921	March–October	Failed attempts by Charles IV to resume Hungarian crown.
	November 6	Parliament officially dethrones House of Hapsburg.
1923	January 31	Hungary admitted to League of Nations.
1924	July 2	League of Nations grants loans to Hungary.
1927	April 5	Italian-Hungarian treaty of friendship concluded.
1932–36		Gyula Gömbös's right-wing government.
1933	June 18	Gömbös visits Hitler in Germany.
1934	February	German-Hungarian economic treaty signed.
1937	October 10	Unification of Arrow Cross Parties.
1938	April	First Anti-Jewish Law.
	August 20	Horthy meets Hitler in Germany.
	November 2	First Vienna Award. Part of Slovakia returned to Hungary.
1939	January 13	Hungary adheres to Anti-Comintern Pact.
	April 11	Hungary withdraws from League of Nations.
	May	Arrow Cross Party gains in Parliament elections. Second Anti-Jewish Law.
1940	August 30	Second Vienna Award. Northern Transylvania recovered.
	November 20	Hungary joins Tripartite Pact.
	December 12	Hungary signs "Eternal Friendship" Pact with Yugoslavia.
1941	April 4	László Bárdossy becomes prime minister.
	April 11	Hungary attacks Yugoslavia.
	June 27	Hungary declares war on USSR.
	December 7	Great Britain declares war on Hungary.
	December 8	Hungary declares war on United States.
1942	March 9	Miklós Kállay replaces Bárdossy as prime minister.
1943	January	Second Hungarian Army destroyed at Don Bend.
	September	Secret peace negotiations with Western powers begin.
1944	March 17	Hitler draws Horthy to Salzburg meeting.
	March 19	First occupation of Hungary by German army.
	March 22	Döme Sztójay replaces Kállay as prime minister.

	May–July	Deportation of Hungarian Jews from provinces.
	August 29	General Géza Lakatos, loyal to Horthy, replaces Sztójay.
	September 23	Red Army troops cross Hungarian frontier.
	October 11	Secret provisional cease-fire signed in Moscow.
	October 15	Horthy proclaims Hungarian withdrawal from war.
	October 16	Arrow Cross takes control of government under Ferenc Szálasi.
	December 22	Provisional (pro-Soviet) government established in Debrecen.
	December 25	Red Army cuts off Budapest. Siege of the city begins.
	December 28	Provisional Hungarian government declares war on Germany.
1945	February 13	Soviet Army completes "liberation" of Budapest.
	April 4	Last German military units expelled from Hungary.
1946	February 7	Hungarian republic proclaimed.
	March	Szálasi, Bárdossy, Sztójay, and other rightists executed.
1948	February 18	Treaty of Friendship and Mutual Aid signed with USSR.
1955	May	Warsaw Pact. Armed forces of socialist countries integrated.
1956	November	Soviet military crushes the Hungarian Revolution.

Major Historical Characters

Bárdossy, László (1890–1946). Right-wing politician and advocate of pro-German policy. Prime minister (1941–42) who supported the attack on Yugoslavia and was responsible for the declaration of war against the USSR. Sentenced and executed as a war criminal in 1945.

Bethlen, István, Count (1874–1947). Transylvanian landowner and leader of the conservative wing in Parliament. Prime minister (1921–31) who consolidated the Horthy regime. Urged rapprochement with the Western powers during the war years.

Gömbös, Gyula (1886–1936). Captain of the general staff during the First World War. Leading figure of the counterrevolution during the Horthy period. Established the Racialist Party during the 1920s to oppose Bethlen moderation. Prime minister (1932–36) who attempted to introduce the fascist models of Italy and Germany into Hungarian political life. Died of natural causes.

Horthy, Miklós (1868–1957). Aide-de-camp to Emperor Franz József, and the last commander of the Austro-Hungarian navy during the First World War. Led the counterrevolutionary army in 1919. Regent of Hungary 1920–44, later prisoner of the Nazi government. Exonerated of war crimes by Allied tribunals. Retired to Portugal.

Kállay, Miklós (1887–1967). Minister of agriculture under Gömbös and prime minister 1942–44. Sought separate peace terms from the Allies. Imprisoned by the Germans in 1944 under sentence of death. Released by Italian partisans. Emigrated to the United States.

Kun, Béla (1886–1939). Hungarian POW in Russia in 1916. Follower of Lenin. In 1918 founded the Hungarian Communist Party. After release from prison in 1919, administered the short-lived Hungarian Soviet Republic. Exiled in Vienna. Purged in the USSR.

Szálasi, Ferenc (1897–1946). Major on the general staff during World War II. After retirement from the army in 1935, founded the Party of Nation's Will. Consolidated right-wing parties as the Hungarian National Socialist Party in 1937. Imprisoned in 1938, pardoned in 1940. Appointed prime minister on October 16, 1944, after the second German occupation of Hungary. Tried and sentenced to death as a war criminal in 1946.

Sztójay, Döme (1883–1946). General of the army, then Hungary's minister in Berlin from 1935. Appointed prime minister after the first German occupation in March 1944. Tolerated activities of the German Gestapo and deportation of the provincial Hungarian Jews. Tried and sentenced to death as a war criminal in 1946.

Teleki, Pál, Count (1879–1941). Prominent landowner and university geographer. Member of the Trianon peace delegation. Prime minister 1920–21 and 1939–41. Upheld Hungarian neutrality during the German invasion of Poland. His government signed the Treaty of Eternal Friendship with Yugoslavia. Committed suicide when army interests prevailed and Hungary joined Germany in invading Yugoslavia.

Introduction:
Between Wars

In October 1918, one month before the fighting ceased on the western front, Hungary withdrew from the war. By the end of the month the army had placed itself under a National Council and had occupied the civic buildings in Budapest. A band of angry soldiers broke into the house of Count István Tisza, the Hungarian prime minister whose government had voted Hungary into the war, and assassinated him. At one swoop Hungary achieved complete separation from Austria (which it had failed to do during the revolution of 1848) but inherited an economy in ruins after losing a two-front war against both Italy and Russia. Conditions in Budapest verged on anarchy. While the National Council looked on helplessly, real power was exercised by armed bands who roamed the streets and looted without fear of apprehension or punishment.

At the worst possible time Hungary found itself leaderless, adrift, and broke. The country could expect no mercy from the victorious Allies, who were assembling in Paris conferences to dictate the terms of peace for each of the Central Powers. On November 16 a coalition led by an anemic group of Social Democrats proclaimed the Hungarian People's Republic, but it failed to hold the bickering factions of the country together. Ethnic minorities, which had been harshly treated by the Hungarians during the prewar epoch, began to show their teeth, and their demands for independence were fed by Wilsonian rhetoric about the self-determination of peoples. Their hostility toward the dominant Magyars was not without reasonable cause. In 1910, for example, ethnic minorities held only 8 seats out of 431 in the Hungarian Parliament, although they numbered half the total population of the country.[1]

1. Nicholas Nagy-Talavera, *The Green Shirts and the Others: A History of Fascism in Hungary and Rumania* (Stanford, 1970), 10.

Nor was this discrimination aimed solely at ethnic minorities. For centuries Hungary had been ruled by a privileged few, who were both unprepared for and hostile to democratization. This caste was opposed to universal suffrage, to secret ballots, to bipartisan tallying of votes. Election results were therefore controlled by less than 10 percent of the adult male population. Added to this sorry state of affairs was the shocking poverty among the rural population, many of whom labored under conditions not far removed from serfdom, which had been formally abolished only in 1848. Always agriculture had been the trump card in the Hungarian economy, yet there were nearly two million families who did not have enough land to grow food for their own consumption—nor did they have social services to fall back upon when larders were empty. Such people were forgotten and despised. (Middle-class children regularly used the word *paraszt* [peasant] as a term of contempt for anyone less fortunate than they.) Little wonder that throughout November 1918 there were spontaneous uprisings throughout the country as peasants seized land, harassed landlords, and pillaged estates.

At this juncture Lenin, seeing an opportunity to expand into the West, sent his agent Béla Kun into Hungary with authority to foment a Communist revolution. Kun, a former Hungarian officer imprisoned by Russians during the war, dutifully established the Hungarian Communist Party on November 24, but was soon arrested on a charge of sedition and jailed with a hundred of his minions. In a similar move, the new government expelled some rightists from the country. These efforts by the governing clique to prove to the Allied powers that Hungary had evolved into a democratic nation had little impact upon negotiators in Paris. By January 1919 it was clear that the Allies would convey Transylvania, a venerated province of Hungary for nearly a millennium, to Romania as a reward for service to the Allies during the war.[2] Since the Hungarian army had been disbanded in accordance with terms of the armistice, Hungarians had to watch with impotent rage as Romanian troops swarmed into Transylvania and even spilled over into the Great Hungarian Plain farther to the west—all under the nose of French military authorities charged with monitoring postwar affairs in the Balkans. By the middle of March 1919, journalists began to hypothesize that the country's "salvation"

---

2. It seemed to Hungarians a particularly undeserved reward. Romania had remained neutral until August 1916, when it joined the Allies, after which it was quickly engulfed by the armies of Bulgaria and Austria-Hungary and occupied by the Central Powers. However, on November 9, 1918, just two days before Germany signed the armistice terms at Compiègne, Romania took advantage of the chaos in Hungary to reenter the war on the side of the Allies and to seize Transylvania.

might lie in a rapprochement with Russia, whose Red Army was approaching the Carpathian Mountains. In an abrupt volte-face Hungarian authorities released Béla Kun and his cohorts from jail and instructed them to form a new government. Kun appointed thirty-three "people's commissars"—most of them from his entourage but also a few, as window dressing, from the Social Democrats—and launched his "Hungarian Soviet Republic." It lasted only 133 days.

Kun proved to be only an impractical theoretician. He believed, for example, that because the working classes of Hungary were better educated and organized than those in Russia, revolutionary zeal would be higher. It was lower. He concluded that vast numbers of disaffected former soldiers would swell his ranks. He overlooked the fact that many of them had been POWs in Russia and wanted nothing whatever to do with either Russia or Communism. And finally, Kun was convinced that Communism was imminent in western Europe because the bourgeoisie had lost their will to resist it. Wholly lacking in personal magnetism and wasting opportunities for meaningful reform by passing bizarre laws such as the death penalty for black-market operations, Béla Kun might have gone down in Magyar history as a temporary aberration had he not unleashed what would be vividly remembered for the next two decades as the Red Terror. In Budapest law and order were administered by workers' committees. Armored trains packed with Kun's Cheka crisscrossed the country, ferreting out trouble spots and hammering home with truncheons and guns the catechism of Marx and Lenin. These squads (one of them colloquially called "the Lenin Boys") were particularly murderous among rural folk, who were not easily convinced that they should turn their pigs and chickens over to members of a faceless collective. Even the idea of collective farms pleased few peasants. What they wanted was their own private plots of land. Of the 342 victims executed during the Red Terror, 248 were peasants.[3] Because half of the commissars, including Kun and his principal executioner, Tibor Szamuely, were of Jewish origin, their regime acted as a catalyst for anti-Semitism in the years to come, particularly among those rural and urban workers who normally had little contact with Jews.[4]

Alarmed by this westward spread of Bolshevism, and fearing the contagion would spread to Austria, the Allies unleashed the Romanian army to teach

3. Nagy-Talavera, 25.

4. Tibor Hajdu and Zsuzsa Nagy, "Revolution, Counterrevolution, Consolidation," in *A History of Hungary*, ed. Péter F. Sugár (Bloomington, 1990).

Hungarians a bitter lesson. At the same time, the Czech army attacked Hungary from the north and seized Miskolc, a major center for heavy industry. Since the Hungarian army had been disbanded in accordance with terms of the armistice, only fifty-five thousand unorganized men of the newly constituted Hungarian Red Army were available to meet these invasions. Although successful in stalemating the Czechs, they found the Romanians tougher opponents. In early August 1919 the Romanian army occupied Budapest. In order to subdue all resistance in the country, the Romanians appealed to former Hungarian soldiers to join them in purging the country of Communists. Those taking the bait were arrested, stuffed into boxcars, and shipped as POWs to Romania, where they were detained until December. This practically guaranteed that the sack of Hungary could proceed without opposition. The invaders demanded delivery of 50 percent of the country's rolling stock, 30 percent of its livestock, twenty thousand carloads of fodder, and even assessed payment for their expenses while looting the country.[5] During this melee Béla Kun and his band fled to Vienna. (Kun subsequently returned to Russia, where in 1937 Stalin purged him.) In the end the Allied Control Commission persuaded the Romanians to withdraw, which they did after a final looting spree that stripped even the telephones and typewriters from government offices. On November 16 a counterrevolutionary force, recruited in Szeged under French auspices and led by Miklós Horthy, a Magyar who had commanded the Austro-Hungarian navy during the war, entered Budapest with Horthy mounted on an appropriately white stallion. Although he was hailed as savior of the country, his small force had not actually engaged the Romanians. There followed what would be called by leftists the White Terror, a purge of Kun followers (many of whom were indeed murderers) along with other dissidents—real or imagined. Some seventy thousand Hungarians were said to have been put into concentration camps, and legal action on one level or another was brought against twenty-seven thousand.[6] In all, the White Terror brought 329 executions resulting from formal trials along with about 1,200 impromptu murders. The principal legacy of the short-lived Kun regime was an abiding hatred of Communism that penetrated nearly all ranks of society, including the working class. Unlike Germany or France, Hungary was never seriously threatened by leftist

---

5. Francis Deák, *Hungary at the Paris Peace Conference* (New York, 1972), 113.

6. The camps were only temporary, and most of the charges were dropped. Western journalists covering the trials were often startled to see defendants, who were being roundly denounced as traitors in the courtrooms during the day, wining and dining in restaurants with their judges at night. Nagy-Talavera, 55.

extremism during the next two decades, because by 1919 a right-wing government was firmly locked into place. In 1920 Admiral Horthy was elected regent for life, with the power of appointing prime ministers and cabinets without consulting Parliament.[7] The postwar epoch for Hungary had truly begun.

Even more traumatic than the Béla Kun episode were the terms of the Trianon Treaty imposed on Hungary in June 1920. It divested the country of 70 percent of its prewar territory and 60 percent of its population. Of the 282,000 square miles of pre-Trianon Hungary, only 93,000 were left under Hungarian control. Romania got about 103,000, Czechoslovakia 61,000, and Yugoslavia 20,500. (Even Austria, whose Hapsburg dynasty had pulled Hungary into the war, received 4,000.) From a prewar population of 18,000,000 the country dropped to 7,600,000—leaving 3,200,000 Magyars trapped in "foreign" dominions.[8] Moreover, at one stroke Hungary lost 89 percent of its iron production, 84 percent of its timber, and 62 percent of its railways.[9] Thereafter "self-determination" became a dirty word for Hungarians. The outcry was enormous, all the more frustrating because the country was militarily helpless and therefore could do nothing but endure the degradation. *Trianon! Nem, nem, soha!* (Trianon! No, no, never!) became the rallying cry for the next two decades. As if this were not punishment enough, Hungary was required to pay reparations totaling 200 million gold crowns, with annual payments extending to the year 1966.[10] Moreover, adding to the bitter pill, the treaty limited Hungary's armed forces to 35,000 officers and men for use exclusively as frontier defense and prohibited all heavy artillery, tanks, and military aircraft.[11] Since no such restrictions were placed on the Little Entente (Yugoslavia, Czechoslovakia, and Romania), Hungary was left at the mercy of hostile neighbors. Hungarians developed a kind of cultural paranoia. Journalists and politicians lamented that their country was now only "a drop in the Slavic ocean," and that Yugoslavia and Czechoslovakia

---

7. Officially Hungary remained a kingdom, with a minority of Legitimists calling for restoration of the Hapsburgs. But in 1921, when King Charles IV twice entered the country and attempted to regain the crown, Horthy forcibly ejected him. Notwithstanding this, the crown of King Stephen remained on the national coat of arms, and Hungary was nominally a monarchy until the end of World War II.

8. C. A. Macartney, *October Fifteenth: A History of Modern Hungary*, 2 vols. (Edinburgh, 1956), 1:4.

9. Hajdu and Nagy, 314.

10. The payments lapsed during World War II. However, in 1945 the Soviets began collecting a new set of reparations from Hungary. For World War I reparations, see Macartney, 1:63 and 88.

11. Macartney, 1:5.

were not real nation-states but only Trianon "fictions."[12] Inflicted with the Béla Kun regime and the infamous treaty within a single year, Hungary had been looted and betrayed by both East and West. The experience sealed into place two overriding mainsprings of Hungarian foreign policy between the wars—hatred of Bolshevism and repudiation of Trianon. Magyars bitterly compared the terms of the Versailles treaty with those of Trianon. Versailles placed only 5 percent of German nationals into foreign states; but with Trianon 14 percent of prewar Magyars now found themselves trapped within foreign countries.[13]

During the period between the wars political control in Hungary was vested in two right-wing factions that maintained an uneasy peace with one another. Count István Bethlen, a Transylvanian aristocrat who had extensive financial and social connections with the West, headed a conservative wing that supported a gradualist approach to reform. The Party of National Unity, which had an ingrained distrust of populist democracy, commanded the wealth of the country—mainly through ownership of land and control of banks. Their power lay in pulling strings behind the scenes rather than attempting to bid for votes at the polls. Members of their exclusive National Casino even boasted that no Social Democrat, Communist, or Fascist had ever been admitted to their club. Many of these traditionalists were covert monarchists, equally at home in Vienna or London, but fiercely proud of their Magyar traditions and lineage. They could be trusted to put a brake on disruptive radicalism, whether of the Far Right or Far Left. The Bethlen principle was to allow the opposition to shout in Parliament, but to demand that the streets remain silent. The best that could be said of this "Government Party" was that it felt responsible for, but not to, the people. As the epoch became more stridently anti-Semitic, Bethlen voiced no objection to rooting out dissident Jewish intellectuals, like those who had supported Béla Kun, but he understood the need for foreign capital in rebuilding his country and placed a wall of protection around Jewish capitalists and industrialists. (He once defined an anti-Semite as "any person who detested the Jews *more* than was necessary.")[14] Bethlen was a pragmatist prepared to maintain the status quo at any cost. He was humane without being a humanist.

12. Nicholas [Miklós] Kállay, *Hungarian Premier* (New York, 1954), 349.
13. György Száraz, "The Jewish Question in Hungary: A Historical Retrospective," in *The Holocaust in Hungary: Forty Years Later*, ed. Randolph L. Braham and Béla Vágó (New York, 1985), 19.
14. Nagy-Talavera, 64.

The other right-wing faction was led by Gyula Gömbös, a charismatic former army officer of humble lineage who spoke for the disgruntled petite bourgeoisie. Of Swabian stock, he called himself a National Socialist as early as 1919—long before Hitler had worked out his political ideas in *Mein Kampf*. He opposed internationalism of any stripe, whether from Berlin or Moscow. His followers were a throwback to ancient Magyar values (or romanticized fictions thereof), and they called for a total restructuring of Hungarian society based upon blood, clan, tribe. Gömbös insisted that anyone of non-Hungarian ancestry magyarize his name if he entered government service. His followers were more willing to seek radical solutions to economic problems than the Bethlenites, and since they were of a lower social station, they were more embittered by the runaway inflation of the postwar years, which had decimated the middle classes. Moreover, Gömbös recruited followers easily from the million former state employees who swarmed into Hungary after Trianon had rearranged the national boundaries. Others had acquired paramilitary experience during the Béla Kun purges. Gömbös men were a generation younger than the Bethlenites, were more willing to reach their goals through violence, and made no secret of their anti-Semitism.

The decade of the twenties brought some improvement in Hungarian life. In 1920 a new franchise law expanded the numbers of those eligible to vote from 10 percent to 39 percent of the adult population.[15] In 1923, after being rejected the year before, Hungary joined the League of Nations, floated a large foreign loan, and stabilized its currency. Its xenophobic sense of encirclement by enemies eased somewhat in 1927, when Count Bethlen signed a friendship treaty with Italy. Soon Italy began supplying her new ally with aircraft in violation of Trianon, and both countries were conspiring to break up Yugoslavia by fostering separatism in Croatia.[16] Il Duce's strongman image was widely admired in Hungary, so much so that satirists began calling Gömbös, who aped his histrionic manner, Signor Gombolini. Many Jews shared this admiration. In a sermon the chief rabbi of Budapest, Simon Hevesi, compared Mussolini favorably with Moses, while Jewish middle-class parents, grateful that their boys had been admitted to the crack Italian high school, watched with pride as their sons paraded in Italian Fascist uniforms.[17]

15. Macartney, 1:23.

16. This conspiracy was conceived as a favor to Croatia because for Hungarians Serbia was a particularly primitive and vile country. A prominent Magyar visitor to Belgrade once compared the Serb Parliament to a "stable with wooden benches" containing rooms "reeking of onions and sheep." Cecile Tormay, *An Outlaw's Diary* (London, 1923), 102.

17. Nagy-Talavera, 104.

During the 1920s Budapest, a city approaching a million inhabitants, impressed visitors for its vague resemblance to Paris, with its wide boulevards, fine architecture, lively theaters, and cafe society. Fifty years later members of the ruling class would reminisce about this period as a kind of lost Romanov era in which there had been an endless succession of tea dances, cocktail parties, candlelight dinners, gypsy music, and champagne breakfasts at dawn along the Fisherman's Bastion in Buda, overlooking the broad Danube and the spires of Pest. Among the urban proletariat conditions had steadily improved since the war—they worked fewer hours, received extra pay for overtime, and received limited medical compensation. Yet once out of the capital, traveling in any direction, a visitor entered a counterworld— primitive, ignorant, and dirt-poor. In the *puszta*—the Great Hungarian Plain to the southeast of Budapest—two-thirds of the agricultural workers remained landless, despite promises from Parliament that the great estates would be broken up and the land distributed.[18] Reformers lamented that in rural Hungary languished "an army of three million beggars" regarded simply as draft animals to be kept under control by a brutal gendarmerie and exploited seasonally for their labor. It was even rumored that in some villages food was so scarce that a pregnant woman would be reprimanded for burdening the population with another mouth to be fed.[19] Vocational organizations among the peasantry were rigorously forbidden, lest they turn into unions. Their plight grew even worse after 1924, when the United States cut its immigration quotas and closed this escape valve. As late as 1935 nearly one-third of the cultivable land in Hungary was owned by .1 percent of the population.[20] Rural workers pathetically begged landowners not to introduce labor-saving farm machinery, because it would throw even greater numbers of them out of work. Better a pittance at back-breaking labor than nothing at all.

The Great Depression hit Hungary especially hard. Banks failed in Vienna and cut off credits. The price of wheat, the principal export crop, dropped disastrously. In the urban centers 20 percent of the workforce, unprotected by any form of unemployment relief, lost their jobs. In Budapest workers lived on beans, potatoes, and sour apples. Out in the provinces gendarmes, the

18. Horthy thought it immoral to set goals that were impossible to achieve. The idea of promising land for every peasant was absurd, he said, for the very simple reason that there was not land enough to go around. Macartney, 1:57.

19. Ibid., 60.

20. Ibid., 67. The census of 1930 revealed that 51 percent of the total population of Hungary earned their living from agriculture. Jörg K. Hoensch, *A History of Modern Hungary, 1867–1994* (London, 1996), 128.

Hungarian rural police, seized whatever they liked for taxes—kitchen pots, bedding, milk goats. Having been ruined by inflation during the twenties, the white-collar classes now faced conditions of poverty that they had associated in the past only with factory workers. They were angry, and as their anger evolved into political militancy, they repudiated Bethlen's conservative line in favor of the quasi-fascist orientation of Gömbös. In 1932 Horthy succumbed to public pressure and appointed Gömbös prime minister after exacting from him promises that he would support agrarian reform and would not campaign against Jews. Although Gömbös kept both promises, he stunned conservatives when he sent an ambassador to Berlin with congratulations only two days after Hitler had become chancellor. Subsequently he visited Hitler, who openly talked of invading both Austria and Czechoslovakia, saying of the latter that he wanted only the western part and that he did not care what happened to Slovakia or Ruthenia. Here was the first signal that Hungary might be able to restore some of the territory taken by the hated Trianon Treaty. The two leaders collided over whether the Volksdeutsche in Hungary owed their primary allegiance to Germany or to Hungary. Hitler was adamant on this subject—all Germans owed their first loyalty to the Reich. (This would cause problems later.) One positive result of the meeting was that Germany took increased amounts of agricultural produce from Hungary, along with 96 percent of the bauxite production.[21] The down side to this was that the Hungarian economy became interlocked, and overly dependent upon trade, with Germany. An unanticipated effect of these trade agreements was that large numbers of agricultural and industrial workers were invited to Germany for seasonal and short-term labor. Well paid and well treated, they usually returned home as ardent publicists of the Nazi economic boom. Horthy, however, remained skeptical about the German connection. While on a shooting excursion in Austria in 1935, he visited Hitler for a few hours at Berchtesgaden. The two leaders agreed that Communism was a dangerous evil, and Horthy most certainly was not displeased when Hitler indicated he wished to erase Czechoslovakia. At this meeting Horthy, not Hitler, was the mentor. He advised Hitler never to alienate Great Britain, because in warfare sea power always prevailed. He also could not resist a parting shot and told Hitler that Germans would never dominate the world, because they were so universally disliked for their bad manners.[22]

---

21. Ibid., 142n.
22. No minutes of this first Hitler-Horthy conference were taken. The substance was conveyed by Horthy to Macartney in a private meeting after the war. Ibid., 150n.

By 1935 Gömbös had succeeded, by cutting wages to the bone, in balancing the national budget, but to Horthy's disappointment he encouraged the proliferation of far-right parties that in this election year took three-quarters of the seats in Parliament. Had Gömbös not died of natural causes in the fall of 1936, Horthy would most certainly have removed him as prime minister because of this dangerous drift to the far right. He left behind a government unwilling to return to the old Bethlen conservatism. Henceforth Hungarian politics would become more volatile, more susceptible to radical ideas, provided these came from well to the right of center. Though repugnant to old-line conservatives, many of these ideas would have passed muster with Western liberals, including as they did land reform, tax equalization, the secret ballot and general franchise, a balanced budget, foreign trade, and credits for modernizing industry and agriculture. The liberals would not, however, have been happy with encroaching anti-Semitic legislation that followed shortly after Gömbös's death, or the continuing courtship of Italy, including endorsement of Mussolini's Ethiopian invasion.

It was at this time that the infamous Arrow Cross Party, under Ferenc Szálasi, began its slow rise. Its genealogy is difficult to trace because a host of short-lived radical organizations, whose members were absorbed by successively larger organizations, passed on distinguishing features that would later come to be recognized as the earmarks of Arrow Cross. From the Hungarian National Socialist Party (circa 1928) came the green membership card and the green-shirt uniform, and from the Hungarian National Socialist Agricultural Laborers' and Workers' Party (1932) came the telltale insignia, the Nyilas Kereszt (Arrow Cross), two crossed arrows each barbed at both ends. These earlier factions had convened, deliberated, deposed leaders, marched, and propagandized without causing more than a ripple in the body politic of the country. Their one "rising"—an attempt in 1936 to seize the country town of Nagykőrös as the first step in a far-fetched plan that would take over the whole country—proved to be only a minor nuisance, put down by gendarmes as easily as if it were a Saturday night brawl.[23] Hungarian fascism waited for a leader with the charisma of a Hitler or a Mussolini.

That leader appeared in Ferenc Szálasi, who was born in Kassa (today Kosice, Slovakia) in 1897. His father was a common soldier in the Hapsburg army whose forebears seem to have been Armenians named Salosan. After graduating from the Royal Hungarian Military Academy, he served briefly in

---

23. The ringleader got a two-year sentence after an insanity plea. There were seven hundred arrests, as a scare tactic, but few sentences. Nagy-Talavera, 109.

World War I, and by 1925 had been elevated to the general staff, where he excelled as a writer of military essays. But it soon became apparent to his superiors that he was not on the conventional track for military promotion. He read widely but erratically, and his mind spilled over with tangential notions. Increasingly he became obsessed with the destiny of the quasi-mystical Hungarian nation, which included not only the restoration of lands and population lost by Trianon—all his superiors would have agreed heartily with that—but also the consolidation of a dream state that he called "the Carpathian-Danubian Great Fatherland," a fusion of Magyars, Slovaks, Croats, Slovenes, and Ruthenians. The language would be Magyar, and the amalgam would be under Hungarian leadership because their tribes had led the migration to the Danubian basin one thousand years before. To implement his doctrine of "Hungarism" he resigned from the army in 1935 and founded the Arrow Cross Party (Nyilaskeresztes Párt) known by its graphic symbol, the Arrow Cross. This symbol would soon become as indelibly associated with fascism as the Nazi swastika (which incidentally was banned in prewar Hungary).

While his opponents often tarred Szálasi with the same brush they used on Hitler, the differences between the two were enormous. Szálasi was a political guru, not a practical administrator. He lacked the skill and the patience to turn an idea into a reality. Moreover, he was a constitutionalist who advocated legal process and had a sincere admiration for Horthy. He personally disliked Hitler, whose atheism and materialism repelled him. In his "Hungaristic" musings he envisioned a collaboration in which Horthy would be head of state and he, Szálasi, leader of the party. When members of his party were first admitted to Parliament and were assigned seats on the right side, they rose indignantly and moved to the left side. Szálasi genuinely wished to relieve the plight of the rural poor and the urban working class, and always he lived modestly (as few Hungarian leaders ever did). Intellectuals avoided him and scorned his ideas, but his nationalist mystique appealed to many Hungarians who had lost faith in themselves and in their country.[24] From Marx he had borrowed egalitarian ideas, but he rejected Marxism as too materialistic, too class-conscious, too internationalist. He regarded Jews as the major culprits in the twin vices of Communism and capitalism (for Szálasi

---

24. The verdict of Miklós Kállay, Horthy's pro-Western prime minister during World War II, was shared by most intellectuals of the epoch: "[Szálasi's government] was so low on the intellectual level that it would have been hard to find one among them fit in the old days to fill the post of village notary." Kállay, 471.

the Protocols of Zion were true writ), and they would have no place in his fantasized nation of the future. For all his limitations, he was not a sadist or racial psychopath of the Julius Streicher breed. He did not want Jews liquidated. In his forecast they would emigrate elsewhere. He envisioned this as an orderly exodus in which the exiles would be allowed to carry away their capital with them.[25]

Perhaps the most curious feature of Szálasi's ten-year political career was that it often flourished most when he was serving one of his many stints in jail for seditious remarks or writings. At such times his henchmen attended to the day-to-day operations of the party, and authorized terrorist attacks— which included bombing a synagogue—while their leader meditated, held séances, and penned his memoirs. Szálasi refused to accept funding from the Germans, but his cronies had no such scruples. The Arrow Cross Party did not become a major player in Hungarian politics until the later years of the war, when the threat of a Russian invasion became a reality. Only after Horthy attempted to arrange an armistice with the Russians in October 1944, did the Germans install Szálasi as their quisling—not because they admired him but because only the Arrow Cross Party could be depended upon to resist Communism to the bitter end.[26] Despite their sponsorship of him, Szálasi disliked the Germans, while to them he was nothing more than a last-hope puppet whose strings they pulled.

Germany's occupation of Austria in March 1938 shifted Hungarian foreign policy firmly into the Axis camp. Hitler was now a next-door neighbor leaning over the back fence, and Hungary's line of communication to the West, through Austria and Switzerland, had been cut. Furthermore, Hungary was heavily dependent on Austrian banking and industrial interests, which now passed into German control. It was evident that Czechoslovakia was next on Hitler's list, but he got no commitment of support from Hungary when Horthy reviewed the German navy at Kiel in the summer of 1938. Although Hitler implied that part of the territory taken by Trianon twenty years before might at last be returned to Hungary, Horthy refused to commit

25. Szálasi had nothing to do with the Jewish deportations to Auschwitz and other concentration camps, which had occurred months before he came to power in October 1944. Nor did he unleash the murderous Arrow Cross gangs that raided and killed Jews in Budapest during the following months. It is true that he did not stop them; it is also likely that he knew little about them. By this time Szálasi was little more than a remote figurehead in his own party.

26. Edmund Veesenmayer, the top Reich official in Budapest during this period, characterized Szálasi as "a buffoon who alternately swaggered and grovelled" and his followers as "a gang of fantasts." Macartney, 2:291. More succinctly, Horthy, who had to endure two meetings with him, called him "an idiot." Ibid., 230.

the *Honvédség* (the Hungarian army), explaining that his country lacked the resources for a major war with the Little Entente. He had not been impressed with the German navy and infuriated Hitler by repeating his warning that if Germany fought England the British navy would destroy him.

Hitler's partition of Czechoslovakia, achieved without retaliation from the West, was received in Hungary with both alarm and enthusiasm—alarm because it was clear that Hitler could take anything he wanted in Central Europe, enthusiasm because the strongest member of the Little Entente had been chopped into several parts. Among the leftovers Slovakia became an independent (and rightist) state, while hapless Ruthenia (the "tail" of Czechoslovakia) was promptly invaded by Hungary in an unusual surge of martial bravado. Moreover, through German intervention, the Felvidék, a segment of Slovakia that had been taken by Trianon, was returned to Hungary.[27] This gift subsequently became known in diplomatic circles as the First Vienna Award. Among cheering crowds Regent Horthy entered Kassa, the regional capital, on his famous white stallion.[28] Germany was returning what the Allies had pilfered. Hungary showed its appreciation by joining the Tripartite Pact as its fourth member and by resigning from the League of Nations. These gobbets of territory, which Hungary scraped from the claws of Hitler, aroused the Western press, which began dubbing Hungary the "Jackal of Central Europe."

In an effort to bolster his country's sagging image in the West, Horthy in February 1939 appointed as his prime minister Pál Teleki, a Transylvanian aristocrat and world-famous geographer. (His predecessor, Béla Imrédy, a notorious anti-Semite, had resigned precipitately when political opponents publicized documents purporting to show that his great-grandmother was Jewish.)[29] A staunch anti-Nazi as well as an anti-Communist, Teleki moved at once to ban the Arrow Cross Party, which had become a hive of extremist

27. Many Magyars, suddenly "liberated" after two decades of Czechoslovakian "captivity," discovered to their consternation that Hungary was a more feudalistic and reactionary country with a lower standard of living, primitive social services, and negligible land reform. They also were disappointed to find themselves underrepresented in Parliament.

28. Many in Hungary were embittered by the First Vienna Award because it failed to return *all* of the Hungarian territory originally surrendered to Czechoslovakia. Although both Hungary and Slovakia were solidly lodged in the German camp by this time, relations between them were never cordial. A large Magyar minority continued to live in Slovakia and to petition for restoration, while Slovakian patriots laid claim to major Hungarian cities along the Danube, including Esztergom, seat of a Hungarian archbishopric.

29. The "evidence" consisted only of a document showing she had been baptized at age seven, suggesting she had been a convert. Nothing better exemplifies the onus of Jewish blood at this time than the fact that Imrédy fainted when Horthy showed him the document.

plots, confiscated its funds, and arrested some of its more obstreperous followers. But international events were of greater moment as Europe tottered on the brink of war. It had become evident that Hitler's next target would be Poland, which alone among the nations of Central Europe regarded Hungary as a friendly power. Since they now shared a common border, optimists in the West hoped that the two countries would establish a common front against the German juggernaut. But the best Hungary would do was to warn the Germans that any attempt to send troops across her territory would be met with force—itself a bluff because at this stage in preparedness Hungary could barely produce enough uniforms for its Honvédség reserves. When Hitler invaded Poland in September, Hungary declared her neutrality. She did salvage a modicum of self-respect by allowing Polish officers and their families to cross the frontier, where they were interned under comfortable conditions or assisted in joining the Polish refugee army in London. Teleki was deeply disturbed by the immorality of the Hitler-Stalin Pact, which led to simultaneous invasions of Poland from both the west and the east. Only one system seemed worse to him than Nazism, and that was Bolshevism, and both were alien to Hungarian interests. There was great apprehension that the Russian attack upon Poland might not stop when it reached the Hungarian frontier in Ruthenia, but the only crossings occurred when ill-fed Russian soldiers sneaked over to cadge food from Hungarian frontier guards.

After the fall of France, Russia gave the Romanians (a nominal but never useful French ally) four days to surrender Bessarabia, and Molotov, in a friendly note, indicated his acceptance of Hungarian claims to Transylvania. Exulting in this opportunity to even the score with the despised Romanians, Hungarian border guards fired some random shots across the frontier and girded for war. Hitler, who had his eye on the Romanian oil fields and wanted no national quarrels in eastern Europe, intervened. He warned that the Romanian army was much better armed than the Honvédség. Through pressure, Germany and Russia persuaded Romania to surrender to Hungary a portion of northern Transylvania containing more than two million people, about half of them Magyars. This negotiation, which returned about 40 percent of pre-Trianon Transylvania, was called the Second Vienna Award. Once again the white horse was trotted out, and Regent Horthy rode through cheering crowds in Kolozsvár (Cluj), the regional capital. The disgruntled Romanian army backed out without firing a shot—German warnings saw to that. Romanians in the territory were promised automatic Hungarian citizenship—but if they insisted on remaining Romanians, they would be expelled. Both countries were embittered by the settlement and vowed to settle the dispute by war at a future time, when the German eagle and Russian bear were not monitoring the situation. The award placed Hungary even deeper in Hitler's debt. When the Romanians invited Germany to send a "training army" into the country, the Hungarians, in violation of their declaration of neutrality in England's war with Germany, allowed this army to use Hungarian railroads. More menacing, Hungarian politicians legalized the *Volksbund*, which could now openly proclaim its National Socialist ideas. Hitler's *Jugend* soon made their first appearances in the parks and along the byways of the country.[30] The two Vienna awards strengthened all Hungarian parties of the extreme right.

A few months later, in December 1940, Teleki, hoping to keep southeastern Europe out of the war, signed a Treaty of Eternal Friendship with Yugoslavia. However, when Germany invaded Yugoslavia in the following April, Teleki was unable to stop his government from granting the Wehrmacht permission to cross Hungarian territory. Convinced that his country had dishonored itself beyond redemption, Teleki retired to his office, put a pistol to his head, and killed himself. He left a note for Horthy, which read in part: "We have become breakers of our word. . . . I have allowed the nation's honor to be lost. The Yugoslav nation are our friends. . . . But now, out of cowardice, we have allied ourselves with scoundrels."[31] A few days later his successor, László Bárdossy, authorized Hungarian troops to cross the frontier and seize the Voivodina region, which had been lost by Trianon. This campaign initiated a brutal military occupation that involved expulsions, graft, and ultimately massacre. Western opinion was outraged by this further behavior of the Hungarian jackal, which had now clearly joined Germany in an aggressive military operation and would thereafter be regarded as a formal member of the Axis. Anthony Eden, the British foreign secretary, told the Hungarian minister in London that in view of the recently concluded Treaty of Eternal Friendship, the attack was "an eternal shame on Hungary," and that Britain would bring Hungary to judgment at the peace conference after the Allies won the war.

30. Loránd Tilkovszky, "The Later Interwar Years and World War II," in Sugár, 343.
31. Macartney, 1:489.

1 | Soldiers

Invasion

In the streets of Budapest the dominant reaction to the war was apathy. Among the rightists no eager volunteers rushed to the colors; among the leftists no demonstrators took to the streets or shut down factories in protest. It might as well have been news of war on the moon. Probably the average citizen with memory of internecine battles between Reds and Whites during the Béla Kun epoch and its aftermath felt that it was good riddance to both if Germans and Russians were killing one another, but that there was no reason for Hungary to pitch in. Nor were the Germans excited about Hungarian participation. Hitler always assumed that the Magyars' major contribution to his war machine would be the supply, not of soldiers, but of grain, bauxite, and oil.

Hungary was poorly prepared for war. By standards of Western nations Hungary was still a primitive country without the means of sustaining a modern war. Two-thirds of its villages had no electricity; a million adults were illiterate; less than 3 percent of the university population consisted of students from either the peasantry or the working class.[1] To save money the army had been demobilized after the Yugoslavian invasion. During the first months of the war, the Hungarian expeditionary force numbered only 36,000 men. Their two-seater Balilla tanks (Italian), useful only for riot control, were so fragile that in advancing through fields of vegetables they were often entangled and immobilized by pumpkin vines.[2] Many of their "mobile" units

---

1. Jörg K. Hoensch, *A History of Modern Hungary, 1867–1994* (London, 1996), 121–22.
2. Interview with Béla Király (July 19, 1996).

consisted of bicycles, and in September they became mired in the *rasputitsa*, the twice-yearly liquefaction of the Russian steppe, when autumn rains came in and winter snows went out. Adding to their problems, they had to requisition basic military hardware from the Germans, only to discover that they lacked the means to move it. Much of this equipment had been captured during the Polish and French campaigns and was a hopeless mishmash of random sizes and calibers for which spare parts did not exist.[3] By the end of August an estimated 50 percent of it had been lost or abandoned as they tagged behind the German blitzkrieg that moved eastward toward the Dneiper River. After only two months of war, Horthy began to have second thoughts about his alliance with Hitler. Even though Hungarian casualties stood at only 478 dead (including 27 officers), he notified Hitler he wanted his troops to return home, that they were doing no good.[4] Hitler made no objection. In the flush of victory as his armies penetrated the Soviet Union on all fronts, he had little use for a Hungarian army except as a token occupational force employed against the Ukrainians. By December the "Carpathian Group" of the Honvédség had returned to Hungary. At this stage of the war the Germans showed greater interest in drawing upon Hungarian skilled labor, and they succeeded in attracting (by paying good wages) 35,000 volunteer workers to German factories in 1941 alone. Hungary also agreed to an SS recruitment drive for 20,000 men.[5]

The war took a serious turn on December 7, when Britain declared war on Hungary, and a few hours later, quite by coincidence, the Japanese bombed Pearl Harbor. When the United States declared war on Germany, Hungary was obliged by the terms of the Tripartite Pact to declare war on the United States. Bárdossy informed the American minister that Hungary was "in a state of war" with the United States but had not "declared war"—a weaselly ambiguity that he hoped would pacify Hitler without angering Roosevelt. The United States, aware that Germany was pulling the puppet strings, did not condescend to declare war against Hungary until six months later.

Early in 1942, as Russian resistance stiffened, the Germans decided the time had come for Hungary to pay its debt for the two Vienna awards. They demanded twenty-eight divisions for duty in Russia. When Horthy pleaded

3. R. L. Dinardo, "The Dysfunctional Coalition: Axis Power and the Eastern Front," *Journal of Military History* 60 (October 1996): 723.

4. C. A. Macartney, *October Fifteenth: A History of Modern Hungary* (Edinburgh, 1956), 2:52.

5. Loránd Tilkovszky, "The Late Interwar Years and World War II," in *A History of Hungary*, ed. Péter F. Sugár (Bloomington, 1990), 347.

that it was impossible to supply such a number, he was promised up-to-date armament and supplies. Nudged by the information that both Slovakia and Romania were contributing more, Horthy agreed to mobilize an army of 200,000 men in addition to 40,000 occupational troops and 37,000 drudges for labor battalions (mainly Jewish conscripts). This became the ill-fated Second Army. (The First Army was retained at home for defense against possible Romanian aggression; the fact that Hungary and Romania were both allies of Germany never diminished their mutual antagonism.)[6] The Germans laid out the details in fine print: Hungary had to renounce its right to take war booty or to use Russian POW labor, and further had to agree to pay in full for German supplies. In late February the government issued a call-up for men between the ages of nineteen and thirty.

Hitler's satisfaction at this sign of military cooperation was dampened a month later when Horthy replaced Bárdossy with Miklós Kállay, a Bethlen admirer and old-school conservative. A former minister of agriculture with a doctorate in political science, Kállay was by birth and upbringing a country squire. He had no appetite for political intrigue, and he was untainted by scandal, whether economic or domestic. He regarded Hungary's entrance into the war a terrible mistake, and during his two-year tenure as prime minister he strove to open a bridge to the West without fomenting a German occupation. He deplored both Nazism and Communism. His major policy objective was quietly to disconnect Hungary from the Germans without opening the country to a Russian invasion. Kállay would never have regarded himself an anti-Semite, but with others of his class he would have agreed that Jewish influence in major professions, from law to education, should be curtailed. His approach to the welter of anti-Jewish legislation was not to undertake the impossible by trying to repeal it, but to weaken and ignore it wherever he could. This was also his method in dealing with German requests for increasing the Hungarian share of agricultural and industrial products— delay, conceal, play dumb. Horthy stood squarely behind Kállay as Hitler launched ever more strident demands that he be sacked.

By early July 1942 Hungary had packed off nine light divisions and one mechanized division to the Russian front, but owing to faulty logistics they had to detrain six hundred kilometers from the front line and hike the rest of the way on foot. Even before they reached their permanent position beside the German Eighth Corps along the Don River north of Stalingrad, they were

---

6. Throughout the war the Germans took care not to place Romanian and Hungarian units adjacent to each other lest they launch their own war within the war. Dinardo, 727.

exhausted and demoralized. Equipment supplied by the Germans was second-rate. As antitank guns they received obsolescent field guns captured from the Belgians, and ammunition was always in short supply. By the end of 1942 there were about 250,000 Hungarian troops in Russia. These had drained the country of three-fourths of its weapons, vehicles, and aircraft.

When the American army landed in North Africa in November 1942, the tide of support for Germany ebbed quickly. Using the Atlantic Charter as his wedge, particularly the guarantee of sovereign rights and self-government, Kállay opened lines of communication with the Allies.[7] He reiterated that Hungary was not at war with the Allies, only with Bolshevism. The Hungarian press was henceforth allowed to publish Allied communiqués as freely as Axis ones. In the main the Allies regarded these protestations as demonstration that Hungary was playing its old diplomatic game—having it both ways. Yet when Americans in 1943 established air bases in Italy and began flying over Hungary on bombing runs to Silesia, a gentleman's agreement prevailed. Both sides were officially at war, but the Allied bombers enjoyed immunity from attack and, in return, dropped no bombs en route.

In January 1943 the Second Hungarian Army occupied a 186-kilometer front north of Stalingrad, where the great battle raged. They were in a quiet sector, but their line was stretched very thin. Behind them were German reserve divisions, but these obeyed orders only from Supreme German Headquarters, through which the Hungarians had to funnel their requests, which the German staff often ignored. Hungarian artillery batteries were restricted to three to five shots per day because of the difficulty of bringing up munitions through the ice and snow. Other supplies, like heavy winter clothing and firewood, if they existed at all, lay in warehouses far behind the front line.

By Christmas German and Romanian troops were being driven back from the suburbs of Stalingrad. On the Hungarian right flank the Italian Alpine Division gave way. The entire front was beginning to crumble. General Gusztáv Jány, the Hungarian commander, requested permission to retire. This was denied. When he asked to be reinforced by the Hungarian armored division being held in the German reserve, this too was denied. The debacle began on January 12, when the Russians, concealed by fog, crossed the river and attacked. Germans, Italians, and Hungarians flooded to the rear. Fugitives clogged the few roads, whose snow banks, six to ten feet high, made cross-country retreat impossible. The panic was compounded when commanders ordered that all men without arms retire. Seizing an opportunity, many with

7. Nicholas [Miklós] Kállay, *Hungarian Premier* (New York, 1954), 352.

arms simply threw them away. The confusion was so great and the human losses so staggering that no exact statistics would ever be compiled. A calculation of Hungarian losses for all of 1943 lists 6,076 killed, 14,682 wounded, 57,001 missing, and 923 captured. Probably most of the missing were either killed outright or taken prisoner. In addition, there were more than 23,000 in the labor battalions—largely Jewish—who disappeared.[8] The likelihood is that all these figures are low.

The remnants of what had been the Second Hungarian Army regrouped in Kiev, over a thousand kilometers to the west. They had endured the worst defeat in Hungarian history since the Turks decimated the army of King Lajos II at Mohács in 1526. Soldiers complained bitterly that during the retreat the Germans had kept them at the rear to slow the Russian advance by interposing their sheer protoplasmic bulk. Many Hungarians flatly vowed they would risk execution before they would fight with the Germans again. The standard Wehrmacht riposte to that threat was that the Hungarians were more trouble than they were worth.

As a youth Gyula Sághy (born 1914) hoped to become a professional soldier. His father, a veterinary surgeon, had been decorated for service in the Tyrol. On his return to Hungary after the war he supported the Legitimists—who wished to restore to Charles IV the crown of Hungary—and had to flee the country before Béla Kun's Cheka. The family settled briefly in Belgium, but the father's death in 1920 sent them back to Hungary. As an officer's son, Gyula was admitted to the crack military school at Kőszeg at age eleven, but he was expelled after only a year for climbing out of his barracks window and visiting a wine cellar.[9] He completed secondary school in Budapest, graduated from the economics university, and in 1936 found a post in a solid Swiss-Hungarian bank. He voted the Gömbös ticket and admired the efficiency and audacity of Hitler's *Anschluβ*. Conscripted into the army in 1939 and trained as an antiaircraft technician, he was demobilized after the Yugoslavian campaign early in 1941, when it appeared that the war would bypass Hungary. Then in March 1942 he was recalled, sent to a rifle course at Fertőd, and in June found himself on a jam-packed freight train nosing into Russia as part of Horthy's hastily improvised Second Army.

The men were in high spirits, but Sághy was not hopeful. At twenty-eight he had become more reflective than most of the recruits, whose idea of life in

---

8. Macartney, 2:135.
9. Interview with Gyula Sághy (February 23, 1989).

the military was getting drunk and yelling at every female within vocal range of the train. Moreover, he had heard that the Germans were having trouble with the Russians, and he was annoyed that the Wehrmacht was supplied with food and equipment superior in quality to that issued to the Honvédség. They traveled through Kassa (Kosice) to Lemberg (Lvov), where they boarded German trucks bound for Kiev. Here they rested a week in a brand-new, six-storied Russian barracks, a curious place with central heating but without indoor toilets. What manner of men were these? Sághy asked himself.

To the east of Kiev the country became increasingly primitive. The rolling country was as depressing as it was endless. Transportation began to break down. The distance from Kiev to the Don River, where the Hungarians were to take defensive positions, was more than a thousand kilometers. Sometimes they walked—marching was out of the question—and at other times hitched rides as best they could from any passing vehicle. The farther they went, the greater the percentage of horses in the auto-parks. What were they doing out there? Certainly not protecting Hungary from the Bolsheviks. At Krastnoye Sághy was examining a map at a rest stop when a Russian woman asked what he was reading. He explained what a map was and pointed out the route back to Hungary. He was arrested by military police, interrogated, and accused of revealing secrets to the enemy. The charge was dropped when he convinced them his map was marked only with notes indicating where they had come from, not where they were going—in this wilderness who could tell anyway? But as punishment they forced him to march in full battle gear for one hundred kilometers in a broiling sun.

In the afternoon of August 7, Sághy's machine-gun section relieved a German unit on the west bank of the Don Bend southeast of Voronezh. To their left was the German Second Army; to their right, the Eighth Italian Army. A wide but shallow river separated them from the Russians on the east bank. Every night Russian patrols floated across the river on logs. Sághy dared not use his machine gun against them, because every fifth bullet was a tracer, which gave away their position and invited mortar rounds from the east bank. The Germans had issued them an obsolete 47-mm howitzer with corroded shells, which they were somehow supposed to employ as an antitank gun if the Russians ever attacked in force. Throughout the fall and early winter the Hungarians alternated ten days on the line with three days relief and rest. About the first of November a mysterious and sinister silence enveloped the front. Sághy assumed that it was because the temperature, at thirty-seven degrees below zero, had become too cold even for the Russians.

(He was wrong—the Red Army was flexing all its muscle for a counter-offensive against the Axis forces at Stalingrad.)

At Christmas Sághy's group came out of the line and rested in a snow-bound village about fifteen kilometers from the Don. They heard of the battle raging to their south, but the official line was that the Germans would break the Red Army in two. Defeatist talk was evidence of sedition and was absolutely forbidden. To Sághy's astonishment a German woman, uniformed in one of the Wehrmacht auxiliary services, announced that the Germans under General Paulus were surrounded and would have to surrender. She also went on to say that the Russians would eventually overrun Hungary and impose a Communist regime on the country. He thought her prophecy the raving of a madwoman.

Returning to the line they heard disquieting rumors about the collapse of the Italians on their right flank. The cold was so intense it was nearly impossible to move. Wrapped up in scraps of clothing and blankets, they huddled in bunkers, waiting for spring. Their Mannlicher guns were now frozen and useless—cartridges jammed in the barrels. Every four hours they reported to division by radio, but they learned nothing. Then, on January 10, no one answered their call. They dispatched a runner. Five days later he returned with electrifying news—headquarters no longer existed. It had packed up everything on horse sled and had skedaddled. Sághy's group panicked when they realized they had been left behind. For all they knew the Russians might have them surrounded.

Sághy took charge of his twelve-man squad as they moved west, guiding themselves by the abandoned debris of an army in headlong rout. Everywhere there were dead horses, tanks buried up to their turrets in snow, Hungarian soldiers frozen in contorted shapes in snow drifts two meters high. Russian airplanes buzzed them at thirty meters, dropping leaflets in Hungarian, in Italian, in Romanian. "WE ARE NOT GOING TO HARM YOU. IF GERMANS JOIN YOU, REMOVE YOURSELVES. FOR WE WILL KILL THEM." They dug into the back-packs of dead soldiers, trying to find food. Once Sághy's group came across a bag of salt, which kept them going for three days. Added to their woes was dysentery, which forced them to relieve themselves, in the bitter cold, six or eight times a day. In time they joined a ragged column of men two kilometers long who reported having been attacked by partisans and savaged by wolves. Everyone had thrown away weapons in a mad scramble to cut weight and flee. Officers were not present among this group; having had advance knowledge of what was happening, they had gotten off ahead of the enlisted men.

Near Kiev Sághy's group found freight cars running again and prayed that they had outrun the Red Army. Of the 385 original men in his unit back in August, only 120 remained. Few had been killed—they had just disappeared in that white chaos. Now worthless as a fighting force the Second Army was recalled in May. At Sumy, the few who had held on to their weapons were disarmed. Once across the Hungarian frontier, beyond Munkács, they were stripped, dipped in chemical baths, and issued clean uniforms for the first time in nearly a year. In Budapest Sághy received his discharge with a paper indicating that he would not be called up again.[10]

Cured forever of his earlier infatuation with a military career, Gyula Sághy resumed his duties at the bank and flourished his exemption paper every time the government tried to call him up. During the Arrow Cross period he lived with his brother, next to the infamous party headquarters at 60 Andrássy Avenue in Pest, a particularly dangerous area after October 15 because Nyilas (Arrow Cross) gangs began to shoot suspected deserters. He dared not go to his bank, for his exemption pass meant nothing to the Nyilas. After they broke into his building and began looting, he found shelter in a cellar on Üllői Street and moved in just as the siege began.

The first Russians to break into his cellar were disciplined soldiers. The next group were scourings who beat up the men and raped the women. When they began shipping random Hungarians to the USSR as slave laborers, Sághy decided it was time to leave. He hopped a freight train moving south toward Szeged, but near Kecskemét he was caught and arrested. His warden was a Russian female soldier who forced him to have sex with her.[11] Afterward she turned him loose, and he escaped in the darkness. He remained in hiding for several months before daring to venture back to Budapest and to resume his pleasantly dull work at the bank.

The Russian experiences of István Hegedüs (born 1902) of Sopron were nearly identical with those of Gyula Sághy. Although he was married, with three children, and was a middle-range executive in the Messerschmitt factory at Győr, he was called up in August 1942 and sent to the Don Bend front, where he served as translator and map specialist at Second Army headquarters

10. It is reported that some soldiers erased their names and gave these documents to Jewish companions during the period late in 1944 when the Arrow Cross controlled the city. Sághy kept his.

11. Russian males had no monopoly on rape during the early months of their occupation. For another account of the notorious Russian women's camp at Kecskemét, see "Postmortem" in Chapter 6.

at Aleksejevka. He returned home on furlough at Christmas, when he astonished his children by devouring, in the course of only a few days, five liters of plum jam. On January 16 he left on what proved to be the last train bound for the front, unaware that the Russians at that moment were smashing to pieces the Axis defenses along the Don. Arriving at headquarters on the twentieth, he found that the hows and whens of precipitate flight were the sole subjects of animated conversation among the staff. He was ordered to salvage all maps and telecommunication equipment, but as they were loading the truck, the Russians arrived and opened fire. The headquarters company assigned to cover them had vanished. Hegedüs, with a few others, escaped in an automobile that soon broke down. Then began a forty-day march on foot. Twice they were surrounded—whether by the Red Army or by partisans, none could say—but each time they dispersed and got away. At farms they dug carrots, potatoes—any roots that looked edible—and learned how to pick undigested kernels of grain from frozen goat dung. At one place the leader of their bedraggled assortment of 120 men called for a rest, Hegedüs refused. His feet were already black with frostbite, and he dared not stop. With twelve of his fellows he pushed on. They never saw the others again. Soon after they had crossed into Hungary, an army surgeon in a Nyiregyháza hospital prepared to amputate Hegedüs's leg, which was black from the knee down. But again Hegedüs stubbornly resisted, refusing to submit to knife and saw. He demanded, and got, a railway pass for Sopron. Once home, he had a private doctor perform surgery, which resulted in the loss of only a part of the big toe.[12]

Now dismissed from the army, Hegedüs resumed his work at the airplane factory, at which he remained until the Russians closed the ring around Budapest in late December 1944. The Germans planned to evacuate all machinery, supplies, and personnel of the factory to Landsberg in Germany in order to resume production there. Hegedüs and his wife and three children joined others in a boxcar for a three-day trip into Austria. They traveled in the same kind of boxcars that carried Jews to Auschwitz, with similar armed guards (except these were Arrow Cross youths, not gendarmes) on top to prevent them from leaving the cars—not even for rest stops. Allied bombers forced them to Linz, where plans for the Landsberg factory were scrapped because the train carrying most of the machinery had been swallowed up in railway chaos. Thereafter the Hegedüs family meandered with millions of other refugees dislocated in the final months of the war. In November 1945,

12. Interview with Piroska Hegedüs (May 24, 1996).

although American occupational officers warned them that whole trainloads of Hungarians returning home from the West were being shipped to the USSR as forced laborers, the Hegedüs family arranged for space on a baggage car bound for the Hungarian border. At the last minute, however, they succumbed to an appeal and gave up their place to a band of homesick Hungarian POWs. (It was later reported that these men were seized by the Russians and shipped east.) The family made no further attempt to return to Hungary. Skilled labor being in short supply immediately after the war, the German authorities welcomed the Hegedüs family until 1950, when the government changed its priorities and forced them into exile. The only country open to them was Australia, but the grandfather adamantly refused to go—he would not live among "savages." By a fluke an opening appeared in the United States quota, and they immigrated to Detroit.

Giovanni Nastasi (born 1922), a native of Milan, had been lured into the war by the promise of adventure, not by any political convictions. He hated hot climates and was pleased when he learned in 1942 that his unit, the Third Bersaglieri, would be sent to Russia, not Libya. "I was in the regular Italian army—not Black Shirt. I was never a Fascist. Neither was my father, though as a stationmaster for the Italian railroad he was supposed to be."[13] Nastasi and two hundred thousand other Italians constituting ten divisions went up to the Russian front in boxcars fitted with bunks. Their route lay through Warsaw, Pinsk, and Kiev. Somewhere in Poland they stopped next to a train packed with Jewish families being sent to a concentration camp. When the Italians tried to pass food and water to them, they were driven off by German guards. "There was nearly a riot—shouts, threats, insults. We hated the Germans."[14]

From Milerova they marched for a week through slush and mud and a blinding snowstorm to reach their defensive positions south of the Second Hungarian Army along the Don River. What Nastasi had never imagined about Russia was the bone-penetrating cold. The Italian expeditionary force had arrived in summer uniforms, and it was November before they were issued sheepskin jackets. "At first we made fun of the Romanians, who used oxen to pull their cannon, but not after the subzero temperatures shut down our modern motorized transport."

---

13. Interview with John [Giovanni] Nastasi (September 25, 1993).

14. Interview with John Nastasi (September 21, 1995). The quotations that follow are taken from this interview and that cited in note 13 above. In the rest of the book's sections devoted to interviewees' tales, a similar pattern will pertain: I shall cite the interview source of quotations only at the outset.

At first it was easy duty. Their bunkers lay on the high cliffs of the west bank of the Don, overlooking the Russians in the flatlands to the east. "The nights were beautiful. It was cold and crisp, and you could read a newspaper by the full moon. Russian loudspeakers played the Vienna waltz for us or called out, 'Italians! Give up! The war is over for you!' It made us laugh." The food was poor. "In Italy when we complained about the food, the officers told us, 'Where do you think you are, at the front?' Now we were at the front, and when we complained, they told us, 'Where do you think you are, in Italy?'" Nastasi was now a staff sergeant. The German rule was that any civilian caught after curfew without the password must be taken to headquarters for interrogation. "We just ignored the order and let them go. The Ukrainians were good people. They flocked around us in the village when we sang. And their women were very nice to us, if you know what I mean."

The Russians attacked across the Don and overran his position on January 22, coming in from the rear. On that morning Nastasi awoke to find his senior officers had vanished. German support troops had also disappeared. Russians poured into their bunker, "carrying tommy guns that looked like the ones used by Al Capone's boys in Hollywood movies." Nastasi's group stood up immediately and surrendered. A Russian pointed his gun at them and said, with alarming ambiguity, "No more war." Instead of shooting, he sent them streaming to the rear, where they fell in with Hungarian and Romanian POWs on the river bank. Nastasi had a bad moment when he remembered, just before being searched, that a friend had given him two regimental insignia from the collars of dead Russian soldiers. In the nick of time he managed to trample them in the mud. Had the Russians found them, they would have shot him. The POWs crossed the Don on the ice, a Russian soldier in front of them delicately testing the firmness of the ice with a long stick. None of the prisoners were abused, kicked, or struck, but the Russians immediately stripped them of their sheepskin jackets. Later many Italians died of exposure.

On the east bank they were turned over to partisans, most of them teenagers, who ushered them to a holding camp at Kalach, far to the east. They walked for a week, without food, and many died on the way, either collapsing from untreated wounds or shot by guards for lagging behind. Nastasi heard the shots and knew what was happening but never looked back at these executions. "They were not cruel—only practical. Those men could never have made it." They passed lines of frozen bodies, some standing up with eyes open and looking as though standing on a street corner, waiting for someone. Once a partisan took Nastasi's wallet, tore out pictures of his mother, and threw the wallet away, saying, "You'll not be needing these." He was terrified. "I thought the guard was taking me out to be shot, but it was only his joke. Maybe he just meant the money."

At Kalach they were locked in boxcars—sixty men per car—and trained eastward. Unable to remove the dead, the living used them as pillows. Once a day guards unlocked the door and pulled the corpses out. For a week they squatted without food or water, licking condensation off frozen hinges and iron plates and lying in feces and urine, which grew to a great heap near the barred door. Once Nastasi begged a can of hot water from a Russian locomotive engineer on the next track—"the best soup I ever had."

Their destination was a huge camp of twenty thousand prisoners at Tambov. The Russians left the management of the camp to the national groups. Initially the Poles held all the cushy kitchen jobs, but only until the Italians mobilized and pushed them out. Whoever strong-armed the cookhouse had the best chance for survival. Food was prepared in gigantic iron pots, which were slung on poles and carried to the camp sections. The passage had to be guarded by big Italians with clubs to prevent the other prisoners from breaking through and stealing the food. Everyone avoided the Germans, whom they blamed for their misery. Hearing that Hungarians were like Italians, Nastasi tried to establish rapport with them, but the Magyars kept to themselves. They were a morose and badly demoralized group of men. Spaniards of the Blue Division were worse off because their leaders in Madrid, fearing to antagonize the Allies, refused to admit they were there. At some indeterminate date (Nastasi had lost track of calendar time) the POWs at the holding camp were separated by nationality. Nastasi never saw the Hungarians again and never heard where they went.

The Italians remained at Tambov for a year, in barracks that had been hacked together from green and warped lumber and admitted rain, snow, or sun—depending on the season. It was nearly impossible to sleep on bunks constructed of untrimmed logs with snags or knots that always found your backbone. To keep warm they slept in heaps like hibernating animals. Their work consisted in felling trees and hauling logs to sawmills. Men with frozen or broken fingers broke or bit them off. There was no sick bay, no medicine. "There were these terrible diseases—typhus, typhoid, dysentery, scabies—and there was nothing you could do about them. If a flea bit you, you figured it was a death sentence." He saw one suicide—a German walked calmly up to the wire and was shot. Nastasi himself often became desperate. To cure his depression he would lie on his back, look up at the clouds, and pretend he was back in Italy and free again.

Once each month they disrobed in a stinking hut and passed over their clothes for fumigation. Then a Polish barber with a dull straight razor scraped off the dirt, filth, and lice from their skin, always drawing blood if the prisoner had no chunk of bread or other tip for him. Then they got a bowl of water the size of a saucer and were told to wash themselves. They passed into a dim hall, where their wet, fumigated clothes were pitched in to them. Sometimes the guards switched off the light. In the dark they scrambled for whatever they could find. "The Russians thought this very funny. We did not. To miss a sock or a shirt in that climate was certain death." Shoes were the greatest need, and Russians regularly pilfered the best ones. Nastasi had a good pair, which he scratched and mutilated to make them look worn. Anyone without good shoes was soon dead. "The Russians were like children. Sometimes the guards gave us cigarettes. At other times they pushed red-hot pokers near our faces and scowled to scare us. But there were no beatings in any of these camps."

In February 1944 the Italians were removed temporarily to a camp near Moscow. They had to move across the city to another railway line, but the civilians were well behaved, none of them jeering or spitting as some of the prisoners feared. "Some Russians handed us pieces of bread, and others burst into tears—probably because we looked so shabby and they wondered how their boys looked in German prison camps." At the station an Italian who had once performed at La Scala sang an aria. Soon hundreds of Russians swarmed round him like filings to a magnet, all of them smiling and clapping. "Caruso! Caruso!" they chanted.

Compared with the other Axis prisoners taken at the Don Bend debacle, few of whom survived their captivity, the Italians fared comparatively well. Their last camp was in Uzbekistan, near Tashkent, where they had a temperate climate and plenty of food. Some nameless commissar told them that Comrade Stalin was sending them south because he knew that Italians were unaccustomed to a cold climate. "It was probably a lie, but we could relax. By this time Italy had dropped out of the war, and the Russians seemed to trust us." They worked in rice fields. Here the greatest danger was infection of wet feet, for without medical attention blood poisoning always led to death. But they ate well, gaining strength from camel's milk and gorging on cucumbers and tomatoes. Although they moved easily among the local population, "the women were not friendly like the Ukrainians—you know, Moslem."

The Italians were packed off for home in November 1945. (Most Hungarians captured at the Don Bend had to wait two years longer.) Nastasi had heard nothing from his family and did not know whether they had survived the war.[15] They traveled as they had come—by boxcars—but now the doors were open, and they stripped the barbed wire from the small window. Since the locomotive frequently detached itself from the cars, then wandered off, and later returned to pick them up again, they had a leisurely trip home through devastated Europe—Warsaw, Berlin, Hamburg, Frankfurt. Nastasi remembered that at one station a young Russian soldier whose leg had been amputated climbed off the train. His wife appeared, looked momentarily alarmed at the empty trouser leg, then ran forward for an embrace that concluded with both of them in tears. "It was exactly like a movie." Nastasi's weight had dropped in captivity from 165 to 95 pounds, but the population along the route—especially the Poles—looked far worse than he did. In December the Italians wept and laughed and cheered as their train dropped down from the Brenner Pass. The tattered remnants of Mussolini's vaunted expeditionary force to rid the world of Communism had come home.

Nastasi found his father at his old job in the Verona railway station. When he got home to his mother at midnight, her wailing aroused the neighborhood and brought the police, who thought she was dying or being attacked by burglars. In Milan he resumed his old job at the telephone company, which had sent his mother his salary check during all the months of his absence. He immediately put the experience behind him. He has never had dreams or nightmares about Russia. "I respect the Russians. Sometime I would like to go back there and see all the places—the Don Bend and even the prisons."[16]

József Bárdos (born 1920), was the son of a Jewish tailor in Jászberény, a small city in the *puszta* east of Budapest. His family had no political affiliations or interests. For the Jews of Jászberény, as in many provincial Hungarian towns, the recipe for prosperity, and survival, lay in minding one's own business and quietly adopting the values of the Magyar majority.[17] Bárdos senior played by the rules, obediently magyarizing his family name when it became politic to do so.

---

15. No letters were exchanged, but his family knew that he was a prisoner in the USSR. His name had been sent to the BBC. While listening to their Italian program his mother heard this announcement: "Giovanni Nastasi sends greetings from Russia."

16. In 1948, when a female cousin from the United States came to Verona on a visit, Giovanni married her, settled in Lawrence, Massachusetts, and became John Nastasi. The present Italian government now sends him $140 bimonthly for his military service, which includes a bonus for his more than two years as a prisoner of war. In all, he has collected $8,000.

17. The policy was not always successful. In Jászberény, for example, during the late spring of 1944, 560 Jews were combed from their homes and packed off to Auschwitz. See Martin Gilbert, *Atlas of the Holocaust* (Oxford, 1988), 197.

At the local high school József distinguished himself in a business course, but after graduation in 1938 he found himself blocked from higher education by the Jewish quotas. He moved at once to Budapest and took a job in a factory on Csepel Island, the center of the working-class movement in Hungary. His political awakening came when a cousin was thrown into prison for expounding Marxist ideas at his high school. József began to examine the question of fairness, and came up with no rational answers. As he looked about him, he saw that his fellow workers lacked the basic amenities for decent lives, but the observation raised more questions than answers. A young woman at his factory guided him into the trade-union movement. The local community house was packed with underground ideologues, and through lectures, discussions, and late-night debates he acquired a working knowledge of Marxist theory and political economy. Although he was ready to join the Communist Party, his mentors advised him to join the Social Democrats, which included at that time large numbers of crypto-Communists forced underground by rightist purges.[18]

The Csepel Island region was loaded with members of Ferenc Szálasi's Arrow Cross Party, and Bárdos reveled in the street fights against them. The Nyilas were "rough and crude people—lumpenproletariat of the worst sort." In 1940 he was a ringleader in an organized attack upon an Arrow Cross mass rally. These fights were brawls, not mayhem. A black eye was more customary than a broken skull. No guns or knives came into play.[19]

By the spring of 1941 it had become evident to his cadre that Hungary would shortly join Germany in its war against the Soviet Union. They worked on a plan to encourage soldiers of working-class origins to desert and to hide in the homes of workers in the Csepel district. This fizzled. No deserters sought asylum, and most families scoffed at such a dangerous and subversive idea. In October 1941 Bárdos himself was drafted into a Jewish labor battalion and found himself an unwilling participant in a capitalist war as he dug wells and laid railroad track in Transylvania.[20]

In November 1942 his unit was locked in freight cars and moved into the Ukraine. The farther they traveled from Hungary, the worse their treatment. Hungarian officers behaved in ways unthinkable at home. To clear a path

---

18. Interview with József Bárdos (January 17, 1989).

19. Fights at the university between rightists and leftists were even more gentlemanly, consisting as they usually did of masses of students pushing against one another like a tug-of-war in reverse.

20. For the evolution of Jewish labor battalions attached to the Honvédség, see "Men" in Chapter 2.

through a suspected minefield they would order a labor battalion at pistol point to fan out and advance over the terrain—and take bets on how many Jews would be killed. (The brother of the woman Bárdos later married was killed in such a demonstration.) By contrast, the Russian peasants of the region were compassionate and helpful. Billeted in peasant houses near the Don River, Bárdos and seven others (all of them Communists) obtained a crude map showing locations of the partisans and planned to escape. When the Red Army smashed the Hungarian line in January, Bárdos's group led into the Russian lines a total of fifty-five men—including some of their former guards, Gentiles who preferred taking their chances as deserters and POWs rather than retreat in this murderous winter climate.

In a huge collection camp containing about ten thousand POWs, Bárdos's group stripped underwear and Hungarian uniforms from corpses. This was the first time as labor-service Jews they had dared put on Honvédség uniforms, but though Magyar soldiers witnessing this defilement of their uniforms may have been offended, they dared say nothing about it. Bárdos and his comrades were disappointed when their captors lumped them with all the other "fascist" prisoners taken at the Don Bend. Early in May a typhus epidemic ravaged the camp. Bárdos estimates that about 8,500 prisoners died, including three-quarters of the medical staff (all of them improvised from the POWs).[21] His own weight dropped to thirty-eight kilos.

During the summer the Russians dispatched the prisoners in different directions. Bárdos ended up in a munitions factory in the Ural Mountains, where he was trained as a welder. He took instruction in Marxist-Leninist doctrine, and in 1944 attended an antifascist institute in Gorki. His future was laid out for him as carefully as if by blueprint; subject to the approval of his mentors, he would be allowed to return to Hungary after the war and to assist in replacing that moribund capitalist state with a genuine people's republic.

In September 1947, just before the Communists took control of the government, Bárdos returned to Hungary. He had been in Russia for more than five years. He rode in a boxcar, not a parlor car. "The train ride took a month, but it was a beautiful trip for me." In Budapest he took part in rigging the elections and cheerfully admits that his party faked IDs and stuffed ballot boxes. "Yes, the elections were corrupt. But we Communists only did what

21. It is curious that the labor battalions contained a higher percentage of medical doctors than the Hungarian army at large. The reason is that Christian doctors could arrange exemptions, whereas Jewish ones could not. Although doctors were badly needed in the Honvédség, Jews were not allowed to serve there.

the other parties had always done. We just did it better." In the years to come he had a varied career in Communist Party activities as an organizer of a World Youth conference in Budapest (the Communist equivalent of a Boy Scout jamboree) and as a professor of Marxist ideology and philosophy at the Lenin Institute. After the 1956 revolution Bárdos joined the State Security Police attached to the Ministry of Interior. He retired in 1975.

There were tangible rewards. The regime provided Bárdos and his wife with a luxurious flat on Rippl-Rónai Street, a patrician avenue just a few steps from City Park and Heroes' Square. With the flat came furniture, Chinese urns, and paintings that once belonged to some prewar aristocrat now long forgotten. Today, as József Bárdos and his wife, Judit, stroll protectively with their grandchildren in City Park, they are virtually indistinguishable in dress and demeanor from the capitalist couples who paraded along these broad avenues in the Horthy epoch, half a century earlier.[22]

Retreat

The Don Bend disaster proved to be the turning point for the Hungarian commitment to the German war. Stories circulated in Budapest of how the cheap iron rifle cartridges froze in the barrels, of how gasoline turned into jelly in the subzero temperatures, of how soldiers starved, and of how artillery support dropped to three rounds per day because mud and snow swallowed ordnance trucks at the front. Moreover, reports that German divisions had withdrawn without informing the Hungarians brought a great outcry. Enmity between Germans and Hungarians intensified at an exponential rate as each blamed the other for cowardice and incompetence. Now in the salons and cafés of Budapest one heard mutterings that Bárdossy and his supporters had been "criminals" for dragging the nation into a German war. Insiders muttered that twenty-one of the twenty-seven highest-ranking generals in the Honvédség were of German ancestry.[23]

Except for a determined minority of hard-liners in the army and in Parliament, Hungarians overwhelmingly wanted now "to jump out," to salvage what human and physical resources remained, but at the same time somehow to save the country from the dreaded Bolshevik hordes. Anglophilia in the public press was mushrooming. As early as January 1943 Prime Minister

22. For a sketch of the wife of József Bárdos, see "Women" in Chapter 2.
23. Kállay, 95.

Kállay sent a secret note to the Allies that Hungary would not oppose an Anglo-American troop advance into his country, although he insisted upon assurances that the Western powers, not the Soviets, would occupy his country. These guarantees the Allies repeatedly refused to give. They had agreed among themselves that Hungary belonged to the Soviet sphere.

In mid-April 1943 Horthy met Hitler at Salzburg. Hitler knew about Kállay's peace overtures and demanded his removal, which Horthy refused. Further, he refused to promise another army for the Russian front or to sign a text stating that the aims of the war were to defeat the Allies as well as the Soviet Union. What the two leaders agreed on was the paramount importance of continuing the war against the USSR. Horthy pressed Hitler for return of the Second Hungarian Army. Hitler agreed, for the Hungarian troops, now a ragtag collection of demoralized and angry men, had become even more uncooperative and mutinous. By May Hungary had pulled out most of them, leaving only a smaller body as occupational troops in the Ukraine. This force, which acquired the appropriate nickname the "Dead Army," was held by Hitler as hostage to guarantee fealty. Horthy even succeeded in bringing home the Jewish labor battalions, which saved them from Nazi death camps. Up to this time the Germans had not interfered in Hungarian politics. Now, seeing so clearly Horthy's growing antipathy to the alliance, the Germans began to pour money into the coffers of Hungarian radical right parties, including the Arrow Cross.

The fall of Mussolini in July 1943 electrified the peace factions in Budapest. Kállay saw an opportunity for both Italy and Hungary to withdraw together from the Axis, but when Italy chose to continue the war, he knew that unless he did the same, the Germans would occupy the country.[24] As yet there were no German troops based in Hungary, and formal permission was required each time the Germans wished to use Hungarian railways for transporting men or supplies to the Russian front. (Even on these occasions, Kállay forced them to use single-track and spur facilities whenever he could get away with it.) General Vilmos Nagy Nagybaczoni was now his minister of defense, an appointment that angered anti-Semites because Nagybaczoni instituted humanizing reforms in the labor service. (But Kállay dared not cancel the system altogether lest he be accused of exempting Jews from wartime service.)

24. After the war, when the Allies blamed Hungary for not dropping out of the war in 1943, Kállay argued that this would have harmed, not helped, the Allied war effort because the Germans would have occupied the country, drafted 700,000 men for the Wehrmacht, and used every possible factory for war production. Ibid., 179ff.

Early in 1944 Kállay grew bolder. Even as he made public pronouncements stating that Hungary's interests were best served by "an essentially defensive Germany [rather than] an expansionist Russia,"[25] he began sending feelers to Stalin, suggesting that if the Soviet drive westward would agree to bypass Romania and Hungary, he would safeguard the left flank from attack. Since Hungary lay within the projected postwar sphere of the Soviet Union, this offer was never seriously considered. German intelligence agencies were fully informed about Hungary's various overtures to the Allied powers, and Hitler's patience was being stretched too far. Late in February Kállay issued an ultimatum to Germany: the Dead Army must be immediately returned; no German troops would be allowed to cross Hungary; Hungary alone would defend the Carpathian line. This was the last straw. Hitler ordered his generals to launch Operation Margarethe—a plan for the military occupation of Hungary.

Still sufficiently in awe of Horthy to fear that his presence could stir Hungary to resistance, Hitler invited the regent to Salzburg to discuss withdrawal of the Dead Army. Therefore Horthy was out of the country on March 18, 1944, when the German army crossed the frontier. When he learned what had happened, Horthy threatened to abdicate, but Hitler begged him not to, promising that the occupying force would be withdrawn after the government had been purged of obstructionists. He then asked Horthy to sign a paper indicating that the occupation was by mutual agreement, but the regent stubbornly refused. (The new Hungarian government signed it on March 22.) Horthy was then allowed to return to Budapest. With him came Hitler's personal representative, Edmund Veesenmayer, the new German minister plenipotentiary, and on a separate train the Adolf Eichmann *Sonderkommando*, responsible for deporting the Jews.[26] Horthy still talked of abdication, but Kállay dissuaded him; Hitler still admired him, and his presence would mitigate some of the worst features of occupation. Veesenmayer went to work and rounded up the most vocal leftists in Parliament. (Most of them were released within a few days, sufficiently intimidated to be allowed to resume their legislative duties.) Kállay, however, had to take refuge in the Turkish legation, where he remained—always with a ring of German guards and searchlights around the villa—until late October, when he surrendered and was imprisoned at Mauthausen. In his place Horthy installed Veesenmayer's choice, Döme Sztójay, a colorless yes-man who had been serving as the Hungarian minister in Berlin.

25. Macartney, 2:210.
26. For a discussion of the Jewish deportations, see Chapter 2.

The Arrow Cross Party was not included in the new government, Veesen-mayer having no appetite to placate such a mercurial chieftain as Szálasi, who for a time even encouraged his party to demonstrate against the occupation—the only major leader, incidentally, who dared do so. The Germans had no intention of stirring the fires of revolution in the country but wanted only to keep Hungary economically sound and politically welded to the Axis frame. At first, Veesenmayer feared that strikes and sabotage might break out among the workers, but there were none. (As a matter of fact, labor conditions improved under the Germans because they demanded greater production and raised wages accordingly.) Nor was there trouble in the universities or in the government bureaucracy. Soon the German minister was driving about Budapest without a bodyguard. As he later said, "A day in Yugoslavia was more dangerous than a year in Hungary."[27]

Conditions reverted to normality so rapidly that by April 25 Hitler had removed nearly all of his occupation troops. (After the first days of the occupation, German soldiers were rarely seen on the streets of Budapest.) Hitler said that he was giving the Hungarians a final opportunity to redeem themselves for their poor performance in the anti-Bolshevik crusade. Horthy promised to raise a new army consisting of a million and a half men, but no one—least of all the Germans, who would have had to equip such a horde—ever believed it could, or would, be done. In the domestic sector censorship was tightened. Parliament busied itself passing laws designed to encourage the development of "Hungarian qualities" without defining specifically what these might be.

The most noticeable change in the day-to-day life of Budapest following Operation Margarethe was the advent of Allied aerial bombing.[28] Efforts by Kállay to have Budapest declared an open city had been blocked by the pro-war clique, who postulated that this would cut armaments production by 80 percent and leave an equal proportion of the workforce jobless (as well as politically restless). The Germans had promised to maintain aerial superiority, but they lacked the wherewithal to deliver. On April 2 the Eighth American Air Force came up from bases in Italy to bomb industrial sites in Budapest and environs. Thereafter the skies were often filled with great armadas containing up to two hundred B-17s and B-25s, protected by Lightning and Mustang fighter planes, making daylight raids, while at night the RAF

---

27. Macartney, 2:444.

28. In the fall of 1942 the Soviets had made a single bombing raid on Budapest, which caused great outrage because it damaged Városmajor Church in the heart of the city, but Hungarian targets had no priority for the Soviets at this time.

dropped mines in the Danube to disrupt the river trade with Germany. While the purpose of the raids was to destroy industrial areas like the vast factory complex downriver at Csepel Island, residential areas took heavy damage from the Americans, who were particularly poor shots.

The Dead Army was appropriately named. It consisted of a dejected and defeated ragtag assemblage of soldiers whose litany, Miklós Bárd (born 1914) recalled, was always "We want to go home."[29] Bárd, who was a graduate of Pécs University with a degree in Italian, had always been a reluctant soldier. A native of Kaposvár, he came from six generations of village schoolmasters and never had a weapon in his hand until he was drafted into the army. Politics was distasteful to him, particularly the nationalist kind promulgated by the Gömbös faction.

In 1935 he studied in Rome and Perugia on a state scholarship. He found Italians sympathetic and friendly, and at this stage of his life envisioned nothing more exciting than guiding students through the nuances of the Italian language. The Italy of Benito Mussolini was something else—noisy, bellicose, menacing. In May 1938, when Hitler came to Rome, Bárd joined the mob of spectators lining the avenue. The procession was heavily guarded, and when he reached into his pocket to take a bite from his *panino*, he was roughly handled by Italian plainclothesmen who thought he was reaching for a grenade. Afterward they had a good laugh about it, but he never forgot his sense of helplessness when the police swarmed about him.

When Bárd returned to Pécs in 1939, he was drafted into the army. Fluent in German as well as Italian, he became a translator. The Volksdeutsche of the region, excited by Hitler's easy victory over Poland, were becoming troublesome. Great numbers of them spoke only broken Hungarian, and they responded eagerly to Hitler's affirmations that whoever was a native speaker of German belonged to the Reich. Many had already refused induction into the Hungarian army, and in Budapest there was a movement afoot to deport dissidents. During the summer months students from Germany fanned out into the villages and even the corridors of the universities, where they glorified the Nazi revolution. In his duties as an Army interpreter Miklós Bárd found himself drawn willy-nilly into a distasteful political maelstrom. Moreover, his clerical duties did not exempt him from basic training, where he had to learn the manual of arms punctuated by kicks, cuffs, and beatings of the drillmaster. He hated the army, and his distaste was so glaringly

29. Interview with Miklós Bárd (April 23, 1989).

reciprocated that he was never promoted. The universal corruption in the army offended him as much as the brutality. Bribery was an open avenue to preferment. "If you wanted a promotion, or a leave, it was easy—you just gave your sergeant a pig." No pig—no preferment.

Bárd was dismayed when Hungary declared war on the Soviet Union, but having followed Hitler's blitzkriegs in Poland and in France, he believed that the Germans would quickly overrun Russia. He was now attached to the staff of a mountain infantry regiment that was shipped to the front after the Don Bend debacle. His regiment crossed the Soviet frontier by train in March of 1943, and went into the front line near Kolomya, where they waded a river choked with ice. They joined a polyglot group of Hungarians, Germans, Ukrainians, and Romanians—all of them unified by their mutual demoralization and exhaustion. Bárd found the diary of a dead German soldier, which graphically described the retreat and predicted worse disasters to come. For the first time he entertained the idea that the Germans might lose the war. "Up to this time I thought they were invincible. Now I saw that they were just men, not gods."

The first attack of his regiment ended in disaster. His colonel, who had never been in battle before, insisted that his officers turn out in spit-polished leather boots, which looked splendid on parade but which proved to be perfect targets for Soviet sharpshooters.[30] Only four officers returned. Then a report came into headquarters that the Russians were running. Cheers and congratulations were short-lived, however, for they learned that the Russians were indeed running—but toward them. Within minutes the Hungarians were in full flight. "We never went forward while at the front—always backward."

During their retreat Ukrainian peasants encouraged Hungarians—but never Germans—to desert, offering them civilian clothes and promising concealment. One of Bárd's companions tried it. He was caught, stripped of uniform, tied to a post, and shot by a Hungarian officer. His naked body was dragged away and thrown into an unmarked hole in that boggy wilderness.

For a time Bárd was luckier than most Hungarian privates. As a university man in an army of semiliterates he was indispensable as a headquarters clerk. Usually he could sleep beside a stove and trade command gossip for extra food and cigarettes. For a time he served as regimental postman, a useful job because he got to know everyone, and by reading letters written to long-dead soldiers, he kept informed about conditions back in Hungary. While German

---

30. Two Hungarian historians have questioned Bárd's testimony on this, as well as several other points.

officers maintained discipline till the end, the Hungarians were generally incompetent and corrupt. Food shipped from Hungary regularly vanished before reaching the Dead Army. A commissary officer miraculously acquired several barrels of apples not through army channels but from the private stock of a brother at home. On one occasion the men were issued five liters of wine after a thirty-kilometer march. There was no way to carry it, so everybody got drunk.

Bárd hated his officers, who, according to him, thrived on unprovoked brutal behavior. For eight months he was a scribe for a combat captain who abused him because he was a university graduate. "You won't die a hero's death," the captain said, "but I'll see that you die at this desk here." At mealtime he would knock food out of Bárd's hands and in the morning kick him awake. On one occasion, when rain blew in a window and spotted a document, he ordered Bárd to be hung up by the wrists. This punishment could result in major bone dislocation or death. Once out of sight of the captain, a kindly lieutenant revoked the sentence and pretended it had been carried out.

All pretense that his unit was an effective fighting instrument ended on June 17, 1944, during a retreat through a Polish village. When Russians suddenly broke the line, everyone began running. A captain emerged from a doorway and tried to stop the rout, but a crazed soldier running beside Bárd leaped on the officer and began biting and strangling him. The captain shouted, "Gendarmes!" Gendarmes materialized from the church and "shot the soldier like a hare." They pointed their guns at Bárd, who feared he would be shot as a deserter, but the gendarmes, distracted by the roiling mob fleeing westward, passed him by. Farther along he saw a general resting the barrel of a machine gun against a tree and shooting his men when they failed to rally. Henceforth only a minority cadre of rightist officers, fearful about what would happen to them if captured, showed a vestige of fighting spirit. As the retreat swept back across Poland, even the Wehrmacht abandoned its fiction that it would regroup and counterattack. In order to impede Russian supply trains, the Germans employed a ten-ton hook on a locomotive to uproot sleepers and flip rails to the side. It was evident to Bárd that the German vow to launch a counteroffensive was as empty as the country itself.

In April 1945 Bárd found himself with a small band of Hungarians deep in Czechoslovakia. They hid for a few days and then crossed into the Russian lines. The Russians gave them a choice—hard labor in Siberia as POWs or service in a newly organized Hungarian division of the Red Army. Bárd chose to enlist in the Fifth Hungarian (Red Army) Division. They received Soviet uniforms and primitive firearms salvaged from some battlefield. Under heavy guard the token division (never at full strength) was shipped south. Knowing most of them would try to desert, the Russians kept them locked up in the train. They went through Budapest and passed the site of a recent battle at Lake Velence, where several hundred smashed Russian and German tanks squatted in the marshes. At Veszprém they waited for artillery and trained for the final Soviet thrust into Germany. On May 9, Bárd was awakened by shooting and yelling. It was not a counterattack as he had feared. Red soldiers ranged through camp, shouting, "Krieg kaput!"

The Soviets demobilized the Hungarians promptly in order to avoid having to feed them. They were told to go home and to get there the best way they could. Miklós Bárd returned to Budapest not on a white horse but in a sugarbeet cart. Having heard countless stories about Russian soldiers raping and looting, he expected the worst. But on arriving home in Ujpest he found his father cheerfully engrossed in a chess game with a friendly Red Army captain billeted in the house. That captain was like a guardian angel, for no member of the Bárd family ever suffered inconvenience or indignity from any Red Army soldier during the Russian occupation of the capital. Miklós never forgot the date—June 20, 1945. After six years of involuntary servitude he had attained his ambition—once again he was safe at home.

József Kiss (born 1923) never doubted that he would make a rotten soldier. His problem lay in convincing his father of his martial limitations, for his father was always extremely proud of his military service in the First World War, even though he had spent the greater part of it as a prisoner of war in Russia.[31] József grew up in rural Vácrátót, a tiny hamlet upstream from Budapest, where his father rented over two thousand *holds* of farmland (about three thousand acres). The senior Kiss played the role of a wealthy country gentleman until wiped out by poor management, a ruinous divorce, and the collapse of wheat prices during the Great Depression. He then settled at Kaposvár as director of the local chamber of commerce. His sons, Elemér and József, attended a Protestant boarding school at Pápa and moved on to the prestigious Eötvös Kollégium in Budapest. József lived a harum-scarum existence. "I paid no attention to the war. I admired English books and values. When a pro-German teacher urged us to join Turul, the right-wing student organization, I joined the Boy Scouts."[32] At the university he played a lot of

---

31. Interview with József Kiss (June 18, 1989).

32. The *turul* was a mythical eagle, sacred to the Magyar tribes. Its appropriation as the name of a rightist organization was in keeping with the "Hungaristic" mysticism purveyed by the followers of Gömbös.

tennis and began his lifelong absorption with Sándor Petőfi, the poet of the 1848 revolution who was martyred while fighting the Russian allies of the Hapsburgs. But much as he admired Petőfi, Kiss had no desire to share his fate.

In the summer of 1944, as the Red Army approached the eastern slopes of the Carpathians, university students were collected and sent to labor camps in Transylvania, where they dug tank traps and gun emplacements.[33] Kiss had barely arrived when a new order notified all men aged twenty or above to return to their homes and await regular army drafts. He spent an enjoyable summer in Kaposvár, reading and playing tennis. Almost daily he watched formations of American bombers flying to Budapest, but they dropped nothing on Kaposvár. In September he went up to Budapest for a new university term, but the bombing was so severe that classes were often canceled. Returning home, József resumed his tennis and quiet reading. The tennis games proved to be his downfall. His favorite partner was the daughter of an army colonel, who was indignant when he discovered an apparently healthy young man wielding a tennis racket instead of a weapon—and this at a time when the Bolsheviks were about to overrun the country. He ordered Kiss to report to his barracks and demanded to know why he was not in the army. Kiss muttered something vague about preferring to play tennis, and a week later found himself on a freight car bound for a remote training camp in eastern Slovakia. He never saw the colonel or his daughter again. By this time the Red Army had reached the outskirts of Arad, a Romanian city within a few miles of the Hungarian border.

At the training camp outside Érsekújvár (Presov) József Kiss received a frayed uniform and boots several sizes too large and became one of the thousand new recruits milling about a barbed-wire compound without much to do. There were no Germans in evidence; the camp was run by the Arrow Cross, and run badly. Their instructors were beardless cadets whose idea of punishment was to make a recruit write 1,500 times "A Honvéd's boots are always clean." Because he knew some math, Kiss was assigned to a trench-mortar team. Since they had no real mortars—Kiss never in his army career saw one up close—they trained with blocks of wood, "which we carried on our backs to keep us in good condition." They would stack the blocks properly under the eyes of an instructor (who probably had never seen a real mortar either), hold a log upright (pretending it was the barrel), and fire off imaginary shells. "I think we looked foolish." The place had once been some

---

33. They retained their civilian status. The practice of compelling university students in Hungary to perform labor service, usually at harvest, persisted until the middle 1980s.

sort of ramshackle farm. They slept on piles of straw in stables, which their
officers insisted that they call "barracks"—presumably because that word
had a military ring to it. Other than a basin with a hole in its bottom, which
provided what the sergeant called "a very quick wash," there were no
bathing facilities for the thousand stinking recruits. As part of a course called
"observation training" an officer led them on a long hike and then queried
them on what they had seen. All József Kiss could come up with was "a red
eiderdown hanging in a window." Most of the instructors knew the camp
was a farce. The larger number of them spent their days and nights in
shirtsleeves or underwear, playing cards and drinking wine.

A few days after October 15, when Germany deposed Horthy and installed
the Szálasi government, the new minister of propaganda arrived in camp and
announced that they were being incorporated into the German army. For a
time the recruits listened to the great man, then someone began singing
"Szózat," a patriotic Hungarian anthem with the opening lines "To your
country you must be steadily faithful, O Hungarian, / It's your crib and later
your grave site that cares for you and covers you."[34] Others chimed in, and
soon the minister's speech was submerged by a rolling anthem powered by
hundreds of throats. Officers ran about, threatening punishment, but the
anthem continued until the minister departed in a huff. The entire camp was
then restricted to barracks for two weeks. For Kiss this small act of defiance
was worth it. Besides, it was no great misfortune to be barred from
Érsekújvár, a town singularly devoid of amenities József Kiss might have
enjoyed—tennis courts, libraries, theaters, cafés.

In December the camp heard with mounting alarm that the Red Army was
closing on Budapest. The realization dawned that the Russians had gotten
between their camp and the capital. They evacuated the place in a panic. A
wood-burning locomotive dragging a string of sooty and bombed-out pas-
senger cars pulled into a siding, and the recruits swarmed aboard. There was
no heat, and most of the windows were gone. It was dog eat dog as recruits,
ignoring the shouts and threats of officers, fought each other for strips of
upholstery or wooden panels to block the windows and battled for corners
not fouled with excrement and debris. The condition of the carriages mir-
rored the chaos that marked that last period of the war.

At times the train barely moved; at other times it stopped altogether. No
one was permitted to stray beyond a few meters from the carriages. Officers

---

34. "Szózat," which means "proclamation," was an anti-Hapsburg poem (later set to music)
written by Mihály Vörösmarty (1800–1855).

each day read the names of men who had tried to desert, had been caught, and had been executed. Kiss was never able to confirm that these executions really occurred, for he never heard shots. But he had no appetite to put the matter to a test. Somewhere—in Slovakia or Hungary, he was never sure where—he was dispatched with orders to obtain lamp oil from some villagers. His begging technique was a failure—the citizens only grunted and slammed their doors. Finally, remembering the rhetorical flight of the minister of propaganda, he beat furiously on a door and launched his request with an appeal to their patriotism: "The salvation of the Hungarian nation and the fate of the army depends directly upon your aid," and so forth. The peasants seemed impressed. They heard him out and meekly asked what he wanted them to do. "Ah, two liters of petroleum, if you please," Kiss responded limply.

They detrained outside the Baltic port of Stettin and began two weeks of instruction. Although the Red Army confronted the city on three sides, their instructors, businesslike German cadets who never seemed to doubt that Germany would win the war, behaved with peacetime spit and polish, as though the Russians were still thousands of kilometers to the east. In March they boarded six different trains, always working slowly westward. Kiss admired the efficiency of the German rail system. No matter how much or how often the railways were bombed, they were always told the exact time for changing trains. To avoid strafings they always moved at night. One night their carriage was packed further with German female soldiers. Because of blackout, no lights were permitted. In the morning one of Kiss's companions studied the faces of the women carefully and confessed to him sadly, "I had such a good one last night, although now I can't tell which one it was."

At some forgotten date in April their train stopped near Münster. Train guards shouted, "Heraus! Heraus!" and they spilled out of the carriages. News came down that the British army was close at hand, and the regiment was broken up into squads of ten men. They were ordered to move north on foot, toward Bremen. They had been ordered to throw away their guns at the last camp so that, if captured, they could plead they were a harmless unarmed column. Allied planes nearly took their heads off with their propellers, but the pilots, seeing they were helpless and useless, never strafed them.

József and three others decided they had had enough of army life. They slipped away to a farm, where they explained they were Hungarians and were invited to dinner. The farmer's sons were somewhere on the eastern front—God only knew where. Later they found a farm where the workforce had been reduced to one young girl, who promised to hide and protect them in return for farmwork. They dared not risk it—it was certain execution if caught.

One day they found themselves in the middle of a battle, with artillery and machine-gun fire raging on both sides. They burrowed in a stable until the front passed over them. In the morning they wandered down a country lane and found an English guard at a bridge. They asked him how they could surrender. He said he did not want the responsibility, but allowed them to cross the bridge and look for the appropriate authority. Within a few minutes the foursome found themselves in a bivouac jammed with Britons, none willing to accept their surrender. At some point, however, a smiling English noncom approached them. "What time is it?" he asked pleasantly. The Hungarians lifted their wrists obligingly to examine their watches, and the Tommy said, "I'll take those." Deftly unstrapping their wrist watches, he disappeared among a laughing crowd of Britons.

The war was over, but not for József Kiss and his Hungarian companions. With German prisoners they were herded into open coal cars and moved to a POW camp near Edingen in Belgium. As they passed across Holland, the Dutch shook their fists and mimed throat cuttings. Holland had been systematically looted by the Germans, and the Dutch were starving. The Edingen camp was huge, but the Germans kept it tidy, and food was adequate—soup, bread, cheese, tins of meat. Kiss used his command of German to land a good position as chief clerk of his section. After half a year the Hungarians were weeded out and sent to a camp exclusively for Magyars at Eselheide in West Germany. Kiss was appalled. The prisoners were expected to sign a two-year contract and work in the mines. No letters were allowed in or out. It reminded Kiss of stories his father had told of slave labor in Russia after the First World War.

In late spring of 1946 everything brightened. British intelligence officers screened the prisoners carefully and offered those cleared of war crimes the choice of returning to Hungary or remaining in the West as protected refugees. If they chose to go, British soldiers could protect them only to the Hungarian border. After that, they would be on their own and at the disposal of the Russians. Moreover, they explained that Russians were arresting Horthy soldiers and shipping them to labor camps in Siberia. Despite the danger, Kiss chose to leave.

At the Hungarian frontier, when the British guards left the train, pirate gangs—not Russian soldiers—swept through the freight cars like clouds of hungry locusts, picking them clean of clothing, food, and blankets. József Kiss was too happy to care, for quite by chance the next stop was Kaposvár, the town where his military odyssey had begun two years before. In May 1946 he reached his father's house, where he found his brother, Elemér, who during the last days of the war had deserted the Hungarian army and joined a supply unit of the newly constituted Russo-Hungarian army. Their father was not happy with the military records of his two sons. He had not expected much of József, who was always thin and frail, but he was bitterly disappointed in Elemér, a powerfully built man who looked every inch a soldier yet admitted without shame that he had deserted his army and joined the enemy's. Furthermore, he returned home not with a chest covered by medals but only with a stamp collection he had looted from some good Hungarian's villa while consorting with Russian bandits.

Both brothers forgot the war more easily than did their father. For József it had only been a kind of Soldier Schweik experience that interrupted the real business in his life—studying the life and work of Sándor Petőfi. For Elemér the real struggle was yet to come—eight years in a Communist prison on a charge of leaking agricultural "secrets" to the Americans.[35]

When it became evident, particularly after Romania jumped out of the war in August 1944, that nothing could halt the Russian blitzkrieg from rolling across the nearly defenseless eastern plain of Hungary, conservatives in the government worked on strategies to guarantee that young intellectuals and scientists would not be squandered in hopeless battles. The idea was to transport these young men to the comparative safety of the West so that an intellectual elite capable of reconstructing the country would survive the war. Above all, these human resources should not fall into the hands of the Russians, who would carry them off to the Soviet Union as forced laborers. To this end, whole institutes and schools were packed up and dispatched by train to Austria and Germany. Hungary had learned a bitter lesson from the First World War, which wasted a generation of young men in a lost cause.

As the Red Army converged on Budapest in December 1944, the prestigious technical university arranged to move two thousand students with their faculty to Germany, where studies would be resumed as if the war did not exist. These young Hungarians constituted an intellectual elite chosen on the basis of academic merit, not wealth or family connections, and since they had been promised exemption from conscription, they were eager to leave.

---

35. József Kiss became Hungary's foremost Petőfi scholar and a curator of the Petőfi Museum in Budapest. For Elemér's postwar career, see the account of Eleonóra Majorosy in "Women," Chapter 5.

"We had no enthusiasm for the war," recalled Géza Galló (born 1924), the son of a railway clerk in Miskolc.[36] "We were told that our primary duty during wartime was to study hard. We worried that if we failed, we could be shipped off as private soldiers to the Russian front." The German authorities endorsed the plan; if Hungary fell permanently under the Soviet yoke after the war, Germany would inherit these young technocrats. Most of them were political innocents. "The announced war aims meant nothing to me," explained Galló. "I felt that Germans were our major enemy. At that time I had barely heard of Ferenc Szálasi." Aware of the lies promulgated as news in Hungarian newspapers, the students listened to shortwave broadcasts from the BBC, and scoffed at the law against owning shortwave radios or tuning to the BBC. If police confiscated their radios, the students could construct another one within hours.

On December 8 they had a rousing send-off at Keleti Station and left by special train, complete with professors, scientific instruments, and textbooks. Because Allied airplanes commanded the air and wrecked trains punctuated their journey, it took four days to reach Breslau. Here they set up school in some unheated military barracks and tried to resume their classes. Concentration proved nearly impossible: it was bitterly cold, they were always hungry, and the Germans were already withdrawing from Poland to defensive positions in the Reich.

At the end of January, when the Red Army approached Breslau, they packed up again, but a special train promised for them never materialized. They left on foot headed west, leaving behind most of their books and scientific apparatus and dragging their personal belongings on sleds. The thermometer stood at twenty below. In ten days they covered three hundred kilometers and afterward spent three days recovering at a Wehrmacht training center. Then they boarded a train, this time to Halle, where the university was set up in an old Luftwaffe barracks. Studies continued, and the professors even gave examinations but, as Galló remembered, "there was little motivation." At this time hundreds of British and American planes were carpet bombing Halle. While the Germans did not demand it, the Hungarians often spent entire days assisting civic authorities in removing debris, restoring water and electrical services, and searching for bodies. They were treated well by families in Halle, and were often invited for spartan teas in their homes, but Wehrmacht and SS soldiers, enraged by the Hungarians' noncombatant garb, cursed and kicked them off trams. At night they lay awake during the

36. Interview with Géza Galló (January 19, 1989).

blackout, watching the searchlights and glow from fires in the burning city, and they felt the earth trembling from bombardments. One afternoon, after returning from the city, they found half their barracks obliterated. The university was ordered to move again.

They boarded a train, which laboriously crawled eastward until the locomotive stalled permanently when they were ten kilometers from Dresden. They bailed out of the cars and saw, ahead of them on the eastern horizon, "an immense fire [that] turned the darkness into daylight. It was fantastic— like the footlights in a theater." Under their feet the earth shuddered. What they were watching was the terrible Dresden firestorm of February 13, which followed a dual raid from English and American bombers. In the morning a squadron of American fighter planes swept down and strafed their train. They scattered into a forest. The planes made six passes and flew so low that Gallo could see Negro pilots in the cockpits. For a day they hung about the wheezing locomotive, but from this time on they knew the university-in-transit idea was dead. They were isolated in the middle of Germany without orders, transportation, or supplies. By this time thirty-six students had been killed or disabled by air attacks.

Their leaders divided them into sections of twenty and instructed them to rendezvous at Regensburg, 250 kilometers south. The idea was to avoid capture by the Russians; somewhere down south they might link up with the Americans or British. They were on their own, had no maps, and would have to forage for supplies. Gallo's section soon split up further. Finally reduced to four, his group hitched rides on lorries and exchanged work for food in villages populated only by children, women, and old men. "Always the villagers accepted us and were kind to us. In every house they showed us pictures of husbands or sons missing or killed in the war." In the Bohemian Forest of western Czechoslovakia, rough wooded country fringed with meadows, they found a village where the mayor gave them a room over his inn. Here they decided to hole up and wait for the war to pass over them. Since most of the German males of the community had been drafted, farm families took the Hungarians into their homes in exchange for field work. They waited in this pastoral enclave until the front moved past.

One morning an American jeep came to the village and announced that the war was over. Gallo and his companions stepped out and identified themselves. The soldiers gave them food and cigarettes and drove off. One of them wrote out his name and address and told them to look him up if they ever got over to the States. Apparently forgotten by the Americans, they worked on their farms until early September, when an army truck arrived and carried them to a huge collecting camp at Pilsen containing tens of thousands of Axis prisoners. Galló was processed and quickly cleared of possible war crimes. An officer told him he could apply for an American immigration visa, or he could try to jump freights back to Budapest. He chose the latter.

On September 11, when Galló stepped off the Bratislava train in Keleti Station, Hungarian policemen seized him and jailed him for three weeks. "They seemed to think I was an American spy." After his release he immediately resumed his course work in the windowless classrooms of the technical university. On graduation two years later he saw that his transcript made no mention of his "German excursion." It was just as well, for in the Communist regime of 1948 and afterward it was dangerous to carry official papers indicating that one had ever lived or traveled in the capitalist West.

Although officially cleared of any political crime, Galló never could dismiss the specter of persecution. In 1951 his wife's parents, devout Catholics in Miskolc, were roused by the doorbell one night at 10 P.M. and were given thirty minutes by the gendarmes to collect some baggage and climb into a truck waiting in the street. They were deported to a remote camp in the *puszta*. They were not charged with anything and there was no trial. After two years of hard labor, personal abuse, and starvation fare, they returned to Miskolc. Their house and furnishings had been expropriated. "Both old people were destroyed by this experience. He had no job. A priest had to take them in. Thereafter when anyone rang their doorbell, their blood froze." Even forty years later Galló's wife sobbed convulsively as she tried to explain what the Communists of her own country had done to her parents.

In the Hungarian army the likelihood of death in battle appears to have been inversely correlated with the depth of one's educational background. Class and caste counted for something in Hungary, and the extent of one's education served as a ready yardstick for measuring either. "Intelligentsia," for Hungarians, was a term of distinction and signified a palpable reality—it was not a term of abuse as in America. Graduates of high school, for example, wore a special stripe on their sleeves to distinguish them from the others. Government policy was to segregate, whenever feasible and reasonable, the lower classes destined for cannon fodder from that privileged class of young men in whom the state had invested heavily. For at least two reasons the artillery was the safest branch of military service: first, it took such a long time to train artillery soldiers that generals were chary of throwing them away in hopeless battles; second, artillerists often did not get to the front, because the Germans disliked to supply the Honvédség with expensive cannon. Conveniently, because competence in mathematics was requisite for artillerists, recruits were drawn mostly from the pool of educated men.

The case of Lieutenant György Hahn (born 1918) was characteristic. Although drafted into the artillery in 1940, he remained in Budapest during the first four years of the war, much of the time at the Andrássy Barracks in downtown Pest, with easy access to the cafés and theaters of the boulevards. "I was very lucky," he recalled, "for in the army I always met people like myself. Duties and discipline were always very reasonable."[37] His father, a teacher of Saxon extraction, had fled from Szolnok during the Red Terror of the Béla Kun regime and had settled into a comfortable middle-class existence in Budapest. The family was deeply religious, and despite their Germanic orientation they always regarded the Nazi ideology as mendacious. From 1935 to 1940 Hahn studied Hungarian linguistics at the University of Budapest, where he joined an antifascist student organization opposing Turul, the Magyar nationalist group. There were fights between the two organizations—tame affairs consisting mainly of imprecations hurled between classes or pushing contests in the hallways. No one was ever seriously hurt. (Because the university was autonomous, city police were not allowed on the premises.)

In the army Lieutenant Hahn attached himself to a loose coterie of officers opposing the German war objectives. These supported General Vilmos Nagy Nagybaczoni, the minister of defense appointed during Horthy's disillusioned phase in mid-1942. Nagybaczoni was detested by rightists and anti-Semites, both in and out of the army, because he demanded that Jews in the labor service be treated as human beings.[38] Convinced that an anti-Nazi coup was feasible at some point in the war, Nagybaczoni covertly removed stocks of rifles and sidearms from government arsenals to civilian warehouses and the cellars of Jewish synagogues in preparation for such a rising. Hahn joined a faction whose goal was not to overthrow the government (they were firmly loyal to Horthy) but to free Hungary from the ever-tightening German net.

At dawn on March 19, 1944—the date of German occupation—Hahn was aroused at dawn by a policeman with an urgent message to report at once to his barracks. There his commander whispered in his ear that the Wehrmacht was already in the country and that the time had come to activate their

37. Interview with György Hahn (May 16, 1989).
38. Nagy was responsible for Bill 1942XIVtc, which forbade any kind of unreasonable severity for Jews in the army. On a visit to Berlin during the war he discovered that many top officers in the Luftwaffe and Wehrmacht were Jews, despite laws to the contrary. Göring told him, "In Germany I determine who is a Jew." Vilmos Nagy Nagybaczoni, *Végzetes esztendők* (Fatal years) (Budapest, 1986), 142.

resistance plan. His artillery units were on full alert and prepared to fight the Germans as soon as orders came down from the top. Hahn was dispatched to the Ministry of Defense in his role as an interpreter to spy out the situation. He found nothing at all happening. Since the regent was still in Salzburg conferring with Hitler, the country was rudderless. The anti-German faction of Parliament was quietly rounded up by the Gestapo, and all commanding officers suspected of anti-German attitudes were replaced. When Lieutenant Hahn returned to his barracks, his commander had changed his politics. Now his attitude was ignorance: "What resistance are you talking about?" Within twenty-four hours the Honvédség had become a satellite army of Hitler's without firing a shot in protest.

After four lazy years of barracks duty in Budapest, Hahn's military duties changed radically once the Germans forced the Honvédség to reorganize and increase its commitment to the anti-Bolshevik crusade. Within a fortnight he found himself on a troop train with the Twenty-Sixth Division en route to the Russian front in Galicia. They disembarked at Kolomya and went up to the line on foot. Their condition was nearly hopeless. Although the Twenty-Sixth Division was classified as a first-class unit, their field guns dated from the First World War. (Less favored units used guns dating back to the nineteenth century.) These were drawn by horses, spavined and anemic creatures—some of them superannuated race horses—that quickly deteriorated and drowned in an omnipresent ocean of mud and rain. No sooner had they reached the front at the hamlet of Slobodarungurska than they were forced to retreat—and they never did anything else during the war. Although Hahn was officially listed as a German translator and liaison officer, there was such a shortage of experienced artillerists that he had to work out mathematical problems for firing the guns. The Hungarians were poor shots, and their shortage of shells was so critical that Russian loudspeakers, brought up to the line to blare out inducements to desert, enjoyed using the refrain "YOU HAVE USED UP ALL YOUR ALLOWANCE OF AMMUNITION TODAY." Even their Wehrmacht allies gibed at the Hungarian "goulash cannon." Whenever the Red Army made a push, they fired off several Katusha rocket launchers—called by Hungarians "Stalin organs." "We could do nothing against them. They were so terrifying that anyone who could ran away." During one such rout an order came down that it was forbidden to throw away weapons during the retreat. The men laughed—for weeks they had had no weapons to throw away. Hahn noted the cruelty of the Germans during this retreat. There were long lines of Russian POWs trudging to the west, closely guarded by the SS. When Hungarians approached to give them water, the guards fired at them.

As the German and Hungarian troops fell back through Galicia toward Transylvania, Hahn passed through villages burned by the retreating Germans and saw the bodies of civilians hanging from trees. "Partisans," the Germans explained.[39]

In October 1944, in the mountains of Transylvania, they learned that Horthy had been deposed and that Szálasi's Arrow Cross Party had control of the government. Officers had to take an oath of allegiance to the new leader. Hahn's colonel assembled his officers in a farmyard. They stood in a circle as the colonel mounted a heap of refuse to obtain a better view of his men. It was a symbolic moment. A fellow officer nudged Hahn and whispered, "Now look what we are taking an oath on—a dung heap!" Immediately they began a long withdrawal to Debrecen and across the *puszta* toward the Tisza River. Since the commanding officers knew that their men would desert en bloc if they passed through Budapest, they wheeled south of the city and joined a German defensive line anchored at Lake Balaton. Here they were expected to hold until reinforcements could arrive from Germany, so that Hitler could launch a major counteroffensive. The fuel shortage was now so critical that guns were being moved and even hauled for longer distances by manpower.

At Székesfehérvár the Hungarian artillerists received modern equipment. The Wehrmacht and Waffen SS had been efficient in safeguarding it during their long retreat from Russia but no longer had enough German nationals to use it. The problem was that the equipment was so much more advanced than anything the Hungarians had seen during their four years of war that they could only puzzle over it. Hahn's colonel managed to wangle permission to withdraw from the line for further training, so they moved farther west toward Győr. By this time the Hungarians were panicked by the prospect of being captured by the Russians. One of Lieutenant Hahn's superiors, a disenchanted Arrow Cross member, spoke for them all: "If the Russians treat us half as bad as the Germans did, it will be a catastrophe."

Nothing came of the Balaton counteroffensive. By March 1945 the entire German army, along with that remnant of Hungarians which had not deserted, was in full flight to Austria, where all Magyar soldiers were supposed to be inducted and sworn into the army of the Reich. When the relics of the Twenty-Sixth Division were ordered to assemble at a monastery to take the oath, Hahn led a small band and fled west through the Vienna

---

39. Lieutenant Hahn has declared that he witnessed no atrocities committed by the Hungarian army, but he confessed that the Hungarian gendarmerie within occupied zones had a reputation for harshness.

Woods. He spoke passable German, and after they stole a car, he was able to convince German MPs along the road that they were Hungarian fliers ordered to report to Hamburg. Had his German been flawless, his group would probably have been shot as deserters. Their objective was to get far enough west to surrender to advancing British or Americans.

Somewhere in rural Bavaria they ran into an American armored unit, which sent them to the huge POW cage at Regensburg. Cleared of Nazi associations, Hahn volunteered for work as an interpreter and spent the next year as a civilian employee of the United States Army. Elected commander of the Magyar officers' camp, in his latter days he was assigned a Hungarian servant and even an automobile. In April 1946, despite warnings from the Americans, he chose to return home. He stripped his uniform of every identifying mark and rode a freight train back to Budapest. As a former Horthy officer he was questioned many times, but his anti-German activities as student and soldier were unimpeachable, and he was never punished.[40]

The father and grandfather of Jenő Borzsák (born 1915) were lawyers in the village of Monor, a few miles east of Budapest. They also had a bit of land— about fifteen acres—enough to turn a modest profit each year in grapes and fodder. One of Jenő's earliest recollections was of a column of Romanian soldiers passing through town during their invasion of Hungary in 1919. Some officers came into the garden, asked for water, and gave the boy oranges and chocolates.[41] They did no damage and were not offensive, but in telling the story in later years, his father used the episode as a platform for reviling Béla Kun, Bolshevism, and Trianon, in roughly that order.

In 1933 Jenő entered the Eötvös Kollégium, an elitist college of the University of Budapest. Its guiding light was Pál Teleki, an internationally known professor of geography (later to have a tragic career as prime minister). Two years previously, a Communist Party cell had been uncovered at the college, and Teleki had intervened to prevent the institution from being shut down. Students leaning too heavily on Marxism had been expelled. This suited Borzsák, who continued to admire Gömbös and began to read the work of Dezső Szabó, who excoriated both Jews and Germans in equal

---

40. György Hahn became a distinguished teacher of German and Hungarian in Budapest high schools. During the liberal regime of Imre Nagy in the early 1950s, he became a spokesman for reform and served as a director of the education department of the municipal council. After Nagy and his associates were executed, following the 1956 uprising, Hahn returned to high school teaching.

41. Interview with Jenő Borzsák (February 16, 1990).

measure. He attended the ceremony when the Russians, in a profession of friendship, returned Hungarian banners captured during the 1848 revolution, but he believed that the resumption of diplomatic relations between the Soviet Union and Hungary was farcical.

In 1939 he dutifully accepted his army draft, anticipating only two years of service followed by discharge. He served with a mechanized unit used in transporting patients and medical supplies, and was released to civilian life in September 1941. By this time Hungary was at war with the Soviet Union, but Borzsák gave it little thought. After all, the blitzkrieg was deep within the vitals of Russia, and an end to the war seemed only a matter of time. Meanwhile he graduated from the University of Budapest with a degree in languages and began teaching in high school.

Called up again in 1942, he obtained a post as language instructor at a military high school at Marosvásárhely (Tirgu Mures), capital of the Székely district of Transylvania. For centuries Transylvania had been an integral part of Hungary, but the makers of Trianon had transferred it to Romania, which had unsuccessfully tried to extirpate its Magyar heritage. Now, because of Hitler's Second Vienna Award, this part of Transylvania had been returned to Hungarian control, and the Budapest government moved to solidify its acquisition militarily. Placing a military school among the Szeklers was a shrewd idea, for these mountain people were celebrated for their tradition of fierce combat against outside enemies—whether Romanians, Turks, Bulgars, or Russians.[42] The assumption was that if the Soviet Union ever invaded Hungary, its offensive would come through one of the Carpathian passes.

Borzsák found the school a comfortable posting. His students were handpicked, tough, and bright. Promoted to the rank of first lieutenant, he married a Transylvanian woman of Hungarian extraction, and largely ignored the war. However, he was distressed by the way Romanians were treated by their Hungarian overlords. "They were not regarded as human beings. Although they did not know our language, they had to attend Hungarian schools—or none at all—which usually meant none at all." The enmity between Romanians and Hungarians was visceral.

Their stable academic world at Marosvásárhely collapsed abruptly in August 1944, when the Red Army launched an all-out offensive against Romania, which bypassed the Carpathians and swept around the German

---

42. The word *Székely* appropriately means "resident," which characterization is borne out by their determined occupation of the same wooded foothills of the western Carapathians for a thousand years.

and Hungarian right flank. On the twenty-third of that month Romania backed out of its alliance with Germany and agreed to turn its army over to the Russians. German and Hungarian divisions were forced to retreat pell-mell and reorganize on the Hungarian plain. The Ministry of War immediately ordered the school to pack up everything that could be carried and to resume school operations at Vasvár, a small city in western Hungary near the Austrian border. The fourth-year class was mobilized and dispatched at once to the front, while the other three classes, along with teachers, staff, and dependents, stripped the facilities, burning what could not be carried off. Because the army was in chaotic retreat, no motorized vehicles were available except a few private automobiles for invalids, women, and small children. All others walked—a few officers on bicycles rode ahead to scout for billets in sheds and farmhouses and to scrounge food from commissary dumps. Borzsák was accompanied by his wife and his wife's mother and sister. Their anabasis covered more than four hundred miles and required three months. The roads were jammed with refugees fleeing from the Russians, and against this tide Axis units moved toward the front in an attempt to block the enemy advance. Borzsák was proud of his students; although many of them passed through their home towns, where it would have been easy to desert, only a handful failed to answer roll call when they arrived in Vasvár.

They had barely unpacked when orders came to transfer the school to Germany. The Russian advance had reached the outskirts of Budapest, and the government was moving to Sopron and Szombathely. On December 19, the remnants of what had been the Marosvásárhely cadet school climbed aboard a train and for two weeks were shuttled about eastern Germany until they arrived at Bergen, a small town north of Hannover. As they collected their gear on the siding, another transport, filled with Jewish women from Budapest, pulled into the depot. These were bound for the Bergen concentration camp, a few kilometers to the south.[43] The two trainloads of Hungarian expatriates briefly stared at one another—wide worlds apart.

The academy took up quarters in brick barracks formerly used by a Waffen SS armored unit. There the Hungarian staff at once lost its autonomy to the Germans, who siphoned off the first-year students (fifteen-year-olds) for the Hitler *Jugend* and put the third-year students (seventeen-year-olds) into a *Fahnen Junker Schule*, which trained noncommissioned officers. Of the

---

43. This was a group of Hungarian Jews that Himmler planned to release in Switzerland in return for medical supplies. The Merényi sisters, part of this exchange scheme, had arrived a week earlier. See "Sisters" in Chapter 2.

original academy only the second-year group remained, badly demoralized by the knowledge that the Germans could do with them whatever they liked. Borzsák and other instructors tried to pick up where they had left off in Transylvania, but their motivation had disappeared. There was plenty of food in the SS commissary, and they were treated well by the SS personnel, but they felt like prisoners.[44] Above all, the mysterious prison camp to the south was not to be mentioned. It was off limits, although, when the wind came from that direction, the air was filled with an offensive miasma. On the pretext of having medical checkups the students visited Celle, the nearest city, but the bombing raids made this very dangerous. Throughout this final spring of the war they listened to radio broadcasts always concluding with "Our brave troops continue to retreat according to flexible plans." The real question was, Who would reach Bergen first—the Russians or the English?

On the morning of April 15 Lieutenant Borzsák woke to find the camp abnormally quiet. Most of the Germans of the SS panzer unit had vanished as if by magic. Later they heard that the English army had occupied the Belsen prison camp. The academy director went down and offered their official surrender. They were exempted from POW status and the staff allowed to retain their sidearms. But following this first flush of reconciliation a nettlesome complication quickly arose. The British were stunned by conditions at the Belsen camp, which contained forty thousand semistarved and ill-housed inmates along with thirteen thousand unburied corpses. There were so many of the latter that the British had to bulldoze them into a massive trench. As it happened, many of the guards at the Belsen camp were Hungarian gendarmes, who, even while the first British officers toured the camp, opened fire on starvelings breaking into the kitchens.[45] Since these gendarmes, like the academy personnel, were housed at the SS base, the British wanted to be absolutely certain that the academy had not been involved in creating the unspeakable conditions at the Belsen. The academy officers were held for

44. Meanwhile conditions at the Belsen concentration camp nearby reached starvation levels during the spring of 1945, and no food was transferred from the nearby SS camp. At his trial for war crimes Josef Kramer, the Belsen commandant, argued that Berlin never gave him authority to requisition food supplies from the SS and that the latter never volunteered them.

45. According to a witness at the Belsen trail for war criminals, the shooting was nearly constant. At the entrance to the mortuary yard prisoners dragging in bodies were killed because they did not understand the Hungarian command to go through at double speed. At the war-crimes trial in Lüneburg one former prisoner testified, "In the last three days the Hungarian guards were shooting at us just as if we were rabbits, from all directions." *Trial of Josef Kramer* (London, 1949), 62.

exhaustive interrogation. The British confiscated Borzsák's pistol and put him on a wood-cutting detail.

The filthy wooden buildings at the Belsen camp were torched, and the invalids among the prisoners moved into the former SS installation, which served as hospital and refugee facility until well into the 1950s. Despite protests from the burghers of Bergen, academy personnel were assigned billets in private homes, where they were held for thirteen months until cleared of criminal charges. In May 1946 they were shifted to a huge gathering camp at Osterode, near Göttingen, where POWs from Hungarian divisions awaited repatriation orders. During their four-month delay there Borzsák's daughter was born in a tar-paper hut. The English authorities warned that former officers of the Horthy army might be tried as war criminals if they returned to Hungary, for many such trials were currently in progress. They were offered the option of remaining in the West. The Borzsáks, who had been unable to learn whether their parents had survived the war, chose to return.

Early in October 1946 they began a monthlong train journey back to Hungary. Each freight car, fitted out with mattresses, blankets, packing-box furniture, and a cook stove, held three families. English guards rode shotgun up to the Hungarian border. Within two days they reached Nagykanizsa, but once across the frontier order and system broke down. For days they sat in railway sidings, and they did not arrive in Budapest until early November. The police conducted only a cursory interrogation at this time. Borzsák even applied for and received three thousand forints back pay.[46] Back home at Monor his parents told him shocking tales about the Russians—they had raped and pillaged there as everywhere else. Complaints to the new municipal government, which the Russians had installed, were always met with shrugs and the stock litany *Voina, voina* (War is war)—except that the war was officially over.

In 1948, after the Communists had seized control of the government, KATPOL (Katonai Politikai Osztály), the military equivalent of the ÁVH (Államvédelmi Hatóság), the state security apparatus, began a meticulous investigation of Borzsák's service record. He answered the same questions dozens of times, as commissars scrutinized his testimony for the slightest hesitation or discrepancy. In the end, he was warned that many former Horthy and Szálasi fascist officers with records clearer than his were banished with their families to lean-to huts in the *puszta*, or were sent underground into the lignite mines at Várpalota. Borzsák's year in the capitalist West was always a

---

46. The forint replaced the pengő as the unit of currency during the summer of 1946.

bone of contention for the KATPOL agents, but since more than two hundred thousand other Hungarians fell into that category, he was insulated by those numbers. Nonetheless, he was never sure that a long arm would not seize him. The way to survival lay in remaining as politically inconspicuous as possible, in teaching what the supervisors told him to teach, and in keeping variant opinions to himself. All these things he ably succeeded in doing.

Collapse

After Operation Margarethe in March 1944, Hungary was no longer a sovereign state. Although Horthy remained regent and still possessed considerable moral authority, it was understood that major policies (particularly those bearing upon continuance of the war) would be determined by Hitler through Edmund Veesenmayer, his mouthpiece in Budapest. Within days Adolf Eichmann had met with the Jewish Council of Budapest and enlisted the cooperation of Hungarian authorities in activating his plans for dealing with the Jewish "problem."[47] With the Germans in control it became more difficult for Magyars to shirk and to falsify their contribution to the war economy. Germany now combed Volksdeutsche districts to collect recruits for two Hungarian Waffen SS divisions, and pressured the Ministry of War to increase military drafts. Veesenmayer's policy was to heighten Hungarian participation in the war with a minimum of German visibility. The trick was to occupy the country yet foster the illusion among Magyars that they were not being occupied. Outwardly life in Budapest went on as it had before. Within a month of the initial occupation most of the German soldiers had been pulled from the country, and those remaining were rigorously supervised by their officers. Reports of misbehavior by German troops during this period are practically nonexistent. Hungary was still nominally an ally, not an occupied and ravaged country like Poland.

Meanwhile the Red Army advanced, by jumps and starts, but always relentlessly westward. When Romania quit the war on August 23 and turned its army over to the Soviets, sixteen Axis divisions were cut off. Romania's defection was roundly criticized by a probable majority of Hungarians, though Romania had achieved what they themselves earnestly desired. In Budapest the Ministry of War hastily scratched up a motley collection of units known

47. For a survey of Hungarian anti-Jewish legislation and accounts of how individual Jews fared during the war, see Chapter 2.

officially as the Third Army, but it never took the field in force. Taking advantage of the German deterioration, Horthy replaced Sztójay as prime minister with Géza Lakatos, a respected general who was fiercely loyal to him and distrustful of the Germans. During this same week in August, Hitler had to send General Guderian to assure Horthy that Hungary would never be abandoned and that no further retreat to the west would be tolerated.

All this while a transmitter in the palace was begging the Western Allies for support, only to be told that Hungary had to negotiate with the Soviet Union. This condition was intolerable—but no longer out of the question. During the first week of September the Red Army reached Temesvár (Romania). A month later it advanced into Hungary, holding the line from Tokaj and Szolnok in the north to Kecskemét and Baja in the south. The Soviets were now poised for an assault on Budapest, and it was clear to Horthy that the Germans could not stop them. Because most of Hungary's war industry was located in Budapest, Hitler adamantly refused to allow it to become an open city. For Horthy the prospect of Budapest's becoming another Stalingrad was unthinkable. On October 8 he appealed to the Kremlin for an armistice. Since it was now evident to Hitler that Horthy intended to take the country out of the war—even if this meant begging for mercy from the despised Bolsheviks— Veesenmayer was instructed to reach an agreement with Szálasi and allow the Arrow Cross to take control of the government. On October 15 Horthy's broadcast that the country was no longer at war with the Soviet Union was countermanded a few hours later by another broadcast that reaffirmed the alliance with Germany. Horthy was summarily removed to a Bavarian castle, while Szálasi as new head of the government declared martial law, appointed a cabinet satisfactory to Veesenmayer, and announced that defeatism would be punishable by death.[48] During the weeks that followed, Hungary was stripped of agricultural stores, and whole factories were dismantled and carried off to the west—always with assurances that payment in full would follow. On October 21 those Hungarian troops still at the front were absorbed into German commands. The Jewish population was combed for healthy males and females to dig trenches and tank traps around the city.

On November 4, when the advancing Russian army came within sight of the suburbs of Pest, Szálasi was sworn in as new ruler in the royal palace beside the crown of Saint Stephen. His promise to raise fourteen divisions

---

48. Apparently, no such sentences were carried out through the legal system. However, Arrow Cross gangs no doubt used "defeatism" as one excuse, among many, to justify their sporadic killing sprees.

came to nothing; even if he had been able to collect the manpower, which was unlikely at this stage of the collapse, he could not have found either uniforms or weapons for them. Early in December he visited Hitler and proposed the evacuation of Budapest to save the city from destruction. Hitler refused. He was tired of Hungarian evasions and equivocations. He reiterated his promise that he was preparing a counteroffensive that would drive the Russians completely out of Hungary. Promises, however, did not prevent the Russians from completing their encirclement of Budapest by December 25. A few days before this, the government had abandoned the capital for safer havens in western Hungary. (One of its final contributions to the war effort was changing the names of all Budapest streets named for Jews.)[49] The capital battened down for a kind of do-or-die siege with its eight hundred thousand civilians and approximately seventy thousand defenders (of which 55 percent were Hungarian) under SS general Karl Pfeiffer-Wildenbruch.

Meanwhile mobile units of the Red Army that had bypassed Budapest pushed steadily toward Vienna. Hitler's furious counteroffensives in the vicinity of Lake Balaton failed to dislodge the Russians. In desperation, the high command talked of a secret weapon, called by Hungarians the *lidérc* (hobgoblin), which would win the war in a single stroke, but like its namesake it failed to appear.[50] The Russians occupied Pest on January 18, Buda on February 13, and by April 4 had driven all Axis troops beyond the Hungarian frontier. The war for Hungary was over. The worst predictions had come to pass—the Russians occupied every square kilometer of Hungary.

When the Red Army advanced over the Carpathian passes, the Hungarian and German forces were split in two. The northern units fell back upon Budapest by way of Tokaj and the *puszta*, while those to the south and east retreated toward Szeged by way of Arad. In both cases the German Wehrmacht and SS groups used the Hungarians as buffers for their own escape. Even when there was a will to resist, the Honvédség was hopelessly outnumbered and outclassed by the mechanized bulk of the Red Army. Corporal Tibor Lakner (born 1922) watched in disgust as his 40-mm antitank shells bounded off the hides of the Russian tanks. The Germans had taken all the

49. Macartney, 2:462.

50. It had many guises, but was usually characterized as a death ray—a boxlike device that destroyed enemy bombers with the push of a button. An officer of the Hungarian general staff, dining with the Lukács family, actually claimed he had watched a demonstration of the miracle weapon on a recent visit to Germany. John Lukács, *Confessions of an Original Sinner* (New York, 1990), 59.

75-mm guns with them and left the Hungary army behind them as a kind of human tank trap. It was a massive crisis of command. Lakner called his company headquarters for instructions and found them gone. Even half a century later Lakner is bitter about this massive desertion by the officer cadre. When asked which Hungarian generals he admired, he replied, "None of them. We never saw them. They were all living-room soldiers. So much money was spent on their training that they were too valuable to come to the front. The fighting was carried on by reserve officers and other expendable cattle."[51]

After a brief firefight at Arad, Lakner's group was surrounded and captured. He joined thousands of other prisoners crowding the huge prison pen at Focsani in eastern Romania. When interrogated he admitted that he had served in the occupation army in Ukraine, but denied that Hungarians had murdered or abused civilians. He cited a case in which his men carted manure for a convent, harvested their potatoes, assisted the nuns in making vodka. The nuns gave his men five liters of it for their trouble and treated them like sons. The Russian intelligence officer was unimpressed. In his sphere assisting nuns was not evidence of a healthy political attitude.

Like most Hungarian soldiers Lakner was furious when Romania, without forewarning, went over to the Russians. Therefore a high point of his prison days at Focsani came when a Romanian soldier strolling with a young woman just beyond the barbed wire of their camp failed to salute a passing Red Army officer. The officer called a guard, confiscated the Romanian's pistol and holster, kicked him soundly in the rear, and threw him into the camp as a permanent captive. Hungarians crowded the fence, laughing and cheering. Such arbitrary decisions were standard among the Russians. To make their quotas for Siberian labor camps, they scoured the countryside and rounded up healthy males—whether civilians or former soldiers mattered not a whit to them. When the prison train carrying Corporal Lakner arrived at the frontier of the Soviet Union, all prisoners were counted. Two had escaped— or else the count was off. It made no difference to the train commander. He barked some orders, and guards pried the Romanian engineer and fireman out of their locomotive and booked them as POWs. No protest prevailed against their quotas. Before the train steamed off into the Soviet Union, Lakner threw out a rock with a note wrapped around it giving his name and home address. Someone found it and sent the news of his captivity to his parents in Miskolc, where his father had a pharmacy.

51. Interview with Tibor Lakner (June 10, 1989).

They expected the worst—Siberia. To their relief the train swung south, toward the Black Sea. At Odessa they were separated by military rank and assigned permanent duties at the dockyards. He knew that the Russians, despite their proletarian palaver, gave the worst jobs to soldiers of lowest rank, so he upgraded himself by claiming that he had been a master sergeant. They were put to work loading ships. They stole everything of any value that was portable. Corruption infested the dockyards from top to bottom. POWs looted ships and hid their plunder under overturned wheelbarrows or in piles of rubble artfully hollowed out. Then they exchanged these items for supplemental food rations, the Russian guards taking half as their share. Later their methods of barter became more sophisticated. Local gangs of black-marketing youths had access to the docks through a network of sewers, and set up a thriving business. Lakner organized a group of twenty Hungarians pledged to pool everything they stole and sell it to the Odessa gangs in bulk. "We kidded around and called our group 'The Real Communists.' But our system worked, and it gave us unity." They made one abortive escape attempt. An American ship arrived and lay at wharfside across the harbor. At night a half dozen Hungarians left camp by the sewers and sneaked over to the ship, but Russian guards swarmed about the capitalist craft like so many flies.

The Russian guards did not beat or abuse them. They had shelter and kept warm with the scraps of lumber lying about any dockside. Through their black-marketing they had adequate food. But they were not allowed to write letters home, and no letters came to them, though once, while working near a Hungarian ship, Lakner wrapped a note to his parents around a rock and threw it to a sailor. (Years later he learned they had received it.) The gravest danger in Odessa, something all of them feared, was illness or infection, for they had no medical aid. Lakner, while smashing rocks with a sledge, had once caught a sliver of quartz in the eye and had had to remove it with a sharpened stick. Later a terrifying epidemic swept through the camp, a fungus that quickly spread across the body and resulted in death. There were no antiseptics. Lakner developed a lesion on his wrist that would not heal. He cured it by taking a piece of glass, grinding it into a convex lens, and then using the sun to cauterize an area of flesh the size of a large postage stamp.

In the summer of 1948, after four years as a POW, Lakner and the other Hungarians were packed in freight cars and conveyed to the Romanian border. At the last Russian station Red Army officers pulled them from the train and examined their armpits for SS tattoos. Three prisoners failed the test and were marched off under guard. Lakner never saw them again. The ones who passed were issued worn but clean clothing from a mountainous dump of uniforms removed from the quick and the dead of a dozen armies. It was a costume party. Lakner got a handsome Luftwaffe pilot gown, but on arriving home he dared not wear it for fear of being mistaken for a German officer. Not until his feet touched the ground at Miskolc could he truly believe that the war for him was over.

When the Red Army broke the German line at Veszprém in March 1945, the artillery unit of Lieutenant Lajos Ürge (born 1919) retreated west in good order toward Győr. Their column was strafed by Russian planes once, but the Hungarians did not fire back, and so the airplanes left them alone thereafter. Although their commissary wagons had been cut off, they had no problem getting food. "When hungry we just went into houses along the way and were fed by citizens. We didn't force them. We were all Hungarians, and the people were hospitable."[52] The trouble began as they approached Győr. There came a moment in which, as if by instinct, the men sensed that they were surrounded. They abruptly broke ranks and fled in all directions like a flock of endangered birds. A short time later Russian soldiers arrived on foot and demanded that the Hungarians throw down their weapons. By this time the Hungarians had nothing heavier than pistols. In fact, Ürge had not fired his during the war. "A Russian major told us the war was over. He was very nice to us. We did not seem to be prisoners," Ürge recounted. The Hungarians were rounded up and moved to the square in the village of Tét, where they were lightly guarded by only a few Russian soldiers. Escape would have been easy, but no one saw the need for it. "That was a great big mistake." The Russians were now calling them "Comrade" and assuring them that only Germans, not Hungarians, were their enemy. To solidify their friendship the Russians organized football matches in the village, in which Ürge, a former athlete, participated. "Of course, we were very careful to let the Russians win."

Ürge was eager to return home. The war had been only an interruption for him. A high school graduate of 1937, he had worked in a trade bank until drafted in 1940 for what was supposed to be a one-year term. "I had no politics at the time. I was mainly interested in girls." Because he was good with figures, he was sent to an artillery school, but the training was sketchy and unprofessional. They were never issued artillery weapons, and in four years had maneuvered endlessly, going nowhere in particular and without leaving Hungary. Veszprém had been his first battle, and he had arrived only in time to be caught up in the final retreat and dispersal of the Hungarian

52. Interview with Lajos Ürge (January 18, 1990).

army. The lucky ones escaped to Austria. But Ürge had a clear conscience. He was glad the war was over without his having had to kill somebody or being killed himself. He was glad to be "liberated."

What Ürge did not foresee was that the Russians had no interest whatever in his peace-loving attitude. What they wanted were as many healthy POWs as possible to serve as unpaid laborers in rebuilding the Soviet Union. He was a healthy athlete, as his agility on the soccer field had proved. He was prime stock. With mounting alarm Ürge found himself among a group of Hungarians locked inside a goods train rolling east. Their destination was the stockade near Focsani. For two months he cracked rocks, removed debris, dug ditches. There were no beatings or punishments; the food was adequate—beans, lentils, salt fish. He was never interrogated or charged. His armpit was never checked for an SS tattoo. He assumed that he would shortly be released.

Early in August 1945 his name was called out, and he boarded a freight car with forty other men. At first he thought that he was being sent home, but the door was bolted from outside, and the train moved eastward. Twice a day a guard unlocked the door, and three of the prisoners fetched food in two big kettles. They entered a mountainous terrain of vast forests where the temperature barely rose above freezing even in daytime. Three weeks after leaving Focsani, the doors were thrown open and they climbed out. They were in a Siberian forest, and in front of them was a high wooden fence topped with two strands of barbed wire. This was a forced-labor camp, harboring about a thousand men, in the Tom River region of Siberia, not far from the Chinese border. They ate cabbage soup twice a day. During the first weeks they got tins of American meat, a great luxury, but this soon disappeared. As an officer Ürge got forty-eight grams of sugar per day, which he could swap for tobacco.

They were put to work pulling logs out of the river, cutting and chopping for a sawmill, and doing donkey work at a cement factory. Ürge never saw a prisoner beaten. The only punishment was shouted abuse or, for recalcitrants, threats that they would be sent to a special punishment camp—but no one ever was. The guards, Caucasians, not Mongols, were as dejected a lot as the prisoners. During the first week of September snow lay on the ground, and it did not melt until mid-April. The guards enjoyed reporting the readings on the thermometer, which once registered forty below. Fortunately wood was plentiful. Some Hungarians built a hot-water shower. Often the men were too tired or depressed to use it, but Ürge made a point of showering every day. It was like a religion for him. Sometimes he would dash from the shower and thrash about naked in the snow, to the great amusement of the guards in the towers, who laughed and tapped their heads with their fingers. Without self-discipline and self-respect men went to pieces. Unlike most of the others, Ürge always made a point of changing his underwear once each week.

Their health was surprisingly good. Only two Hungarians died during the first year, both from accidents at work. No one in the camp went insane. For reasons never understood, the German prisoners were more likely to break down physically and emotionally, although treatment was the same for both nationalities. "Some men thought they would remain in Siberia forever. I always expected to go home." The Russians were hard masters but not sadists. "Security here was not tight. What was the point of escape? Where the devil could you go?"

During the second winter conditions improved somewhat. They replaced their rags with sheep-lined coats and Siberian boots. They organized a thespian society—female parts taken by men with funny, squeaky voices. The Russian guards always sat in the front row and applauded noisily, like creatures starved for entertainment. They sat in slack-jawed wonder at the performance of a Transylvanian circus juggler and like elated children stamped their feet to bring him back again and again. The only communication with home was via a single Red Cross postcard distributed to each detainee in 1946. This card consisted of two parts: on one half you signed your name and wrote a brief message saying you were alive (but not indicating where); the other half you got back (without any message) if the card made the three-month round-trip. Most of all, detainees wanted to know how much longer they would be imprisoned, but their guards only shrugged and turned away. "Nighttime was the worst. Often I could not sleep. Scenes of home stuck in my mind. Like what I would be doing back in Hungary—playing tennis with a girl or walking with my father."

In 1947, as they prepared for their third Siberian winter, a group of about sixty Hungarians came in from another camp and said they were all going home. They had lived with such rumors for two years. But a short time afterward the camp commandant woke them up at night by proclaiming that they would leave the next day. "We were wide awake in seconds. All night long we screamed and yelled." In the morning, on the parade ground, the commandant pointed out those with ragged or improper uniforms and ordered new clothes for them. Nothing else happened. A week passed, and they went off to work as usual. It seemed like a cruel joke. Then one night the lights came on, and an officer said that they would leave in the morning. Ürge stayed in bed, refusing to believe it. Yet at morning parade the commandant announced there would be a special farewell lunch. It turned out to be the same cabbage soup as always. This torture of expectation was intolerable. But after the "lunch" the commandant returned and made a short speech: "Through the generosity of the Soviet government and Comrade Stalin the following men are pardoned and may now leave for home." Ürge's name was on the list. But he never forgot the unlucky ones: "It was heartbreaking to see the faces of those left behind." Those cleared of fascist crimes were marched to a train and given seventy rubles—their full pay for two and a half years of work. There was no place to spend the money. It did not matter. Some pitched the rubles into the woods or tossed them to children as they passed through nameless hamlets.

Back in Hungary, the police called him in many times. Their technique was to make him feel as if he had done something wrong, even though he had not. The long-range effect was to convince him of the advantages in leading a (politically) blameless life. Each time he was cleared, but it was always terrifying. He returned to his job at the National Bank and eventually rose to head the foreign-exchange section. But his Gulag experience left him close-mouthed about the postwar regime in Hungary. He had learned that one did not have to be guilty to be sentenced as a criminal. Nevertheless, he bore no ill will toward the Russian people. One Siberian memory still stands fresh in his mind. He was coming back to camp on a ferry over the Tom River and sat exhausted next to a withered old peasant woman. She tapped his knee and secretly handed him a small packet wrapped in a newspaper, signaling him not to open it in front of a guard. Opening it later, Ürge found a piece of bread, an onion, and a carrot—most certainly her meal for the day. Tears flooded his eyes. An old woman whom he had never seen before had touched him across all the barriers of nation, creed, and politics.

If most of the Hungarians in the Romanian camp at Focsani dared to hope that after interrogations had cleared them of war crimes, they would be sent home, Captain Béla Király (born 1912) of the former Hungarian general staff shared none of their optimism. It was transparently evident to him that these teeming prison pens were only a way station on the route to the Soviet Union, for here the narrower European-gauge railway tracks met the wide Russian tracks, and outgoing prisoners were always herded aboard cars on the latter. Resolving never to endure forced labor in Russia, Király recruited a score of fellow officers, who pledged to escape, and worked out operational proce-dures. Escape from the camp was out of the question, for security was tight. Russian guards in wooden towers had a bird's-eye view of the prison pen, while other guards squatting in pits surveyed the prisoners at ground level.

Besides, if one got outside the girdles of barbed wire, where could one go? The camp lay on a wide and level plain, where fugitives would be easily detected and rounded up. Their sole hope lay in jumping off the train at some indeterminate point before it crossed the Russian frontier and climbing the Carpathian range to the west. Among Király's cadre were several Transylvanians whose fluency in Romanian would be invaluable in foraging cross-country. Each day the officer prisoners received two spoonfuls of beet sugar, a high-energy food. Király required his men to put this ration aside for the hard trek ahead. The distance from Focsani to the nearest Hungarian border was over two hundred miles, most of it rough mountainous terrain. Each man was required to obtain some sort of tool—whether hammer, strap of iron, or sharp rock. Since Focsani had formerly been a Romanian army engineering base, mechanical debris lay strewn about. Király pocketed, from the dirt of the camp, a rusty but serviceable wire cutter.[53]

Béla Király considered himself an authority on train jumping. His father, who was chief of the railway station in Kaposvár, had groomed his son for a railroading career and arranged for him to attend the one-year vocational course at the railroad school in Budapest. Young Király set his sights on becoming a veterinarian (he was already an authority in pigeon breeding), but since there was no money for the five-year course, he gamely went up to Budapest to take the entrance exam for the railroad school. Within a week he returned home. He had failed the eye examination, which screened out those unable to distinguish nuances in the colors green and red. At loose ends, he decided to enlist in the army—not through infatuation with it but only so he could limit his enlistment to one year of service and escape the mandatory three-year term for conscripts.[54] Because of his high school diploma he was drawn at once into an officer-training course and found, to his surprise, that he liked military organization. "It was a clear and rational system—no hocus-pocus about it."

But the Hungarian officer corps still lay in the penumbra of the Hapsburg military hierarchy, with the fastest track for advancement reserved for well-connected or wealthy graduates of the prestigious Ludovika Academy. Then, unexpectedly, his father learned that a county scholarship to the academy had just fallen vacant, and he bullyragged his son to apply. Béla dutifully obeyed his father but never assumed he would not be accepted. He was awarded a scholarship that paid all major expenses. He graduated from the academy in

---

53. Interview with Béla Király (July 20, 1996).
54. In 1930 conscription had been reintroduced in Hungary.

1935, with distinction, number ten in a class of six hundred, and was posted to the Royal Hungarian Sixth Infantry.

In July 1940, when the Hungarian army was mobilized because of the Transylvania crisis, Lieutenant Király was the first Hungarian to cross the Szamos River into Romania when the region was returned to Hungary. Two years later he graduated from the General Staff Academy and was posted to the Ministry of Defense as a specialist in army organization, a post that was interrupted by active service in Russia and in Romania. Near the end of the war, when the Hungarian army fell back to the Austrian frontier, he took command of a provisional brigade and moved across to the Soviet side, in accordance with Horthy's aborted armistice of the previous October. Expecting to join battle against the Germans, Király was betrayed and shipped to Focsani as a POW.

Three weeks after Király's arrival at Focsani, the Third Reich collapsed, and the camp was suddenly flooded with German prisoners. This overflow pushed the Hungarians out. They were ordered to assemble at the railway siding, where fifty cattle cars awaited them. "There was even a military band—imagine!—celebrating our departure to the USSR as forced laborers!" In the moiling confusion guards failed to search their prisoners. Probably because his customized uniform was new and his boots spit-polished, the Russians put Captain Király in charge of the embarkation. This piece of luck assured that his cadre would remain together. After inspecting the cars, Király chose a dilapidated hulk in the middle of the train for his own group. Sixty Hungarians climbed into each car, and the guards mounted to their three machine-gun boxes on top.

Once under way, the Hungarians employed their "tools" in tearing out some floorboards for a secondary exit. The doors were fastened only with twists of wire. A long-armed lieutenant reached through a hole and cut the wires. By nightfall the train was running north along an embankment of the Siret River, which lay to their right. Off to their left lay the Carpathians. Scattered through those mountains were pockets of Szeklers, a fierce tribe of Hungarians who had been stranded in Romania by the Trianon partitioning. The Szeklers and Romanians hated one another. If the fugitives could make contact with them, their safety was almost assured. By another stroke of luck all telegraph poles and other dangerous obstructions lay on the landward side. As a railroader's son, Király had perfected his technique for jumping off trains, and he explained the procedure to his men: You held on to the door jamb with your right hand, supporting your body with your left elbow placed on the floor, and lower yourself until your feet were only inches from the ties, and only then let go. The result would be a running start, after which you would roll down the embankment. The problem was that it was a cloudless night with a full moon. The machine-gunners on top of the train had almost daylight visibility.

Before reaching the Russian frontier, the train stopped at the village of Roman, where the prisoners received their last Romanian meal. A female Russian guard, inspecting the train, saw that their door had been tampered with and warned them, "If any of you try to escape I will shoot the whole lot of you." As if challenging them to escape, she made no effort to seal the door. As the train pulled out of Roman a furious windstorm blew up from the Black Sea. The sky turned black. Király saw this was their last chance. Half the men in the car refused to jump. One of them, a prominent Social Democrat, claimed that it was pointless for him to escape, for as soon as the Communists became aware of who he was, he would be sent home. As he said, "They need me back home to help build up a democratic Hungary." (He was sent home—but three years later.)

Király jumped first and tumbled down the embankment. Others followed. There were no shouts of alarm from the guards, and the taillight of the train disappeared. As they floundered through the underbrush, calling to one another, they aroused some farmyard dogs. As agreed beforehand they split up into four bands of six men each and moved west toward the mountains. They were in very dangerous open country. At daybreak Király's band came across a broken-down van in a field. When they opened the door, birds flew out—proof that it had been abandoned. They hid in it until nightfall, when they set out again on foot, and by dawn of the next day they had reached the foothills of the Carpathians, carefully bypassing small villages and keeping away from main roads. For food they scavenged wild bird eggs and berries, which they supplemented with their husbanded sugar rations.

On the third day they spotted some woodcutters around a fire and took a chance that they were Szeklers. The Transylvanian officer greeted them in Romanian. When the woodcutters replied in Hungarian, Király knew that the worst was over. These were Szeklers, who invited them to dig into their pot—a rich mixture of mutton and potatoes, which they topped with sheep cheese. "Never in my life did I eat so much and so well." In the village they were hidden in a hayloft while the Szeklers collected money and forged documents for them. They dumped their uniforms and donned sheepherder garb. Then they took regular trains to Nagyvárad (Oradea), where they waited for another storm, and crossed the border to Hungary under cover of a downpour. Király returned to Kaposvár in June 1945.

Most Hungarian POWs remained in Russian labor camps for two to three years longer.[55]

When Jenő Tarján (born 1916) was assigned to guard Horthy Bridge (now Petőfi Bridge) on the morning of March 19, 1944, he was issued a leather belt and an empty pistol holster. When he complained, he was told that there was a shortage of side arms and that he must scrounge one for himself. Evidently there were still enough pigs and cattle to meet the demand for holsters. Tarján was only a reservist clerk without military training other than a course in first aid, but he was ordered to join others nearly as green as himself in order to prevent the Germans, who had just invaded the country, from seizing that bridge. By profession a philologist—his dissertation, written in German, studied miners' vocabulary in the Miskolc region—Tarján, who was married, with a baby on the way, clearly was among the scrapings at the bottom of the military barrel. The idea of his holding back German panzers with an empty holster—or a full one, for that matter—was ridiculous. But to Tarján it was less ridiculous than terrifying in its madness.[56] As it happened, no German tanks came over that bridge. They did not have to, because the Hungarian army capitulated without firing a shot.

For the following six months Tarján remained on duty at the bridge, returning home nightly by tram and supplementing the few pengős of his soldier's pay by tutoring in English and German. His pistol holster served as a sandwich pocket until the father of one of his students heard of his difficulty and fished out of his attic a five-shot antique revolver. To test it Tarján fired one shot at a pigeon. He missed.

On October 15 he was aroused by the sound of firearms. From his window he could see Tiger tanks rumbling through the streets. When he reported to the bridge, German tank officers were already in parley with the Hungarian commander, who said his orders were to prevent the bridge from being dynamited. The German extended his hand. These were his orders, too. Military courtesy required that the Germans pretend that the Hungarians, with their pitiful collection of side arms, could really have halted tanks.

With the Germans in control of Budapest, Tarján was transferred to the War Ministry on Castle Hill, where he served as a translator until the government packed up for Sopron. Tarján's translation unit was evacuated

---

55. All of the men who made the jump with Király made it safely back to Hungary, except for two Transylvanians who remained in their native country. For an account of Király's postwar career, see Chapter 6.

56. Interview with Jenő Tarján (March 12, 1990).

west, first to a microscopic village near Győr, where they vegetated for three weeks, apparently forgotten by the peripatetic government, which was preparing to move again, this time to Austria. Early in January they finally received orders to entrain for Germany. By this time many Hungarians had simply evaporated in the confusion and were never missed, but Tarján had good reasons for tagging after the Germans. Although his papers showed that Miskolc was his birthplace, they also revealed that his father, a metallurgical engineer in the Hungarian coal fields, was a German citizen with the surname Thern. Although Tarján had magyarized his surname in 1935, temperamentally he never abandoned his Germanic roots. At the university he had proclaimed right-wing views, had boasted of his German blood, and had spoken of Russians with withering contempt. He did not want any of this to leak to the Russians, or to their leftist bootlickers in Budapest. In Germany he felt safe. Accompanied by his pregnant wife, he settled into a billet outside Zwickau. A short time after moving into their rooms, they watched as a six-hundred-plane Allied armada passed overhead in the direction of Dresden. It was the night of the firestorm that incinerated the city. The whole eastern sky turned into day. The bombing was so heavy that, even from forty kilometers away, his wife went into shock and had a miscarriage.

During the first week in May the villagers were informed that the Americans were coming and that they should place white flags and towels in their windows. When they arrived, Tarján met them in full uniform. The soldiers were cheerfully drunk. One of them examined his pistol, and when he found a bullet missing, he became truculent. "Did you shoot at an American soldier?" he demanded. Tarján protested his innocence, in nearly perfect English, and explained that he had fired a round at a pigeon. "And I bet you missed it," replied the soldier. At this the Americans went into gales of laughter. With a dozen other Hungarians Tarján was conducted to the local school and ordered to strip. After a medic blew DDT over him, he was told that he could go wherever he wanted. An officer warned against returning to Hungary, where the Russians were carrying off everyone they could find for slave labor. Tarján bought a plain jacket and threw away his uniform.

His wife left at once for Budapest to reconnoiter the political situation. Tarján stayed close to the Americans until July, when he got word it was safe to go home. However, by this time the American army was engaged in a full-fledged Nazi hunt. Anyone whose status was not immediately clear was suspected of criminal activity. To Tarján's chagrin he paid a price for his caution. He was seized for questioning by the Americans and shut up in a huge POW camp in Austria containing twenty thousand men. His knowledge of three languages quickly opened doors. He found a job in the infirmary and cultivated the head nurse. She was in love with her commanding officer, so Tarján drew upon his lore of Hungarian and German poetry and wrote eloquent love letters that she passed on to her officer, pretending they came from her swollen sensibilities.

"I was treated well by the Americans, who gave me chocolate, chewing gum, cigarettes. When I decided it was time to leave the camp for good, I did what all the GIs did. I handed a pack of cigarettes to the guard at the gate, and walked down to the station and rode a freight train to Budapest." Back in Hungary he was too insignificant to be disturbed by the Russians or their regime. He had a story and stuck to it: he had never trained as a soldier; he had never joined a political party; he had never taken an oath to Szálasi. It worked. In the technique of navigating the tricky shoals of peace and war, Tarján had become a master.

Gyula Farkas of Kassa (born 1900) barely missed being pitched into one of those catastrophic final campaigns of the Hungarian army in the First World War. As a green conscript he was still in basic training with the Ninth Kassa when the armistice was signed at Padua, but what he observed in the months ahead gave him no stomach for war—particularly when it was catalyzed by politics. Magyars in the Kassa region of Slovakia accounted for only 10 percent of the population, and the Farkas family did not share the jubilation of the ethnic majority, which celebrated their anticipated incorporation into the new nation of Czechoslovakia. Gyula's father, who owned a combine that he leased at harvest time, suspected that his machine would be a casualty of the new anti-Hungarian regime, but he also feared that his son would be drafted into the Czech army and forced to go to war against Magyars. The family arranged for Gyula to go into hiding with relatives at Sátoraljaújhely, a mining town in the far northeastern tip of Hungary.[57]

When the Czechs invaded the industrial region of northern Hungary in the spring of 1919, they occupied the Sátoraljaújhely region until Béla Kun's Red Army counterattacked and drove them out. Like other Hungarians, Gyula exulted in the expulsion of the Czechs, but he was aghast at the behavior of the liberators. Commissars ferreted out the town officers, denounced them for conspiring with the Czechs, and dragged them to the public square. Each captive had one end of a rope tied to a chestnut tree and the other end looped around his neck. They were then forced to climb into an open truck, which

---

57. Interview with Gyula Farkas (March 28, 1990).

drove off at top speed. The bodies dangled for three days, until some towns-people collected enough courage to cut them down.

The Farkas family left Slovakia permanently and moved to Budapest, only to find the capital crammed with Hungarians from territories lost through the mincing of Trianon. Some lived in abandoned cattle cars for years, using scrap lumber to partition rooms. Gyula took a job in the postal service, and worked up to a position as head of quality control. He married, fathered three sons, and bought a large flat in the handsome Kós architectural project in Kispest. Although he should have been exempt because of age, he was called up in 1941 when Hungary entered the war, commissioned as an officer, and dispatched to the Ukraine in the occupational army. "We always had good relations with the Ukrainians and Ruthenians. We gave the children bread. The partisans did not attack us Hungarians—only the Germans, who treated everyone poorly, even us. When they distributed food and weapons, the Hungarians came last."

Farkas happened to be on furlough in Budapest when the Russians closed the ring around the city at Christmas, 1944. Reassigned to headquarters duty in Pest, he was moving equipment across the river to Buda when the Germans blew up the Danube bridges. Shell-shocked and deafened by the explosion, he was carried through streets "filled with horse carcasses and human bodies—mainly German"—to a hospital on Gellért Hill. Here he became friends with the concierge and his Russian wife. On February 9 the Russians broke into the hospital and ordered everyone into the courtyard. As Farkas came out he saw the Russians open fire with their machine guns on wounded Germans huddled against a wall. It was apparent that the Russians planned to kill all the prisoners. "I was saved because the Russian woman rushed out and, pointing to me, said I was pro-Russian and should not be killed. But they killed everybody who was injured. The healthy ones were spared for slave labor."

That night he joined a vast throng of prisoners crossing a pontoon bridge and marching to a collection area in Kispest, only a few blocks from his home. They were counted repeatedly by guards, and when they numbered two thousand, they began a trek to Gödöllő, a railway center east of Budapest. For three days they had no food or water other than snow scraped from fences as they passed. On the way Gyula picked up a propaganda leaflet dropped from a Russian plane. It featured a Russian and a German soldier facing each other, smiling as they shared ham, bread, and wine. The caption read, in German—"THIS IS HOW WE RUSSIANS TREAT OUR PRISONERS OF WAR."

In Gödöllő they were crammed with thousands of other Hungarian males into a grammar school. Every day a cargo of live bodies boarded freight cars bound for the USSR, and fresh arrivals joined the remainder camped in the hallways. At 3 A.M. and 5 P.M. they received a dish of boiled wheat. Many prisoners died on the floor where they slept. There was no medicine or medical attendant. Filth lay everywhere. Dysentery was the great scourge, and Farkas feared that killer. He remained two months at this pesthouse without water for washing. The Russians zealously sought healthy animals. A female Red Army lieutenant combed through the host of prisoners each day, testing their potential for labor by feeling their thighs. Muscular legs meant a prompt journey to the USSR. The fact that Farkas was debilitated saved him.

Early in April the leftovers at Gödöllő were taken outside, lined up in rows of five (easily countable), and marched to Jászberény, fifty miles distant—a killing distance for emaciated men. Along the way guards shot eight or ten unable to keep up the pace, seizing civilians along the route to fill the empty places. "At Jászberény they put us in a former panzer barracks with two wells. We could wash. We had regular meals. A surgeon gave me charcoal to chew to clean out my dysentery." Farkas knew that the Russians would expect something in return for this generosity. Sure enough, officials from the puppet government at Debrecen soon arrived, seeking recruits for the new (pro-Soviet) Hungarian army. Since this seemed to offer a shield against being sent to Russia, Farkas volunteered. Besides, the war was nearly over.

When a rumor swept the camp that these troops would be sent to Austria and Germany as an occupational force—perhaps for an indefinite period—Farkas looked for a dodge that would keep him in Hungary.[58] He applied for a post as equine veterinarian, though he knew nothing about horses. This kept him in Jászberény while his fellow volunteers went off to Austria. When his commanding colonel discovered that the horses attended by Farkas were living or dying without any apparent relationship to the bottled nostrums he administered, he was let go. At age forty-five he was too old for such nonsense. Although the kindly colonel warned him that if he accepted a discharge from the army, he could be picked up by the Russians for labor, Farkas chose to take that chance. He returned to Kispest in the back of a vegetable truck. He had served his country three times in three different armies—and in none of them voluntarily.

Many of the flats in his Kós project, complete with the furniture of their former Hungarian tenants, were now occupied by the families of Russian

---

58. Farkas was told that Red Army policy favored nationals of other countries for service as occupation forces in the West because, if Russians were used, they might return home with attitudes and tastes contaminated by degenerate capitalist culture.

officers, but they were quiet people apparently grateful to be housed in such luxury. His wife said that except for some soldiers breaking in and prancing about in her evening gowns, she had not been molested by the Russians, probably because the apartment complex was requisitioned immediately for officers. A Russian captain had been billeted briefly with her, but except for getting drunk and vomiting on her carpets, he had offended no one. When she complained about it, he was removed. As a going-away present he had given one of her children a prized horn that he had stolen from a western automobile.

Farkas resumed his work at the post office. One day he returned home and heard the Russian women in a neighboring flat wailing as though afflicted by an unendurable tragedy, like the outbreak of a new war or the loss of a child. They were lamenting bitterly that they had just received orders to return to Russia. Farkas promptly notified the owner of the flat, who arrived with trucks as soon as the Russian family vacated his property. Within an hour swarms of helpers had loaded all his furniture into the trucks for deposit in his daughter's flat in Buda. Early the next morning three Russian army trucks pulled up in front of the building, and soldiers jumped out. Their boots echoed in empty rooms. Russians were then filling Danube barges with stolen furniture for shipment to Russia, but from that flat they carried not even a broken chair. For Farkas and his neighbors that was a minor, but very satisfying, triumph.

Lovers

On graduating from the Horticultural University of Budapest in 1942, Ilona Joó (born 1920), a representative middle-class young woman, seldom wasted many thoughts about the war being fought far away in Russia. She took a research assistantship at the Seed Institute in Ercsi, a village on the Danube south of the capital, and began her career.[59] An attractive brunette, she soon caught the attention of soldiers stationed nearby at a small radio installation. She, in turn, liked the looks of the curly-haired sergeant who ran the station. His name was Károly Jobbágy (born 1922). To her surprise, for she had grown up to believe that all soldiers were uncultivated boors, she discovered that his ambition was to become a great poet. He loaded her with his poems, wrote several for her, and they fell in love.

---

59. Interview with Ilona Joó (May 19, 1989).

Her family discouraged the match. Jobbágy had graduated from only a commercial—not a classical—high school; his father was a baker's assistant; and his mother kept a tiny one-room grocery shop near Déli Station. By contrast, the Joó family came from a line of Protestant ministers and bourgeoisie from Transylvania. Alarmed by the proximity of the Russian Revolution and anti-Hungarian feeling among the Romanian population, Ilona's father had scuttled his law practice in order to emigrate to Budapest in 1917. There he specialized in property law and soon was managing the property of 120 children orphaned by World War I. He built a large villa on Tarcali Street, a leafy thoroughfare of trees and gardens in the valley west of Gellért Hill. Although he did not fancy himself a political man, he nevertheless believed that Horthy had saved the country from Bolsheviks like Béla Kun, and that Gömbös had the right idea. He respected working-class people, but kept them at a distance—certainly as far as possible from his only daughter. Since Ilona made it clear to her father that she had no intention of giving up Jobbágy, the best he could hope for was that the army would eventually ship him to some post out of sight and out of mind.

Károly Jankovich was born in Balassagyarmat, a city on the Slovakian border. He came to Budapest at age nine with his parents, who promptly magyarized their surname to Jobbágy. His family had to sacrifice to support his commercial course, but further education was out of the question. "Because of our poverty I could not dream of a university education."[60] Instead, he began to dream of writing socially engaged poetry like that of his idol, Attila József. While a student he attached himself to the Social Democrats and was drawn into a leftist writing circle that they sponsored at the Püski bookstore in Pest, near Franz Joseph Bridge. At this time the Social Democrats included a spotty collection of Communists, whose own party had been outlawed. They were both pro-Soviet and pacifist—exactly opposite the teachers in his school. His first real impact as a versifier came when he wrote an antiwar poem that vividly expressed his fear of death. The headmaster professed outrage at this repudiation of patriotic fervor, brought him before a board of the faculty, and recommended his expulsion. After a few teachers took his side, the headmaster backed off, fearing negative publicity. But he did succeed in revoking Jobbágy's scholarship. (A rich Jewish furrier, hearing about the case, came forward and paid his tuition.)

Károly was willing to knock a few heads for his political principles. On one occasion he joined a student band of Social Democrats who raided an Arrow

60. Interview with Károly Jobbágy (May 5, 1989).

Cross house near Petőfi Bridge and sent the Green Shirts flying. He might have been drawn into the Communist student underground led by László Rajk except that he had a habit of questioning authority and demanding to have dubious points of ideology clarified. What would a doctrinaire Communist do with a heretic who argued that Gyula Gömbös was an honest man?

After graduating from high school in 1939, Károly Jobbágy worked as a clerk in the Defense Ministry and took a room in the Jewish quarter. Here he met a Jewish woman nine years his senior who had been expelled from Israel for terrorist activity against the British. Olga—she had several surnames—had been a member of a Communist Party cell in Tel Aviv, where she had stored boxes of grenades under her bed for distribution to Jews engaged in bombing British installations. She had high principles. In Tel Aviv she quit her job in protest when she learned that she was making twice the salary offered Arabs for the same work. Although a Jew, she was anti-Zionist. Mystified yet enthralled by this complex woman, Jobbágy fell in love with her. They had an intermittent affair that lasted for years, until she moved to a villa outside Budapest and was swallowed up in one of the Jewish deportation levies.

On holiday in June 1941 he cycled up into Slovakia to visit relatives in a country village. The place was deserted, all stores closed and the population scattered. He was mystified until the villagers, ashamed of their panic, drifted back home and explained that on that day Germany had invaded the Soviet Union. No one gave a rational explanation for the war, but all agreed that the Russians would be easily crushed because, as Jobbágy explained, "the Russians had no knowledge of modern weapons and were a peaceful nation." A few days later Jobbágy had to swallow a bitter pill when Hungary joined the Germans. As a Slovakian, his distrust of Germans was bred in the bone, and he foresaw that Hungary's entry into the war would strengthen the hand of the Arrow Cross and the right radicals of Parliament.

A few months later he was drafted into the Honvédség, assigned to a telecommunications school, and trained as a radio operator. It was after his posting to the radio center at Ercsi that he first met Ilona and they began their courtship. They often met in Budapest and attended poetry readings at the Püski bookshop. The Joó family lived well; the shops were full; and everything rolled smoothly as though it were still peacetime. Károly's military duties were nominal. He set his own schedule, rarely participated in maneuvers—which the government kept at a minimum because of the great expense—and during the lulls at the radio station had plenty of time for his own versifying.

Sometimes the war became a magnificent pageant. Ilona loved to watch the great waves of American bombers that filled the sky from horizon to horizon, their contrails stretched behind them like woolly strands of hair, bound for targets in Silesia. Although the United States and Hungary were officially at war, the "gentleman's agreement" held—neither country attacked the other. All this changed abruptly after the first German occupation in March 1944. The spectacle became terrifying when the fleets of American bombers, assisted by the British, began targeting Budapest and other industrial centers, like Szolnok and Győr. Since the principal telecommunications center for the country was situated on Gellért Hill, not far from her home, her district took heavy bomb damage. She saw only rubble, never bodies, for the municipal authorities quickly whisked away the human debris to discourage defeatism. She felt a kind of immunity from these air raids and liked to leave the shelter to watch the commotion in the sky. Once she saw an American bomber burst into flames. Parachutes blossomed like aerial flowers, and a gauzy object fluttered down, which she retrieved. It was a map of Europe printed on a silk handkerchief—part of the emergency kit issued to American airmen.

When the Germans occupied Budapest in March 1944, Jobbágy's unit was confined to barracks and warned to keep quiet. He read some anti-German poems to men in his barracks and waited for the order to attack the German invaders. For two days they were closeted in barracks. Then an announcement came: Hungary was a friend of Germany and should be thankful that Germany had restored parts of Slovakia and Transylvania. Jobbágy was not fooled. He remembered that Péter Veres, a peasant-poet whom he admired, had said about the two Vienna awards, "Hitler will give us the bill later."

Conditions steadily worsened throughout 1944. A succession of defeats on the Russian front, coupled with the rapid advance westward of the Red Army, brought undercurrents of fear, depression, meanness. The ominous heading "Missing in Action," with its implications of ambiguity and chaos, began to replace "Killed" in the casualty reports. After the German occupation of Hungary in mid-March, anti-Semitism flared into the open. Brutality toward Jews become overt, defiant, and boastful. One of Ilona's closest friends, a Jewish girl named Mária Munk, suddenly disappeared. She was picked up with her parents, their three-thousand-acre estate confiscated, and the family deported to a camp somewhere in Austria. For three months Ilona received letters from Mária that alluded to the slow deterioration of living conditions among rural Hungarian Jews assigned to the camp. Later a postcard said they had arrived safely at "Waldsee." (Not until long after the war did Ilona realize that this was a German code name for Auschwitz.) Then the letters ceased. The Munk family simply vanished without a trace. Neither Ilona nor Károly suspected the truth—that they had been liquidated. Some

Jews in Károly's old neighborhood spoke of how considerate the Germans were in keeping whole families together by sending everyone, not just the males, to those work camps. (Ironically, Mária's brother evaded the German and Nyilas nets and survived the war, only to be executed by Hungarian Communists for a trumped-up slate of "fascist" crimes.)

Meanwhile Károly Jobbágy gained rapid promotion to sergeant, and was being groomed for officers' school until censured for insubordination. Because Jews were known to be listening to outlawed radio broadcasts from Western stations, Jobbágy's squad was ordered to confiscate the radios of certain Jewish families. They gave the Jews signed receipts and promised them that the radios would be returned to them in time. At night, in barracks workshops, the soldiers stripped them of tubes, condensers, and other usable parts, pitching the skeletons into a corner for scrap. Jobbágy was incensed at having been forced to play a part in this shameful scheme. On the following day, when ordered to collect more radios, he refused. His superiors threatened him with court-martial and, when this made no impact, with revocation of his application for officers' school, but he would not budge. The officers could do nothing with him except restrict him to barracks temporarily and black-mark his military transcript. At heart he retained the stubbornness of a Slovakian peasant.

The irreversible point in the war came with Romania's defection to Stalin in late August. After that no sound head could believe in a German victory. Ercsi, a village with a heavy Volksdeutsche population, was combed for fresh youths. From her window at the Seed Institute Ilona watched as rosy-cheeked farm boys in new Waffen SS uniforms climbed into army trucks, which lumbered out of town along the eastern road and then returned empty for a fresh load. On October 15 she heard Horthy's radio broadcast announcing that Hungary had jumped out of the war, followed by counterstatements, including one that indicated he had been deposed. Sensing trouble, she packed up all the beans, peas, and other edible seeds she could find at the Institute, combed country shops for carrots, flour, and onions, and in a borrowed delivery van drove to Budapest, where she stored her food cache in the basement of the Horticultural Institute. She knew the Red Army was close at hand. Like many other Hungarians she was deeply angered by the German occupation, and in spirit embraced the popular saying "If the Allies win, we will lose; but if the Germans win, we are lost." But worst of all were the Russians.

By mid-December the Russians were so close that Ercsi had to be evacuated. Károly's radio center moved west to Veszprém, where a "final" defensive line was being prepared by the Germans. Ilona reluctantly joined her parents in

Budapest. Communication between them was permanently cut. Their wedding, planned for early January, was now out of the question unless the long-promised German counterattack, assisted by their hush-hush "secret weapon," succeeded in breaking the Russian advance.

With the Arrow Cross prowling the streets of Budapest, one was safe only when in the protective custody of the Germans, who despised the Szálasi faction. One morning in November, while walking to the Horticultural Institute, near Kálvin Square, Ilona saw a band of Jews with sacks slung across their shoulders being herded from the ghetto toward the Danube embankment by Arrow Cross adolescents brandishing machine guns. Later she heard that they had been shot and their bodies kicked or thrown into the river. (Sometimes the Arrow Cross tied three Jews together and shot only the two on the ends. This saved a bullet.)

Instead of forcing their way directly into Budapest, the Red Army circled the city and cut off overland communication with the world outside. To save electrical power, the trams stopped running on Christmas Day. On the next day, when a Russian artillery shell burst nearby and broke all the windows on the front of their house on Tarcali Street, the Joó family moved into their cellar. There were seven of them: she and her mother and father, an uncle and aunt from Gödöllő (a town east of Budapest already overrun by the Russians), her godfather, and a teenage cousin named Pötyi. Electricity in the house was cut permanently at noon on December 27. In the darkness they busied themselves making candles out of shoe polish, cutting wood for a primitive stove, and agreeing on territorial demarcations with the furniture. Their toilet consisted of a jar in the corner behind a curtain, supplemented by an outdoor privy in the garden, which could be used when there was a lull in the barrage. Pötyi avidly studied a Russian grammar, saying he would be ready to survive when the Russians came. Ilona found it difficult to concentrate. She briefly tried to read a textbook on Russian history but in the end pushed it aside and recorded in her diary, "I am afraid that world is not for me." They divided up the duties: her job was to make the seven beds and try to keep the cellar tidy. Everyone had a special worry: her father fretted about what might be happening to his workshop and tools in the garden hut, Uncle Sanyi about his sausages in Gödöllő, Ilona about where Károly was and what was happening to him. To suppress the terrifying noise of drumfire, they took turns playing the harmonica—all badly. On December 29 Ilona began writing Károly letters that she could save until he came back to her. The conclusion of her first one reads:

> Let the Good God grant that we overcome the hardship and sadness
> of war. Since the sky is always blue over the passing clouds, we could
> shine at each other—you with the thousand sparkles in your eyes, and I
> just smile at you.
> Needless to say, we do not have electricity any more.[61]

On New Year's Eve they prepared a festive menu—sausage, wine, and
sweets. Her mother even tried to bake bread in their crude oven fabricated of
tin sheets. She failed, but did produce a grotesque roll, which all agreed was
delicious. A windup Victrola played Beethoven. During a lull in the cannonade, Uncle Sanyi ventured into the garden but returned in a hurry, describing
a red, slow-moving projectile. Aunt Rózsika dryly remarked that it probably
saw him and burned with a desire to explode. It was not much of a joke, but
after a week of tension it was good enough for a long hysterical laugh. They
consoled themselves with the opinion that the bombing was so bad it could
not get any worse—but it did. Leaflets from a German (or Hungarian) plane
fluttered down into their garden, bearing promises that the Russian
barbarians would soon be hurled out of Budapest.

After January 1 there was no more washing, because the water line had
been cut. Fortunately they found a tap at a deserted gardener's shop several
blocks away, but the place came under fire. They took turns fetching water,
except for Ilona, whom her father forbade to venture outside. It was much
too dangerous for a young woman. The Wehrmacht was forming a new
defensive perimeter along a parallel street three blocks away, indicating that
the Russians were about to cross the river to Buda. Three men from the
neighborhood reported on a trip to Pest: The bridges were still open, but
there was not one undamaged house on the way. Nearer at hand, all along
Karolina Avenue corpses of people killed in the bombardments had been
buried in the road in front of their houses. The men reported that across the
river they saw more corpses than living creatures.

A few days later Károly Jobbágy's father came to their shelter. The good
news was that he had heard no bad news from or about his son, so he
assumed he was still alive. Otherwise all his news was bad. The Russians
were fighting their way, tree by tree, through City Park over in Pest; they had
taken the Honvéd barracks near Kálvin Square; and they were rumored to be
in the Danubia factory, a few miles downriver. Policemen on the street still

---

61. This, along with other block-quoted material, comes from the diary of Ilona Joó,
translated by Eleonóra Arató.

painted a rosy picture, saying that the German army would soon arrive and drive the Bolsheviks away.

By January 10 it was bitterly cold, with a foot of snow outside. Ilona's father brought in a tub of snow to melt for water, but the others shouted at him angrily because it seemed to freeze the air in the cellar. Fights among those in the cellar were now too frequent to be catalogued; to escape the bickering, Ilona went out to sweep the path to the outhouse. The Russians were dropping leaflets demanding unconditional surrender, claiming that the Debrecen ministers (Communist approved) represented the legitimate government, but city policemen insisted that this was a lie. The side streets were now crowded with lines of German tanks, trucks, and artillery lying in reserve for what was supposed to be an impregnable defensive line running from nearby Villányi Road to the river bank. This concentration meant that their neighborhood would soon be the front line. Already their house had been hit seven times by bombs, and their roof was so perforated, Ilona noted in her diary, that it "looked like ragged embroidery." During a slack moment they went into their garden and watched Russian airplanes dive-bombing Horthy Square (now Móricz Zsigmond). A neighbor, a lieutenant, dropped by and said the lower Danube bridges were badly hit but still usable. "You would know," he said, "that Pest had gone up the spout, when the Germans dynamited the bridges."

A mid-January thaw turned their cellar into a mudhole. The weather turned sunny. The dead horses in the street began to stink. During lulls in the bombing they took brief turns on the terrace, where they could see aerial combats downriver. They still had ample food. There was no sugar, but there was an abundant supply of dried beans, lentils, and seeds, which her father replaced on nocturnal trips to the nearby Horticultural University, supplemented with flaccid potatoes and cabbage. They were grateful when the snow fell again on the twentieth, for they needed it for their water supply, since the public tap was under fire from snipers. The news was worsening. Pest had surrendered to the Russians, the Danube bridges were blown up, and a German "relief" army was immobilized somewhere near Veszprém. The German defenders in the castle area were now trapped. Since most of these units were SS, there was no incentive for them to surrender, because the Reds took no SS prisoners, or so it was believed. From a distance they heard loudspeakers repetitively blaring German phrases like *Krockodil gross*, *Kommt Vogel*, and *Strandbad*. At first they thought this might be part of a news broadcast; then they took it to be secret instructions from the German command, until they finally concluded it was only a garbled message from chaos.

Even worse than the drumfire and occasional earth-shaking explosions when a munitions dump would go up was the tedium and boredom. They tried to entertain themselves in the dim light of the cellar by playing cards, culling memory for lines of poetry, and fighting among themselves. Priming herself for the Communist regime sure to come, Ilona read Attila József, a radical poet. In her diary she recorded his lines "People with good will take the problems of the proletariat in their hearts, / but not on their shoulders." His admonitions against bourgeois dissipation made her feel guilty, even though she knew that she had never lived in the kind of decadent luxury he condemned. As to the Red propaganda that promised a speedy "liberation" of the city, neither she nor anyone else in her family took it seriously. For the Russians "freedom" only meant a permit to free Hungarians from their property. If the Russians took the city, it would be a repetition of 1919, when the Romanians, encouraged by the treaty makers of Trianon, occupied Budapest—only much worse.

On January 25 they took stock after a month in the cellar. Ilona got physically sick whenever she looked into a mirror. Her skin showed layers of dirt from making beds, the dirtiest job in the cellar. When the neighbor's chimney fell on the house, spattering everyone with a coating of oily soot, their first reaction was uncontrollable laughter at the blackface appearance of one another, but humor passed quickly into annoyance, for the stuff was impossible to remove without soap and water, and they had been unable to wash for over three weeks. Her mother and father now looked like scarecrows. Ilona felt everything was bearable except her mother, who had turned into a quarrelsome shrew apparently dedicated to making everyone miserable. When Ilona occasionally replaced her mother at the stove and prepared a lentil stew, the others dared not praise it for fear of sending the mother into a paroxysm of jealousy.

Signs of defeat and collapse were everywhere by January 26. Eight German soldiers wandered in looking for shelter and remained long enough to warm up. They were members of the SS Feldherrnhalle Panzer Division who had been driven down from Svábhegy during the night.[62] A month ago they had had two hundred tanks—now only ten remained. For the past ten nights they had slept only by fits and starts; the food supply had been cut, and they had been gnawing chunks of frozen horse. They estimated that forty thousand

---

62. Svábhegy is the wooded mountain standing above Budapest to the west and commanding the whole region. Many had regarded it as impregnable, and so it might have been had the Germans been provided with reinforcements, food, and fresh ammunition.

Germans were trapped in the castle area, with at least ten thousand dead up there. It was now a battle under the black flag, for they were ordered to take no Russians prisoners, and they expected no mercy from the Russians. Their accounts of the house-to-house fighting in Pest particularly alarmed the Joó family. Over there Russians had invaded the cellars while Germans defended the upper stories. Whenever the Russians moved upstairs, they sent the civilians ahead to shield them from German fire. They also used civilians as packhorses for removing corpses and carrying wounded and ammunition. This meant that Hungarian noncombatants were exposed to fire from both sides.

The same night brought ominous signs that the German ring was shrinking. Two tanks lodged themselves in their neighbor's garden, which meant that the Joó villa was now the front line. All night long weary German soldiers trailed in, asked questions politely, and moved on to houses nearby. They said that partisan activity against them was increasing, and they had orders to trust no one. Dozens of Hungarian refugees, fleeing from the Russians, prowled the streets seeking shelter and food. Villányi Street was cut off to the south, toward the river, as Germans retreated northward toward Déli Station, the principal depot of Buda. Then on January 30 the Russians took the station, which trapped the German units remaining in the Joó neighborhood. This was a time, she recorded in her diary when "terror moved along the whole street."

Among their visitors was a thirty-five-year-old German soldier from Berlin, who soon became a friend of the family. In the diary she kept for her fiancé, Ilona chronicled the last days of this German soldier:

January 29

I was still in bed when our German was here again and asked whether our house was shelled. It is nice of him. There is quite a big turmoil outside, new cannons are moved by the houses; they move to and fro. Is the end near? One more day? One more week is the world? What will the future bring?

I have cleaned the mold off of your box. Boots and the bag of socks are piled up waiting for you. It would be nice to know that you are alive and want to come back.

As a servant I do much better than as a lady. I have always said that I did not deserve a different life; I am not refined enough. And if we survive this, I will be able to earn my living like that, too.

My hands are cold. That is why my writing is so slow and ugly. I wish you would have the chance to read it. At least that much of me would get over to you.

January 30, 11:00

Your little servant finished washing the dishes, making the beds, also let a German court her, and at last can have a rest. Karcsi, my darling, it would be so nice to live. In the evening we put our heads together with a German and talked about the point of war. He is a thirty-five-year-old Berlin boy. Married; what is more, has a fifteen-year-old daughter. He is an intelligent man, belongs to the simpler people, though. Has been a soldier only for nine months, belongs to the Wehrmacht, yet here in Pest with the army consolidation he was relegated to the SS. He was desperate and firmly believes that he will not survive this siege. He speaks nicely, with a clear accent, and I was so glad that I understood every word. He also shares my opinion that if you have been taken to Germany, then I will never see you again.

. . . The ring is becoming tighter around us. At night, as the German tells us, again some territory was lost, and the airplanes delivering ammunition were disturbed so much by the Russians that they dropped everything over enemy lines. So today the soldiers will not get any more bread. Last night they were given a speech [telling them] that they should behave heroically, like good Germans, since the relief army is further delayed.

It feels so good to talk with him: Ernst Richter is his name, and he has already shown me his wife's wedding picture. His thirty-fifth birthday was yesterday. He will be on duty in the evening again, and if we live that long, I would like to talk with him again. He, just like you, my Sweetheart, does not consider himself a good soldier. He hates the murderous tools and would be pleased to throw them away if he knew that it was worth doing.

February 2, 8:00

Last night I waited for my German till 9:00. In vain. I could not imagine why he did not come at all and why everything is in such a turmoil around them, around the tanks.

I got up at 5:30 in the morning, and soon learned it all from the Bremen boy. I asked him what that big commotion [nearby] was. He told me. The Russians occupied the last house in Ábel Jenő Street [the next street to the south]. Dressed in German and Hungarian uniforms, at least thirty [Russians] attacked them. [The Russians] shelled them with grenades all the morning. My German was on duty at about ten in the morning in front of the Palinai house. A grenade fell in front of him; he got a splinter in his head, and the blast threw him out of his place. He died instantly. I did not want to [believe] my ears. I asked him three times: Ernst Richter? Thirty-five years old? Is it sure?

Yes, yes, the other guard confirmed an hour later. He will not be on duty any more. You know how easily I cry anyway. But I got to like Ernst so well. He was a serious, intelligent man, and we had such good conversations. He always said that he was guarding us, too. So he will guard us forever. He was buried opposite the kitchen door, on the empty lot, on Strausz's site, at the corner of the Nigreisz house.

His comrades all dug a little on his grave, and I watched them from here as his only relative, instead of his wife and daughter.

Rest in peace, Ernst, in the soft Hungarian soil. As long as I live, I will be thinking of you fondly, and we shall meet over there.

The first week of February brought closer the sounds of hand-to-hand fighting. Individual bullets now sprayed the walls of the Joó villa. A bomb smashed the bathroom, up to then regarded as the most secure place in the house. Overhead the Germans were air-dropping supplies, but most of these fell into the Russian zone. From the garden at night Ilona watched a supply airplane drop a container, and she admired the beautiful silk parachute— perfect for a blouse or an evening dress. After more than a month underground, the family fell into a sink of lethargy. Neither food nor future had any savor. They spent most of their time in bed, in darkness, for it helped destroy time. Germans came and went in the cellar as if they had lived there always, but they disturbed no one. Members of the family now had to ask permission to visit the toilet in the yard; otherwise they would attract fire. In spite of it all, they had a good laugh when Father Joó, stopped by a soldier, asked in magyarized German, "Die WC ist erobernt [conquered]?" A soldier from Bremen visited them, crying with misery and exhaustion. He showed them a picture of his family, and said that his unit had just combed the area in five armored cars looking for petrol and that only two cars had returned safely, and these with only twenty liters.

By February 9 fixed front lines no longer existed. Russians in their long white gowns were now turning up in houses officially held by Germans. Weary and desperate Germans flooded into their garden. What happened on that day and others following, Ilona carefully recorded in her diary.

February 11

I have no idea what the time is. On the ninth, at around 3:00 P.M., the retreating German soldiers swarmed onto our yard. My father stood outside at the door. A grenade fell here, and he shouted, "I am finished. Leave me alone," and fell through the door. I ran to him and also got injured on my right upper arm, three places.[63] We were really frightened but attended my father's wounds and then mine. The headquarters were here till 10:00 P.M.; then guards stayed in the house, but by the morning they were not here either.

On the tenth there was suspense in the air as we looked to the future. At around eleven I heard that the wall was being dismantled in the bedroom (above us) and then that somebody jumped in through the window. At around twelve two old Russians came down. They looked and tapped [searched] us and then they left. We were very relieved that they were rushed. Later came four more. These were already slightly inebriated. A bearded one dissuaded his fellow soldier from picking me out. Later came two more. These took Aunt Sarkó's, my godfather's, and Uncle Sanyi's watches. Two of them stayed to talk with Pötyi. Then the Germans on Ábel Jenő Street noticed them. These [the Russians] forced my godfather and Pötyi to break a hole through the ceiling into the apartment above. It went slowly, of course. They were impatient and urged them with their machine guns. Finally the parquet floor appeared, but there was a big box of books on top. The Russians cleared out of the area just in time. There were seven tank shots into the kitchen, but they were already upstairs.

February 14

Only now can I continue, my Karcsi. We are sound and healthy, sort of. My father is also healing; I have no complaints except I cannot lift with my arm.[64]

On the tenth we did not dare to fall asleep till twelve, and I did not sleep a wink. My father was very restless.

On the eleventh the shootings were still raging. In the morning Pötyi and godfather were immediately taken away for labor. They pushed cannons and midday came home—thank God—sound and healthy. At the Horváths there were two deaths, Uncle Horváth and Margitka's brother-in-law, when they pushed a cannon on top of a land mine. In the

---

63. Her father had been pointing out the back entrances to neighboring houses for some German soldiers when struck by Russian shrapnel.

64. The condition of her father proved to be worse. He had been struck by sixty shell splinters and later had to have a large intestine bypass, which rendered him unable to eat any more than tiny amounts every hour and a half, which he did until his death in 1946.

afternoon a Russian entertained himself by asking to see Pötyi's papers. In the evening we went to bed early. At around nine four drunken Russians came in to us. I was hidden under five blankets and that way escaped what Aunt Rózsi went through. I admired how skillfully Pötyi dealt with the drunken Russian who only left at 2:00 A.M. In the meantime, at 11:00 Aunt Horváth and Zsuzsika ran in, escaped to us. They had jumped through the window to escape the three Russians who went over there from us. It was a terrible night. I almost suffocated, then shivered with cold, cried, but the dear God saved me.

The next day all day we lived in terror. The apartment was first looted by the Germans and then the Russians. It is maddening what it looks like. We are trying to tidy it up now.

I almost forgot that on the eleventh, at dawn, we ran out, hearing screams and cries. The Vastaghs, the grocers, were escaping their house, no. 14, on fire. Since then we have been living here together. It is a bit unusual but better that we are more [i.e., safer from Russian predators].

On the twelfth, at 2:00, the rumor spread that free looting was over. Pötyi et al. were burying at the Hanrély's [a neighbor], but I did not have the courage to stay at home for the night. Although a [Russian] sergeant moved in with us, still I asked for admission at the Lamons' house, where officers lived. There was an officer and guards.

The six of us slept in one bed. Before going to bed a Hungarian driver said that the siege was over in Buda. All the afternoon the castle had been heavily bombed; nothing remained of it. He also described the fighting. On the evening of the eleventh, with eight Tiger tanks in front, the Germans started breaking out (of the castle area) at the Bécsi kapu [Vienna Gate]. He had to transport a [Russian] officer from then on. They arrived at Kálmán Széll Square by 6:00 A.M. (on the twelfth). The long line was hopeless, and the Russians were shooting heavily. They turned back, and by the time the bombardments had begun, they had reached one of the shelters of the Alagut [the tunnel to Chain Bridge]. After the bombardment the Russians pushed their way into the castle, and he, as a civilian, was used as a driver.

It is said that in Moscow fifty cannon shots celebrated the event: the fall of Budapest.

In her diary Ilona did not record "what happened to Aunt Rózsi," the fifty-year-old wife of her mother's brother, Sanyi, but she spoke of it in her interview. Through a peephole in the coverlets Ilona watched with terror as four drunken Russians raped her. To keep her from crying out and perhaps alerting an officer of the Red Army, they stuffed her mouth with sausages until she was on the verge of suffocation. Uncle Sanyi could do nothing. Thereafter the family pretended it had never happened—it was a subject never discussed. "Considering my father's injury, our general suffering, and constant fear of being killed—the rape was minor." One Russian remained all night, Pötyi distracting him with his Russian phrases, while Ilona lay motionless under her stifling blankets. For the next few nights she dared not stay at home. She slipped off to a nearby family whose six women slept in one bed, under the illusion that there might be some safety in numbers. Later her godfather made her a special cot concealed under a stack of wood. The problem always was to crawl in without detection, for the Russians barged in at will.

Thereafter they lived in fear of the Russians, who came in, seized the males for work parties to bury the dead in the neighborhood, and made eye inventories of all the women. The family gave the Russians anything they asked for—whether gold trinkets or jam. There was a particularly dangerous moment when the family first returned upstairs, for they found the corpse of a Russian soldier on the floor and were petrified by the thought that the Russians might blame them for his death. They waited for nightfall and dragged him into the garden for a shallow burial. All the while the father's condition was worsening. They had no medicine, no bandages, no water. They picked gunpowder granules from snow, which they boiled to sterilize bandages used over and over again. It took ten days before they could get the elder Joó to a hospital for treatment.

The fighting in Buda was over, but the Eleventh District was a shambles. Not one undamaged house stood in their neighborhood. Fences had been pulverized by tanks, doors and windows blown out by missiles or concussions. Yet there was a semblance of bureaucratic order being imposed as early as February 18. All persons were ordered to register in a hall at nearby Bocskai Street, from which hung a red flag with the pendant "the property of the Communist Party." Hungarian policemen now wore a red armband with letters in Cyrillic script. Family or Christian names seemed not to exist at this place: everybody who was anybody carefully and monotonously used the sobriquet "Elvtárs" (Comrade). Once a day the Russians distributed a goulash soup of lentils and potatoes. In this predominantly middle-class district chits for meat were distributed only to those favored few who could prove they belonged to trade unions, a procedure that eliminated most applicants. Ilona's mother lined up eight times and finally got some horse bones for soup. One lucky day she gathered handfuls of baking soda from the roadway where it had spilled from a sack. A friendly neighborhood butcher brought them five pounds of horse meat—providing their best meal in months. Shops were being looted, but the Joó family refused to join in, believing that "Hungarians should not rob Hungarians."

Although the Red Army officially prohibited rape or looting, enforcement was rare. Those families who billeted Russian officers acquired some protection, but others were open game for nocturnal prowlers. On February 21 a group of drunken soldiers broke into the cellar seeking Ilona. They overturned beds and stabbed blankets with bayonets without finding her, because that particular night she was upstairs attending her father, whose condition had grown worse. She said it was hard to believe that any man would want her: she was black with dirt and her skin riddled with scabies, but a drunken Russian was not fastidious. Some neighborhood girls established liaisons with Russian officers—there were even some mixed marriages—but Ilona was repelled by them. "They loot and threaten us constantly with their damned machine guns." For a time she tried to find resemblances between the Russians in Budapest and the characters in Gogol's *Dead Souls*. But when she saw the ungainly way they walked, their endless spitting, and had to endure their defecation in public places, the vile stink of their uniforms, she "lost interest in literary comparisons." It was not that they were animals—animals cleaned themselves. If they remained two days in a house or a garden, "a pig sty is nothing compared to what the Russians leave behind."

Early in March the Russians launched a badly managed plan to clean up Budapest. They demanded ten thousand able-bodied civilians per day as a labor force, including women between the ages of eighteen and forty. Signs appeared throughout the district: LONG LIVE THE COMMUNIST PARTY! DEATH TO THE ARROW CROSS! JOIN THE RED ARMY! Wall newspapers reminded Hungarians that the Red Army had liberated them from the Germans and that it was a moral obligation to join in the war against fascism. All the while they heard mysterious shooting everywhere in the capital at night, and the looting and raping continued. Ilona felt it her patriotic duty to join the labor groups— "They are right; how else will the country be rebuilt?"—but her family opposed it. Some informer must have notified the Russians that a young woman lived at the Tarcali Street house, because soldiers repeatedly nosed about the place at night asking for her. She resolved to cross the river to Pest and look for work.

The main Danube bridges had been blown up by the Germans. For exorbitant fees, private boats ferried small groups across the river, but on the day Ilona chose to cross, all river traffic had been canceled by the Russians because thirty SS had broken out of their POW camp. She walked far south and crossed into Pest from Csepel Island, where twisted girders and crumbled cement marked a huge industrial graveyard. All along the Dunapart (the quay) lay unburied corpses and completely pulverized houses, and on the Buda hilltop above the river the castle was still smoking. Despite this devastation, the Hungarian genius for bureaucratic thoroughness asserted itself. Ilona was able to track down the new office of the agricultural ministry and recover three months back pay—1,632 pengő. Even better, she obtained an identity card, with translation in Cyrillic script, certifying that she was a civil servant of the new regime. After this, the Russians left her alone. She remained in Pest and in a short time found a position in the huge network of the Department of Reconstruction, with offices near City Park. Her job was to find spare parts for tractors so that spring planting could proceed immediately. In Budapest there was a dire seed shortage because any object resembling a bean or a pea had been used for food during the siege. But the fertile region of southeastern Hungary—the Great Hungarian Plain—had been barely touched by the war because the Russians had advanced so rapidly that they had not had time for systematic looting. Agriculture had always been the mainstay of the Hungarian economy, all the more important now with so much of Europe blackened.

Despite the crushed appearance of her city, she found signs of revival everywhere in Pest. The black market was flourishing, in defiance of Communist ideology. Nearly everything was available if you had money for it: a kilogram of tobacco came to 400 pengő, fat 500, sugar 400. Small change nearly disappeared—one counted in ten-pengő notes. By mid-March there were shops featuring spring dresses at prices only the wives of millionaires (or commissars) could afford. The Magyar Theater had reopened, although it was now named for Attila József, whom the cognoscenti were avidly reading to acquire a proper proletarian perspective. When Ilona's mother came over for a visit in late March, they found a cinema open and saw a prewar Zola film. Perhaps the most revealing evidence of the city's impatient return to peace was a band of Boy Scouts, in neatly pressed uniforms, which she saw, less than a month after the final shots of the siege, filing into the National Museum.[65]

65. The Boy Scout organization, along with the Rotary Club and the Pen Club, was denounced and liquidated after the Communists took control of the Hungarian government in 1948. The principles and rituals were never forgotten, however, and the organization was revived with much fanfare in 1989.

Her most pressing worry was the fate of her fiancé, Károly Jobbágy, who had disappeared during the rout of the German-Hungarian army in February. Whether escaped to Germany or dead or a POW she did not know. There had been massive desertions among the Hungarians, some of whom had found civilian garb and crept back to their homes. A greater number had been captured. Ilona found out that POWs were being transported by rail to the Focsani concentration camp in Romania. From there they were to be sent to the Soviet Union as convict labor for as long as the Communist authorities cared to use them. For Ilona a long period of waiting began, not only to see Károly again but just to discover a few shreds of evidence about what had happened to him—if he were still alive.

After evacuating Ercsi, the radio unit of Károly Jobbágy set up its equipment in the village of Szentgál, near Veszprém. Jobbágy was secretly gratified by the collapse of the German defensive line and waited expectantly for the arrival of the Russians. When orders came to remove his center farther west to Austria, he balked at the prospect of crossing the frontier to defend a foreign power. Meanwhile the Soviets were broadcasting promises that all Hungarian soldiers who remained behind the German retreat could return home unmolested. One evening, as the Red Army edged closer, Jobbágy encouraged his unit to mutiny. An Arrow Cross officer, supported by two gendarmes, threatened him with court-martial—patent nonsense, since the whole front was dissolving. When they warned him that the Bolsheviks would carry him off to Siberia, Jobbágy replied, "They will not do that. They are *my* people."

They had camped in a small forest. In the morning, when news came that the Russians had passed both flanks, the Arrow Cross officer and his gendarmes jumped in a car and fled. Rifle fire came closer, and soon Jobbágy saw his first Russians. Supported by mammoth tanks, they crossed an open field and stopped at the edge of the forest. Jobbágy volunteered to speak with them. Collecting a Russian-speaking soldier who, half paralyzed with fear, insisted on crawling on all fours, he held up a dirty handkerchief and walked over to a Red Army officer standing near some tanks. His instinct was to embrace the Russian, but they seemed less enthusiastic, as though failing to appreciate the historical significance of the moment, which, if it had been painted by a social realist, might have been titled "Hungarians Greet Their Liberators." The officer began tapping his body for weapons. Jobbágy lifted his arms high and spread his legs wide to indicate his cooperation. The Russian officer speedily removed his watch and wallet and put them in his pocket. He stole everything—even a photograph of Ilona. Jobbágy was disappointed; nothing he had read about Communism, or had heard from his mentor, Olga, had ever mentioned pickpockets. An officer on a tank, using a megaphone, shouted that all enemy soldiers in the copse must come out and surrender. Over a hundred soldiers emerged, including a crestfallen lieutenant general.

Trucks carted them all to Szombathely, where they were separated by rank. Many officers tore off all insignia of rank, assuming that they would be singled out for harsh treatment as "fascists." This proved to be a mistake, for the Red Army, like any capitalist army, provided better food and treatment for officers than for ordinary "prisoners of starvation." A Russian interrogation officer told Jobbágy, "Now we will fight together." Jobbágy assumed this was an invitation to join the Red Army, which was what he had wanted all along—an opportunity to fight against fascism, whether in its Nazi or Arrow Cross guise. Next came a march on foot to Kőszeg, where the prisoners spent two days in the castle. Spirits rose when they boarded a train that moved eastward toward Budapest, but lowered when they realized that the presence of heavily armed Russian guards on the roofs did not suggest real "liberation."

From Budapest the train was shuttled south to Subotica in Yugoslavia. Before leaving Hungary, men scattered scraps of paper with their names and addresses to the winds, hoping that someone along the railroad would notify the International Red Cross or their families that they yet existed. (Ilona received his note on May 8.) Thirty-six days out of Kőszeg they arrived at Focsani, a vast gathering camp for POWs in Romania. As far as the eye could see, men milled about in dirty uniforms of a dozen nations. Over the gate was a gigantic red star, but there was gypsy music in the background. Here they were fed and sealed into carriages that clanked eastward for two weeks. Their destination was a camp in the Urals near Karpinsk. Surrounding them at this camp was an immense forest, and they were told that their job was to chop it down—all of it. The captors said that because Hungarians had joined the Nazis in attempting to destroy the Soviet Union, they must now atone for their antisocial behavior by assisting in the Soviet Union's reconstruction—in other words, they were slave labor. If they worked industriously, admitted the errors in their old political attitudes, and committed no crimes against the state, the Soviets promised their eventual return to Hungary. It was the fall of 1945.

Jobbágy resolved to make the best of a bad time. In his spare moments he wrote love letters to Ilona Joó (which, of course, he could not mail) in the form of poetic fragments on scraps of paper salvaged from cement sacks. Such writing was strictly forbidden and had to be carefully hidden. He became proficient in Russian. He was warmed by the thought that over a thousand years ago this region had been the Magyar homeland. Much of what they had known of the natural world lay about him now. The work was hard, but food and firewood were plentiful. They were not brutalized. The Russians did not worry about prisoners escaping, for where could they go? This was a region where the temperature in winter sank to minus fifty degrees Centigrade.

In the spring of 1947 the Soviets delivered on their promise. The forest had been chopped down and the wood sawed and shipped away. Whatever political attitudes any of these common soldiers had once harbored had been whittled away by boredom and apathy. And their recent political crimes had amounted to nothing more serious than stealing potatoes and, in an undisclosed number of cases, dying of typhoid and typhus—two diseases inconvenient for commissars in charge of the work gangs. A train came to the camp, and they climbed aboard. At Máramarossziget, a border station between Romania and the Ukraine, the Russian train commander lined them up and asked, "Who has anything to complain about?" No one expressed the slightest dissatisfaction. They heard Hungarian spoken by the railway men. Free men speaking Hungarian? It seemed like a miracle. Before they boarded the train that would carry them over the frontier to Hungary, the Russians examined their armpits for SS blood-type tattoos and made a final inspection of personal gear to be certain no materials incriminating the USSR were being carried away.

To Jobbágy's numbed perplexity, he was pulled from the ranks of the POWs and locked up, while the others departed on the train. The Soviet officers had found poems he had written while in the Karpinsk camp. They could not read them, but they accused him of being SS. From the window of a guardhouse he had to watch the train disappear down the track toward Hungary without him. (Some of these men carried in their shoes copies of his poems for Ilona Joó.) The next day he was taken under guard to a station and put on an eastbound train. A Romanian cleaning women who saw his Hungarian uniform and knew what was happening burst into tears. At the first station in Russia he was tied to a tree for two days and told his documents were "bad." A major interrogated him about his SS service, which he denied. His papers were stamped "fascist," and he was put aboard a train filled with civilian criminals. The next compartment contained women, whom the Russian guards raped at their convenience for several days.

At a labor camp near Lvov the warden asked him whether he had killed anyone, stolen anything, or traded on the black market. "No, I was only writing poetry." "You fascist!" retorted the warden, "You will never get home. You will die here." This camp of lumpen proletariat was more severe than Karpinsk. He worked from dawn to late evening, slept in a building alive with lice, watched prisoners assault each other for an extra loaf of bread, and learned which weeds were edible (wild radishes were the best). It got worse in another camp near Kiev, designed for political incorrigibles. They were starving. Here they crushed raw bones to dig out the marrow and would murder for bread. Because of his poetry he had to serve an additional one year and three months. Charges were never specified; nor was there ever trial or sentence. The Russians did with him whatever they wanted to do, for reasons they did not have to explain. Jobbágy found it impossible to reconcile his treatment with socialist theory.

In the summer of 1948, without forewarning, he was taken under armed guard to Debrecen and turned over to the Hungarian authorities, who were now Communist Party functionaries. He had spent 1,258 days in Russian captivity. He feared more problems with papers that labeled him "fascist," but was allowed to continue home to Budapest and his family's one-room flat near Déli Station. His father was in despair. He had worked all his life as a baker's assistant and had finally bought a small shop. Now, with the Communists running the country, it had been nationalized, and he was a baker's assistant again.

Yet Ilona Joó was waiting for him faithfully. Within a year they married and started a family.[66] He bore no bitter feelings toward the Russians. That was behind him. Regarded with suspicion when he first returned, he became deeply depressed. Eventually he was permitted to take courses at the Lenin Institute in Budapest and to begin a career as a high school teacher of Russian and Hungarian. Students found him formidable. When there was no heat in classrooms during the hard winters of the 1950s and students demanded to be sent home, Jobbágy would button up his overcoat and say, "This is nothing. I was in Siberia for two years."

As a self-taught poet, Jobbágy lacked confidence in his work. In 1949 he copied his prison poems and gave the packet to a friend at the National Bank, who in turn passed it on to a literary critic. The critic, who expected only a sheaf of anti-Soviet doggerel that at best might have some documentary interest, expressed surprise at its quality. But in view of the political censorship,

66. Ilona and Károly were divorced in 1959. Both remarried—Ilona twice.

publication was out of the question. Even to possess or read such materials was dangerous. When he returned the packet to Jobbágy, he thrust it into his hands as if it were a live grenade and offered two words of emphatic advice, "Burn it!"[67] Only after the Communist restrictions relaxed in the 1960s did he begin to have his work published.

Many years later at Sopron, where Jobbágy had been invited to read his poems, a vaguely familiar gentleman approached him afterward to compliment him on his work. He identified himself as the Arrow Cross officer at Szentgál who had ordered the radio men not to surrender to the Russians but to join him in evacuating to Germany. "And what happened to you?" Jobbágy asked, wondering how many years he must have spent in Communist jails. "Nothing," replied the gentleman. "I came back to Hungary a few months later. Nothing happened to me."

67. A selection of these prison poems was published in Budapest as *Vesszőfutás* (Ordeal) in 1990.

2 | Jews

Men

It is a commonplace among Jewish historians to highlight the period between 1867 and 1918 as the "Golden Era" of Magyar-Jewish relations because of a cordial and symbiotic relationship that existed between the elites of both groups. Having little taste for industrial and commercial development, the Hungarian ruling class encouraged Jews to enter these professions and in return provided a protective shield. Anti-Semitism, when it was felt by Jews at all, came not from aristocrats but from the rising middle class aware of economic competition. Large numbers of Jews eagerly accepted magyarization. Many fought valiantly in the First World War, and it was not uncommon for Jews to intermarry with Magyars and convert to Christianity.[1] It was a Jewish publicist who wrote of this phenomenon that Hungarian Jews often were "more fervently Magyar than the Magyars themselves."[2] (Not all that unreasonable when one considers that, like other Central Europeans, the Hungarians were such an amalgam of Magyar, Slovakian, Serbian, Austrian, Romanian, and other hybrid stock that picking out a purely Magyar bloodline was virtually impossible.) That there were Hungarian theoreticians of anti-Semitism, like Dezső Szabó, is undeniable, but their impact upon public policy at this period was minimal. This is not to say, however, that the Hungarian ruling class fraternized intimately with the Jewish elites, only that

1. During the census of 1910 some 77 percent of Jews living in Hungary listed their nationality as "Hungarian," probably a rough measure of their assimilation. György Ránki, "The Germans and the Destruction of Hungarian Jewry," in *The Holocaust in Hungary: Forty Years Later*, ed. Randolph L. Braham and Béla Vágó (New York, 1985), 87.
2. Quoted in Randolph L. Braham, "The Uniqueness of the Holocaust in Hungary," in Braham and Vágó, 179.

they respected their competence and efficiency in managing so well the complex business of a modern state. But segregation on a preferential basis was a fact of life. For affluent Jews Siófok on Lake Balaton was a favored resort, but Magyars of the same economic class gathered at Balatonfüred; in Budapest the New York café drew a Jewish clientele, while Magyars frequented the Pannonia. There was nothing fanatical about these nuances, but they were clearly understood by both groups.

This live-and-let-live equilibrium underwent a change in the decades following Hungary's defeat in the First World War. The Treaty of Trianon, which deprived Hungary of two-thirds of its former territory and three-fifths of its former population, at one stroke reduced the country to a minor nation. Schoolchildren recited the national slogan of the thirties: "Csonka Magyarország nem ország. Egész Magyarország menyország" (Crippled Hungary is no country. Whole Hungary is God's country). Surrounded by the hostile Little Entente, which was backed by the Allied Control Commission, Hungary found itself in a vulnerable position—with neither the friends nor the finances to defend itself against enemies, real and imaginary. Moreover, the economy had collapsed, and increasingly there grew an awareness that the Jews, who represented only 6 percent of the total population, possessed wealth and power considerably in excess of their number. To make matters worse, the short-lived Bolshevik regime of Béla Kun in 1919, with its concomitant Red Terror, had been officered by a disproportionate number of Jews. From political obscurity before the war, Jews had suddenly become visible, and Hungarians began to resent what they saw.

For many Magyars it appeared that Jews had infiltrated into every nook and cranny of the better-paid occupations and professions, and Christians thus felt in danger of being pushed out altogether. To deal with this, Parliament passed the so-called *Numerus Clausus* Act (Article 25 of Law XXV of 1920), which limited the percentage of Jewish students enrolled in universities to the proportion of Jews in the total population.[3] The law proclaimed more than it delivered, for Jews quickly filled up their quotas (which in many instances were ignored by registrars and directors intent upon enlisting the

---

3. Iván T. Berend, "The Road to Holocaust: The Ideological and Political Background," in Braham and Vágó, 35. Estimates range widely because many Jews classified themselves as Magyars. According to the census figures of 1920 the total population of Hungary was 7,980,143, of which 473,214, or 16.86 percent, were listed as "of Jewish religion." C. A. Macartney, *Hungary and Her Successors* (London, 1937), 447. The proportion of Jewish students fell from 34 percent in 1918 to 8 percent in 1935. Jörg K. Hoensch, *A History of Modern Hungary, 1867–1994* (London, 1996), 107.

best-qualified students), while many wealthy ones bypassed the quota system altogether by seeking education abroad. Nevertheless, Hungary had the dubious distinction of being the first country in Europe to pass legislation that attempted to limit the influence of Jews in public life, and in so doing it augured more drastic laws to come. The census of 1925 revealed that Jews constituted 50.6 percent of all lawyers in Hungary, 46.3 percent of physicians, 34.3 percent of editors and journalists, 39.1 percent of engineers and chemists, and 22.7 percent of directors and actors. In addition, 40.5 percent of the industrial firms were owned by Jews.[4] Although the *Numerus Clausus* Act was designed to limit the influence of Jews in prominent sectors of Hungarian life, little effort was made to put teeth in the law or to extend it. While some conservatives railed about the problem, most Hungarians, preoccupied by reconstruction of their own lives, gave Jews little thought. Occasional debates occurred in Parliament, but no further restrictive laws were passed against Jews until the nationalist fever arrived in the late 1930s, a period when Hungary fell under the aegis of racial theories current in Germany.

As already noted, the overriding objective of Hungarian foreign policy during the period between the two world wars was restoration of the territories and population lost by the Trianon Treaty. During the 1920s this restoration seemed possible only by maintaining a supine or hangdog attitude toward the victorious Allied powers. Accordingly, Hungary tried to show good faith by playing by the rules laid down by the victors: it joined the League of Nations, established credit with Western banks, acquiesced in the gutting of its armed forces, and extended political rights to the non-Magyar groups stranded within its boundaries. Unfortunately this good behavior resulted in nothing tangible. The Western powers had no intention of scalping Yugoslavia, Czechoslovakia, and Romania in order to restore the lost territories. By an ironic twist, it was the world depression of the 1930s that offered a dim ray of hope, for as the former Allied powers became absorbed in their own economic woes, they became increasingly unable, or unwilling, to monitor control mechanisms they had installed in the Trianon Treaty. Italy and Germany, on the other hand, encouraged Hungarian recalcitrance. By 1940 Hungary had quit the League of Nations and joined both the Anti-

4. Raphael Patai, "The Cultural Losses of Hungarians Jewry," in Braham and Vágó, 165. The census of 1930 for Budapest listed these percentages: merchants, 50 percent; clerks in private firms, 45 percent; attorneys, 51 percent; physicians, 42 percent; engineers, 26 percent. Gyula Zeke, in *Hét évtized a hazai Zsidóság életében* (Seven decades in the life of Hungarian Jewry) (Budapest, 1992), 187.

Comintern Pact and the Tripartite Pact. Germany had become the principal trading partner of Hungary. Gyula Gömbös, an admirer of Mussolini and Hitler who became prime minister in 1932, had published an essay as far back as 1920 that posited that the solution to the "Jewish problem" lay in limiting the number of Jews in all professions to their percentage in the population as a whole. Gömbös died in 1936, but his mission was continued by other prime ministers as Hitler strengthened his position through aggressive action in Spain, Austria, and Czechoslovakia.

In May 1938 Parliament passed its so-called First Anti-Jewish Law. This reduced the ratio of Jews in professions to 20 percent, and called for the dismissal of 1,500 Jews from intellectual occupations every six months until the proportion was attained. Jews who converted to Christianity after 1919— the year of Béla Kun's insurrection—would be classified as Jews, not as Christians, just as any child born after that date to a mother and father of Jewish faith would be officially a Jew, even if reared as a Christian.[5] This law would shortly have disastrous consequences because it defined a Jew according to racial type rather than religious affiliation. As though rewarding a child with a prize for obedient behavior, Hitler six months later announced the First Vienna Award, which returned to Hungary the *Felvidék* (upper province), a swath of Czechoslovakia containing one million Magyars, of which seventy thousand were Jews. The hated Trianon Treaty was at last being overturned. Justice was arriving at last—adjudicated by Adolf Hitler. Hungarians were exultant about the return of their territory and the recovery of lost Magyars, but they deplored the increase in Jewish population.

Six months later, in March 1939, Parliament responded by passing the so-called Second Anti-Jewish Law. This cut the proportion of Jews in professions to 6 percent (reactivating the old *Numerus Clausus* Act of 1920) and banned Jews from serving in Parliament and other public offices. Henceforth a Jew was defined as anyone having two Jewish grandparents or one Jewish parent (except children of mixed marriages born before 1919). To deter immigration of Jews from Germany, the law forbade Jews from acquiring Hungarian citizenship by marriage; moreover, naturalization acquired after 1919 was subject to annulment.[6] It took no particular clairvoyance to see that Hungary was aligning itself more closely to the "nationalist" orientation of the Third Reich. It was symptomatic that Hungarians of Swabian descent made up only

---

5. Randolph L. Braham, *The Politics of Genocide: The Holocaust in Hungary* (New York, 1981), 125, and C. A. Macartney, *October Fifteenth: A History of Modern Hungary* (Edinburgh, 1956), 1:218–19.

6. Braham, *Politics of Genocide*, 155, and Macartney, *October Fifteenth*, 1:325–26.

3 percent of the population at large but 40 percent of the officers and personnel at the Ministry of Defense.[7] The impact of this influential minority on Hungary's decision to enter the war is self-evident.

Hitler's reputation as gift giver soared in August 1940, when western Transylvania was cut loose from Romania and returned to Hungary in the Second Vienna Award. The gift came with no strings attached—at least not at the moment—although the addition of seven hundred thousand more Jews to the population at large added to the burgeoning problem of anti-Semitism. (The problem was exacerbated by the fact that the density of Jews in the annexed territory was substantially larger than in Trianon Hungary.) Meanwhile Germany seemed all-powerful, having occupied the Low Countries, whipped France, and partitioned Poland after concluding a peace treaty with the USSR. In Europe the future appeared to lie with Germany, and Hungary waxed in its success. As a token of gratitude and support, Parliament in August 1941 passed, by a vote of sixty-three to fifty-three in the upper House, the so-called Third Anti-Jewish Law, which was designed to free the country from the Jewish spirit and to eliminate Jews from cultural and professional life, including the military. It forbade marriage or sexual intercourse between Christians and Jews and implemented the main provisions of Germany's Nuremberg Laws.[8] Per Anger, a Swedish diplomat in Budapest during the war who was involved in the effort to save Jews from deportation, believed that anti-Semitism in Hungary differed from the German strain in being motivated less by racial theory than by sociopolitical factors—specifically economic competition.[9]

One other major difference between Hungary and Germany was that Hungarian Jews of military age were eligible for conscription whenever needed, but were only allowed to serve in labor battalions attached to regular military units.[10] This was an arrangement unique in Axis Europe. In effect, they were subject to military enslavement without recourse to the law. Initially they wore Honvéd uniforms without insignia, but later this so infuriated regular soldiers that they were allowed only civilian clothes marked with yellow armbands (not stars). Among the bitter pills they had to swallow was a requirement that they supply their own clothing and personal gear. Whether

7. Eugene Lévai, *Black Book on Martyrdom of Hungarian Jewry* (Zurich, 1948), 20.

8. Braham, *Politics of Genocide*, 195, and Macartney, *October Fifteenth*, 1:436.

9. Per Anger, *With Raoul Wallenberg in Budapest* (New York, 1981), 49.

10. The precedent for these labor units dated from 1919, when Horthy, requiring manpower, drafted into his White Army two classes of "unreliables"—workers and Jews—neither of whom had the right to bear arms. Braham, *Politics of Genocide*, 286.

their treatment in service was harsh or compassionate depended, in the field, on the personal attitude of their particular commander, which varied from sadistic to humane. Some of the more rabid anti-Semites among the officer class were said to have boasted that if any Jews returned home, they would arrive in an attaché case—in other words, as cards in an index file.[11] Testimonials collected after the war describe how in some units Jews had been forced to climb trees and crow like roosters and shout "I am a dirty Jew," how they had been hosed down in winter to become "ice statues," and how they had to subsist on bones and vegetable matter, all grain foods being denied them.[12] In general, the farther the units were from Hungary, the less humane their treatment.

Jewish participation in the Hungarian military services underwent a gradual modification between wars. Originally Jews were drafted into the Honvédség, where they served with Christians just as they had in the First World War. After anti-Semitism hardened in the post-Gömbös era, they were deprived of rank and cast into labor battalions. Endre Sásdi (born 1911), whose four grandparents were Jews, grew up in Szolnok with little awareness of any difference between himself and his Magyar schoolmates.[13] He entered his father's business as an apprentice buyer of English woolen fabrics and on coming of age entered the army as a volunteer reserve lieutenant. When his father died in 1931, the family business collapsed. Added to the general business malaise of the early depression years was a disturbing obstructionism among government employees, who delayed, held up, and eventually canceled his passport, which made buying trips to England impossible. At the time, Endre assumed this treatment resulted from bureaucratic inertia, not anti-Semitism. He gave up his business and moved to Budapest, where he took a job in a dynamo factory near Nyugati Station. "Discrimination against Jews began about 1938, but it didn't touch me personally. I never thought much about it."

Sásdi was called up when the Hungarian army "liberated" Ruthenia after the First Vienna Award, served three months in the highlands without hearing a shot fired, and returned to his factory in Béke Square. Then, in 1940, during the occupation of Transylvania, he was again called up, but the mood

---

11. Nicholas Nagy-Talavera, *The Green Shirts and the Others: A History of Fascism in Hungary and Rumania* (Stanford, 1970), 182. Reserve officers were probably responsible for the majority of the atrocities. Few professional officers would have condoned them.

12. Braham, *Politics of Genocide*, 317.

13. Interview with Endre Sásdi (January 4, 1990).

of the army was changing. Although the Sásdi family had magyarized their name in the 1920s and Endre had no features that suggested his Jewish origin, he noted with mounting concern that anti-Semitic jokes and allusions were proliferating. At a military canteen he met a deputy of Szálasi, the Arrow Cross leader, who boasted that he could detect a Jew by smell. He sniffed Sásdi, declared him clean, and, handing him an application, invited him to join his party. Sásdi did not tell him that he was a double enemy—both as a Jew and as a member of the forbidden Communist Party.

After passage of the Third Anti-Jewish Law, Jews were stripped of their reserve-officer status. Sásdi was deprived of his rank and drafted into an inactive Budapest labor battalion. Hungary was now at war with the USSR, but since he was a specialized worker in a major defense industry, he continued working at his foundry and receiving regular wages. (One was not a Jew when it was convenient for the government to decide one was not.) He was now married and hoped to avoid a call-up that would take him to the front.

All this changed dramatically in April 1942, when Hungary agreed to reinforce the Wehrmacht on the eastern front. With a tag-end group of other Jews, Sásdi was picked up and locked into a baggage car bound for Hatvan, a major railway junction for traffic eastward. There Jews were formed into units and sent under guard to the Russian frontier. They walked the rest of the way—1,200 kilometers—to the front along the Don River north of Stalingrad. There they dug tank traps and trenches and worked as pack animals. It was forbidden to send letters home. When Sásdi attempted to smuggle to his wife a note that read "I am well," he was caught and sentenced to two months hard labor. In his view Hungarian officers showed more antagonism toward Jews than did Germans. "One Jew had brought his violin. Attracted by the music, a German colonel came over and brought him food. When a Hungarian officer rebuked the German for enjoying Jewish music, the colonel told him to shut up, or he would have him shot. Later, when the colonel left, the Hungarian beat up the violinist in revenge, but he was afraid to smash the violin."

In January 1943 the Soviet offensive overran the Axis front south of Voronezh and rolled up the Hungarians. Within hours all discipline vanished. "Among the Jews there were only a few of us left. To keep up we had to walk thirty to fifty kilometers a day through the deep snow in minus thirty degrees. You dared not sit down, or you would immediately freeze. All this while we were loaded with lice and infected with typhus. The clothes we had brought from Hungary were in rags. No one cared whether we were Jews or not. They even gave us Hungarian uniforms that had been stripped from corpses.

They issued no food because there was none. If the Russian peasants had not fed us, we would have starved."

The army straggled back to Kiev and regrouped. Sásdi barely made it. In March he nearly died in a huge typhus camp near Dorosic, and when he emerged he weighed thirty-six kilograms, about half his regular weight. He was lucky to survive at all. Nearby a stable containing seven hundred Jewish typhus cases accidentally caught on fire. The doors were locked, and men jumping out of the loft like "flaming torches" were machine-gunned to prevent them from setting fire to other buildings. There were only a handful of survivors.[14] Meanwhile Horthy pushed Hitler for the return of his Second Army, along with the Jewish labor battalions, and by bits and pieces this was done. In the spring of 1944, Sásdi was among sixty Jews locked into a forty-man freight car. They had no idea where they were going, and suspected the worst. To their inexpressible joy they arrived at the Hungarian border. After a month in quarantine, they were sent on to Budapest and given twenty-four hours' leave. Sásdi swore that he would never return to a labor battalion. Better to be dead.

He nearly died of food poisoning. Relatives descended on him and crammed him full of rich foods he had not eaten in over a year—cutlets, pastries, cheese, cream. He had to obtain a medical extension to his leave. At the War Ministry he found an old friend of his regular army days who was able to pull strings and obtain his release from the labor service. He thought that his long nightmare might be over. He was well out of it. Estimates of Jewish deaths in labor battalions serving in Russia range as high as forty-two thousand souls.[15]

On March 18, when the Germans occupied Budapest, Sásdi found himself again in the lion's mouth. When Jews were ordered to the ghetto and forced to wear the yellow star, they knew worse was coming for Jews. His wife had a nervous breakdown when two of her cousins were raped and forced into prostitution by an Arrow Cross gang. She begged him to join her in a suicide pact. Sásdi agreed. On March 27 he dissolved sleeping pills in water. Although he drank more than his wife, he had been overfed and only fell asleep. His mother-in-law woke him in the morning. His wife lay in a coma and died three days later in the suicide ward at Rákóczi Hospital. His mother-in-law bitterly reproached him—not because of their suicide pact but because she had not been included. (A few months later she died in Auschwitz.)

---

14. Vilmos Nagy Nagybaczoni, *Végzetes esztendők* (Fatal years) (Budapest, 1986), 126.

15. Braham, "Uniqueness of the Holocaust in Hungary," 184. The minister of defense, General Nagybaczoni, estimated that of the 50,000 who served in Russia only 5,000 to 6,000 survived.

Sásdi had no time to grieve. He had to resume work at the foundry at once. Since he was a highly skilled foundry worker, he escaped persecution—at least for the moment. His factory, located within a residential area, was never bombed. But when the Allied air forces began massive raids on the factory district around Csepel Island and killed hundreds of Magyar workers, the rightist press complained bitterly that Gentiles were being killed, while Jews squatted safely in their ghetto. Beginning in July the government began collecting Jewish workers from the city and putting them to work at the Csepel factories. Sásdi and others were billeted in a synagogue and commuted to the factory each morning under guard.

After the October coup that installed the puppet government of Szálasi, the Csepel factories began to be dismantled and the machines shipped to Germany. The rumor got around that the Jewish workers would be sent to Germany with the machines, and Sásdi resolved at all costs to remain in Budapest and wait for the Red Army, which was not far away. Somehow he had to escape from the guards. His opportunity came on November 23, when he badly injured his hand while loading a railcar. Discipline had become so lax that he was allowed to go to a hospital without a guard. He ripped off his yellow star (the punishment for which was immediate execution) and under cover of darkness took a tram for the city. He was wearing an old army overcoat. When three armed Arrow Cross entered and sat down beside him, Sásdi faked sexual interest in a woman across the aisle. Shortly after leaving Keleti Station British bombers came over. Knowing that if he entered a shelter he would receive an ID check, he hid in his sister's house near Parliament Square. This was far too dangerous. The Arrow Cross were pounding on doors in the neighborhood. At night the family could hear shots on the Danube embankment, where random Jews were being massacred. His brother-in-law moved him to the garret of a stamp shop he owned overlooking Erzsébet Bridge. Sásdi lay here for several weeks. There was no heat, but his sister and a female friend brought him tinned food and water at night.

Peeping from a small bull's-eye window he watched German engineers blow up Erzsébet Bridge as they tried to halt the Russian advance at the river. Then, in late January, he saw Russian soldiers crawling through the snow toward the river embankment. He opened a kilo tin of beans to celebrate his liberation, but his exuberance was short-lived. After moving into his sister's flat he had a ringside seat for what the Russian soldiers were doing with Budapest women. They regularly invaded the shelter at night, gave food to whomever they fancied, and forced them upstairs. At the end of the month Russian secret police checked his ID. When he told them he was a Communist, they scoffed, but they accepted his factory card, telling him he would be a privileged person in the new regime.

When the Russians began recruiting for eight divisions of Hungarians to fight the Germans, Sásdi volunteered eagerly. (Ultimately they organized three paper divisions, only one of which did any fighting.) He was appointed provisional lieutenant and assigned his first chore—removing manure from offices where the Red Army had stabled their horses. Training was rudimentary. Clearly the Hungarians were mainly a propaganda army. Hungarian officers had no authority over Russians of any rank and dared not attempt to assert· any. Once Sásdi did save a young girl from being raped, not because he commanded the attackers to desist but because he told them she had a disease.

Early in May his skeletonized division entrained for Austria. On May 8, as they neared the front, they heard what sounded like a major battle in progress. The Russians were firing off mortars, field pieces, rockets, and every explosive they could lay their hands on. News had just reached them that the war was over. Not far away an SS unit had fortified a wooded area and had sworn to defend it to the death. The Red Army commander amused his staff by ordering the new arrivals to root them out. Fortunately for the green Hungarian unit, the Germans surrendered after firing only some token shots.

The Hungarians were told they could go home, but were provided no transport. The Red Army refused them trains or trucks. The Russians treated them as turncoats and suspected—with justification—that many of them were former Arrow Cross men. In the end they had to steal handcarts from Austrian civilians and push them back to the Hungarian frontier, where they were able to wheedle transportation back to Budapest. At checkpoints Russian guards picked through them at will, randomly collecting prisoners to fill POW quotas for forced-labor gangs in Russia. At one checkpoint they seized Sásdi. It was the last straw. He ripped off his jacket, threw it on the ground, and said, "No. Never. Better shoot me now." They laughed and let him go. For the second time during the war he returned to Budapest, tail between his legs. His side had prevailed, but Sásdi felt no elation, only relief.[16]

During the thirties Antal Blumenthal (born 1915) performed his regular infantry service without anyone suspecting he was Jewish—or if they

---

16. Sásdi married the woman who had come with his sister to bring him food at his hideout. He remained in the Hungarian army until 1946, when he joined the Border Guards. Later he attended the Frunze Academy in the USSR for nine months, became disenchanted with the politics, returned to the army, and in 1968 retired as a lieutenant colonel of the quartermaster corps.

suspected it, they seemed not to care. He had been born in Berlin, but his father, a jack-of-all-trades of Slovakian origin, moved to Budapest in 1918. Although Antal received religious instruction at a succession of Jewish schools, he always moved easily among Christians, especially those of the sporting set. His hangout was a coffeehouse run by his grandfather across from the Gellért Hotel, where he indulged his image as bon vivant and man-about-town. His apprenticeship to a fancy furrier (specializing in mink) was interrupted in the late thirties by conscription into the regular army. Unlike Sásdi he never got beyond the rank of private. "I had no military ambition whatsoever. And my family had no politics—other than making money."[17] He admired Horthy and loyally believed that he would protect Hungarian Jews. Thus it came as a shock when in 1942 he found himself summarily drafted into a labor battalion bound for the Russian front.

Within days of his induction his comfortable worldview collapsed. His section was guarded by an Arrow Cross Jew hater whom they named Kintornai (the Torturer). For minor infractions, or for no reason at all, Jews were tied to trees and beaten bloody with rods. They were issued no uniforms, knapsacks, or personal gear. Clothing had to come from home, and since they were not allowed to receive mail, their clothes quickly went to pieces. "We soon became ragbags. Nobody cared about us." During a six-thousand-kilometer trek, east then west, they dug roads and trenches, chopped trees, constructed huts, manhandled military equipment through thigh-deep mud, served as guinea pigs in detecting mine fields. They walked—horse and motorized transportation were not for labor battalions. "Nowadays you hear stories about men who escaped these camps. It never happened with us. A few tried, but they were always torn up by dogs or shot by guards." Late in 1942 the front stabilized just west of the Don River. The Russians were only a kilometer away, across the shallow river. Some Jews talked hopefully about being liberated by the Red Army; others, having heard their fathers discuss privations as POWs of the Russians in the last war, dreaded the prospect of being taken as prisoners.

Early in January 1943, when the Don Bend front collapsed, Blumenthal fled westward in the chaotic retreat. With Russians in hot pursuit many Magyars changed their attitudes toward the Jews. Soldiers were now ripping off badges, emblems, and insignia to become as anonymous as possible. They eagerly struck up friendships with the Jews, gave them full rations, and invited them to share huts, sensing that they might need endorsements if the

17. Interview with Antal Blumenthal (April 21, 1989).

Russians ever overtook them. "They were kind to us—that is, until we got safely beyond the Russians. Then the old treatment returned." The retreat lasted until mid-April. A month later Blumenthal came down with typhus at Dorosic, in the Ukraine. Diseased men were locked into a quarantine camp that in effect became a death camp. The only medicine was milk. Blumenthal had a gold chain, a parting gift from his mother. This he gave to a doctor who bartered it for a few liters of contraband milk from a guard. His fever went down, and after ten days he recovered.

Horthy's appointment of General Vilmos Nagy Nagybaczoni as minister of defense gradually alleviated the plight of the Jewish labor battalions in Russia. A simple soldier with traditional views of justice and decency, Nagybaczoni demanded that the disgraceful conditions within the Jewish labor battalions be immediately improved and the men returned home along with other units of the army. Torture, beating, expropriation of property were to be ended, and the Jews were to have proper food, clothing, and leaves like those of regular soldiers. At one stroke the worst phases of involuntary servitude for Jewish males ended.[18] Blumenthal crossed the Hungarian frontier in August 1943. Of the 1,150 Jews who had left Budapest with him, only 27 answered the final roll call. After six weeks at an "easy" camp at Komárom, where they swam and lounged on the bank of the Danube, he was discharged from the labor service and resumed his old life as a civilian furrier. He had done his duty and assumed that he would surely never be called up again.

This situation changed, of course, when the German army occupied Hungary in March 1944. Jews had to wear the yellow star and were restricted to quarters, either in the ghetto or in so-called protected houses. Disconcerting stories circulated about Jews in rural areas being carried off to Poland and Germany as laborers, while the Jewish Council in Budapest met every German demand in order to save the urban Jews. Blumenthal was again drafted. This time he remained in Budapest making collars and coats for German officers and their women. He slept on a straw pallet in a church near the Erkel Theater, but he held on to his bicycle and could roam the city without guard or harassment. He was now engaged to Olga Koós, a rising

---

18. Nagybaczoni's championship of the labor battalions, which he probably would have eliminated altogether if he had had the power, was reviled by both the Germans and the Hungarian Right. Unfortunately, Nagybaczoni had maintained business connections with prominent Jewish families, which, when discovered in June 1943, forced him out of office. While Jewish labor battalions continued to be formed and used until the end of the war, and abuses continued, credit can be given to Nagybaczoni for making such abuses illegal rather than acceptable. Macartney, *October Fifteenth*, 2:155.

young Jewish actress of the Hungarian stage, who introduced him to a lively circle of artistic friends. All of them waited eagerly for the Russians to hurl the Germans back to Berlin. In the meantime they enjoyed the good life—or the best wartime facsimile thereof. During the early fall of 1944 monotony replaced fear as the dominant feeling for many Jews in the protected houses. The general sense among Budapest Jews was that with the Red Army so clearly dominating the Wehrmacht, it was only a question of time before they would be rescued.[19]

Fear returned when Horthy went out and Szálasi came in. Thereafter Blumenthal was rarely allowed to leave the church without an armed guard. On December 1, as the Red Army was closing on Budapest, he learned that he was scheduled for deportation. He met Olga, who was living in a vacant school building with a group of wealthy Jews who had agreed to pay a ransom to the SS in order to guarantee their survival. She begged him to join them, but he was afraid. "I smelled a trap. If they found out I had skipped the draft, they would kill me. Besides, I always played by the rules. None of us knew anything about the death camps at that time."[20]

At Józsefváros Station (a minor Budapest depot favored for trafficking in Jews because fewer eyewitnesses were about) he was locked into a freight car with ninety-two other Jewish males.[21] For ten days in an unheated carriage they huddled together as the train crawled westward. Guards passed in food and water once a day. When the doors were unlocked, they found themselves in Berlin. For Blumenthal this was a bad omen: "I was born here and now I'm to die here." A short time later they were hauled to Oranienburg, regarded as a show camp for Swiss inspectors. But no neutral observers were on hand when SS guards unloaded the train, shouting, "Los! Los!" and kicking them into lines. They were stripped, shaved, and issued striped uniforms. Methodically, German quartermasters placed all their clothes, watches, and jewelry into labeled boxes and stored them in cupboards for their future recovery. "But we never saw them again." In their coarse uniforms they stood in stark contrast with the political prisoners at Oranienburg, many of them wealthy Dutch and Belgians wearing tailored clothes.

---

19. Interview with Andrew Nagy (August 9, 1995). Nagy, who was twelve years old during this waiting period, amused himself by making model airplanes like any other boy of that age.

20. For an account of Olga's experiences during the war, see "Women" below.

21. Unknown to him, he was probably part of a contingent of Jews whom the Germans wished to trade to the Allies for medicine, trucks, or whatever matériel they could negotiate. The Eichmann deportations of Jews to Auschwitz had been halted by Horthy in July, except for rare stragglers who slipped through the net.

After three days a truck carted them to the Sachsenhausen camp as laborers in a vast Heinkel factory. "This was the best of these places—no gas chamber." Most worked repairing the railway, which was repeatedly damaged by Allied bombers. The punishment for the slightest infraction was smashing rocks in a nearby quarry ruled by a brutal SS sergeant who personally hated Jews. "Du, Jude, komm hier!" he would shout, followed by kidney punches with an iron rod. Seven to ten prisoners died each day until the SS command itself removed the sergeant for excessive cruelty.

In late March 1945 they heard the sound of a distant cannonade. Orders came to evacuate the camp. It was raining as they lined up in a forest next to a railroad siding; Blumenthal was ill and emaciated. The guards ordered all men unable to go on to collect under a tree, and he joined perhaps a dozen broken men—a melange of Jews, Russians, Poles. Their moaning irritated him, for he wanted only oblivion. He muttered some curses and cried out in German, "Ruhe!" (Quiet!). This outburst attracted a friendly SS guard, who told him, "I heard you. You must not stay here. These are dead men." Inexplicably he helped Blumenthal to the train and arranged for him to work in the kitchen detail. With this extra food, he regained the will to go on.

The train unloaded them at Buchenwald, a camp already crammed with seventy thousand prisoners. Massive Allied bombing of the factories beyond the camp wire continued, but no bombs fell on Buchenwald. There were no executions here, but the crematorium worked round the clock in disposing of bodies dead of starvation and disease. On April 4 or 5 SS guards entered their barracks, shouting, "Alle Juden heraus!" Blumenthal was deathly ill, but always one to obey an order, he tried to get up. But when his bunk mate cried out, "Stop!" he weakly dropped back on his bunk. "That voice from a man I barely knew saved my life. It was like a miracle. The ones who obeyed the guards were killed in the forest."

A few days later the first American tanks arrived. The Americans were stunned by what they found, but most prisoners were too emaciated to show any reaction at all. At the liberation Blumenthal weighed only thirty-eight kilos. "I was nothing but a bag of bones." Soon Yugoslav and French partisans with the American army scoured and whitewashed the stinking barracks. He spent three weeks at an improvised sanitarium fitted out in a former SS barracks. Here was a heaven of clean sheets, fresh clothes, and food the taste of which he had nearly forgotten. (In the hospital more patients died of gorging on rich food than of diseases contracted in the camp.)

When repatriation papers were arranged in August 1945, Antal returned home. He found both his parents alive. They had remained in the fenced-off ghetto rather than seek safety in a Swiss or Swedish "protected" house. (Some of their neighbors who had made this transfer had been killed by Nyilas gangs contemptuous of the national flags hanging from the windows.) Olga had also survived. They married, and she resumed her career on the stage. Through her contacts Antal became a business manager in the booming Olympic industry of the postwar years. When their son was born in 1956 Olga made him change his name to Bakos because she did not want her boy to be branded a Jew. In 1958 Antal and Olga separated, and in 1964 they were divorced.

Since Hungary had inherited from the Hapsburg dynasty a comprehensive system for recording vital statistics, it was difficult for a citizen to slip through the network of registration. The chances that a Jew could hide his identity were small, but often one could evade persecution by moving about among relatives scattered throughout Hungary and adjacent countries, particularly Slovakia. One such evader was László Felkai (born 1920), the son of a bankrupt merchant of the predominantly Jewish district near the Dohány Street synagogue.[22] Although he performed well as a student at the prestigious training school for rabbis, the Jewish quota system kept him out of the university. Determined to earn a degree, he moved in with relatives in Prague at exactly the wrong time— just after the Munich Agreement. He then moved to Nyitra in Slovakia, where he worked as a confectioner. The environment became increasingly oppressive with racial hatred. The rightist Hlinka Guard paraded openly, scrawled anti-Jewish slogans on walls, and roughed up Jews in the streets. The Slovakian Parliament passed laws forbidding Jews from wearing leather, jewelry, or fur, from owning more than two suits or a radio. The yellow star became mandatory, and only two Jews were allowed on a street at the same time. Compared with anything he had ever encountered in Hungary, Felkai found the treatment of Jews by the Slovaks "primitive, malicious, hateful." In 1942 he returned to Budapest, arriving just after most available Jewish males had been scraped up into the labor battalions and sent to the Russian front. Encouraged by his old rabbi, he applied for one of the few openings at the university yet available for Jews and was admitted. He did not receive coupons for meals or books; he was not allowed to join student organizations; but he distinguished himself in his major studies—history and Hungarian.

The bureaucracy caught up with Felkai in August 1943, when he was drafted into a labor battalion. Within two days he was over the border in a

22. Interview with László Felkai (May 24, 1989).

freight car bound for the Pripet Marshes, where the Hungarian army had occupational duties. Most of the Jews he found there had been in Russia for two years and were survivors of the Don Bend debacle. They were closely guarded by the Keret, a special military police, which worked their charges ten to twelve hours per day—constructing roads and bridges through the swamp. They were allowed one "dumb" postcard per month—a printed card with multiple choices that could be checked off. "I am healthy/I am well treated/I am well fed." If one failed to make the proper mark, the card would not be sent; additional marks brought a beating. This was the only way to inform family back in Hungary that one was still alive. Conditions were harsh beyond anything that Felkai had imagined, but the sadistic phase of torturing Jews had largely ended, even though men of the notorious Gecső Battalion still loved to boast about the number of Jews they had personally killed. Granted that this was probably exaggerated, still no Jew in a labor battalion could afford to be complacent in the company of Hungarian soldiers. Felkai heard stories—but did not personally witness any incidents—about wealthy Jews tied up on horizontal poles and released only when they promised to have money sent to Keret relatives in Budapest. The greatest fear was disease, for typhoid, hepatitis, and typhus were endemic in these camps. Felkai came down with scabies, contracted from filthy horse blankets, but skin disorders were nearly universal in Russia. The labor battalions were in constant movement, always westward in retreat from the Russians. Felkai remembered the worst difficulty was walking up to forty kilometers per day with a heavy rucksack containing tools. Food was near starvation level: the Germans took first table, the Hungarians second, while the labor units scrounged whatever was left. Russian peasants were friendly. They allowed the broken men to sleep in their houses and outbuildings and provided them with carrots, potatoes, milk, and bread. Once over the border into Poland the situation abruptly changed. Polish peasants kept the Jews at bay and provided them with food only in exchange for money or jewelry.

During the fall of 1944 Felkai was part of the massive pullout of the Hungarian army from the Polish front. Germans and Hungarians rode south in trucks; Jews walked. (Felkai estimated that he walked more than two thousand kilometers—often forty per day—while in the labor battalion.) But each weary day brought him closer to Hungary, and his health had never been better, which he attributed to walking and fresh air. In Hungary his battalion was rushed to Kecskemét to dig tank traps, for the Russians were now sweeping nearly unopposed toward Budapest. The guards, knowing that the Jews would denounce them if they were captured, panicked and fled. One evening, after digging at his tank trap, Felkai threw down his shovel, stepped out of line, and began walking southwest toward Romania.

Within a few days he passed completely through the advancing Red Army, which paid no attention to him. He spent the next three months in Temesvár. In February 1945, when Budapest was liberated by the Russians, he returned home. Both his parents survived. His father had remained in the family flat at Wesselényi Street, on the eastern edge of the ghetto, while his mother had found refuge in a protected house. Only a few sticks of furniture remained, the rest having been burned as fuel. His other relatives had been less fortunate. Four had been killed by Arrow Cross gangs at the Danube embankment in December. They had refused to accept protection in a Swedish house set up by Raoul Wallenberg because they clung to their belief that as "good Hungarians" they were protected against illegal persecution. Six of Felkai's uncles on his mother's side had disappeared forever. Months later, when communication opened with Slovakia, Felkai learned what would probably have been his fate had he remained in Nyitra. All his relatives there had been swallowed by Auschwitz except for one aunt, a doctor.

Felkai knew how to bend in a gale. The arrival of the Russians was for him truly a "liberation," and he flourished in the regime that the Russians installed in Hungary. He completed his studies at the university, launched a career as a teacher of German and Hungarian in Budapest high schools, and became a widely published author of articles about education—"all of them written within Marxist theory." Unlike many present-day Hungarians he does not look back nostalgically to the *belle epoque* of Admiral Horthy, and the bitter drafts he was made to swallow during the war have not been purged from his system. "Hungary was always ahead of its time in persecuting Jews. It is now illegal to do so, so they persecute Gypsies instead. In my youth there was no 'Gypsy Problem.' Nowadays some xenophobes here hate Gypsies because they *look* Jewish."

Too young to be drafted into a Jewish labor battalion, Rudolf Singer and his twin brother, József (born 1928), experienced their own civilian version of hell during the Szálasi regime in 1944. They were born and grew up in the largely Jewish Seventh District of Pest, where their father served as manager of a large Czech-Hungarian textile firm. The twins were bright. They jumped two grades in their public school, which some of the Magyar students resented. One teacher, a parachutist reserve officer, openly showed his distaste for them, but they attributed this to idiosyncrasy rather than to pronounced anti-Semitic feelings. Jewish and Christian students had fights—but not more frequently than Jews against Jews or Christians against Christians. The words "dirty Jew" were not heard at their school, but Rudolf did observe that Jews were beaten with ten strokes of a rod, whereas the Christians only got eight. More disturbing were activities outside of school. By 1938 ordinary, quiet citizens were wearing Arrow Cross emblems in their buttonholes. On weekends Nyilas troopers defiantly paraded in their black uniforms with green shirts and ties.[23]

The directors of their father's firm had to fire him in 1942 because of the anti-Jewish laws, but knowing he was indispensable to operations, they encouraged him to take another name and to continue working for them—at a reduced salary. On these terms he was able to hold on to this post until the German occupation in March 1944. That period also terminated the twins' secondary education; thereafter they went to an electrician's trade school. With family friends, many of whom had connections in Germany, they speculated about what was happening to Jews elsewhere in Europe. "We knew they were dying of overwork and disease, but we had no notion at all of the death camps. But after the German occupation, all of us got scared."

In June there came an order for the family to vacate their flat within three hours and move into a special ghetto area being set up near the Dohány Street synagogue. They stored their furniture in the empty flat of a neighbor, a Jewish doctor who, with his wife, had committed suicide by injection, and found lodging in a yellow-star house where their mother's niece supported herself on the pittance she got from making military uniforms. Jews were allowed on the streets only for four hours each afternoon. Food was always in short supply but never at starvation level. Some Christian shops defied the law by selling Jews more than the specified limit. (And a few of these did not raise their prices.)

The twins' older sister, Valéria, concluded that their best chance for survival lay in gaining admittance to one of the protected houses near Margit Bridge, well away from the ghetto. She had a close friend who was one of Raoul Wallenberg's typists, and the Singers moved over to 42 Pozsonyi Street. It was crowded—seventeen people in two rooms and taking turns sleeping in the bathroom—but reputed to be safe. However, in November the twins were caught outside after curfew and taken to the notorious brickyard camp at Óbuda on the Vienna road, a collection camp for Jews about to be deported. Valéria went into action at once. Her typist friend gave her Swedish passes for her brothers, and because she dared not make the trip herself, she found a

---

23. Interview with Rudolf [Singer] Sas (April 21, 1990).

Christian woman who volunteered to take them. Minutes after this woman crossed Margit Bridge, the Germans dynamited it without warning, dropping automobiles, trams crammed with passengers, and pedestrians into the Danube, but she succeeded in delivering the passes to the boys. They proved useless—the Arrow Cross wardens simply tore them to pieces. The camp rumor was that they would shortly be marched on foot to Vienna. The twins planned to break out. The Arrow Cross were always more effective in putting people in jails than in keeping them there. During the afternoon the twins hid with a sixteen-year-old girl in a stack of drying lumber and at night scaled a ten-foot wall. Then they ripped off their yellow stars and rode a tram to the river. Once ferried across, they went into deep hiding at the Pozsonyi Street flat. A few days later the building was raided, and Valéria was carried off as part of a draft of women under forty. This group went on foot to the Óbuda brickworks, where Valéria spent a horrifying night besieged by the screams and moans of fellow prisoners who feared deportation. In the morning they had to line up and show their IDs. Many of the Swedish and Swiss passes were torn up; but for no plausible reason hers was accepted, and within hours she was walking back to Pest.[24] The family was still hanging on together. It was late November, and they believed that if they could hold on for only a few more weeks, the Russians would liberate them. A cryptic message found in the personal column of a Pest newspaper had wide circulation among Budapest Jews: "Soon I'll be with you. Be calm. Uncle Joe."

On December 3 Valéria sensed trouble. There were gangs of Arrow Cross combing Pozsonyi Street looking for Jews, and gunshots echoed throughout the district. At the risk of their lives, she and her mother donned coats without the yellow star and set out to find a safer place. They found one in a Red Cross orphanage nearby, but when Valéria returned to Pozsonyi to notify her brothers and father, she found an Arrow Cross gang had carried them off— no one knew where. Her mother was so unsettled by this that she insisted on returning to Pozsonyi to wait for her boys and man, none of whom Valéria ever expected to see again.[25] When Valéria returned to the Red Cross house, it was dark, and the director refused to open the door, so she spent a terrifying

24. Interview with Valéria Singer (April 21, 1990).

25. Valéria and her mother were moved forcibly one more time, seeing out the siege on Wesselényi Street in the Jewish ghetto. Here they lived in the cellar, which by chance had once been a small canning factory and was crammed with tins of food. They were liberated on January 18 by a rare Russian soldier whose libido was more political than sexual. Ripping the yellow star off their coats he exclaimed, "You are free!"

night walking in City Park, dodging patrols. Had she been detected, she
would probably have been summarily shot.

The Arrow Cross had succeeded in flushing the twins from their hiding
place in 42 Pozsonyi and marched them at dawn on December 4 to Józsefváros Station to join a large collection of Jews bound for some unspecified
place. Because of his age, their father could have remained in Budapest, but
he chose to accompany his sons. Packed eighty in each freight car they had to
take turns sitting down. Each carriage carried two Hungarian gendarmes,
who occupied small cabins mounted on the roof. They were frequently
shunted onto side tracks to make way for trains carrying industrial machinery
to the west, for the looting of Hungary had begun in earnest. It took three
days to reach the village of Acs, only sixty miles from Budapest on the Vienna
line. Here they were allowed to leave the train in groups of ten to collect
water. Five Jews in one group made a break for it but were swiftly pursed by
guards and shot down in front of the others. Beyond Győr some Jews in the
twins' carriage tore up the flooring. About eight escaped by dropping
between the tracks. As punishment the SS commandant permanently sealed
all carriages until the train crossed the frontier of the Third Reich.

On December 12 they disembarked at the Bergen-Belsen camp, where they
were segregated on the basis of health. The Singers were in good health and
were placed in a forest to cut wood and do senseless jobs like moving piles of
dirt from one place to another, then back again. There was a rumor that their
group would be exchanged in Switzerland for medicine. To fatten them up, at
Christmas they got Red Cross packages containing butter, crackers, sugar,
sausage, cigarettes—although many packages had been looted in transit.
After Christmas, when they received the same rations as others in the camp,
they concluded that the exchange had been called off. Daily rations now
consisted of five decagrams of bread, half a liter of soup (potato peel, carrot,
no fat), two decagrams of ersatz coffee. Every Sunday they got a spoonful of
"Hitler Jam," beet-root pulp. Conditions steadily worsened, less by German
design than mismanagement and overcrowding. As the Germans lost ground
in Poland, they carried their concentration camps with them. These starving
and broken people descended on Bergen-Belsen, which could not feed its
original population. Each barracks contained three hundred prisoners.
Normal human beings became dehumanized in "an ocean of feces, lice, and
disease." Of the occupants in Rudolf's barracks 40 percent died, mainly of
typhoid, dysentery, and typhus. To escape the filth piling up on the barracks
floor, men built precarious aeries in the rafters, from which they peered down
at the human cesspool below them like frightened monkeys. They had no

water for washing, and toward the end the only drinking water came from a stagnant pond around which lay unburied corpses. The capos, mainly Ukrainians or Wehrmacht rejects, took satisfaction in brutality. With their clubs they could break a skull with a quick triple blow. The prisoners had to stand at attention outside the barracks and answer roll call from two to seven in the morning. When they left or entered the barracks, they had to pass through a narrow door where two capos clubbed them. Captives went insane and became oblivious to commands. Rudolf saw capos beat a mentally deranged Dutch boy to death because he did not respond to their questions. Perhaps as a malignant joke the SS appointed Polish Jews as capos for Polish Gentile prisoners. Rudolf saw no suicides—with death all about them the inmates clung to life.[26]

On April 7, one week before the British army liberated Bergen-Belsen, the Singers were crammed into a trainload of other Jews. Their SS guards told them their destination was Theresienstadt, near Prague, which still had extermination facilities. The Germans were desperately trying to eradicate all traces of their "final solution" policy. For six days, the Jews without food or water, the train, consisting of twenty-five locked cars and guarded by six SS guards in sentry boxes nailed to the rear, crawled along to the southeast. No prisoners were allowed outside. On the morning of April 13 the train came to a permanent stop, the locomotive was detached, and the SS guards vanished with it. The sun was high when American soldiers of a tank division discovered the train and cracked the doors. Fully half the Jews inside were dead in the fetid atmosphere. The Singer twins' father died only minutes before the doors were opened.

A short time later some Americans brought back the locomotive with the SS guards. Three or four were picked at random and tied to trees. Americans then handed loaded pistols to some Polish Jews, who killed and buried them on the spot. The train had halted outside Haldensleben, a wealthy town near the Elbe River untouched by the war. On the outskirts was an elaborate recreational camp for German officers, which the Americans commandeered for the former prisoners. The Americans then made the local citizenry cart the heaps of Jewish dead to town and bury them in a mass grave in the garden of the officers' club. The clubhouse became an instant hospital, staffed by German doctors and nurses, who, encouraged by the presence of armed and

26. Even Rudolf Hoess, the commandant at Auschwitz, claimed to be shocked by conditions at Bergen-Belsen during a visitation around this time: "Sanitary conditions were far worse than at Auschwitz. The camp was a picture of wretchedness." Rudolf Hoess, *Commandant of Auschwitz* (London, 1959), 163.

angry Americans, "gave us excellent treatment," Rudolf recalled. He weighed in at 32 kilograms (about 70 pounds)—down from a normal 55 (about 120 pounds). He had not seen his brother since early morning because József had contracted typhus and had been carried off to a quarantine room. After being bathed and deloused, the Jews were encouraged by the Americans to help themselves to uniforms, found in abundance at the club. Within a short time Jews had exchanged filthy rags for the splendid costumes of German artillery colonels. Many Jews died of the rich food proffered by the Americans, who did not realize the dangers of such fare. Rudolf himself went down with typhoid. When he recovered and sought his brother, he was directed to a grave in the club garden.

This sector fell within the Russian zone, and the Americans soon pulled out. They promised asylum to anyone who went with them, but Rudolf was eager to return home. As soon as the Red Army occupational force came to town, they ejected the Jews from their camp. Rudolf petitioned the Russian authorities for a travel pass, but always there were delays and excuses. All the Jewish refugees were carefully supervised and watched—as though they were still prisoners. Long trains full of German POWs passed every day, all of them going east, and Rudolf heard unsettling tales of how any able-bodied male might find himself on a train bound for a Russian labor camp.

Late in August Rudolf and two others slipped away from Haldensleben at night. The Americans had given them clothes, blankets, and tinned food and had written out safe-conduct passes in three languages. Such papers meant nothing to the Russians, but eastbound travelers were not impeded—it was the westbound traffic that was stopped. They traveled by freight trains and horse carts. At the Hungarian border the guards accepted their passes but stole everything in their backpacks except for one blanket. Rudolf reached Budapest in September and found his mother and sister safe. On September 15 he went back to work as an electrician.

After the war Rudolf Singer magyarized his family name to Sas as a symbolic commitment to Hungarian tradition. In 1949 he was admitted to the Military Academy of the Hungarian People's Republic and after graduation joined the ÁVH—the Hungarian equivalent of the KGB. In time he became a lieutenant colonel in charge of "flight control in the air force"—a position in which he investigated, not air traffic, but suspected political deviation. Survival on the party track was not always easy. "My first disappointment came in 1951 when Auschwitz survivors whom I knew were deported to the worst camps in the Hortobágy [the most primitive part of the *puszta*]. Also I was distressed by the so-called economic reforms. In 1949 our standard of living had returned to the prewar level, but by 1951 we were back to a wartime economy."

Lieutenant Colonel Rudolf Sas retired from the Ministry of Interior in 1983. He never married and lives with his widowed sister, Valéria. He laments that racial intolerance is resurfacing in present-day Hungary, for it was held in check by the Communists. "Anti-Semitism can now be openly talked about. Under Kádár [the USSR Party head installed after the 1956 revolution] even to discuss it was against the law."

Women

Hungarian rightists sometimes boasted that they had introduced the first anti-Semitic legislation in post–World War I Europe, yet paradoxically as late as 1944 Hungary remained a haven for Jews even as they were being systematically exterminated elsewhere, from the Balkans to the Low Countries. Horthy's Hungary had no extermination camps for Jews. In the country 800,000 of them still lived in comparative freedom and retained some semblance of protection under the law at a time when 3,000,000 were being liquidated next door in Poland alone. And because of the rapid advance of the Red Army it seemed likely that they would escape altogether. However, with the German occupation this condition changed dramatically. The haven turned into an assembly-line hell as approximately 450,000 Jews were deported and liquidated in the forty-six-day period between May 15 and July 7, 1944. Again paradoxically, the country that had so successfully protected its Jews from the Nazi death camps became, almost overnight, the country that eliminated more Jews per diem than any other nation in Europe, not excepting Germany.[27] Even the SS were surprised at the alacrity with which the governmental agencies arranged the deportations. One SS report stated that in no other part of occupied Europe had they received such cooperation.[28]

Only one day after the bloodless German occupation, the *Sonderkommando* of Adolf Eichmann went to work. His underlings called a meeting of the Jewish leaders at the Dohány Street synagogue, where they promised that no Jews would be harmed if they cooperated. There would be no arbitrary arrests or deportations, and both life and property would be protected. Jews

27. At his trial in Nuremberg, Edmund Veesenmayer testified that if the Hungarians had been resolute in refusing to cooperate, the German goals would have been impossible to achieve. Béla Vágó, "The Hungarians and the Destruction of Hungarian Jews," in Braham and Vágó, 102.

28. Braham, *Politics of Genocide*, 462.

were prohibited from travel or changing domiciles without permission. They were to form a *Judenrat* (Jewish Council) to implement German demands. The Jews present seemed "hypnotized" by this seemingly polite and reasonable presentation, and they promptly contributed the blankets, bedding, and other items that the Germans demanded. They even brought Germans items not asked for. Yet already Jewish families were fleeing the city. Over three thousand of them were picked up and placed in a camp at Kistarcsa, a suburb east of Budapest, within the first week. When the Judenrat complained, Eichmann himself appeared and insisted that they had been arrested not because they were Jews but because they had disobeyed the law. He explained that Jews would be asked to "volunteer" as workers in war industries. They would be well treated and paid on the same scale as other workers. Compulsion would be used only if a sufficient number failed to come forward.

The Hungarian government cooperated fully in executing the German plan for suppressing Jews. In the Ministry of Interior two secretaries of state, László Baky of the political section and László Endre of the administrative section, both Arrow Cross partisans, were placed in charge of Jewish affairs and bent to their labors eagerly. (Eichmann once joked about Endre's zest for his job, saying that that he "wanted to eat the Jews with paprika.")[29] Ministerial decrees (none of them approved by Horthy, who consistently refused to sign any anti-Jewish documents) began to roll off the presses within a week of the occupation. By the end of May some of the restrictions were firmly in place. All Jews above the age of six had to wear a yellow star at all times; they were expelled from banks and stock exchanges; they were dismissed from public services; they had to surrender all cash over three thousand pengős; they were forbidden to practice as teachers, actors, journalists, or lawyers; Jewish doctors could treat only Jewish patients; Jews were not allowed to use cars, taxis, trains, ships, or other vehicles except trams and buses within town; they had to surrender their bicycles, firearms, and radios; they could not enter hotels, cafés, restaurants, theaters, cinemas used by non-Jews. To block a possible avenue of escape, one law prohibited Christians from adopting Jewish children. Jewish businesses were to be closed down. (Yet any Christian laid off by such closure would have his salary continued.) There was a public book burning in which the work of 250 Jewish authors went to the flames. From libraries and schools 450,000 books—the equivalent of twenty-two freight cars—had been collected and incinerated.[30] (Ironically,

29. Ibid., 403.
30. Ibid., 500.

the number of books burned is approximately the number of Hungarian Jews sent to death camps.) When the Germans promised rewards for denunciations of Jews, they were surprised by the response; during the first eight days of their occupation they received thirty thousand denunciations (which compares dismally with the 350 during the first year of their occupation of Holland).[31]

When Allied air raids began killing people in working-class districts, leaving Jews in the central city untouched, there was a great outcry, followed by an Arrow Cross leaflet demanding that one hundred Jews be executed for every Magyar killed by the bombings. Nothing came of this other than the compulsion of some Jewish males to work in the threatened factories. (Moving Jewish families to the factory quarter was out of the question, for the authorities feared that they would contaminate the workers with Bolshevik ideas.) On the positive side, there were exemptions for the families of Jewish invalids of the First World War and for those who had distinguished themselves in overthrowing Béla Kun.

At this stage the Hungarian authorities apparently had no intention of deporting Jews, only of separating them from the rest of the population. The subsequent liquidation of Jews in rural areas occurred through a series of miscalculations that placed all the trumps into German hands. To begin with, in eastern Hungary, where the Russian advance had reached to within twenty miles of the frontier, military commanders feared that great pockets of Jewish subversives (and partisans) might lurk in their zones. The Baky plan called for placing Budapest Jews in special houses flying a yellow flag and removing Jews in the provinces to camps. As an interim step, the provincial Jews would be rounded up by gendarmes and penned in dozens of temporary enclosures scattered in towns and cities in the countryside. However, Baky quickly discovered that he could not raise either the funds or the manpower to construct camps for nearly half a million Jews, much less to feed and clothe them. Within a short time the temporary camps, often local brickyards where families squatted in the rain without adequate shelter, food, water, or proper sanitation, quickly became a national disgrace. Even gendarme officers complained to the ministry that illness and disease were turning these improvised, ramshackle ghettos into death traps in plain view of any bystander. Baky discussed his problem with Eichmann, who had been patiently waiting for such an opportunity to solve the Hungarian Jewish "problem" in his own way. Horthy was not consulted. Within fifteen minutes Baky had finalized a decision to ship the rural Jews to Germany, ostensibly as factory workers.

31. Vágó, 97.

Eichmann immediately made arrangements with German railways.[32] An official order from the Ministry of Interior to gendarmes spelled out the procedures: "They can be loaded like sardines since the Germans require hardy people. Those who cannot take it will perish. There is no need in Germany for ladies of fashion."[33]

A large number of these Jews came from regions that had only recently been added to Hungary through the two Vienna awards. Thus there was a sense that they were not really Hungary's responsibility. The Budapest Judenrat, for example, had been informed by escaped messengers that Auschwitz was an extermination camp, but they kept this information to themselves. Their policy seems to have been to turn the other way while "unassimilated Jews" were thrown to the wolves, on the assumption that urban Jews might thus be spared.[34] This attitude is evidenced by a letter from the council to the minister of interior, written on May 3, seeking a meeting to discuss the deportations: "We emphatically declare that we do not seek this audience to lodge complaints about the merit of the measures adopted [the Auschwitz shipments] but merely ask that they be carried out in a humane spirit."[35]

Moving such a mass of humanity required enormous expenditures of manpower and money. Because the Honvédség refused to participate, Baky's force of twenty thousand gendarmes had to supervise the operation. The German participation was minuscule, for only eight officers of Eichmann's *Sonderkommando*, along with forty SS, were involved in the removal. The Jews were shipped north by way of Kassa, a remote region. The original plan called for some trains to proceed by way of Budapest, but this idea was scrapped because it would have highlighted the deportations. Once beyond the Hungarian frontier, the Germans took charge. They also carefully counted heads and sent Hungary a bill for transportation costs. They gave the Hungarian finance minister a 50 percent discount because of the "low comfort level" of the freight cars. Moreover, there was an additional discount for senior citizens and children.[36] Without adequate food or water and packed in

---

32. Years later, at his trial in Jerusalem, Eichmann said that these deportations proceeded flawlessly, or as he put it, they "went like a dream." Hannah Arendt, *Eichmann in Jerusalem* (New York, 1963), 142.

33. Quoted in Braham, *Politics of Genocide*, 602.

34. A Jewish historian places much of the responsibility for this deportation on the shoulders of the Budapest Jewish Council—"the most spineless, the most servile and with that of Vienna and Germany the most contemptible in all of Europe." Nagy-Talavera, 203.

35. Quoted in Raul Hilberg, *The Destruction of the European Jews* (New York, 1973), 542.

36. Félix Péter, "Pokoljárás" (Going to hell), *Heti világgazdaság (HVG)*, February 25, 1995, 99ff.

stifling freight cars in the heat of summer (even the ventilators were nailed shut) an uncounted number died in transit. To allay suspicion in Budapest, the deportees were allowed on arrival to put their names on postcards that reported they had arrived in "Waldsee." (The Judenrat knew this was a code name for Auschwitz but chose not to alarm Budapest Jews by divulging the information.)

By the end of June news of the deportations had leaked to the West. When letters of protest reached Horthy from both neutral and Allied countries, including one from President Roosevelt, he conducted an investigation, which confirmed the reports. Shocked by the large numbers of Jews who had been deported, and outraged at the brutality of the operation, Horthy fired Baky and Endre as "filthy sadists" and canceled further deportations. This saved the Budapest Jews, who had been scheduled for collection and transportation by Baky's gendarmes on June 30. Although Eichmann was able to squeeze a few more Jews through the Horthy net, he began meeting walls of resistance.[37] In August, Eichmann, realizing that his goal of removing all of Hungary's Jews was impossible, packed up his office and left Hungary. On trial in Jerusalem years later, he remarked, "Hungary was the only country where we were not quick enough for them."[38] Although the German authorities continued to demand that the Budapest Jews be moved to country camps, this demand was ignored and the matter dropped.

Conditions among the Budapest Jews improved slightly in the months following. Horthy ordered the Ministry of Interior to be depoliticized, and he absolutely refused to accede to the German request that Baky and Endre be reinstated. Baptized Jews were exempt from most anti-Jewish legislation, and Horthy delegated to himself the power to exempt any Jews who, in his judgment, had brought distinction upon Hungary. The Red Cross was allowed to set up relief organizations among the Jews. With the approach of the Russians, the German high command determined that mobilization of manpower on the eastern front was of greater importance than monitoring Jewish activities in Budapest. As their grip on the country loosened, the climate of fear abated. However, there was one disturbing portent: the Arrow

---

37. According to the testimony of Veesenmayer at his interrogation for war crimes, Horthy told him at this time, "I haven't the faintest intention of doing to the Jews the things the Reich is asking me to do. The Holy Father has written to me from Rome, the King of Sweden has written to me, and the King of England has written to me through an intermediary. I don't like being blackmailed like this by the Reich to act against the Jews." Quoted in Macartney, *October Fifteenth*, 2:306.

38. Nagy-Talavera, 202.

Cross Party, once spurned and even banned by Horthy's government, began to swell in membership and influence, attracting conservatives who had once regarded it as little more than a club for lumpen proles. Yet with the Russian offensive in high gear, it seemed likely that the Budapest Jews would not be harmed and would survive the war.

Their hopes were dashed on October 15, 1944, when Horthy's attempt to draw Hungary from the war failed and the Arrow Cross movement took control of the government. Veesenmayer, alarmed by the prospect of an intra-city guerrilla war made possible by the presence of several hundred thousand Jews incited by the approach of the Russians, pushed the new minister of interior, Gábor Vajna, to do something. Vajna's first effort was to nullify all foreign passports and safe-conduct passes issued to Jews, but this aroused such a clamor among the foreign missions that he immediately had to rescind the order. He then devised a complicated table of exemptions that included Jews under foreign protection. The Swiss, Swedish, and Spanish legations were inundated with applications, and forgers were kept busy. Within a few weeks the number of Jews carrying foreign papers rose from 15,000 to 33,000.[39] This clearly was not what Veesenmayer wanted. Moreover, it infuriated the Nyilas gangs, who began invading the protected houses, where they seized whomever they liked and carried them off to the Danube embankment for execution. By contrast, the 125,000 Jews who remained in the ghetto, where they were protected by the German army (motivated not by love of Jews but by their abhorrence of any civic disturbance), were comparatively safe, despite terrible living conditions. All male Jews of the ghetto between sixteen and sixty were enrolled in labor groups, which began digging trenches and tank traps around the city. A few days later the Jewish women between fourteen and forty were collected to wash and mend soldiers' clothes, although a few of the hardier ones joined the men in digging. Although Szálasi laid out a grandiose plan for all Hungarian males between twelve and seventy to be mobilized for national service, this was never implemented. Paradoxically the Jews of Budapest, by their work on fortifications, did more to hold back the barbarians at the wall than the average Magyar male steeped in the lore of Hungarian heroics.

Meanwhile the Germans were building their "East Wall," a defensive line in Austria, and asked for a labor force of 50,000 Jews. Szálasi reluctantly agreed to send half that number, providing that they be employed only on Hungarian soil. Fitness was not a condition of removal; these Jews included

39. Macartney, *October Fifteenth*, 2:449.

pregnant and nursing women, children, and old people. The first group of 20,000 went by rail (except for the able-bodied, who walked). But no transportation was provided for the second group of 20,000. All of them, irrespective of age, health, or sex, had to walk. The result was a death march in which the victims were brutalized by gendarmes and buffeted by winter storms. Conditions became so appalling that a "rescue" team had to be sent from Budapest to collect the survivors.

How many Jews were butchered by improvised Arrow Cross gangs after October 15 is not known, but all agree they numbered in the hundreds. These were unauthorized killings. When the Red Army prepared a census of Pest at the end of the siege, it found 124,000 Jews still alive. Buda held a smaller number.

Although Jewish through all grandparents, Judit Herceg (born 1921) was raised in a family proudly magyarized. Her father, a bank clerk, had seen hard service in World War I and was pensioned for loss of a leg and the fingers of one hand. Although the son of a rabbi, he had put Jewry behind him. His family did not attend synagogue or observe kosher restrictions in their consumption of food. Judit was especially proud of her mother's side of the family. Her grandfather had been a sculptor and architect, so their flat in downtown Pest, on Váci Street, was crammed with artwork and antiques. Her mother fancied herself as a grande dame. "She was used to money and fashionable friends. Her family regarded her marriage to a bank clerk as a poor match."[40] Although Judit's mother had planned to study medicine, she had been closed out because of the *Numerus Clausus* legislation of the early 1920s.

Judit attended a mixed school opposite the big market at Ferenc József Bridge. Despite the large number of right-wing and very privileged students at her school, she was never ostracized. Like her schoolmates, she came from a family that accepted Regent Horthy without question. When she graduated, she expected to enter medical school but, like her mother, was foiled because of the Jewish quotas. Instead, she went to Szeged for a two-year laboratory assistant's course. She was a conformist, not a rebel. The degree of her complacency is evident in the following anecdote. The students at her school planned a ball and invited army officers from the Szeged regiments. Just before the girls went downstairs, the headmistress came into her room

---

40. Interview with Judit Herceg (January 20, 1990). For the interview with József Bárdos, husband of Judit Herceg, see "Invasion" in Chapter 1.

and told her, "You cannot go down. It might be embarrassing. These are officers, and you are Jewish." It was not spoken in an unkind way, but it came as a great shock as well as an augury of the future. Judit remained in her room.

When the Second Anti-Jewish Law forced her father out of his bank, Judit returned to Budapest and found private employment in a Buda sanitarium. This job was on the prohibited list for Jews, but the location was remote, and she had a forged ID. Besides, she demanded less money than a Christian. (To whom could a Jew complain about such discrimination in pay?) Since Váci Street was too expensive and too conspicuous, the family moved to a crowded quarter near Kálvin Square.

About noon on March 19, 1944, while on her way home, Judit found German armored units at Ferenc József Bridge and guards around the Gellért Hotel. She was frightened, but the Germans smiled and waved her on. It was that fatal and unforgettable Sunday when the German army first occupied Hungary. The streets were deserted and unnaturally silent. The whole city seemed intimidated. From that day on she moved about warily, spending the least time possible in public view. Because of her father's military service and 100 percent war disability, the family did not have to move into the ghetto, nor did they have to wear a yellow star. Meanwhile, preparing for the worst, her mother began to hoard peas, beans, lentils, and a laundry basket full of dried vegetables that looked and tasted like grass, and on one occasion turned up with great chunks of pork, which she fried in grease as a preservative and then hid away.

One morning at the clinic Judit's doctor whispered that someone very important was coming and that she must gave him an EKG. To her horror the patient was Döme Sztójay, former ambassador to the Third Reich and currently prime minister, an infamous Hitler toady and anti-Semite. Despite his fearsome reputation he treated her affectionately, and she almost came to like him.[41] In the months ahead she regularly treated Germans at the clinic— gonorrhea was the most common ailment. "Fortunately I did not look Jewish. Whenever I met German soldiers they wanted to go out with me." The period between May and July 1944, was alarming. Budapest Jews knew that something dire was happening, but they did not know what. "I never saw Jews carried off to death camps. We had no knowledge of death camps.

41. Sztójay was prime minister during the height of the Jewish deportations, from March to August 1944, when he retired to a sanitarium. An ailing man, he was executed as a war criminal in 1946.

We only knew that they were being deported to Germany to work in factories. We thought it considerate of the Germans that they took whole families."[42]

When the Germans occupied Budapest for the second time, on October 15, 1944, and replaced Horthy with Ferenc Szálasi, the reign of terror officially began. Male Jews of all ages were ordered to report to military barracks, where the healthy ones were shanghaied into labor battalions. A Communist whom the Hercegs had helped while he was in prison intercepted Judit's father, who was walking to the barracks on his artificial leg, and told him to return home at once and report on his crutches. He did this and was classified as "disabled" and sent home. However, Judit was ordered to report with other women to the Dohány Street synagogue, where the Judenrat was negotiating with Eichmann's *Sonderkommando*. The women were packed into the synagogue, where they camped out in the hallway and galleries. Thousands lived there, cooking their meals beside their suitcases and sacks. Beyond the small garden two rows of ten toilets, all open to public view, were set up in the aisle of the wedding chapel. "This place was the worst nightmare of all for me." After five days at Dohány Street her mother arrived, imperiously announced that her husband's exemption privileges still held, and took her home. Judit never forgave the council for its favoritism. It was supported financially by wealthy Jewish families, particularly by donations from the Manfred Weiss conglomerate, which owned the bulk of the Csepel Island factories and employed forty thousand workers.[43] Judit learned that wealthy Jews could save themselves by paying off the Germans, the council acting as go-between. "The Jewish Council was corrupt. To the poor it gave nothing but vague promises and soothing words. They could have saved more of the common people. I personally knew one rabbi on the council who had to emigrate after the war to keep from being tried as a war criminal."[44]

Judit busied herself helping Jews to find hideouts. An aunt who had once been an opera singer traded all her jewelry for false documents and was taken into the family of a retired colonel from an aristocratic Transylvania family. Judit joined a ring of clever forgers who, with the connivance of a parish

---

42. Judit Herceg first heard of Auschwitz and death camps several years after the war. "At first we didn't believe it. We simply could not imagine it." This comment is frequently heard among Budapest Jews.

43. Weiss was shortly to arrange with the SS the transfer of himself and forty-six other wealthy Jews to safety in Portugal in return for handing his factories over to the SS organization.

44. This rabbi later sent her father a letter in which he tried to clear himself in anticipation of his denunciation. He was accused of turning Jews over to the Arrow Cross after he had collected money specifically for their safety.

church in the Seventh District, washed out names on its register and replaced them with Jewish names having similar sounds. On one occasion her team found in a bombed-out county building seals and legal forms, which they used to forge all sorts of documents. The Jewish population of Budapest offered no armed resistance as in Warsaw, but there were a few bands of young Jews—most of them outlawed Communists—who dressed in Arrow Cross uniforms and conducted people from the ghetto to hiding places among the Christians. Sometimes these masqueraders would intercept real Arrow Cross gangs with Jewish prisoners, put on a great show of Jew baiting and rank pulling, and persuade the gangs to hand over their prisoners. Although the Herceg family did not have to wear the yellow star, it was extremely dangerous to walk in public because the Arrow Cross gangs had little respect for documents, credentials, exemptions, or diplomatic immunity. They carried off Jews from protected houses with impunity, contemptuous of Swiss or Swedish flags. By contrast, the German soldiers Judit met on the streets were always well mannered. They despised the Nyilas as bullies and scavengers only pretending to be soldiers.

On December 24, as Judit came home from her aunt's hiding place, she heard a heavy cannonade in the direction of Kispest, the eastern suburb. That night the family took up quarters in their cellar and remained there until mid-January, as the battle for the city raged around and above them. They made sorties to the bread shops, which miraculously remained open until nearly the end, and they queued up in long lines for their precious loaves despite the shrapnel and the splintered rooftops that dropped shards into the street. Usually her father performed the bread duty, which was especially dangerous for him because he was no longer agile enough to throw himself to the ground quickly if a shell landed near. Whenever he returned to the cellar with a loaf of bread under his arm, his face bore a triumphant smile. The gas and water lines had been cut—water came from a tap two blocks away. Dead horses littered the streets, but it was nearly impossible to cut up a frozen carcass at any time, much less during a bombardment. When the horse in front of their flat softened somewhat in early February, her mother prepared a rich horse soup, but it tasted putrid, and they could not eat horse meat a second time.

On January 9 they heard rifle and machine-gun fire in the next house. Then their cellar wall was torn apart, and a Russian soldier cautiously poked his head in. Even though the Germans in a nearby building had not been dislodged, the Hercegs had been liberated. Their first real taste of freedom came when Russians broke into a German warehouse nearby and gave them flour, potatoes, sugar, and poppy seed. But any euphoria they felt at deliverance died quickly. German propaganda leaflets had warned that the Russian barbarians were thieves and rapists, but they had long ago dismissed such propaganda. For the Hercegs trouble began when some Russian soldiers broke into a pub across the street and found the cellar full of liquor. A drunken soldier burst into their cellar. He was huge, red-haired, and carried a machine gun on a strap. Waving the gun at Judit he said, "We go into the attic to see if there are any Germans there." She had no choice except to go. In an empty room he groped her. She clasped her hands tightly round her breasts and prayed that her layers of overcoat, ski pants, and heavy boots would act as a protective shield. In the meantime her mother followed her into the attic room and began screaming and pummeling the soldier on the back. At the same time, her father ran into the street and shouted to some military police- men that his daughter was being raped in the house. The soldier, drunk and unsteady, gave up his assault on Judit and ordered the two women back into the cellar. There, as he turned his attention to two other women, a very small Russian officer carrying a tiny revolver entered the cellar and rapped the soldier on the back. When the soldier saw the officer he turned white and sobered up as if by magic. He was hustled outside. A short time later the Hercegs heard that the soldier had been shot, which may have been true, because afterward similar bands of Russians kept away from their flat.

Pest was cleansed of Germans by the third week in January, although the enemy held out in the hills of Buda across the river. On January 20 her father's bank reopened. The Germans (or Arrow Cross) had broken open safe deposit boxes and stolen everything. Earlier Judit's father had deposited valu- ables belonging to his Jewish friends in these boxes, and now he felt guilty and miserable about their loss. His shame was unnecessary, however—all these friends had vanished forever. Of Judit's immediate family only her parents and aunt survived. All of the others, who had left the ghetto for the imagined safety of "protected" houses, were executed by Arrow Cross gangs or perished on the notorious Vienna death march in December.

Food services returned only slowly. At every street corner and alcove women and men stood all day offering household items or scraps of food for trade. Judit knew an old woman who hung out of a window bartering small sacks of cornmeal for gold jewelry. Window glass was unavailable at any price, so they pasted greased paper in their window frames. In this barter economy the Hercegs kept alive by exchanging antiques for food.

They knew the war was over when, in mid-February, some friends came over from Buda on an improvised ferry—the retreating Germans having blown up the Danube bridges—and reported that the SS and Hungarian units trapped in the castle had finally surrendered. It was time to celebrate their liberation and survival. Judit's mother disappeared into the kitchen, from which there shortly came the "divine smell" of cooking pork. She was preparing a grand feast, the centerpiece of which was the great chunk of pork that she had so carefully preserved back in December. There were sixteen friends in the room, all of them excited by the kitchen aroma, when her mother triumphantly brought in a big tray of breaded meat—real meat, of a quality not seen for so long that they had almost forgotten such things existed. But as she entered the room, her foot caught on the carpet; she stumbled and, failing to catch herself, scattered the ritual feast on the floor at their feet. (Judit Herceg gave her account of the war years calmly and without obvious emotion, but when she told of her mother dropping the tray, she burst into tears.)

The Herceg family were deeply grateful that they had survived the war. Five months later Judit's mother set off to buy a cooker, ignoring the entreaties of her husband, who said the streets were still too dangerous. She never returned, and the police found no trace of her. Weeks later her father saw an announcement in the newspaper that an unidentified woman had been found in a basement nearby. The corpse was badly decayed and had to be identified by its clothing. Whether the cause of her death was rape, robbery, or suicide, they never knew.

The greatest blessing for a Jewish woman in Budapest during the German occupation was somehow to attain ethnic invisibility. Olga Koós (born 1925) lived during that period under a dangling sword yet refused to admit that it could cut her throat. She grew up on Hernád Street in a Jewish quarter near Keleti Station in Pest, where her father was a door-to-door peddler whose income was supplemented by his wife's piecework as a seamstress. Somehow they arranged for her to attend prestigious schools and to think of herself as destined for something exceptional. At no time during her school years did she witness discrimination against Jews. Her first intimation of prejudice occurred during a visit in 1938 to her father's sister in Berlin, when this aunt took her to an open-air entertainment park where Jews were not admitted.[45] She found the experience more bewildering than humiliating. That might be how Germans were—Hungarians were different.

---

45. Interview with Olga Koós (April 17, 1989). Later this aunt was deported from Germany on a train bound for Budapest. She disappeared en route.

In the late 1930s Olga revealed her talent as a dancer and actress, and she fought her way through the restrictive quotas on Jews to obtain admittance to the national ballet school. She became deeply absorbed in her work among an artistic coterie who cared not a whit about international politics, Hungarian nationalism, or ethnic purity. The reality of the war and Hungary's hapless role as a German satellite touched her only in 1942, when an older brother was drafted into a labor battalion and was quickly swallowed up in the Don Bend catastrophe. Otherwise life in the Hernád Street flat continued on a normal course. The Koós family was never uprooted from their flat, because her father had an exemption certificate based upon military service in the First World War. Olga had a flood of suitors, some of them Magyar soldiers, but in 1944 she fell in love with Antal Blumenthal, who had recently been returned from Russia after hard service in a labor battalion.[46]

Within days of the German occupation of October 1944, her father was seized and taken to the infamous brickyard in Óbuda. Before he left, he told his family, "Don't worry. The worst will never happen to me." He was among the contingent of twenty thousand slated to work on the "East Wall" defensive line. Since rail transportation was rationed, he joined the huge procession of those forced to go on foot. He died—or was shot by gendarmes—on the route.

Olga and her mother were given twenty-four hours to vacate their flat. They received no instructions where they should go. They packed up essential food and clothes—Olga also took a volume of Endre Ady's poems—and began a crosstown trek toward Margit Bridge, where they had heard that the Swedish legation had set up some protected houses in Pozsonyi Street. Wearing their conspicuous yellow stars they were fair game for any of the Arrow Cross gangs ranging the town with clubs and pistols. On their way they were stopped by a Magyar soldier who had once courted her. He advised them not to venture further toward Pozsonyi, because the protected houses were full and the Nyilas were preying upon the flood of Jews in the street vainly seeking asylum. He told them to go to a building near Keleti Station that had formerly been used as a trade school for Jewish children and had now been taken over by twenty-five rich Jews who had bribed German officers to protect relatives hiding there. Olga and her mother turned back at once and found sanctuary in the school.

The house was arranged along strictly plutocratic lines—rich Jews lived topside, charity cases in the basement. (Ironically, the basement became the

46. For an interview with Blumenthal, see "Men" above.

choice location in December, when the Russian bombardment of Pest began in earnest.) Their greatest fear was that Arrow Cross gangs would do to them what they were doing at protected houses—hauling Jews out at night, marching them to the Danube embankment, shooting them in the head, and pushing the bodies into the river. One terrifying day an Arrow Cross contingent arrived and ordered everyone into the courtyard. An officer slowly read their names and arranged them into two groups. It took a long time, for there were about two thousand Jews at the school. Meanwhile underlings stripped them of rings, watches, jewelry, while others rifled through their luggage inside. At the outer gate a young boy wearing an Arrow Cross uniform watched what was happening and then rode off on a motorcycle. Soon he returned with a well-armed detachment of German soldiers led by a brisk young officer, who furiously ordered the Magyars to get out. To save face the Arrow Cross leader continued to read the list to the end, but he slurred the names. They left and the young man disappeared. Whether he was a Jew disguised as a Nyilas, a watchman hired by a Jewish financier, or a real Nyilas moved by compassion, they never found out. Thereafter a squad of Germans stayed at the school until the end of the siege. "They were all nice boys. When the Russians surrounded us, we gave them civilian clothes and helped them get away, but few of them escaped, poor chaps."

Not even this close call crimped Olga's style. Pocketing her forged documents, she often put on a coat without a yellow star and slipped away to visit Christian friends in the city. She regularly drank espresso at the Royal Hotel café, a hangout for German and Arrow Cross officers. She was blond, attractive, and looked more Aryan than many of the swarthy types among the officers. Always she returned to the school at night. Conditions deteriorated during the heavy bombardment of Pest in early January. There was no water, no electricity, no heat, and little food. "Our shit piled up to the ceiling, until we dug eight open pits in the yard." Through malnutrition and anxiety women skipped their periods. An epidemic of German measles swept the school. Olga contracted it, and her mother feared that she would die. As the house-to-house fighting edged nearer, the fugitives found themselves in a dilemma: Russians were technically "liberators," but the inmates had heard the stories about their raping, looting, and wanton destructiveness. Whether they attacked Jews as well as Magyars was anyone's guess. There was little in Russian history to suggest that they liked Jews.

On January 11 the German guards slipped away, and on the next morning Russian officers entered the courtyard and told them they were free. Olga and her mother left immediately for home. Before they left, a friend handed Olga

two eggs, an incredible delicacy, which, fearing they would be broken in her
rucksack, she carried in her hands through streets mounded with rubble and
past buildings bisected with shrapnel. Their hearts sank when they reached
Hernád Street and saw that carpet bombing had flattened whole blocks of
flats. But although the flat next door had been gutted, theirs was untouched.
The door was still locked, and inside there was a cache of canned food. They
celebrated with a pancake supper cooked over an open fire.

In 1946 Olga began taking bit parts in the theater and in the following year
entered the state school for acting. Expelled from the Actors' Guild in 1949
for disrespectful remarks about the Rákosi regime, she was rehabilitated later
in the 1950s and had a successful career both on the stage and in film.

"Even today, whenever I smell Hypo [a Hungarian bleach], I smell
Auschwitz," said Veronika Vadas (born 1926), one of the two thousand Jews
of Békéscsaba, a city of southeastern Hungary, who were rousted out by the
Hungarian gendarmerie early in June 1944 for deportation to Poland.[47] Her
father had already been interned at Sárvár and then executed somewhere—
they never learned where—for the dual crime of Jewish ancestry and socialist
politics. Gendarmes wearing rooster-tail caps summoned the Békéscsaba Jews
from their houses, punctiliously locked the doors (to support the fiction that
the houses would not be looted), and marched them through streets crowded
with curious but silent bystanders to a brick factory on the edge of town.
There was water for them in a stagnant pond, such shelter over their heads as
they could improvise from clothing carried in suitcases, and sufficient food
only if they had carried it from their homes. Many of them died within the
first week, some of them without apparent cause other than depression.
When a Zionist leader visited them from Budapest, they swarmed about him,
begging for assistance, but he only carried off to safety less than a dozen—all
of them Zionists. A short time later they were told their condition would
shortly improve because they were going to Germany to work in factories.
Veronika was relieved to hear that the brick factory ordeal was over, but
when the freight train pulled in, it looked very small for the number of people
assembled on the platform. Gendarmes pushed and shoved them until eighty-
five Jews per were crammed into cars that would have been crowded with
half that number. Gendarmes robbed captives of clothes and shoes as they
climbed aboard. Veronika saw one guard even strip prosthetic shoes—which

47. Interview with Veronika Vadas (February 8, 1990). Her estimate of the number of Jews
deported conforms to that cited in Martin Gilbert's *Atlas of the Holocaust* (Oxford, 1988), 196.

he could never have used or sold—from a cripple. Inside were some bottles of water and pails for toilets. The door to each car was locked; it was opened again only once in seven days—at Kassa, in Slovakia.

In June the train reached the Birkenau annex of Auschwitz. With the other women Veronika had to undress and to stand all day with her hands up. This allowed the Germans to determine who was unfit for physical labor, and as a bonus it gave the Jews a lesson in intimidation. She and her mother spent six weeks in a barracks at Birkenau. All the bunks were taken, so they slept on the filthy floor. Her first impression was that normal humanity had all but disappeared from the place. The prisoners, clad in rags (not the infamous striped uniforms), scooped up drinking water from puddles. They stood outside in close lines from daybreak till afternoon as capos went through the mockery of repetitive and unnecessary counting. They heard stories about poison gas in shower rooms, but Veronika dismissed them as rumors. On one occasion she was ordered to the shower, but nothing came from the jet but cold water. The two real killers were exhaustion and dysentery. As soon as an inmate became ill, the others ripped off her clothes and pushed her outside.

Among the Jews she observed at Birkenau there were great differences. The Germans tried to organize things and were leaders in any collective endeavor to improve their lot; the Hungarians kept to themselves and turned against one another with mad-dog rage; the Poles willingly took jobs as capos, the camp police; the Italians sang. Veronika saw no attempts by the German guards to exploit the women sexually. They seemed to regard Jewish women as filthy and animal-like. She quickly lost what religious feeling she had ever had. "I heard a girl being beaten to death crying out, 'God, save me!' And others said, 'Don't be afraid. God will help.' But He didn't."

After six weeks at Birkenau, Veronika and her mother were again packed into a train and sent north to Breslau to work in a textile factory, making thread. Her mother had been a beautiful woman, but now, at forty-three, she was haggard. At eighteen Veronika became her parent, pushing her on. In February, when the Red Army threatened Breslau, the Jewish prisoners were moved west on foot. At Görlitz, on the border of Germany, they slept in stables and by day dug trenches and tank traps and hauled to the rear corpses of German soldiers killed in the fighting. The Russians were winning, and that was their only hope. "I always felt that I would survive. I wanted to have three children. I recited poems in the *lager* to keep our spirits high."

One day the Germans disappeared from their camp and the prisoners timidly ventured out. Although house-to-house fighting continued in Görlitz,

Veronika and her mother moved into a half-destroyed apartment building on the edge of town. Here they found sacks of chicken feed, which they boiled and ate. "It was so good." Neither woman had any illusions about the "liberating" Red Army. Veronika's mother smeared coal dust over their faces and at night they hid in the darkest corner of the cellar when the Russians came through collecting women. "The Germans had never molested us, because for them we were only animals, but to the Russians we were human beings. They were fighting, and the next day they could die. So I did not blame them for what they did to us. They gave us bread. Once a Russian soldier traveling up to the front jumped off a train and handed me a flower." Because of the Russian presence the people in Görlitz suddenly radiated hospitality and opened their houses to the Jewish fugitives.

In May Veronika and her mother joined a group of other Hungarian women and started home. They found trousers in a warehouse and, for greater safety, tried to look like men. At one checkpoint a guard refused to allow them to cross unless one of the women served him. The women looked at each other quizzically; one of them shrugged and without comment went behind the custom house; and after she returned, they continued on their way. After what they had endured, sex was meaningless. The Vadas women reached Békéscsaba in early June and found their house had been looted—furniture, food, clothing, jewelry. After inquiries they learned the names of the thieving parties, who were not Arrow Cross but fellow Social Democrats. (Later they got back about 5 percent of what had been pilfered.) Of the estimated two thousand Jews deported from Békéscsaba, all of whom went to or through Auschwitz, only forty-eight returned home.

In 1947 Veronika married a Roman Catholic and for his convenience converted to Catholicism. "But it means nothing to me." Reflecting on her experiences during the war, she says, "They do not seem real to me anymore. It is as if all those things never happened. Then I see films of concentration camps. None of them begin to convey the horror of the reality."

Görlitz is a picture-postcard town straddling the Neisse River between Poland and Germany. Many years after the war Veronika returned for a visit with her husband, György, and they tried to find the location of the *lager*. No one in town knew anything about it. However, she did succeed in finding a beautiful doorway that she had passed many times on work details. When she knocked on the door and asked the lady of the house where the lager had been located, she was told, "There was never a *lager* here." Veronika protested, saying "But there was. I was there. It was on the railroad line." The German lady listened politely, then quietly shut the door.

Money talks everywhere, and Auschwitz was no exception. When officials in Budapest during the Eichmann era discovered that Imre Borsodi, a wealthy Budapest jeweler, had tried to conceal some of his assets, they placed him in a labor battalion and locked up his wife, Eszter, with other detainees in the Rabbi Training Institute on József Boulevard. Expecting worse things to come, Eszter (born 1901) inserted into the covered buttons of her corset a collection of exquisitely cut diamonds of the highest quality. After a week at the institute, when no one came forth to bail her out, she was transferred to the pestiferous Kistarcsa brickyards, to await shipment to Auschwitz. Her daughter and two sisters watched helplessly as the gang of prisoners departed from the institute.

Before her consignment of deportees arrived at Birkenau, she picked the diamonds from her corset and swallowed them. Retrieving them later, she opened negotiations with her guards. Although she spoke no word of German, she somehow conveyed to them that the value of each gem was roughly equivalent to the value of a German house. At once she was elevated to a privileged position among the Jewish prisoners. Transferred to the kitchen, she obtained adequate food and had a better chance for survival. But her diamonds did not save her from the typhus epidemic that raged through the camp that winter.

Early in 1945, as the Russian offensive drove through southern Poland, the Germans evacuated Auschwitz. The prisoners, all of them women among Eszter's group, began a long march northwest toward the Baltic. It was bitterly cold, and Eszter was weakened by her disease. On the march, if a woman fell behind, she was shot. She teamed with two other women in supporting one another as they hobbled through the snow. During one blinding storm they slipped out of the line and burrowed in a snow bank, digging a single hole to share body heat. After three days they came out and discovered that the Red Army had liberated the sector. Eszter's face was now blackened by typhus. Her two companions found a Russian military hospital and left her there. She was well cared far and recovered, except for an apparently incurable infection in her vagina. A terrible odor baffled her doctors until she confessed that she had stored her last diamond in her vagina. The doctor who removed it surgically was "an honorable and honest man."[48] He did not claim it. Eager to return home and tortured by lack of information about her family, Eszter offered to barter the diamond for a Russian airplane to carry her to Budapest. This was impossible. Not even rail or road transportation

48. Interview with Júlia Berkes, the granddaughter of Eszter Borsodi (November 26, 1996).

was available at that time. She started out on foot. Along the way she begged and stole food. Warsaw was still smoldering as she passed through.

In the fall of 1945 she arrived in Budapest on the roof of a train. She weighed only seventy-eight pounds and was deeply ashamed because her hair, shaved to the skull in Auschwitz, had not grown back. Yet she appeared before her family, all having survived the war, wearing a red bed sheet artistically draped about her body and with a matching red scarf over her head. For months she refused to allow anyone to come near her or look at her closely, until her weight and her hair had been restored. Whenever asked about her experiences during the war, she burst into tears. Her granddaughter learned her story only bit by bit over the course of many years.

Eszter Borsodi held on to her diamond until 1956, when she gave it to her son, who escaped from Hungary during the Russian invasion. The quality of the stone was so exceptional that it not only paid his transportation to Australia but allowed him to set himself up in business there.

Gabriella Kardos remembered October 15, 1944, as a beautiful autumn day made more glorious by the morning radio speech of Regent Horthy, which announced that Hungary was arranging an armistice with the Soviet Union. For Gabriella (born 1899) the news was especially welcome because her husband, a teacher of Hungarian history at a Jewish secondary school, had already been drafted twice into labor service—each time fortunately close to home and with light duties—and she feared that another draft would carry him off and kill him. Failing health had exacerbated his naturally indecisive and timid nature. (Because of a domineering mother, he had waited twenty-four years to marry Gabriella.) Now, with the announcement that the war had ended, the worst of her worries were over. She organized an impromptu celebration among Jewish friends at her flat in Szalay Street near Parliament Square. They sat close to the radio and drank bottles of Tokaj wine that she had carefully hoarded for this occasion. By evening their euphoria had vanished as totally as their Tokaj, for the radio had brought another proclamation announcing that the regent had been deposed and that the war would continue. Worse, the new leader would be Ferenc Szálasi, the mercurial, feared leader of the Arrow Cross Party. Her husband's headmaster called and told him not to report to the school until further notice because it would be a natural target for Arrow Cross gangs. The day that had opened with such promise had become for Gabriella "the worst day of my life."[49]

---

49. Interview with Gabriella Kardos (January 6, 1988).

News came shortly that SS officers had met with the Judenrat and imposed the first of a list of restrictions and confiscations that promised to be never ending. Gabriella and her friends also knew there could be physical danger, because they had heard about the persecution of Jews in Germany. The Jews in her apartment building were particularly alarmed because one of the tenants was a Nyilas and he was raging and threatening them. Gabriella joined some neighbors in pooling their sleeping pills. If conditions became intolerable, they vowed they would kill themselves.

On October 17 there was an air-raid alarm, and the resident Arrow Cross stalwart angrily herded them into the cellar. Convinced that they would be slaughtered down there, the women went down wailing and the men cursing. "We thought they were going to kill us in that black hole." Her mother, who was bedridden, asked for her ration of the pills. Gabriella took some too, but when she realized that there was no danger, she spat them out. But her mother had swallowed hers and fell into a deep sleep. They had to wait for the all-clear siren before calling for an ambulance. She was rushed to a hospital, where she died.

Within weeks of the German occupation the Kardos family was evicted from their flat and moved into a Red Cross house near Margit Bridge. Food was rationed, and Jews received less. When she complained at a shop that her week's ration of eight decagrams of meat was full of bones, the butcher cursed her and refused to sell to her again. The daily fare at the Red Cross house—a thin soup of onions, fat, and water—was so worthless that it was a waste of time to eat it. The atmosphere was not communal, for people shamelessly stole food from one another. Her family was saved by her husband's Christian students, who brought them staples like flour, grease, and beans.

At Christmas the siege of Budapest commenced. Thereafter all residents lived in the cellar, lighted by a single candle. Gabriella set up pallets in a coal bin, which was relatively private. They did not escape the notice of the Nyilas patrols. One such group ordered her father to report to their local headquarters in the morning. He started out, but the air-raid siren went off, and police ordered him back inside. "This saved his life. He was a tidy person who always believed in 'the law.' He would have been led to the embankment and killed." They could expect no humanity from the Arrow Cross. In their flat one of them raped a little Jewish girl on the stairwell in front of her mother.

They emerged into the light on January 18, when Pest was liberated. The streets were strewn with dead horses. At first they were terrified of the Russians, but children came back with food the Russians had given them. On one occasion Gabriella's husband was carrying a jar of stewed fruit when he was stopped by two Russians, who impounded it. When they tasted it and discovered it was not liquor, they made a face and handed it back. Yet for Gabriella the stories about Russians and women came back in a terrifying rush in March, when a particularly repulsive soldier—"a black man" (probably a Mongol)—rooted her out of the house and made her come with him. She was forty-six years old and had been always nurtured in a protected, upper-middle-class environment. Worse than what might happen to her was the thought of how her husband would endure it. The Russian, however, was bent upon other things. They joined a large work party of females, Jews and Magyars, and marched to Cinkota, a dismal collection of houses on the far northeastern edge of Pest. Here they were taught how to dig trenches and tank traps to block a rumored German counterattack. After a hike of more than twenty kilometers, however, the job proved too much for a team of undernourished women only three weeks out of cellars. The Russians did more work demonstrating pick and shovel than the women accomplished. At nightfall they marched back home again, their labor service terminated.

In April Gabriella and her husband set off for their Szalay Street flat. The street itself was little damaged, but their Arrow Cross neighbor had looted all the empty flats and then disappeared. Christians living next door had concealed some of the Jewish families in their homes during the Nyilas raids. "There were many good people like that." Except for her parents and husband, all of Gabriella's family died or were killed during the war. Asked by this interviewer whether she had ever thought that she was not going to survive, she replied, "Oh, no, I could not think of that. I had too many responsibilities and an ill husband."

Years later she unexpectedly encountered her former neighbor, the Arrow Cross bravo. He was now a conductor on a streetcar. When he took her ticket, she noticed the red star in his uniform lapel and his red armband. He was startled to see her, but quickly turned his eyes away.

Not until Hitler's invasion of Austria in 1938 did Márta Ofner (born 1920) experience at first hand tangible signs of anti-Semitism. She was about to graduate from a racially mixed high school when her geography teacher entered the classroom, his face beaming. He asked a Jewish girl, "What do you think happened today?" When she did not reply, he cheerfully expounded on Hitler's rise to power and how he was destined to conquer all of Europe.[50]

---

50. Interview with Márta Ofner (January 4, 1990).

Márta had excelled in high school and expected to study chemistry and physics at the university. But the anti-Jewish laws were being locked into place at this time, and to her great surprise her application was rejected. Although Jewish on both sides of her family back to her grandparents, she had never thought of herself as separate from her classmates in any way. Her parents regarded themselves as Hungarian to the core. They had status in Budapest. Her father was a highly respected internist, and her mother taught Hungarian history in a public secondary school. Music, art, books, and all the embellishments of a sophisticated urban environment were vital to their lives. They entertained frequently and lavishly in their large flat off Deák Square, in the heart of downtown Pest. Despite the setback, Márta resolved to bide her time. She had faith that the values of Regent Horthy would prevail in the end: he would oust the fanatics from his government, and she would pursue her university studies. It was impossible to doubt this. Until that happened, she would work in the confectionery shop of a family friend.

In 1940 Márta married a clerical employee of the mammoth Ganz factory and they moved into a flat near the Dohány Street synagogue. That same year he was drafted into a labor battalion and assigned to a maintenance job in a machine-tool factory at Várpalota, near Veszprém. He was multilingual and at Ganz had performed interesting work as a translator in the international trade department. Várpalota was a comedown for him, but he was well treated. During this period labor battalions contained large numbers of Christians who had been placed there to sweat leftist political ideas out of their systems. There was no racial segregation except that full Jews displayed a yellow band (not a star) on their sleeves, while Christians—whether converts or of mixed births—wore a white band on theirs. The leaders of this labor group were Jews, former officers in the Honvédség. Márta's husband could receive packages and letters, and once a month he came home for a short leave. In 1942 he was called up again, this time for six months of road building near Veszprém; then in 1943 for similar work at Pécs; and finally in 1944 for a year of very hard labor in Poland. They considered it a miracle that he had missed the Don Bend disaster. He was always frail, and that would have killed him.

On Sunday, March 18, 1944, Márta collected some food packages and went up to the river town of Göd, where her husband was in a labor camp. The two of them went to a restaurant and were having a quiet meal when they heard a great commotion on the highway. It was a long cavalcade of Germans in full battle gear moving toward Budapest, riding cars, trucks, motorcycles, and tanks. They watched in awe and in fear as this unexpected land armada rumbled past. They knew about concentration camps. Her husband told her to go home at once, and he hurried back to the relative security of the labor camp. Sunday-afternoon trains were normally flooded with excursionists returning to the city, but not on this day. She was almost alone on the train. And when it arrived at Nyugati Station, she was interrogated in a waiting room. Márta was terrified, but her pass was in order, and a railway guard, seeing how distraught she was, kindly escorted her to her tram.

Almost immediately she was fired from her job, and three months later ejected from her flat in favor of a working-class Christian family bombed out during an American air raid. (Throughout the war her husband's salary from the Ganz factory continued to be paid to her.) Meanwhile her father had moved into the house of one of his patients, a Christian woman, at 33 Pozsonyi Road. When he obtained for Márta a *Schutzpaß*, or safe-conduct document, from the Swiss legation, she moved in with him. Thirty people were crammed into this three-room flat. From noon to four o'clock they were allowed to leave the building provided they conspicuously displayed the hated yellow star. (It had to be sewed on—the penalty for loose stitching, defined as that which would allow insertion of a pencil between the stitches, was a six-month jail term.) They needed this time to forage for food, even though the Arrow Cross gangs ranging through the district made it very dangerous. Yet the denizens at their refuge were better off than most because Christian patients of the doctor faithfully brought him food. The two cellars in the building were segregated by sex. "We had no thought of the future. We just lived one day to the next. If we had something to eat we were happy."

On December 2 an Arrow Cross squad entered the flat and began sorting the people into two groups—the sick, elderly, and young mothers in one room, the able-bodied in another. Márta told her father to write a certificate showing that because of sciatic nerve damage she could not walk. He used her married name so the officer would not suspect he was her father. The officer scornfully brushed aside the *Schutzpaß*, but the medical report brought him up short, as though unable to make up his mind. She cried out, "I cannot walk! You can shoot me, but I cannot walk!" When her father confirmed this, the officer handed back the papers and said, "Try and cure her so that next time we can take her away." The able-bodied ones were taken directly to the Józsefváros depot and loaded into freight cars.[51]

---

51. Although Márta believed these people were shipped to Auschwitz, that destination is improbable because the proximity of the Red Army forced its closure about this time. It is more likely that they were among the group who perished on the forced march toward Vienna.

After the Russians closed the ring around Budapest and began fighting their way through the city, the Nyilas bands became more desperate. They burst into the flat one night in early January, ransacked the building from cellars to attic, and hauled out Jews at random. These were herded to the Danube embankment near Parliament Square, where they were lined up along the river's edge and shot, the bodies pushed into the water. The next morning even the Christians of the building, when they told Márta of the executions, seemed shaken and frightened. Thereafter Márta and her father lived each hour in terror. One night there was a loud knocking at their cellar door. Arrow Cross men entered, and one of them flashed a light on their faces. "Are you people Jews?" he asked. There was nothing to do but say yes, for it might be worse if they denied it. "All right," he replied, with a laugh. "Sleep well." He was having fun with them, but Márta shook with fear.

In January, when there was a lull in the fighting, Márta peered into the street. Two men wearing stained greatcoats and peaked caps too small for their heads were picking through the debris. "My God, I can't believe it! They're Russians!" she called to those inside. Her father had heard countless stories about their behavior around women and warned her not to be too joyful, but Márta realized that she was saved. "I was never afraid of the Russians—they were truly our liberators." No one in their protected house was molested, and by the end of the month she had returned to her flat and used righteous indignation to evict the squatters, whose political fortunes had abruptly changed.

On February 18, the day that Buda was liberated, Márta's husband appeared at the flat. She had not heard from him for nearly a year. He had been in poor health when the Red Army liberated him in October, but he was afraid to return to Hungary until the Germans and Arrow Cross were thrown out. In November he learned that the Russians had set up a provisional Hungarian government in Debrecen, and concluding it must be safe, he made his way there, where he was hospitalized for several months. As soon as he heard that Budapest had been cleared of Germans and Arrow Cross, he found a freight train and came home. In May he resumed work at the Ganz factory.

In September Márta fulfilled her dream. She was admitted to the university to study English and French, the first steps in a long career as language instructor at Karl Marx University, the economics university of Budapest. "There were no more nightmares. We just tried to forget." In a burst of gratitude her husband joined the Communist Party during the euphoric months of 1945, when the Hungarian fascists were being tried and executed and a new

Hungary seemed to be in the making. However, he quit the party in 1956, after the political purges—reinforced by Soviet tanks—took the bloom off that rose.

Sisters

The Merényi sisters, Lea (born 1914) and Zsuzsa (born 1925), grew up in Budapest without any inkling that they were Jews.[52] Their great-grandfather, a converted Christian, had attended the same Masonic lodge as Kossuth, and their father, an engineer, had served with distinction as an officer in the Austro-Hungarian army during the 1914 war. Like their parents, they attended Catholic convent schools. They knew what Jews were because there were a few Jewish girls scattered in their classes, but they never gave the subject much thought. At school they saw no signs of anti-Semitism.

All members of the Merényi family were pro-German to the core. For them Germany was the hope of the world—in education, in engineering, in music, in the arts. After the First World War, when political agitation and economic stagnation vexed Hungary, Merényi senior moved to Berlin and expected to settle there permanently. His son was born there, and his daughters enrolled in a succession of ballet schools. However, Hitler's rise to power in 1933 brought them back to Budapest in the year following, where he took a post as a steam engineer in the locomotive division of the Ganz factories. The family was well-to-do and moved easily in professional and artistic circles. Their father voiced no political ideas at home and carefully concealed from his children what he knew the *Anschluβ* would mean for Jews in Austria first, and Hungary afterward. No hint of their Jewish ancestry leaked to anyone. Passage of the First Anti-Jewish Law in 1938 was symptomatic of what lay ahead for his family, but for the moment they were not affected. After all, Merényi had earned the Károly Cross for his frontline service during First World War.[53] He died in 1939 and missed the anti-Semitic purges resulting from Hungary's alliance with Germany. Persecution of Jews accelerated

52. Interviews with Lea Merényi (January 11, 1990) and Zsuzsa Merényi (January 26, 1990).
53. The First Anti-Jewish Law of 1938, among other things, limited the number of Jews in the professions and white-collar employment and defined a Jew as anyone born a Jew or converted to Christianity after July 31, 1919. The Second Anti-Jewish Law of 1939, which further restricted the quota of Jews in the professions (and eliminated them altogether from Parliament and public offices), defined a Jew as any person with one Jewish parent or with two Jewish grandparents, except those born of mixed marriages before 1919. Macartney, *October Fifteenth*, 1:218–19 and 325–26.

exponentially when Hungary participated in Germany's crusade against the Soviet Union in the summer of 1941. Encouraged by this German connection, anti-Semites now combed record offices, and found, thanks to generations of Hapsburg efficiency, that Hungarian birth records were both accurate and extensive. As the circle tightened, it fell to the mother to explain to her children the truth about their racial origins.

Zsuzsa remembered clearly the moment when she learned she was Jewish. It was a few days before the German army occupied Budapest in March 1944. When their mother wrapped herself in her furs and took the three of them on a walk in Városliget (City Park), they knew it had to be important, because that lady never walked anywhere if she could avoid it. In a remote area of the park she whispered to them that on both sides of their family they were Jewish. At this news, they laughed outright—it was so grotesque and inconceivable. Zsuzsa made a weak joke about it: "Fortunately we have never been anti-Semitic." It was impossible for them to conceive that they were in any personal danger. The girls, who had graduated from the national ballet school and were now apprentice dancers, felt secure in their Hungarian citizenship and their privileged circle of friends. Moreover, the Arrow Cross was still only a minority party despised by most respectable Hungarians as a gang of lumpen-proletariat fanatics. Their brother, however, seemed stunned by the revelation. It was a shock for a young man who spoke German as a first language, fraternized with Hungarians of Swabian descent, wore clothes with a German cut, and thought all things German were the best in the world. Up to this time he had given little thought to reports of Jewish persecution in the country of his birth.

With the Germans now in Budapest, the status of the Merényi family changed overnight. On one day they were Christians attending the wedding of a cousin at a Lutheran church; on the next they were Jews, forced to display the lemon yellow star on their left breast.[54] The presence of the German army on city streets unleashed a rash of anti-Semitism by members of Ferenc Szálasi's Arrow Cross Party, which had formerly been held in check by conservatives in the government. One day a gang of lumpen proles hanging about in the tough "Chicago" district near Keleti Station beat up the Merényi girls' brother. There was no recourse under the law, and the episode broke something deep inside him. His sense of an ordered universe lay in ruins.

---

54. The star had to be no less than ten centimeters in diameter, and had to be sewed—not pinned—in full view. Jews caught in public without the star were liable to a six-month prison term. Lévai, 85.

In June 1944 the Merénys were ordered to move from their flat to a yellow-star house near Margit Bridge. It was nominally under Vatican protection, although such sanctuaries were not respected by Arrow Cross gangs, who broke in, shot, and looted at will. Here three families shared three rooms. In the city at large, Jews were forbidden from taking jobs. Lea and her brother had been private teachers of German, but no one dared come in for lessons now, and it was dangerous to be seen outside. Zsuzsa, the extrovert of the family, found an illegal job in a basement factory making boxes for medical syringes, but she earned enough only for bread and apples. Her income was further diminished by the daylight American air raids because her boss, a Social Democrat, fearing that the police would discover her in their shelter and that his business would be closed down for harboring a Jew, insisted that she go home at each alert. The distance was too great for her to return after the all-clear. Yet the family was more fortunate than most in having laid up a store of dried and canned foods. Moreover, the so-called protected houses near Margit Bridge had fewer restrictions than the official ghetto area around Dohány Street, which had been boarded up and was closely watched.[55]

Horthy's proclamation of October 15, 1944, which attempted to take Hungary out of the war and repudiate its alliance with the Third Reich, seemed like an act of God for the Jewish community. They heard the news from contraband radios early in the morning. In the Merényi flat a neighbor baked a communal cake to celebrate the end of the war. But by afternoon Horthy had been deposed, and a pro-Nazi government under Szálasi had been recognized by the Germans. Gangs of Arrow Cross, no longer under government restraint, ranged the streets on the lookout for fugitive Jews.

There now began the second occupation of Budapest by the Germans, far more drastic because of Horthy's "betrayal" of Hitler's war and because nearly all civil authority had been overthrown. The Germans professed respect for the wishes of the Jewish Council with regard to treatment of the Jewish population, but in effect the council had no alternative except compliance with whatever the Germans wanted—whether pianos, Watteau paintings, feather beds, or labor gangs. On October 23 all Jews between fifteen and fifty-five were commanded to report with three-days rations to the Erzsébet Sports Field. Here Zsuzsa and Lea saw their brother for the last time as he

---

55. These Jews were usually more affluent and influential than those who went to the ghetto. For a graphic account of events in a protected house on Pozsonyi Road when frivolity changed to tragedy, see George Konrád, "The High Priest of Frivolity," *New Yorker*, March 9, 1992, 31–39.

straggled off with a male group. The two girls were led on a march up the east bank of the Danube to the village of Göd, where they were ferried across to an unpopulated region on Szentendre Island and made to dig huge pits facing north. Many Jews began moaning, convinced that they were being forced to dig their own mass grave. But the authorities, alarmed by the rapid advance of the Red Army across the plains of Hungary toward Budapest, were only preparing tank traps. Why these were needed on this remote island no one ever learned—or asked. The Green Shirt leader of the labor detail seemed bewildered by his instructions. On the second day he had them fill in the holes and dig traps facing south. (Years later Zsuzsa recognized this same Arrow Cross man as the official Communist Party supervisor of ballots in her Budapest district.)

On November 15 three angry men in green Arrow Cross uniforms stormed into the camp and demanded release of the two sisters. Driven back to the city and showered with abusive language all the way, they wondered what they had done and feared the worst. To their surprise the men brought them to an abandoned flat near Margit Bridge, where their mother waited for them. The "arrest" had been a bold hoax. Three Jewish Communists disguised in Arrow Cross uniforms had volunteered to rescue them after their mother had reported their abduction.[56] Here they learned that their brother had escaped from his labor column and had returned home at night, only to be picked up again and marched to the west, presumably as a slave laborer in Germany. Nothing was ever heard of him again.[57] The three women returned to their yellow-star house, hoping to be overlooked. Every day they heard doors being smashed and rifle shots in the streets. Their sole hope was that the Russians, who were closing rapidly upon Budapest, would be able to liberate them.

When it became apparent that Budapest would fall, the Germans arranged for their last shipments of Jews to concentration camps beyond the Hungarian frontier. On December 4, an Arrow Cross patrol burst into the Merényi flat and hauled the two girls to the Józsefváros railway station. There Nyilas

---

56. These men were György Aczél, who later became cultural minister and right-hand man of János Kádár after the 1956 uprising; Tamás Major, later a distinguished actor; and Jenő Pásztor, a leading Hungarian Communist.

57. The likelihood is that he was among those thousands of Jews held briefly in the notorious brickyard prison in Óbuda and herded in the death march toward the Austrian frontier. There was an appalling loss of life from exposure, typhoid, and exhaustion, with an estimated 1,200 dead en route. See Gerald Reitlinger, *The Final Solution* (Northvale, N.J., 1987), 443. Even an SS general who witnessed the death march was appalled at the treatment of these fugitives. See Braham, *Politics of Genocide*, 841–42.

females looted their jewelry and took what they wanted from bundles of food and clothing. Hungarian gendarmes then packed them into a freight car and bolted the door from the outside. It was pitch dark except for small, high windows covered with barbed wire. There was no room to lie down, so they had to squat. They had no water and only the scraps of food not stolen by the Arrow Cross. The train moved slowly west, its progress interrupted frequently by Allied bombing of the railheads. In order to chart their journey they mounted a lookout on someone's shoulders and held her up to the barbed window. Whenever the train passed through a village, they threw out letters listing their names and recounting what was happening, hoping that some sympathetic compatriot would forward them to the International Red Cross. At every stop they begged for water through the cracks in the freight car's sidewalls, rarely with success because guards kept the populace away from the train. Hungarian rail workers made easy money selling them water at fifty pengős per bucket—about a week's wage. So long as they were in Hungary, they were allowed to deposit the dead in open fields. Once they were allowed to wash and drink from a muddy pond. But the doors were permanently sealed as soon as they crossed into the Reich. Unknown to them, they were the last contingent of Hungarian Jews transported out of their country.

On December 24 they arrived at a remote forest compound, where the train was quickly emptied by a gang of Ukrainian capos wielding truncheons and assisted by snarling dogs. This was Bergen-Belsen, a concentration camp north of Hannover in Germany. After a long march through deep gloomy woods like the setting for a Grimm Brothers' tale, they were herded into log huts and assigned double bunks seventy centimeters wide. Lea and Zsuzsa found themselves in Barracks 5, with four hundred other women, under control of sadistic Ukrainian viragos who, while officially prisoners themselves, wore special armbands and enforced their screaming orders with kicks and beatings.

Barracks 5 was reserved for special prisoners, Jews, they learned, that Heinrich Himmler intended to swap for medicine and other supplies delivered in Switzerland.[58] As such they were called by the guards "special goods"—

---

58. To this end some 1,368 Jews had arrived in Switzerland from Bergen-Belsen on December 6, 1944, for whom five million francs was deposited in Swiss banks for Himmler. See Reitlinger, 444. Because of their privileged status, the account of the two Merényi sisters should not be taken as typical of the Bergen-Belsen experience. For accounts of terrible conditions among less privileged prisoners in the camp, see the testimonies in *Trial of Josef Kramer* (London, 1949) and Hanna Levy-Haas, *Inside Belsen* (Sussex, N.J., 1979).

negotiable items. Scratched on a bunk was the name of a well-known Hungarian psychologist who had already left for this exchange. The barracks had become a showpiece for the Red Cross delegation occasionally allowed to visit selected areas of the camp. The occupants were never tattooed; their heads were not shaved; and a few packages of food—many marked with their individual names—arrived irregularly from Switzerland. They never learned why they, among the hundreds of thousands of Hungarian Jews deported to concentration and extermination camps, had been singled out for survival. Even so, about one-quarter of the group that had started from Józsefváros Station died of starvation, infection, or dementia.

They had arrived during the Christmas season, and the German officers of a nearby armored-SS camp organized a songfest, with the prisoners singing carols in German. Lea and Zsuzsa volunteered. The Germans showed their appreciation by applauding enthusiastically and giving the carolers a whole loaf of pressed meat as a Christmas gift. Thereafter the festive air vanished. Only rarely did Germans appear in camp. They did not need to—there were always volunteers among the prisoners themselves to perform the dirty jobs. (Some Hungarian Jews who assisted the capos and pried gold teeth from corpses were tried as war criminals in Budapest after the war.) The guards on the towers of this camp were Hungarian gendarmes.

After a week in camp the two sisters found that their menstrual cycles had ceased, probably because of malnutrition. In any case, they were grateful, for it simplified their hygienic tasks. Showers were rare—only two in four months—but regular prisoners got none at all. When permitted, the women ran naked in the bitter cold from barracks to the shower room four hundred meters away. Some of them had heard rumors of poison gas being sprayed from the shower heads, but the Merényi girls refused to believe it. Germans were civilized people and would not do such things. They were more disturbed by the absence of soap and by having to don their stinking clothes again. Once, on returning to their unheated barracks, they found that their clothes had been disinfected and boiled. Although the temperature outside was below freezing, the garments were dripping wet, and their barracks was unheated, it was a luxury to have clean clothes.[59]

Neither sister ever believed that she would perish during the war. It was just unthinkable. Although ten years older, Lea was less outgoing and had a

---

59. Bergen-Belsen was surrounded by a thick pine forest, but German bureaucracy was so rigidly stratified that efforts by the camp commandant to collect firewood were blocked by forest rangers, who claimed that authorization had to come from the proper forestry official in Berlin. This permission never arrived—or so the commandant claimed.

childlike vulnerability. Shortly after her arrival at the camp, she saw trucks carrying stripped corpses to the crematorium. Thereafter she never saw such sights, because she refused to see them. From nearby barracks there were screams and moans, but she shut them out by pretending that they were the cries of animals in slaughter pens. Such was her rage for normality that she tried to introduce ballet lessons in her barracks, but after one trial this experiment was abandoned. No one, including herself, had the strength to perform the exercises.

Zsuzsa, on the other hand, plunged into life at the camp. She resolved to make a minute chronicle of her incarceration. Somehow she had salvaged a calendar book and some child's crayons and began a series of cartoons depicting events that came under her view. The object was to keep her spirits up and to amuse other inmates, for she was convinced that despair led to death. In all she drew 116 panels, many of them revealing a wry sense of humor. Her removal from the "protected" house was titled "Expelled from the Vatican," and the march to the train station "They invite us on an outing." Much more grim are scenes of their journey to Bergen-Belsen: Arrow Cross women looting at Teleki tér; paying fifty pengős for a can of oily water; washing in a rimed mudhole; peering out of the carriage window at the ruins of Győr Station. The horrors of the camp are conveyed only by euphemism: "X-ray of my stomach" (empty); "When the mortuary is empty" (nude men and women washing themselves); "A visitor" (Hungarian gendarme courting a female prisoner in the barracks); "Our poultry garden" (drawings of lice, rats, bedbugs); "My dream" (bathtubs, English toilet, apple, record player, books, dancing).[60]

Every morning there was the *Appell*, or roll call, outside the barracks. The prisoners were listed only by numbers, not names. Sometimes they had to stand in sleet and snow from half past three till nine o'clock. The worst suffering resulted from irregular food. After morning coffee and weak soup there was often nothing for twenty-four hours. The penalty for stealing a potato was to crouch with a potato in one's mouth for hours. Anyone who stole from the barracks ration was tied up with her wrists bound tightly to her ankles, an excruciating punishment. This bent the body like a hairpin. Zsuzsa never forgot the sight of one such poor wretch, a living skeleton in striped uniform whose only crime was succumbing to hunger. Once they were

60. This extraordinary document she maintained throughout her ordeal at the camp and succeeded in bringing back to Budapest after the war, where it yet exists, faded and frazzled from age and handling.

formed into a work detail and went into the forest to pick up branches for fuel. On their way they passed the adjacent SS camp, an idyllic place with German children chattering on the playground and geraniums cheerfully displayed in cozy, curtained windows. On this trek they met some Dutch prisoners, who became for them symbols of survival, for they had been in camps for four years, yet they had always had items to trade for food.[61]

During the spring months of 1945 more prisoners poured into the adjacent barracks, always arriving from camps farther to the east. It was evident that the Germans were losing the war, but specific news was unavailable. Sometimes they received a "pot message"—a message scrawled on one of the cooking pots by one of the Hungarians delegated to work in the kitchen. British and American planes flew over more frequently. Once a leaflet fluttered down. It came as a gift from heaven because it said that the Americans were near and that they should hold out a little longer. The Hungarian lawyer who caught it allowed others to read it only after they gave him their daily bread ration—a scrap one inch long. Trains continued to arrive from the east with fresh cargoes of prisoners, sometimes one-quarter of them already corpses. At this time there was maximum use of the crematoriums, skeleton figures pulling horse carts full of corpses each morning. Zsuzsa knew the end was near when she saw high-ranking officers pushing wheelbarrows with documents to the crematoriums. "Paper fed corpses, and corpses fed paper." The Germans were destroying their files of incriminating evidence. During the first two weeks of April twenty-eight thousand new prisoners were dumped into Belsen, and the food supply was cut off entirely. Corpses rotted in heaps, and rats attacked living prisoners. Typhus killed 250 to 300 of them each day.[62]

Sometime in early April, just hours before the British army arrived, the inmates of Barracks 5 were called out at night, hurriedly formed into lines, and marched to the railroad. Apparently Himmler expected, up to the end, to arrange some bargain with his "exchange Jews." A train loaded with corpses

61. Bergen-Belsen was never an extermination camp, like Auschwitz, although day-to-day conditions were in many ways worse. Originally a Wehrmacht base, it had been converted in 1943 into a model camp that could withstand scrutiny of Red Cross inspection teams—ideal for exchange Jews. Nearby was a ramshackle camp for Russian POWs, later the infamous Camp I. When the eastern front began to disintegrate in 1944, Belsen received an overflow of prisoners from camps overrun by the Russian advance. With facilities for 7,000, it burgeoned into a fetid dying-ground, warehousing about 80,000, of which half died of starvation or typhus and spotted fever. The water supply, held in open concrete reservoirs, was soon contaminated by floating bodies. *Trial of Josef Kramer*, 116ff, and Konnilyn G. Feig, *Hitler's Death Camps* (New York, 1979), 370–93.

62. Feig, 378.

stood on the siding. Screaming guards ordered them to pull out the bodies and get inside. Zsuzsa noticed that near the carriage was a great pile of sugar beets, and she pitched up to the others as many as she could grab. They were then locked inside, seventy to the carriage. There was great alarm when they discovered the train moving eastward, for this meant they were not destined for Switzerland. For ten days they moved toward Berlin and survived on mud-caked beetroots. Air raids were frequent until a Russian plane demolished the locomotive and stopped the train permanently.

One morning it was preternaturally quiet. Someone noticed that the door was unlocked, and they climbed out into a mysteriously empty world. The guards had disappeared. They were situated in a deep forest and immediately began browsing for wild onions and mushrooms. Some of the men set off for a nearby village and returned with a horse cart. They said the villagers had fled. Resolved to find bread, Lea took bearings on a distant steeple and set off. In the village three armed men with red stars on their hats met her and excitedly, in broken German, told her she had just walked across a live minefield. She found her bread loaves and walked back across the minefield to her sister. Later Russian soldiers, seeing the vegetable muck they had been subsisting on, warned them that "muddy potatoes" were bad for their health. The date was April 23, 1945. They were officially liberated.

Three hundred Hungarians were on this train, all of them loaded with lice and too emaciated to proceed on foot. They were not even sure where they were, except that it was somewhere in northern Germany. They moved into Tröbitz, a mining village, and occupied deserted houses. In one house Zsuzsa and Lea found a friendly old couple who prepared baths and beds for them. The old lady said, "Hitler has deceived us," took his picture off the wall, and stuffed it into her stove. (Later Lea found another Hitler picture carefully stowed under her bed.) They remained in Tröbitz for two weeks, making clothes from curtains, removing lice, and gaining strength for the trip back to Budapest. Many were coming down with typhus.[63] Others died because they could not resist the temptation to gorge themselves with rich food.

On May 6 two dozen women and one man moved off on foot to the south-east, determined to reach Budapest. In a handcart they pushed an old woman who could not bear being left behind. (The man did not last long; at a control

---

63. Behind them at Bergen-Belsen a typhus epidemic raged. A Hungarian SS contingent (Reitlinger is emphatic about their nationality) at the neighboring panzer school did nothing to alleviate it. When the British took over, their unit of 360 men stamped out the epidemic in just two weeks. The panzer school became a convalescent hospital, and the original pesthole was torched. Reitlinger, 468.

point he was gathered in by Russians to fill one of their prisoner-of-war quotas and never seen again.) They followed the railroad lines, riding freights whenever they could fight their way or squeeze on board. All of Europe seemed on the move, packed with displaced persons bound for somewhere. They lived on spinach and gooseberries and picked up beef and flour from the Russians. At times the sisters begged food from the Germans, always saying they were refugee Germans from Hannover. (It was too humiliating to admit they had come from a Jewish concentration camp.) There was no predicting how Germans would behave. Some invited them inside for plum cake. At Spremberg they fell in with Allied POWs, many of whom had not seen a woman up close in three years. These men wanted a dance, and the Hungarian women obliged—twenty women surrounded by concentric circles of eager Britons, Americans, French, and Italians. Elated to find themselves romantic objects once again, the women eagerly responded to this male attention, but many were still so weak that they collapsed on the dance floor and had to be carried home by the Italians.

Both sisters lost all track of where they were and when they were there. Always they pushed southeast toward home. Once across the Hungarian frontier, they rode freight trains. At the end of June they arrived in Budapest, and learned that their mother had died in the ghetto in April. Their former home was occupied by squatters, who promised a room but refused to move out—providing the sisters with their first taste of the proletarian leveling introduced by the Russian victors. Within a week of their arrival Lea reported for work at her beloved ballet school.

Their mother had always insisted that if they ever needed help, they should write to their godfather, an Argentine millionaire. Who in ravaged Budapest did not need help in 1945? They wrote. It took some time, but eventually he sent them two kilograms of semolina.

Both sisters resumed their work in ballet and became instructors. Zsuzsa married and raised a family. Her older sister, Lea, remained single. She seemed more permanently affected by her experiences in the war. Her fiancé had been killed at the Don Bend, and she always seemed somewhat distracted. During the fall of 1945 Zsuzsa sporadically followed newspaper accounts of the trial at Lüneburg, where forty-four officials and guards at Bergen-Belsen were charged with crimes against humanity. Eleven of these, including Josef Kramer, the commandant, were executed. But the Merényi sisters no longer cared.

3 | Fliers

Above the Battle

The Treaty of Trianon, signed on June 4, 1920, limited Hungary's armed services to thirty-five thousand officers and men, these to be used only for maintaining internal order and defending frontiers. (How to defend their frontiers against such bitter enemies as Romania, Czechoslovakia, and Yugoslavia was nowhere spelled out for them.) Armaments were also rigidly restricted: absolutely no heavy artillery, no tanks, no military or naval aviation. Supervision of these prohibitions came under the authority of an Inter-Allied Control Commission.[1] Surrounded by its three enemies of the Little Entente, each of which had mounted its own invasion of Hungarian territory in 1919, Hungary had a choice of doing without an air force at a time when air power was vital for defense or developing one covertly—and, of course, chose the latter. Since there was no possibility of concealing airfields, aircraft factories, or airplanes, the country followed the example of Germany, which had labored under a similar prohibition until it arranged a deal with Mussolini to train a German air force secretly in Italy. Within months of Hitler's accession to power early in 1933, young Germans had been dispatched for pilot training to Grottaglie, an airship base in the heel of the peninsula, not far from Taranto. Issued Italian air force uniforms, forced to shout "Viva il re!" at parades and to endure what they all regarded as lax drill procedures, the young German fliers passed themselves off as "South Tiroleans."[2]

1. C. A. Macartney, *October Fifteenth: A History of Modern Hungary* (Edinburgh, 1956), 1:5. For the full text of the treaty, see Carnegie Endowment for International Peace, *The Treaties of Peace, 1919–1923* (New York, 1924), 1:461–617.
2. Adolf Galland, *The First and the Last* (Mesa, Ariz., 1986), 14.

The Hungarians followed suit in 1937, when eighty-three candidates went down to Grottaglie for a two-year flying course. In return, Hungary agreed to supply Italy with an undisclosed amount of wheat. Before boarding the train with their "tourist" passports, the candidates received a three-week course in marching and the use of sidearms at the Hungarian Military Academy in Budapest. They were an elite, handpicked body of aviation enthusiasts. Most of them had already mastered the principles of flying through sailplane clubs at Hungarian universities. (Motorless aircraft were not prohibited by the Inter-Allied Control Commission.) "Ours was a sports psychology," said Kálmán Wittinger. "We had no thought of war."[3] Unlike the Germans, the Hungarians were fliers first and patriots afterward. "We never talked about politics. Bolshevism and fascism were uninteresting to us."[4]

Jenő Murányi, who later rose to command a fighter squadron during the war, soloed at Grottaglie within ten hours' flight time and logged sixty-five hours of solo flight on the Breda 25 and the Romeo Ro. 1 ("for figure flying, a very nice plane").[5] Hungarian instructors taught them technical subjects; Italians took charge of flight instruction. The base was remote. Fraternization with the local population was discouraged, other than the usual red-light sorties, and they had only one long holiday—a tourist trip to Rome, where their accents fooled no one despite their efforts to playact Italian in their spiffy Italian uniforms. There was little free time, for the course was demanding. Only one Hungarian cadet was killed in training, but about eighty planes were wrecked. Once they had soloed, the candidates were screened for special training in one of three schools—fighting, bombing, or observing, which the men ranked in that order. Those with greater manual dexterity joined the fighting group, although some top candidates, like Kálmán Wittinger, chose bombing because they planned to become test or airline pilots. At Grottaglie there was nothing resembling a Link Trainer, so the candidates never learned blind flying (which proved a major handicap when they went up against the RAF night raids during the war). Murányi's fighter group flew a variety of planes—all Italian—mostly biplanes like the Fiat CR32, fresh from service in the Spanish civil war, where it had been badly abused by Republican planes supplied by the Russians. Wittinger's bombing group trained in the twin-engined Caproni 310 and the three-engined Savoia Marquetti 81. These planes were already obsolete as fighting instruments, but the fundamentals the Hungarians learned at Grottaglie were a solid preparation for the operations these pilots would face in the years to come.

Like the Germans earlier, the Hungarians regarded the Italians as too loose, too undisciplined, too emotional.[6] Murányi, whose father had served as a *k.u.k.* captain in the Austro-Hungarian army during the First World War, was shocked by the Italian "do it tomorrow" attitude. They were not like real soldiers but instead "jolly good fellows"—until trouble came. He recalled one flight instructor who "flew like an angel," but when he sprained his arm, he whined and collapsed, crying out, "Mama mia! I'm dying! Come to me, Mama!" Apparently fascism, Italian-style, failed to produce a warrior caste. Cracks in the much-publicized neo-Roman armor were beginning to show. Their airplanes were fine flying instruments, but the Hungarians wondered about their military utility.

When the fliers returned home in 1939 they formed the nucleus of the Royal Hungarian Air Force.[7] By this time the secret pilot program had been scrapped. It was now post-Munich, and the Western powers no longer pretended that they could police the obsolescent terms of the Trianon Treaty. Flying officers no longer had to play the fool by wearing uniforms of railroad conductors or displaying insignia of customs officers. When the First Vienna Award returned the Felvidék to Hungary in 1938, Horthy founded a flying academy in Kassa, the principal city, to train a second generation of military pilots.[8] It now seemed only a matter of time before the Hungarian air force would exchange its cumbersome Italian craft for the faster German machines. Politically, the pilots (like the majority of Hungarians) were less pro-German than solidly anti-Bolshevik. Yet they did like the way that Germany settled scores with old Hungarian enemies, Czechoslovakia and Yugoslavia. Better, by far, to be an ally than to be overrun—though best to stay clear of war altogether.

6. Adolf Galland regarded the achievements of Italian fliers as somewhat foolish. In 1933, after one of them at Grottaglie had just set the world record for upside-down flying, a pointless feat, Galland irritated the Italians by effortlessly flying upside down between Bari and Taranto, thus setting a new record, which he ridiculed. Galland, 15.

7. "Royal" because officially Hungary was still a monarchy, although its regent, Admiral Miklós Horthy, had used military force to thwart the attempt of the Hapsburg aspirant, Charles IV, to seize his throne in 1921. Under Horthy the country was a symbolic monarchy, with the crown of King Stephen as its most cherished political totem.

8. There had been an interim pilot course sponsored by a quondam civilian organization known as Miklós Horthy National Flying Days, which, under the umbrella of sports flying, secretly trained young men to the level of a primary flight school. Successful students were then "drafted" (all sought this assignment eagerly, of course) into the Hungarian Air Force and sent on to Kassa for advanced training.

The Grottaglie program had been conducted with velvet gloves, but the generation of Hungarian pilot apprentices assembled at Kassa met iron-fisted instructors. Although discipline was known to be brutal, there was such demand for the course that four out of every five applicants were turned away. An eighteen-year-old assistant wheat buyer named Tibor Tabak was one of the successful recruits in 1940. Bored with his job at a flour mill, where he walked behind his boss with a basin of water so that the great man could flush his nostrils frequently, Tabak dreamed of flying and particularly liked to fantasize about landing a plane on a Hungarian aircraft carrier. (Hungary, of course, had no navy except a few gunboats on the Danube.) Accepted into the paramilitary Miklós Horthy Flying Program, he began his training at the Budaőrs airfield, just west of Budapest, where a Junkers commercial pilot was in charge of the flight instruction. Landings could be tricky; to save mowing costs sheep were allowed to graze on the airfield, and sometimes the dumb creatures strayed onto the runways. If a recruit made a poor landing, he had to run around the field with a seventy-pound propeller on his back, dropping to his stomach every ten meters. Tabak made this trip some five times while at Budaőrs. His instructor told him that he had no hand control because his hands were "as soft as shit." He was advised to stroke the vaginas of some Conti Street whores to sensitize his hands. There were compensations. Civilians, especially young girls, loved the cadets and never let them pay for drinks or for tickets to their favorite events—the Budapest bicycle races.[9]

From Budaőrs, Tabak went up to the Kassa Academy in September 1941 for the standard three-year course.[10] There were few distractions in this rustic and remote corner near the Soviet border. The cadets complained about the surliness of the civilian population, who seemed unable to decide whether they disliked the Magyars more than they feared the Russians. The cadets had little free time, for the curriculum was exacting. The idea was not to produce a mere technician but a well-rounded officer and gentleman of the old Hapsburg stripe. Therefore, along with flight instruction they studied geometry, calculus, physics, economics, military history, law, medicine, fencing, riding, and German. Although by this time Hungary had joined Germany in its war against the Soviet Union, the weak Soviet air force never

9. Tibor Tabak, *Pumák földön-égen* (Pumas on the ground and in the air) (Budapest, 1989), 10–15.

10. Because of the war Tabak's class of one hundred cadets received only two years of instruction; later classes received even less because of the shortage of pilots. Interview with Tibor Tabak (March 22, 1990).

tried to break the German defensive ring, even though Kassa was within easy bombing range.[11]

The war brought only a sense of heightened excitement to the Hungarian pilots. All of them expected an easy victory for their German allies. In the air, as on the ground, the Russians steadily gave way. Since the Luftwaffe had largely destroyed the Soviet air arm in the initial weeks of the war, the Hungarians served mainly as observers and as support for ground forces. At this stage of the war the Germans were reluctant to turn over their top air-craft to foreigners. Yet despite their hopelessly obsolete craft, like the Weihe and Fiat biplanes, the Magyars found that the Russians, for reasons they never understood, rarely put up a fight but wheeled and flew away.[12] Some-times the condition of planes in the Royal Hungarian Air Force was less than royal: Lieutenant Tabak flew a Weihe that had been patched up with tin cigarette advertisements. They logged flying time on patrols in the Kharkov sector until the summer and fall of 1943, when relocated near Kiev during the Russian advance. Then designated the Pumas, the Hungarian fighter groups during their Russian summer shot down seventy Soviet planes with a loss of only nine pilots (two of these to a midair collision).[13]

Although Hungary was officially at war with the United States and Britain after December 1941, none of the Hungarian fliers took this belligerency very seriously. Militarily, both countries seemed as remote as the moon—that is, until the Allied invasion of Italy in 1943, when the Fifteenth Air Force estab-lished American bases on the peninsula within striking range of Hungary and Poland. Yet so carefully had the Hungarian government crafted its foreign policy to emphasize that its quarrel was exclusively with the Soviets, and not at all with the West, that no Allied planes were molested when they passed over Hungary on bombing runs to industrial targets in German-occupied Poland. (By contrast, neutral Switzerland zealously attacked any Allied plane straying into its airspace.)[14] And, in conformity with this unspoken gentle-man's agreement, the Allies dropped no bombs on Hungary. This condition changed abruptly after mid-March 1944, when Hitler ordered German troops over the border in force. Only then did the Americans and British

11. None of the pilots I interviewed had anything definitive to offer about the mysterious bombing of Kassa that occurred on June 26, 1941, just a few days after Germany launched its war against the USSR.

12. On entering the war Hungary had only 350 aircraft, all of them obsolete. Walter Musciano, *Messerschmitt Aces* (New York, 1982), 140.

13. Ibid., 142.

14. Nicholas Nagy-Talavera, *The Green Shirts and the Others: A History of Fascism in Hungary and Rumania* (Stanford, 1970), 188.

commence their bombing raids against Hungarian objectives—the American Fifteenth Air Force launching massive daylight raids against industrial centers (particularly the aircraft factories and oil refineries on Csepel Island south of Budapest), and the RAF laying mines at night in the Danube to disrupt river traffic to Germany.

The first of twenty-one American raids came on April 3, when 450 B-17 Flying Fortresses and B-24 Liberators, escorted by 137 fighters, came up from Foggia, Italy, and bombed the aircraft factory at Csepel Island and the Budapest railway yards.[15] Formerly the vast American aerial circus flying over the city, bound for Poland, had always drawn a crowd of spectators in the streets of Budapest. Now onlookers were shocked and dismayed when their city became a target. Lieutenant Tabak recalled that cloudless spring day. His section was en route from barracks to the small airfield at Csepel Island to begin a routine patrol when he heard the sirens, then the "deep threatening sound of four-engine planes." The pilots dived into a ditch as the bombers flew north along the river, pursued by inaccurate puffs of anti-aircraft shots. Then there was the deafening sound of carpet bombing in the vicinity of the railway station. Tabak's first thought was regret at not being in the air. Then he remembered the planes available to him, both observation types, the Storck (one gun) and the Weihe (two guns). It was ridiculous. He suddenly realized that Hungary would never be able to stop these attacks. He had never seen anything like them on the eastern front. The American planes were too numerous, too disciplined, too punctual. After the raiders had disappeared, he saw columns of smoke over the Csepel factories, and the air was filled with white sheets of paper. He thought they must be leaflets, but they turned out to be personnel files of an oil company. Later he heard that the Tokol aircraft factory had been heavily damaged, with one thousand casualties. It was a day he never forgot.[16] Within days the Hungarian press was spinning lurid tales of Texas and Chicago air gangsters dropping explosive toys and poisoned chocolates to victimize innocent Hungarian children. One such newspaper characterized the American pilots as "the scum of American latrines who come to Hungary to murder Hungarians. These dastardly beings, filled with Jewish sadism, come to carry out the devilish, sinister vengeance of Jewry."[17]

15. Kit Carter, comp., *U.S. Army Air Forces in World War II: Combat Chronology* (Washington, 1991), 308.

16. Tabak, 81. The USAF claimed twenty-four enemy planes were shot down, probably most of which were on the ground.

17. Nagy-Talavera, 198.

Budapest before and after the siege of 1945. Buda is to the left and Pest is to the right of the Danube River, with the Chain Bridge connecting the two. The ancient village of Tabán is in the foreground with Castle Hill immediately above it. The prewar photo was taken from the top of Gellért Hill; the wartorn photo was taken from the bottom of the hill.

The Peace Treaty of Trianon is more cruel than any other Peace Treaty.

The peace treaty of Versailles has taken away one of every twenty german-speaking germans.

The peace treaty of Neuilly has torn away one of every twenty bulgarian-speaking bulgarians.

The peace treaty of Trianon has torn away seven of every twenty hungarians of magyar tongue.

This illustrates the relative armament of the hostile neighbours as compared with disarmed Hungary.

The Hungarian army of Trianon.

According to the Treaty of Trianon the Hungarian Army numbers 35.000 in peace and war alike.

By contrast the peace numbers of the countries hostile to Hungary are:

Czechoslovakia... 160.000 men

Rumania .... 232.000 men

Yugoslavia ...... 150.000 men

Total: 542.000 men

But only in peace time! In the case of mobilisation the combined armies of the three countries aggregate nearly four and a half millions.

— 37 —

The Trianon Treaty of 1920 divested Hungary of 70 percent of its prewar territory and 60 percent of its population. Militarily helpless, Hungarians could do nothing but endure it for many years. The illustrations above and on the facing page show

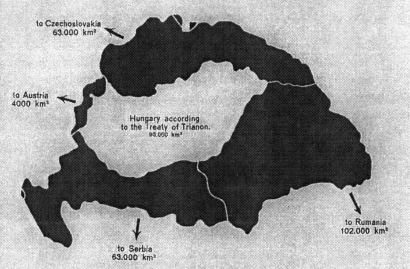

Partition of the territory of Hungary.
The Peace Treaty of Hungary has deprived Hungary of 72 per cent. of its Territory.

to Czechoslovakia
63.000 km²

to Austria
4000 km²

Hungary according
to the Treaty of Trianon.
93.000 km²

to Rumania
102.000 km²

to Serbia
63.000 km²

Partition of Hungary's population.
The Peace Treaty of Hungary has forced 64 per cent of Hungary's Population under Foreign Rule.

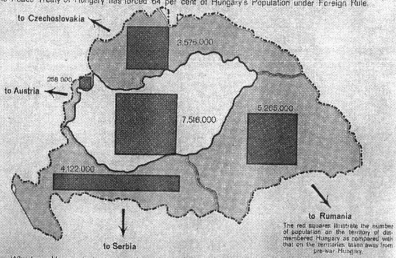

to Czechoslovakia

3,576.000

258.000

to Austria

7,516.000

5,265.000

4,122.000

to Rumania
The red squares illustrate the number
of population on the territory of dis-
membered Hungary as compared with
that on the territories taken away from
pre-war Hungary.

to Serbia

Why have Hungary's territory and population been subjected to such terrible mutilation?

From the ethnographical, geographical and economic points of view the new frontiers are worse than
the old ones were.

The new frontiers serve exclusively the imperialistic and strategical purposes of Czechoslovakia, Rumania
and Yugoslavia.

— 14 —

the bitterness Hungarians felt. Reprinted from *Justice for Hungary: The Cruel
Errors of Trianon*, Budapest, 1930.

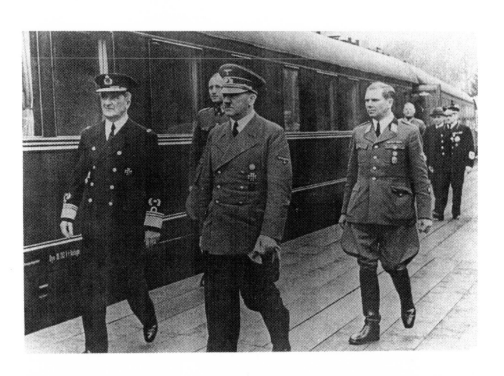

(above) Arrow Cross rally in Hősök tere (Heroes' Square), Budapest, in 1944. Recognized by their green uniforms and barbed-cross insignia, they carried out violent and brutal terrorist attacks, mostly against Jews.

(opposite page, top) Admiral Miklós Horthy, a Magyar, was elected regent for life in 1920 after liberating Budapest and forcing the overthrow of Béla Kun's short-lived Communist regime. Although Horthy was skeptical of the Nazi economic boom, over the next twenty years he helped steer a right-wing course for Hungary that involved closer ties with Germany. Here Horthy is shown with Hitler in Salzburg, Austria, in 1944. Hitler wanted to keep Hungary locked into the Axis frame, but Horthy was becoming increasingly uncooperative.

(opposite page, bottom) Ferenc Szálasi was the leader of the fascist Arrow Cross Party, which he founded in 1935. Only after Horthy attempted to arrange an armistice with the Russians in October 1944, did the Germans install Szálasi as their puppet head. Here Szálasi takes command of the nation. The soldiers are German paratroopers.

At the edge of the Jewish ghetto in Budapest in 1944. The sign reads "Jewish Quarter—Christians forbidden entry." Once the Germans occupied Hungary, in March, the government cooperated in executing the German plan for liquidating Jews.

Waiting for the Auschwitz train. Hungary, which had protected so many of its Jews from Nazi death camps before German occupation in March 1944, became a hell for them after that. Approximately 450,000 Jews were deported and killed in the forty-six-day period between May 15 and July 7.

Faces of war. Fleeing in terror from the advancing Red Army, refugees from remote districts of eastern Hungary flood Budapest in the fall of 1944.

Margit Bridge after the explosion, November 1944. All bridges had been mined by the German army in November, but this explosion was premature and apparently accidental, for the Russians had not yet threatened Budapest.

After a bombardment. The Soviet army shelled and bombed Budapest throughout
January 1945. Families and neighbors were frequently seen digging bodies out
from beneath the rubble of shattered buildings.

In September 1944, Red Army troops crossed the Hungarian frontier. On Christmas night they completely encircled Budapest and intensified their shelling. The siege of the city lasted until February 1945. This photograph shows Hungarians salvaging firewood or other debris from the Danube near ruins of Lánchíd (Chain Bridge).

A Soviet soldier pauses warily during the fighting near the Parliament building at Kossuth Square in Pest. It is likely that the bicycle was once Hungarian property.

The Soviets "liberated" Budapest on February 13, 1945, and proceeded to massacre any Germans they found in the city. Here, Russians raise a Red flag over Kálvin Square in Pest.

Garrison Church in the castle area, where the SS made its last stand. At the end of the fifty-day siege, much of Budapest lay in ruins. Of the 35,677 buildings in the capital, 29,987 were destroyed or damaged.

German "Storck" plane embedded in a ruined building along Attila Street. The dead German pilot remained in the airplane until the summer of 1945.

Hungarians were stunned by the ruthlessness of their liberators. Soviet soldiers looted and terrorized the civilian population as they looked for Germans hiding in the city.

City officers collecting unclaimed corpses from the Üllői Street morgue on a winter morning after the "liberation" of Budapest. Clothes and shoes were carefully saved. While a Russian soldier examines the cart attentively, the civilian workers carefully inspect him. Other civilians give the cart not a glance.

One of these "air gangsters," Lieutenant Robert Carpenter of the USAF, had no recollection whatsoever of this day, which blended into too many others. He flew a P-38 Lightning of the Eighty-Second Fighter Group on a four-hour-and-fifteen-minute run out of Foggia. His group covered the bombers at twenty-four thousand feet. Fresh from training in the United States, he was told just to hang on the wing of his leader and do nothing. Nothing needed to be done. It was, as the pilots liked to say, a "milk run." When interrogated half a century later, all he knew about this historic first raid against the Hungarians came from a battered notebook.[18]

The principal airfield in Hungary, then as now, was Ferihegy, a few miles southeast of Budapest, but it was out of the question to expect that any of the variegated aviation relics there could overtake—much less shoot down—the American bombers or pursuit planes. Farther east, at Szolnok, Lieutenant Tibor Murányi with a half dozen other Hungarian pilots got airbound in Reggio Hawks (domestic planes of Italian design produced at Győr) and bravely took out after the invaders. It was hopeless. Not only were their 12.7 mm guns little better than popguns, but the Hawks' ceiling limit on a good day was fifteen thousand feet, nearly a vertical mile below the American bombers and two miles below the Lightnings. (Besides, they had no oxygen masks). Moreover, it was humiliating. Murányi expected to be promptly knocked out of the air by one of the enemy fighters, which had more than twice the speed of his Hawk. Instead, he found that the American pilots merely buzzed him without firing a shot, as though he were not worth shooting down—or else they were going so fast they failed to see him. The raid caught the Hungarians completely by surprise. There were in Hungary at this time a limited number of Messerschmitt bf109s, capable of engaging the escorting fighters on equal terms, most of them assigned to Luftwaffe squadrons, but because of the surprise, few got off the ground. The Fifteenth Air Force returned to Foggia without losing a plane.

On April 13 there was an even bigger raid—535 Liberators and Fortresses escorted by 200 fighters—which targeted a bomb factory up the Danube at Győr and the Budapest airport at Ferihegy. A mixed group of thirty-two Hungarians in Messerschmitt 210s, a two-engine, two-man plane, went up to meet them. "They were so numerous that I never regarded them as individual planes," remembered Lieutenant Kálmán Wittinger, Hungary's top test pilot. Unfortunately, the antiaircraft batteries were "so nervous they were shooting at sparrows," and a Hungarian gun at Ócsa knocked out one of his

18. Interview with Robert Carpenter (January 16, 1993).

engines.[19] He returned to Ferihegy just as the B-17s began their carpet bombing of the airfield. "In record sprint time I raced for a ditch, made it, but the 210 was completely destroyed." On the tarmac sat a P-38, which the Germans had captured somehow and which Wittinger had been itching to fly. It, too, went up in flames. After this raid, he and the other test pilots were forbidden to fly missions against the Americans, because their technical skills and experience could not be replaced.

Wittinger's companion, Lieutenant János Szentiványi, also piloting a 210, had no better luck. The alarm came at 11:30, when the bomber force was assembling over Lake Balaton, fifty miles southwest of Budapest. There was no sign of them at Balaton, or at Győr, which was covered by thick black smoke. Returning to Budapest they found the city under heavy attack. They passed close to a floundering B-17, its left wing amputated by antiaircraft fire, and watched as seven crewmen bailed out. Five of the parachutes were on fire. "No flier, not even an enemy, ever wants to see that." Radio command on Gellért Hill ordered them to collect at six thousand feet over Csepel Island. There were so many American fighters around him that Szentiványi knew his only hope was speed. At eight hundred kilometers per hour his speedometer fluttered on the red mark, and he expected his wings to come off. By this time there were only two 210s left in his group. Circling Csepel like hawks waiting for doves were a dozen P-38s, which jumped them. Szentiványi's leader went down like a lead shot but made a crash landing in a field, but as he stepped out on the wing, the plane exploded in a fireball. Meanwhile Szentiványi had his hands full with the P-38s, which had superior speed and firepower. For three or four times he was able to dodge back and forth in a cloud, taking a ten-second breather in the gray darkness, but soon their props broke up the cloud. His gunner yelled that they should jump, but Szentiványi had been warned, and believed, that the Americans machine-gunned enemy parachutists.[20] He dropped to within thirty feet of the ground, where the P-38s lost their appetite for pursuit, and tried to make the small airfield on Csepel Island. His right engine was burning, and then his left one stopped. He

19. Other Hungarian pilots complained about their aircraft batteries, which were particularly dangerous because inexperienced gunners fired at anything that flew. Interview with Tibor Murányi (April 13, 1990) (no relation to Jenő Murányi).

20. Szentiványi interview. Lieutenant Robert Carpenter, who flew his P-38 in combat over Hungary during this period, has flatly denied that Americans were instructed or encouraged to machine-gun parachutists, but Hungarian pilots are emphatic that it occurred. Lieutenant Gyula Pintér once overheard a downed Mustang pilot admit that it was a policy of the Fifteenth Air Force to kill enemy airmen in parachutes because they could not be readily replaced. For Pintér this was "not war, but murder." Interview with Gyula Pintér (April 10, 1990).

crashed at just under three hundred kilometers per hour in an orchard, shearing off twelve trees. Szentiványi fractured his neck and was pinned under the fuselage, but his gunner was unharmed. The right wing was now burning and threatened to explode. The gunner commandeered some peasants nearby, and with hoes they hacked a hole in the cockpit and freed him. Meanwhile a half dozen P-38s, attracted to the crash site, hosed the Hungarians with their machine guns, but no one was hit. They carried the pilot about twenty yards before the plane exploded with such force that it broke windows in the village of Ráckeve, four miles away. Szentiványi was safely evacuated to a Budapest hospital, although his ambulance was strafed by P-38s en route. He never flew against the Americans again. After a six-month medical leave, he returned to duty and flew against the Russians, who were closing their ring around Budapest.

The Americans were stung in their three raids into Hungary in April, having lost twenty-four bombers, most of them to ground fire.[21] During the next six weeks the Fifteenth Air Force bypassed Hungary altogether, providing the Pumas with an opportunity for reorganization. They set up interceptor groups north of Lake Balaton at Veszprém and Kenyeri. Each had three squadrons of three patrols, and each patrol had two pairs of fighters. (The Italians had trained them to fly in echelon, but the Germans now taught them how to fight in pairs for greater maneuverability.) It was at this time that most Hungarian fliers were assigned to the killing machine that they fell in love with and would fly with great effectiveness during the remainder of the war—the Messerschmitt bf109G (Gustav version). This plane was now being produced at Győr, and the Luftwaffe set up a special 109 course at a roughed-out landing field near Tapolca, north of Lake Balaton.[22] It was a tricky plane. On takeoffs too much acceleration could shake it apart, and the fragile undercarriage was likely to collapse on any landing less than gentle. A pilot in a 109 felt he had a fair fight with a Lightning because he could turn quicker, but he was instructed never to attack a Mustang unless unavoidable. Mustangs had superior firepower, greater speed, and could turn faster. The only way to escape one was to make a steep dive and pull up sharply, for the 109 had a fuel injection system, whereas the Mustang carburetor choked off temporarily and the plane lost distance. Moreover, the 109 had a special

---

21. Carter, 308, 316.

22. Although the Luftwaffe provided briefings and special courses, the German fighter squadrons were wholly separate from the Hungarians. Between fliers of the two nationalities relations were good and had nothing to do with politics other than anti-Bolshevism: "There was the usual brotherhood that exists among fliers anywhere." Jenő Murányi interview.

methanol boost that could bring the plane up to the speed of a Mustang temporarily, although, if employed longer than ten minutes, the engine seized up. After flying airplanes armed with popguns, the Hungarians marveled at the armament of the 109—a 20-mm cannon firing through the propeller shaft, two 13-mm guns above the engine, and two 20-mm cannon under the wings.[23]

Repeatedly the Pumas were instructed that their job was to knock out enemy bombers and that they were to avoid dogfights with Lightnings or Mustangs. To attack a bomber you got well above it, made a single descent at full throttle, and then tried to shake loose the host of American fighters that invariably stuck to your tail. The idea was to "attack, shoot, disappear."[24] If you felt particularly brave, you might attempt a second strike, but it was not recommended. Should your guns jam in the melee, it was safer to maintain the formation than to run off. One evening Captain Erich Hartmann, the leading German ace, gave some pointers to the Puma squadron at Veszprém. Lieutenant Gyula Pintér, fresh from his academy course, asked how one shot down an enemy plane. "It's very simple," explained Hartmann. "You go so near that your sight is wholly blackened by the enemy plane—about thirty meters. Then all you have to do is push the button."[25] Liberators were less dangerous than the Fortresses, for their gunners could not cover certain zones along the wings and vertically underneath. At first the Hungarians were somewhat intimidated by the term "Flying Fortress," assuming it might be what it claimed to be, but after the first raid, they found it was just propaganda.

After a six-week hiatus the Fifteenth Air Force resumed its missions over Hungary with Operation Frantic, in which the Italian-based planes flew on to bases in the USSR. The plan was to introduce shuttle flights, but it was soon abandoned. The Russian bases were nearly destroyed by lightning German attacks, and the Russians always grumbled about capitalistic American planes invading their air space.[26] Yet by mid-1944 the Axis air war was in deep trouble. Massive Allied raids on the Romanian oil fields in May had cut fuel production by 50 percent. Pilot schools had to be shut down for lack of fuel,

---

23. Musciano, 158.

24. Szentiványi interview. The estimate was that it took at least twenty hits with a 20-mm cannon to bring down a B-17. Galland, 200.

25. Pintér interview. Later Pintér watched a group of Mustangs attack Hartmann as he returned to Veszprém from a mission. Although his wheels were down, he flipped over and shot down two Mustangs while flying upside down. By war's end Hartmann, at age twenty-three, had 352 confirmed kills.

26. Galland, 296.

although aircraft production soared. Ironically, there was a glut of Axis fighter planes on the ground, unable to take to the air at a time when the Allies were smashing major oil refineries. The Axis had always used the Russian front to school new pilots in attack skills before moving them to the west, but fuel was now too precious for this enterprise. Added to the fuel problem was the loss of Luftwaffe fighter pilots, estimated by the summer of 1944 at 25 percent.[27] Pilot losses among the Hungarians were probably higher—so high, in fact, that from mid-July there were long periods when the Pumas were grounded whenever the massive American bombing formations assembled over Lake Balaton. The explanation was that they were too valuable to be thrown away in an effort to stop the unstoppable. After all, it cost 600,000 pengős to train a flying officer, at a time when the salary of a bank clerk was only 320 pengős a month.[28] Captain Jenő Murányi, squadron leader at Veszprém, estimated that in less than a dozen flights against the Americans fifty-six Hungarians pilots had been lost. (Many of these were replacements, in that his original roster listed only fifty-two names.)[29] It was feared that if this rate of decimation continued, there would be no pilots alive to beat back the real enemy—the Red Army, advancing rapidly from the east. The result was that losses of American aircraft, when they occurred at all, were largely the result of mechanical problems or antiaircraft batteries.

For those pilots of the 101st Regiment who survived, the summer of 1944 became a glittering recollection. They were billeted in private lodgings at Almádi and other swanky Lake Balaton resorts, where hotel bands played the latest American dance tunes, beautiful girls basked in the sun, and the water was always warm. "For me war was a kind of sporting event. We fliers were automatically adopted by the Hungarian leisure class," recalled Lieutenant Tibor Murányi. For the Pumas it was strictly an eight-to-four war, in which they commuted by bus to the Veszprém base.[30] (There were no night flights against the British bombers mining the Danube because the Pumas had no radar-controlled aircraft.) As reward for each flight they each received a one-kilo cardboard box filled with chocolate bars, biscuits, candied fruit, potato fudge, and raisins. The ladies adored these boxes.[31]

27. William Murray, *Luftwaffe* (Baltimore, 1985), 259, 262.
28. Tibor Murányi interview. In 1940 the exchange rate for the pengő was a fraction more than $.28, the price of a chicken.
29. Official reports of the Fifteenth Air Force indicate no American losses in the last fourteen raids on Hungarian targets, between late July and December of 1944.
30. Tibor Murányi interview.
31. Tabak, 220.

If Zagreb radioed that the American armada was moving toward Hungary, the Magyar pilots reported to their airfields. Shortly before the Americans arrived, they took to the air, where they could hover on the fringe of the enemy formation and hope for stragglers. A radio station at Gellért in Budapest directed each squadron to specific map grids and specified the appropriate altitude. Sometimes Americans would break into the frequency and, in perfect Hungarian, countermand these orders. Lieutenant Tibor Murányi once made the mistake of falling into this American trap. Fifty Mustangs pounced on his patrol, which barely escaped back to Veszprém.

Their prior service had not prepared the Hungarian airmen for the sheer size of the American raids. The first wave would be just out of sight when the next wave appeared on the southern horizon. Against the Russians there had often been one-on-one dogfights. Now a single Gustav might be pursued by as many as twenty Mustangs or Lightnings. "If you ever saw the belly of a Mustang above you, all your saliva and the snot in your head dried up," recalled Tibor Tabak.[32] In the raid of July 2, for example, 620 heavy bombers with fighter escorts hit the Csepel Island oil refineries, the railway yards, and the aircraft factory at Győr. Although the Americans lost twenty-eight planes, the replacement factor for both airmen and aircraft seemed always infinite.[33] (Unknown to the Americans their bombs leveled a house in Budapest where 150 British and American citizens had been interned, of which only ten were pulled out alive.)[34]

It seemed inconceivable to the Hungarians that the American fighters could stay in the air for more than four hours, escorting the bombers all the way from Italy and returning there, for the airborne limit of their Gustavs was only about eighty minutes. It was not uncommon for the Mustangs to hover about the airfield at Veszprém and attack a Gustav when it came in for refueling. The single disadvantage of this preponderant superiority in numbers and matériel was that it impaired the combat effectiveness of the American pilots.[35] With the odds fifteen to one in their favor, they almost had to queue up to have a shot at a faltering Gustav.

---

32. Tabak interview.

33. Losses in the Fifteenth Air Force were severe, particularly in their raids at this time on the Ploesti oil fields. According to the notes of Lieutenant Carpenter, sixteen fighter pilots of his original group of twenty-one were shot down; of this group only two survived the war. Carpenter interview.

34. John Lukács, *Confessions of an Original Sinner* (New York, 1990), 48. Lukács was with the labor battalion assigned to the excavating team.

35. Tibor Murányi interview.

Despite the massive bombing of Hungarian cities and installations, for the carefully groomed Magyar pilots it remained a gentleman's war with an inviolate chivalric code. Nearly all of them had stories of friendly exchanges with American airmen. On one occasion, in a fight over Veszprém, Lieutenant Domján was startled when a Mustang pulled up alongside him and pointed at the Gustav's tail. Looking back, Domján saw that he was on fire, waved to the American, and safely bailed out. Unfortunately the two planes then collided and the American was trapped in the tangle. The 101st Fighter Group recovered the body and buried it with full military honors in their own cemetery at Sümeg.[36] Downed American airmen often received a royal welcome from the Pumas. Lieutenant Pintér remembered that one of his mates who had shot down a Liberator, on learning that the crewman had safely parachuted, hurried to the site with bottles of champagne for the unexpected guests. Later, when a higher-up in Budapest demanded an explanation for this unlawful fraternization with the enemy, the pilot's CO at Veszprém wrote a tart note in support of his officer: "As long as I am commander, this atmosphere of cordiality remains."[37]

Parachuting from an American plane was fraught with unknown dangers. The greatest danger was getting down safely. Once, at the Veszprém airfield, a group of Hungarians watched as a Liberator spun down, out of control. "Jump!" they shouted in empathy. Relieved, they saw parachutes blossoming from the stricken plane. Then a large package tumbled out—two men on the same parachute. When it opened, one man lost his grip and plummeted to earth.[38] Moreover, since it was always problematic what peasants might do to enemy parachutists, gendarmes or soldiers took them into protective custody as quickly as possible. A Negro crewman was brought to Captain Murányi's squadron. All the Hungarians stared at him, some in disbelief. One of the officers said, "I can't believe he isn't painted." Then, putting saliva on his finger, he wiped the Negro's forehead. The American laughed and offered him a Chesterfield. For three days he had free run of the base—until some Germans came and carted him away. On another occasion Lieutenant Tabak landed his 109 in a field near some Americans who had parachuted from a B-17. They chatted and exchanged cigarettes. Then the American pilot asked permission to examine Tabak's 109. He complied, and only then realized that he was not armed and the American strapped an automatic. The American

36. Tabak interview.
37. Pintér interview.
38. Jenő Murányi interview.

pilot wondered if he might climb into the cockpit. He looked at Tabak in a peculiar way, then both broke into laughter. Tabak always wondered what he would have told his CO if the American had stolen his plane at pistol point. Before they separated, the pilot gave Tabak a one-dollar bill, which he saved till long after the war, when, destitute, he used it to buy a pair of shoes on the black market.[39]

Lieutenant Robert Carpenter was one of the Americans shot down over Hungary on June 16, his fortieth mission. In his Lightning he had been part of the escort for six hundred heavy bombers in a Vienna raid. In the melee he chased a 109 far to the east, shot it down, but found himself alone over Lake Balaton. He had been instructed never to fly alone over lakes because it made a plane visible from above, but he needed the margin of fuel saved by this shortcut. Without warning his instrument panel exploded, and hydraulic fluid spurted from the rear. He was only three hundred feet up with his arm on fire when he jumped. His parachute broke open almost at the instant he landed in a vineyard on the south shore of Balaton. Farmers with pitchforks hurried to the spot, and a young man threatened to hang him; but when a priest arrived, Carpenter established a faltering monosyllabic communication based on his high school Latin. At a gendarme post, where he was forced to strip, a policeman pointed to his penis and exclaimed, "Zsidó!" Carpenter knew no words of Hungarian, but a burst of linguistic adrenaline told him that was the word for Jew. From his pocket he pulled a rosary and said, "No, Catholic!" Shortly SS officers arrived, bringing a woman interpreter who had lived in Cleveland. When he made some wisecrack replies to their questions, the woman whispered, "Be careful what you say." Noting the look of alarm on her face, he thereafter gave only his name, rank, and serial number.

Before the German occupation, downed American and British pilots received a royal welcome. Some Americans lounged luxuriously in a nobleman's house outside Szombathely and were even allowed free access to the city, provided they wore civilian clothes.[40] Conditions were grimmer during Carpenter's stay. He was lodged in a filthy Budapest hospital until the place was destroyed by British night bombers early in July. Then he was jailed with other downed fliers in a city prison, where he was interrogated. A policeman (or soldier) stood behind him with a clubbed musket as an

---

39. When he recently wrote of receiving this money, he was denounced by an eighty-year-old Hungarian colonel as a traitor and collaborationist. Tabak interview.

40. Nicholas [Miklós] Kállay, *Hungarian Premier* (New York, 1954), 342.

officer told him that unless he responded to all questions, his head could be split open, and no one would ever know he had died there. Carpenter stuck to name, rank, serial number. It was only a bluff; besides, the interrogator seemed to know more about the Fifteenth Air Force than he did. The Allied pilots earned a place in Hungarian folklore for their behavior during air raids: when the RAF bombed at night, the British sang "God Save the King," and during the daylight raids the Americans sang "The Star Spangled Banner."[41]

The rest was easy. He was moved by train to Stalag 3 in Bavaria, where there were Red Cross food packages galore and all the cigarettes he could want. When the American army approached the camp, the five thousand Allied officers were evacuated and spent three days on the road moving toward Nuremberg. With a companion Carpenter escaped and spent two weeks wandering about the countryside, trading cigarettes for food. The Bavarian civilians were friendly but warned them that SS were killing stragglers, and convinced them they should voluntarily return to the camp. While the prisoners were at Mass one Sunday, General Patton's tanks liberated the camp, the general himself riding around in a jeep, enjoying the commotion. Carpenter and his fellow POWs were sent stateside and by early June of 1945 had disembarked in New York. A few months later he was studying at the University of Detroit under the G.I. Bill, putting his wartime adventures far behind him. A couple of times he tried flying small aircraft, but the thrill was gone. Nor was he ever tempted to fly for an airline. "After a P-38, one might as well be driving a bus."[42]

Late autumn 1944 brought a host of troubles for Hungary. Even though the massive American bombings by the Fifteenth Air Force had largely ceased by the end of September, the defection of Romania from Hitler's war had opened the floodgates for the advance of the Red Army toward Budapest. This enormous pressure from the east did focus the efforts of the Hungarian Royal Air Force. Pilots had always had trouble regarding the British and the Americans as enemies, but with the Russians at the gates, they prepared themselves for a war to the death. The Arrow Cross regime even brokered a policy of tangible rewards for shooting down Russian planes. For two victories a pilot was promised a grant of sixty-five *holds* of land (about ninety-two acres), payable after the final victory over Bolshevism. (None was ever

---

41. Ferenc Nagy, *The Struggle Behind the Iron Curtain* (New York, 1948), 47.
42. Carpenter interview.

paid.)[43] Some of the younger pilots dreamed of becoming instant landowners, but old pilots, like Jenő Murányi, laughed it off, just as they laughed off the "secret weapon" being prepared by the Germans, which was supposed to win the war.[44] Toward the Arrow Cross in general the pilots always expressed almost universal contempt.

From their old bases near Lake Balaton the Pumas eagerly engaged the Russians. With them there was no chivalry, no gentleman's rules. While the Hungarians were never sure whether the stories about Americans shooting parachutists were true, they had no grounds for doubt about the Russians. If you bailed out and were not protected, you would be shot at—it was as simple as that. "The Russians were not pilots; they were murderers," recalled János Szentiványi. Tibor Tabak, always gregarious, visited a hospitalized Russian pilot to make sure that he was being well treated. It was a mistake. "Among the Russians there was no brotherhood of the air." The Russian refused to speak one word and glared at him with hatred. The greatest fear at this period of the war was being shot down behind enemy lines, for this meant indefinite incarceration or worse. Nearly every Magyar pilot had heard horror stories from Hungarians captured by the Russians in the First World War. The flying junk heaps flown by the Russians in 1942–43 had been replaced by the Lavochkin-7 and the Yakovlev-3, both with speeds comparable to the Gustav, but they never darkened the sky like the ubiquitous Lightnings and Mustangs. The Yaks generally stayed close to the ground, and with their armored cockpits they were ideal for strafing ground forces. Above eighteen thousand feet they were outclassed by the Messerschmitt 109. In fighting a Yak you lifted as steeply as possible and then turned back on the sluggish enemy. Against a Mustang this tactic would have been tantamount to suicide.

Just before the Red Army closed its circle around Budapest on Christmas Eve, Lieutenant Wittinger collected his pregnant wife and small son from the city

---

43. This idea was a corruption of the Order of Vitézi Rend (Order of Gallantry), which Horthy had founded in 1921 to encourage, by a system of tangible rewards, patriotism and heroism. After earning a medal for courage, an individual could apply for membership to the order. If accepted, he could then put Vitéz in front of his name, like a nobleman's title, and was entitled to a small grant of land. Macartney, 1:31.

44. Rumors about various "secret weapons" that would make the Allies sue for peace circulated throughout Germany during the final months of the war. Captain Murányi and the Pumas were told of "a comet with a man aboard," which sounds like the Messerschmitt 262, the first jet fighter, which was never produced in sufficient quantity to alter the outcome of the war.

and took them to the Budaőrs airfield, which was being evacuated. He flew out a transport plane crammed with munitions, his wife sitting on a box of hand grenades. When attacked by a Soviet fighter, Wittinger, who knew the terrain intimately, dived into a deep foggy valley where the Russian dared not follow. Then he flew on to Szombathely, the new headquarters of the HRAF, and arranged for his family to be evacuated to Austria. Always the Germans swore that the evacuation of families and materials was "temporary." In time they would return and sweep the Russians back beyond the Carpathians. Few of the Magyar pilots took this very seriously. Defeatism was seeping into the ranks of the Pumas, exacerbated by the recognition that the Germans were now running the whole show and were not protective of Hungarian lives, whether on the ground or in the air. According to Captain Jenő Murányi, Puma morale had reached such a trough that, if a mission seemed suicidal, a pilot might abort the flight by allowing the prop to churn dirt into the engine till it misfired, or a pilot might call out, "Soviet fighters on the right!" so that the patrol would drop its spare gas tanks, thereby shortening a mission from two hours to forty minutes. The problem now was no warning system against enemy planes, for they were everywhere, seemingly at all times. On his last flight of the war Captain Murányi was shot down by an American fighter patrol that had strayed from Austria. He parachuted safely, but before he could undo his harness, a Lightning swept down and buzzed him. "This is it," he thought, remembering the tales he had heard about Americans picking off parachutists. The flier threw out fair-sized object that almost struck him. He braced for an explosion. None came. It was a wax-covered lunch package.

Other pilots seemed to thrive on hazardous duty. Since Lieutenant Wittinger had flown all sorts of planes and under all sorts of conditions, he volunteered to carry food and ammunition into Budapest. Initially he landed on the racetrack near Keleti Station, within a few city blocks of the front line, but soon the Russians were waiting for him with their trench mortars and so damaged his plane on the tarmac that he had to change his tactics and drop his materials by parachute. These relief flights were at night, over Russian-held territory. Wittinger had never received radar training—not that it mattered, for his transport craft had no radar anyway. It was not uncommon to return without instruments or an electrical system. On one occasion a crewman bled to death from a shrapnel wound in the thigh while the radio-man futilely tried to apply a tourniquet in the dark and Wittinger navigated for home with the aid of a cigarette lighter.

As promised, the Germans did marshal their armies to recapture Budapest, but their February counteroffensive soon petered out, and the great retreat to the west continued. As the Hungarians flew over the front lines, which nearly reached to Veszprém, they could see big German Tiger tanks permanently dug into the ground because there was no gasoline to move them. The Pumas now flew against the La-7, and the enemy pilots seemed more confident.[45] Three or four times each day they attacked the German positions and ravaged the main Hungarian airfield at Veszprém. On March 14, with the Russians about to overrun the region, the Pumas were ordered to strip and evacuate the base. Pilots flew planes to Szombathely and were then ferried back to Veszprém on a bombed-out bus. The bus had no floor, no windows, no roof—but the engine worked fine. Pilots hung on as best they could, and when the bus stalled against the great tide of refugees fleeing from the Russians, they walked. On the road, as though a monument commemorating the defeat, was a smashed German plane. The pilot had been roasted in the cockpit and had shrunk, but such sights were now so common that no one had bothered to bury him. On one transit they met a column of Waffen SS moving up to plug a hole in the line. When the fliers called out, "Wiedersehen," a retreating soldier called back, "Wiedersehen im Massengrab."[46]

What followed was a seemingly endless series of evacuations and relocations—to Szombathely, Kenyeri, then over the Austrian frontier to Grosspetersdorf, Tulln, and finally a wooded airfield near Linz. The airstrips were so primitive that it was difficult to land a Gustav without smashing the undercarriage. Not that it mattered. Right up till the last shots of the war the aircraft factories spewed out a glut of spanking new 109s. It was said that for a hundred cigarettes—even Hungarian ones—you could take your pick of any plane on the tarmac, most of them destined to be burned. During the exodus from Hungary many Puma units had been dispersed. Just before the Russians arrived, Lieutenant Wittinger helped to destroy the airbase at Sopron, and with a group of Hungarian airmen and their families boarded a Salzburg train. In Austria a band of SS stopped the train and threatened to shoot all of them for desertion. They were held prisoner on the train for weeks until the SS verified that they had really been ordered to retreat. Then one day, without a word, the SS unit disappeared, and an American tank company arrived at the railroad. The Americans confiscated their heavy weapons but very politely allowed the officers to keep their pistols, warning them that roving SS guerrillas were still a danger. A short time later trucks

45. Despite this technical superiority in aircraft, the Luftwaffe pilots regarded the Soviet fliers as their inferiors in aerial combat, even up to the final days of the war. D. Walter Schwabedissen, *The Russian Air-Force in the Eyes of German Commanders* (New York, 1960), 267.

46. Tabak interview.

took them to a German military barracks, renamed Fort O'Connell, near Salzburg. For this contingent of Hungarians the war was at last over.

Back at the airstrip near Linz the main contingent of Pumas, now reduced to twenty pilots and two hundred technicians, waited out the long days and nights of late April.[47] A rumor came in that Hitler was dead, but sporadic fighting continued. There was no secret weapon—the Reich was kaput. On the road, gangs of Allied POWs passed by—the Russians silent, morose, and hungry, the Americans cherubic, fat, and cheerful. On one occasion, when a V-formation buzzed the human tide, the Americans POWs cheered, broke ranks, and gathered in an open field, protected by a homemade American flag. The Mustang pilots recognized them and waved. Then, in a spirit of largesse, the POWs invited their German guards to join them in safety, which the guards lost no time in doing.[48] Now who was guarding whom?

The Pumas debated what they should do. Some wanted to fly to the British or Americans, but this was voted down as dishonorable; others computed the distance to Barcelona and figured they could just about carry enough fuel to make it. But how could they carry the technicians, many of whom wanted to go? All that really mattered now was somehow to survive the war and avoid capture by the Russians. They pledged to stay together as a cohesive body.

On May 4 they calculated that the American army would arrive the following day. They burned everything they had—airplanes, weapons, munitions, codebooks, papers. "Burning the planes—this was the saddest moment of the war for me," recalled Lieutenant Pintér. Then they assembled along the road to await the victors. That evening twenty German soldiers came down the road singing the "Horst Wessel Lied," each carrying a *Panzerfaust* (a German bazooka). "Where are you going," asked the incredulous Hungarians. "To find the enemy tanks," replied a soldier. These were the "crazies," who spread death like a plague.[49] The Hungarians moved up at once into the hills, from which they soon heard fire from the *Panzerfäuste*, followed by a heavy barrage from the enemy tanks, then silence. They waited patiently, but no Americans materialized to accept their surrender.

Two days later a Piper Cub with a white star flew over. It swooped down, and the observer threw out a paper weighted with a pistol bullet: "Are you Russian?" In the meadow they formed, in capital letters, the word "HUNGARY." The next message read: "March to Eferding." This miffed the Hungarian

---

47. Pintér interview.
48. Tabak, 257.
49. Tabak interview.

commander: "Gentlemen, I don't like his tone. We will go anywhere except Eferding. We must surrender to more polite Americans." They filed along a road until nightfall. A sergeant named Huso made first contact with the Americans. He had slipped away in the confusion, found an American tank, and returned to the group riding on the tank and drinking whiskey with the crew. On the next morning four soldiers in a jeep from General Mark Clark's army arrived and told the Hungarians to lay down their arms. They had none. The Americans then herded them to Eferding. At every village they saw men hanged from trees—executed Nazi Party leaders—and each man became apprehensive about his own status. In the market square of Eferding an American soldier with a bucket of white paint was smearing on walls and fences "ALL IS KAPUT." No one seemed prepared to accept their surrender. Finally an American officer stood on a truck and told them they were now POWs, but they would have to fend for themselves and must not stray beyond a radius of five kilometers. At this the Hungarians gave a great cheer. Some wept; others sang the Hungarian anthem. In a rush of enthusiasm many volunteered to join the American air force, for they did not doubt that America would eventually go to war against the Bolsheviks. The offer was rejected, but they were promised transportation back to Hungary after conditions stabilized.

Roaming the region were marauding gangs of SS killing POWs. The American officer told them they must organize their own resistance. "But we have no guns," explained the Magyar commander. The next day an American truck dumped a pile of guns in their bivouac, and they were told to help themselves. Arming POWs? The Hungarians were shocked at such unmilitary behavior. It was a telling introduction to those queer creatures known as Americans.[50]

At Eferding the war officially came to an end for the Royal Hungarian Air Force. They had compiled a record they could point to with pride. Since moving from the Russian front in 1943, they had accounted for the destruction of 110 Liberators or Fortresses, 36 Lightnings or Mustangs, and 218 miscellaneous Soviet aircraft, with loss of 100 aircraft and 39 dead airmen. Their total score for the war was 454 victories against 68 men lost.[51] It was an impressive showing for a combat organization without legal existence until 1938.[52]

50. Pintér interview.
51. Musciano, 44.
52. On August 22, 1938, representatives of the Little Entente and Hungary had signed a treaty at Bled (Yugoslavia) granting Hungary's "right" to acquire parity in armaments.

They knew they had lost the war. What they could not have imagined was that they were about to lose the peace. For all too many of them their travail and trouble were only beginning.

Flying Home

The Hungarian fliers collected by the United States Army in Austria had few complaints about their captors other than ambiguity concerning their status: they were never entirely sure whether they were bona fide prisoners of war (they did not even agree on whether they had been so informed), but all spoke favorably of their treatment, and none underwent political interrogation. At this time the Americans were so burdened by the great masses of German prisoners, which had to be screened for Nazi war criminals, that they let the Hungarians fend for themselves. American soldiers seemed to have only vague notions about the location of Hungary on a map of Europe, and great numbers of them expressed surprise when they learned that little Hungary had once declared war on the mighty United States. But none of them ever implied that the Royal Hungarian Air Force had been mixed up in persecuting or torturing Jews or any other group. The "prison" camps harboring the fliers were laughable enclosures of slack and broken wire that could easily be stepped on or over in order to gain "freedom" on the far side. By the end of the summer of 1945 the airmen were free to return to Hungary. American political advisers warned them of what they already knew—that Russians occupied their country and would not welcome the return of Horthy's "fascist" pilots, many of whom had shot down Soviet airplanes.

There was no accounting for the mercurial behavior of postwar Hungarian officialdom toward the returning fliers. Some were ignored, others actively persecuted. Much depended on the whim of a tribunal or the passion of a prosecutor. Armed with a document from the Americans certifying that he was not a prisoner of war, Lieutenant Tibor Murányi set off with some enlisted men in early September on a four-day journey aboard military trucks, horse carts, and perforated rolling stock. In Budapest he reported at once to the Ministry of Defense, where his identity papers were stamped with an incriminating phrase—"Western Officer." Hopes that he might fly again under the new regime were permanently dashed. He spent his next eight years as an unskilled laborer, moving from job to job, often paid at an illegal lower rate because the boss knew that a former Horthy officer would not dare turn him in. The provisos and makeshift machinery of the "class revolution" in Hungary did not extend to protecting the rights of "fascists." He married in 1949 and fathered three children. Fortunately his wife had a council flat in Kós Károly Square, a parklike enclosure in Kispest.[53] His luck changed in 1953 when he found a job at the National Bank as a chauffeur. At the bank was a network of former fliers who maintained the old brotherhood of the air and looked after one another. He was assigned other menial chores, like repairing coin-sorting machines. He retired in 1982. Curiously, he was never deprived of his reserve rank as a lieutenant of the air force, though he would never have been allowed to make use of it. In 1989 Lieutenant Murányi got a chance to fly in a private plane at Ferihegy Airport and took the controls briefly. On landing, the pilot asked him when he had last flown. "Forty-five years ago, in April 1945, in a Messerschmitt 109." The pilot was not impressed. "I think you need some practice."

Captain Jenő Murányi debated about returning to Hungary, because he knew that as a former squadron leader of the Pumas he would be a marked man in a country run by the Soviets. He liked the Americans, who gave him complete freedom to do whatever he liked and gave him a garage job at a base in Austria. But in December 1947 he threw in with 1,500 other Hungarian refugees and POWs and set off by train for Budapest. The Americans arranged for stoves in the freight cars, gave them blankets and enough food for two weeks, and supplied them with American guards. Three days later, in Kaposvár, after the guards had returned to Austria, the train was boarded by Hungarian soldiers and police, who stole everything—even the stovepipes. The authorities refused to supply a locomotive to pull them to Budapest. They had to bribe some railway officers to get permission to ride to the capital on open flatcars. It was a brutal December, but none of them froze.

Captain Murányi arrived at the worst possible time, for the Communist Party was about to consolidate its control on the government. A committee examined him for war crimes and came up with nothing, but he was permitted to work only at manual labor. For a year he drove a tractor on a collective farm. He felt fortunate, because his brother, a former infantry officer, had spent nine months in Vác prison and now drove a horse cart delivering soda water. He moved on to a job as a technician in an ice factory. His hopes rose in 1949 when he received a letter from a Soviet airplane

53. Many Red Army families were billeted in Kós Károly Square after the war. When ordered back to the Soviet Union in the early 1950s, the Russian wives wept and raged at their misfortune. Interviews with Tibor Murányi and Gyula Farkas.

company that was expanding its operations in Hungary and invited him for an interview. A Russian flying officer tested his flying skills and hired him. As a favor Murányi taught him the rudiments of navigation (the Russian had never heard of flying by sine and cosine).

When Hungary entered its Titophobic phase, anyone who had ever had connections with the West came under suspicion. Some pilots of the new Communist-dominated air force were dismissed because of their penchant for wearing white gloves, regarded as a petit bourgeois mannerism. Official paranoia intensified when a few pilots flew beyond the Iron Curtain and defected. In 1956, after the Russian invasion, Captain Murányi was fired. Thereafter he went back to a succession of construction jobs. When the political noose in Hungary loosened in the late 1980s, it was too late for the captain, overaged and long retired.[54]

A Hungarian air force commander once said of Lieutenant Kálmán Wittinger, "If there were a box of soda and slightest hope of flying it, Wittinger would get it off the ground." It was always perfectly clear to anyone who knew him that he was always floating high in the air, miles above sordid battles waged on the fields of politics. So intense was his passion for airplanes that one can imagine him flying for both sides, on alternate days, in order to log more solo time in the air. Wittinger is probably the only Hungarian who ever piloted an American plane while still officially a POW. In Bavaria, during the summer of 1945, he hung about the American airfields, volunteered to teach a course in boxing (a sport he had coached before the war), and pounded the piano for off-duty GIs. His reward came when he strapped himself into a Piper Cub (with a mechanic in the seat behind) and flew for half an hour, happily buzzing and waving to nearby camps of Hungarians.

The Americans offered to repatriate Wittinger during the fall of 1945, but warned that it would be safer for him to take German citizenship. He was unusual among Hungarian fliers in having his wife and family with him—his son having been born on the refugee train from Hungary—and the offer was tempting. But he had his heart set on becoming a professional flier in his own country, so in October he returned by train. Inflation was exploding, and skilled positions for former Horthy officers were nonexistent. The first month he worked as a car mechanic at a wage that bought half a liter of milk and a croissant per day. By early 1946 Ferihegy airfield had been cleaned up, and he was invited to apply for a position as a commercial pilot. A lawyer on the screening committee asked if he had ever taken part in aerial fights against

---

54. Jenő Murányi interview.

Soviet airmen. Wittinger allowed that he had. "Why did you do this?" asked the lawyer. "Because I had orders," replied Wittinger. "Why did you not take your plane and escape to the Soviet Union?" continued the Communist spokesman. "Because I had no such orders," said Wittinger. The committee hired him.

During the following six years Wittinger flew a variety of makeshift craft as Hungary laboriously fabricated a national airline. He seemed to be immune from the travel restrictions plaguing most Hungarians. He flew to London, Venice, Stockholm. Every time a new type of airplane landed at Ferihegy, Wittinger showed up to invite himself for a ride and was usually able to talk the pilot into giving him the controls. This freedom came bluntly to an end in 1951, when the Cold War neurosis festered at its worst. He was called before a board convened by authority of the Communist Party. They probed his connections with the Horthy government, his exposure to the Americans as a POW, and his flights to capitalist countries. Always they demanded to know *why* he had voluntarily served the Horthy government. At the end of the interrogation, when it had become apparent that he would be terminated from the air service—or worse—Wittinger could not hold back his contempt for the tribunal. Alluding to the (little-discussed) fact that Arrow Cross members had flooded the ranks of the Communist Party after the war, he said, "Perhaps some of you gentlemen served the previous regime more enthusiastically than I, because I was only a flier." Back he went to odd jobs for the next six years. Yet no one who knew him ever doubted that somehow, somewhere, Wittinger would return to flying again.

In 1957 he obtained permission to train sports fliers, and when the political climate again cooled, he became involved in organizing an emergency health service for rural Hungary. (The following year he tried to introduce helicopters as aerial ambulances, as the Americans had done in Korea, but this idea was too progressive for its time.) Kálmán Wittinger was back again in the air, and he stayed there until his retirement in 1976 from the Hungarian Air Security Authority, where he specialized in analyzing the causes of accidents. He calculated that he had flown 124 different types of airplanes. Asked which was his favorite, he replied, "All of them." Then he added a little wistfully, "Nowadays I dislike to fly, because the next day I am so unhappy. I feel like a small boy licking the jam jar from the outside."[55]

The Americans tried to dissuade Lieutenant Gyula Pintér from returning to Hungary, but when he and others insisted on going, the Americans obligingly attached a guard team to their train to protect them from improper seizure.

---

55. Wittinger interview.

However, at Komáron, when the guards had to leave them, they were taken to a barracks and interrogated by a people's tribunal. "The questions were so simple-minded that at first we wanted to laugh: 'How did you dare shoot at Russian airplanes?' and 'Why didn't you go over to the Russian air force?'" They expected prison or worse but were finally dismissed and told to go home as best they could. Pintér lived at Adony, a Danube town south of Budapest. During the final months of the war he had married his childhood sweetheart, who had been evacuated to Austria with him and had returned home earlier. Local committees formed to root out suspected "fascists" saw to it that Pintér was unemployable in his town, but because his father-in-law owned the local mill, his family initially suffered little inconvenience.

When the Communists took control of the government after 1948, Pintér's condition became precarious. The mill was nationalized, which dropped his father-in-law into a deep depression that ended with his death soon afterward. The worst was yet to come. In 1951 Hungary underwent a phase of ideological cleansing known as the "conceptual trials." By this time Pintér was working as a construction engineer in the factory city of Dunaújváros. He was arrested and accused of conspiring to overthrow the regime. Party goons made him stand against a wall for thirty-six hours and demanded names of his fellow conspirators—none of whom existed.[56] When released, he was placed under police observation and had to report twice a week at odd times designed to interrupt his working hours. He lost his job, and thereafter no employer dared hire him—a major facet of the punishment. The strain told upon his wife, who within two years died of an overdose of sleeping pills at age twenty-six, leaving three children, the oldest only six. The surveillance lasted for six years, until in a major police amalgamation his ÁVH file vanished in a party shakeup. When the police betrayed puzzlement at his continuing to turn up at their station, Pintér realized what had happened. By the 1960s the world of Miklós Horthy lay in the distant past. Pintér entered the technological university in Budapest, took his degree in 1970, and made a strong marriage. On vacation in Austria in 1989 he went up in a sports plane for the first time since the war, but compared with a Messerschmitt 109, it was nothing but a carnival ride.[57]

---

56. The "wall torture" was favored by the ÁVO/ÁVH because it left no telltale marks. Since the victim was not allowed to move his head, the torture could cause "wall blindness" and psychological derangement. After a few hours ankles were likely to swell up to double their normal size and turn black. István Fehérváry, *The Long Road to Revolution: The Hungarian Gulag, 1945–1956* (Santa Fe, 1989), 72–73.

57. Pintér interview.

True to form, Lieutenant Tibor Tabak fidgeted in the lethargic comforts of the American POW camp. His capacity for solving simple problems through complex maneuvers had not left him. Delays in obtaining clearance for transportation back to Hungary were driving him to frantic impatience. So early in September he joined two others and jumped a freight bound for Graz. They had no papers, but an American sentry passed them through to the British zone of occupation when Tabak flashed an old Boy Scout ID. British MPs later picked them up and locked them in a toilet. But they simply removed the window and kept moving east. Another British patrol brought them to a halt by firing shots over their heads. When the MP officer found that they were going east, not west, he put his pistol to his head and tapped his skull, saying, "Are you crazy?" But he let them go. Dodging Hungarian border guards and Russian patrols, they reached Budapest on September 25. Tabak's fiancée fainted when she saw his face, disfigured since his crash in April, but she married him two weeks later. In defiance of the Russian occupation, Tabak insisted on being married in his Hungarian Royal Air Force uniform, probably because it was strictly forbidden.[58]

He worked as a manual laborer at the Ganz factory on Csepel Island for a short time, until his foreman discovered who he was—"a fascist, a Westerner, a Horthy officer"—and summarily fired him. He found a clerical post in the Meteorological Institute, which paid 140 forints per week, and he cut wood in the evenings for cash. During the summer of 1946, chased by guards and dogs, he stole corn and potatoes from farmers. Although his wife came from a wealthy merchant family, that part of the family business not destroyed during the war was gobbled up under the banner of nationalization. For three years he lived with his wife and baby on the porch of a house in the Thirteenth District.

As the Cold War drifted toward a projected shooting stage in the late 1940s, Hungary stood in dire need of pilot instructors. Tabak applied, was accepted, and to his great joy was dispatched to a flying school at Kecskemét. However, former Horthy fliers were never trusted. They were bled for what they knew, but wore a uniform different from that of the pilots whose pre-flight instruction had included massive injections of Marx and Lenin. The badge of distinction prized by Communist fliers was a helmet lined with genuine rabbit fur.

58. Tabak interview. Displaying military uniforms, badges, regalia, or insignia of the Horthy and Szálasi eras was prohibited by law during the entire period of Communist domination. Not even flea-market vendors dared display or sell such materials.

Then came 1951, when Tabak was placed under arrest and interrogated along with other Horthy pilots. The authorities accused him of being a CIA agent. He received beatings and starvation fare and was kept under lights so bright that sleep was impossible. From time to time he was taken to a cellar, and guards pointed out the exact spot where they would shoot him. If he signed a paper confessing that he was a foreign agent, he would not be hanged. This was only one of many psychological tricks used to break him down. For example, they also informed him that his wife had been imprisoned and his son placed in an orphanage. (Neither was true.) After sixty-four days of this treatment Tabak signed a confession that he had "taken part in an armed coup against the People's Republic of Hungary." This done, they brought him a lavish meal, as he said in interview, "complete with salad!" as if he were a dog that had performed a difficult trick. Two days later he went before a tribunal. He had no defense counsel. His sentence was ten years at hard labor. Ironically, this constituted a bit of luck, for another Horthy pilot, Lajos Tóth, the number two Hungarian ace, had been hanged.

Tabak was assigned to a forced-labor camp near Dorog, a coal-mining community north of Budapest. Digging coal from a kneeling position destroyed his knees. As punishment he was given half rations per day, with one day of fasting per week. Troublesome prisoners had to carry a twenty-five-kilo sewage pot. If any liquid spilled, the guards made the man kneel and lick it up. For the first three years he had no contact with his family. His wife had no idea where he was, if indeed he had not been executed. Her lawyer advised her to apply for a divorce in order to find out if he was still alive. (If he were dead, the authorities would have to reveal that divorce was unnecessary.) In this way she found out that he was in Dorog, but at the cost of Tabak's mental anguish because he thought that she was really applying for a divorce and had found another man. Beginning in December of 1953 she was allowed to visit him for ten-minute sessions in which they were separated by a one-meter gap between two screens. A year later they gave her permission to send him two-kilogram packets of bread, grease, and sugar.

During his five years in prison Tabak never heard his name used. He was a nonperson known only as 477B4429, with the last two numbers as nickname. He gave up counting days or months. Finally, in July 1956, he was brought before a tribunal, which offered him cigarettes and invited him to sit down. He quailed because it was customary in prison to be invited to accept something and then be beaten on acceptance. They asked why he was in prison, and he was afraid to answer, for he had been asked this countless times, and savagely beaten if his answer was not what the guards wanted.

Two weeks later the warden came into his cell smiling and told him to collect his things. "We are taking you to be hanged." This was the warden's private way of telling a man he would be freed. A political commissar warned him that he would only have partial freedom; he would have to prove that he was worthy of citizenship in the Hungarian People's Republic. The next day he got the clothes he had surrendered five years before, except for the shoes, which had been stolen. The bailiff gave him two right-foot shoes from stock at hand, but Tabak put them on without a word of complaint. A few hours later he climbed out of a truck in Budapest and was free.[59] His wife found him a job at a printing office pouring lead into linotype machines. His seven-year-old son had suffered major psychological damage because of his father's ordeal. Teachers had regularly pointed him out, announcing, "Look at him carefully. His father is a fascist." The child had been beaten because he was left-handed. In Hungary left was right, except in manual dexterity.

Tabak was arrested two more times, for violating parole, but in the early 1960s a military court released him and dismissed all charges against him for "lack of proof." This was just the lever Tabak knew how to use. When the power of the Communists began to decay during the 1980s, he brought suit against the military department of the Ministry of Justice. He argued that since he was guilty of no crime and had never been court-martialed, the people's republic owed him fifty-four months back pay for his time in prison. Although Parliament has since acknowledged such claims to be legitimate, no bureaucrat has been willing to take responsibility for opening a floodgate that could bankrupt the country. In 1989 Tabak published *Pumák földön-égen* (Pumas on the ground and in the air), a book about the Royal Hungarian Air Force that was well received and that has encouraged other victims of the Communist scourge to come forth with their stories.[60] Now, as president of the Veteran Fliers Association, he has been feted and honored by a growing body of Hungarians whose historical curiosity predates 1945.

59. When asked of his years in Communist prisons, Tabak replied, "Read Koestler's *Darkness at Noon*. It's all there."

60. Tabak wrote the manuscript twenty years before but allowed it to circulate only among friends. In 1988 a sympathetic publisher expressed a desire to publish it. At first afraid of retribution, Tabak agreed provided that a top Communist somewhere give it clearance. The head of the military academy reviewed it and asked for a change of only one detail—that Hungarian peasants were frightened of Russian troops. Tabak refused, and the book was published as he had written it.

4 | Players

Volksdeutsche

The attitude of Magyars toward Germans has always consisted of roughly equal parts of awe and irritation. Maria Theresa and other Hapsburg leaders admired the German work ethic and encouraged them to settle in Hungary. Large numbers of Swabians, uprooted by increased population density and diminished economic opportunities at home, brought labor skills and mercantile expertise to a country that had been predominantly agrarian. While the Swabians contributed to the national wealth of the nation, great numbers resisted assimilation. (In popular speech "Swabian" lost its original meaning and became the popular word for any member of the German minority in Hungary.) Large numbers of them tended to cluster in colonies that upheld German customs, kept German as their first language, and remained detached from events in their adopted country. Among these groups there grew a common belief, only thinly disguised, that the German stock was fashioned from a clay superior to the Magyar. Because of their astonishing financial success, in business and in agriculture, many Swabians felt superior to the poorer Hungarians of the laboring classes, regarding their lack of education and their poverty as indicative of defects in the Magyar character. At the same time, they resented bitterly the social pretensions and the political power of the Hungarian aristocracy.

Although a conservative minority of Legitimists continued to call for Charles IV to regain the Hungarian throne, restoration of the Hapsburg monarchy was never a serious issue during the period between the wars. What was very serious, however, was an alarming infatuation with the goals of Adolf Hitler, particularly among the Volksdeutsche. Numbering half a million in the 1930s, they were the largest and potentially the most dangerous ethnic minority in Hungary. They formed a disputatious faction attentive to the pan-Germanic propaganda associated with the rise of Hitler, who held to the principle that any native German speaker, whether within or outside the Reich, owed him allegiance as leader of the German people. This idea conflicted with Hungarian law, which required that anyone with Hungarian citizenship owed allegiance to the Hungarian state.

During the early 1930s the *Auslandsdeutschtum* movement collided head-on with militant Hungarian nationalism. Swabians were not allowed to form their own political party. Funds were withdrawn from German-language schools, and Germans were expected to magyarize their surnames. When conservatives learned that a prominent spokesman of the Volksbund had accepted funds from the German Foreign Office, he was denounced as a traitor and a danger, despite the fact that the funds went only for a youth hostel and a library. Alarmists noted that as early as the Easter vacation of 1933, German students attending the Passion Play at Budaörs, a suburb of Budapest, proudly wore brown shirts, displayed swastikas on their button-holes, and proselytized for National Socialism in Swabian villages.[1]

After the *Anschluß*, German nationalism became more vociferous among the Swabians. During summers ubiquitous German students distributed illegal literature, contrasted the prosperity of the Reich with the economic backwardness of Hungary, and explained how the country was being destroyed by Jewish domination of the professions. The result was that Swabians began to look toward Germany for vindication of their rights and for political equality. Their hand was strengthened when Hitler returned Hungarian territory and population with the two Vienna awards. These annexed lands contained nearly two hundred thousand more Volksdeutsche, who owed their liberation to Germany, not to Hungary. The Swabians gradually won important concessions from the government, such as the right to use their language in public meetings and in the press and to have schools in which the first language was German. Males of draft age were allowed to choose between the Honvédség and one of the newly organized Hungarian Waffen SS divisions, and an overwhelming number chose the latter. The government tried to save face by proclaiming that these Volksdeutsche recruits had automatically lost their Hungarian citizenship and that Germany was obliged to pay their family allowances. (After the German occupation in 1944 their citizenship was restored, and the Hungarian minister of finance

---

1. Eugene Lévai, *The Black Book on Martyrdom of Hungarian Jewry* (Zurich, 1948), 15.

secretly agreed to meet their family obligations.)[2] The upshot was that gradually the Volksdeutsche began to think of themselves as Germans first and
Hungarians second.

It was evident to everyone that this liberalization of laws treating the
Volksdeutsche owed more to German military power than to a sudden surge
of tolerance among parliamentarians. It was not coincidental that Hungary
signed the Tripartite Pact in the fall of 1940 after Germans had overrun
France and the Low Countries. Hungary was sliding into a satellite role with
regard to the Third Reich, and many Volksdeutsche looked forward to the
day when Hitler would do with Hungary what he had done with Austria.[3]
Emboldened by Hitler's success, Swabians proceeded to organize paramilitary
organizations, to flaunt their German language and customs, and openly to
fly the swastika and to use the Nazi salute.[4] In January 1941 their Volksbund
went so far as to proclaim that only one form of National Socialism was
legitimate—that of the Nazi Party, not the Arrow Cross.[5]

To the northwest and west of Budapest lie a number of prosperous villages
settled by Swabians invited to the region by Maria Theresa in the early
seventeenth century to fill a population vacuum resulting from the expulsion
of the Turks. Then, as now, these villages and their streets had dual place
names, but during the thirties the German name was not officially acknowledged. The wealth of the region lay in its crops, livestock, vineyards, and
wine cellars. The inhabitants were provincial and liked it that way. Largely
self-sufficient and aloof, they distrusted Hungarians and did what they could
to minimize contacts with the central government.

The largest Swabian village in the region was Solymár, where Erzsébet
Ökeli, an innkeeper's daughter, was born in 1925. Her father spoke Hungarian

2. C. A. Macartney, *October Fifteenth: A History of Modern Hungary* (Edinburgh, 1956),
2:96.

3. The Honvédség was thoroughly supportive of German military objectives. General
Henrik Werth, its chief of staff, who listed himself as German in the 1941 census, consistently
supported the Reich. Ibid., 1:274.

4. After Munich, Hitler *Jugend* took to the streets in western Hungary. There was a public
outcry in Sopron when marchers spat on the flag of Hungary as they passed a war memorial.
University students demanded—and received—both a verbal and printed apology, after which
the *Jugend* had a less visible presence in the city. Interview with Piroska Hegedüs (March 23,
1996).

5. An amusing aftermath followed this initial enthusiasm. When a rumor spread that the
Volksdeutsche would be repatriated to Germany and sent to fight the Russians, many speedily
remagyarized their names or thumbed through genealogical charts to prove they were of French
descent. Macartney, 1:456.

only when he had to, her grandparents not at all. The German language was forbidden at the local school until her third grade, after which the authorities permitted two hours per week as evidence of the governmental "tolerance" of minorities. Only children with Magyar or magyarized names attended these schools. Once children left school, they could as well have been in Bavaria. Looking back on her childhood, Erszébet evokes a rural paradise of well-manicured farms, sleek horses, fat pigs. In this Roman Catholic village there were poor people but no desperate poverty as existed in the cities. Each morning the men departed in horse-drawn vehicles—gasoline engines were a novelty—to tend their acres in a rich alluvial plain surrounding the village, and they returned at sundown. During harvest time the women and children collected broad wooden pitchforks and joined the men in fluffing hay so it would dry. In the evening farmers collected in her father's inn, the cultural center of the village. They debated the issue of the Volksbund and the growing dissatisfaction of the German minority. The wealthier classes, along with younger hotheads, followed the military campaigns of the Third Reich eagerly. Erzsébet's father, as spokesman for working-class Swabians, opposed the Volksbund platform because he believed that nationalism led to trouble—particularly for those without the money or the influence to escape it. Only about twenty families in Solymár joined the Volksbund, all of them of the wealthy class that possessed what passed for power in village affairs.[6]

After the German offensive stalled in Russia in 1942, the Reich government began to apply pressure on Horthy to supply soldiers. Few eligible males in Solymár rushed to defend the Hungarian colors. Waffen SS divisions were being formed in the country, but service in them required surrendering one's Hungarian citizenship—which was folly to do. After some hard bargaining with the Horthy government, in May 1943 the Germans gained the right to establish a protectorate over the Volksdeutsche population, which consisted of all who registered German as their mother tongue in the 1941 census. Volksdeutsche males between eighteen and sixty-two could choose to join either the Waffen SS or the Honvédség; if the former, they would no longer have to give up their Hungarian citizenship.

In August 1944, when the Axis was in pell-mell retreat in Russia and in France, the local Volksbund authorities cleaned whole Solymár streets of their young men. Erzsébet Ökeli recounted the occasion: "It was a disgrace. Members of the council took poor boys from sixteen up and exempted the sons of rich people. My brother and all the young boys of Madách Street

---

6. Interview with Erzsébet Ökeli (April 29, 1990).

were put in the SS and went off. Only five out of one hundred and fifty ever came back here." Townspeople received a few letters from Brno, in Bohemia, where the young men received training before being hurled into battle in Belgium. (The SS command did not employ them in defending Hungary, which at this time was being swept with waves of the Red Army, because they knew that the opportunities for desertion were too great.) Her brother simply vanished in one of the battles on the western front—the Red Cross could not say which one.

Meanwhile the women of the village carried on. Because the nearby railway line to Vienna was a major target for American bombers, they listened each morning to the ten o'clock report, which announced whether airplane spotters in Yugoslavia had detected bombers moving north. If so, they went to shelters. If American—or, later, Russian—pilots saw anyone moving in a field, they would strafe. Sometimes they shot up hayricks for fun. When the Szálasi government took over in October, a group of Arrow Cross came from Budapest and tried to recruit members in her father's inn. Her father threw them out. One advantage of the German occupation was that the Swabians could openly show their contempt for the despised Nyilas.

After the siege of Budapest commenced, the German army occupied Solymár in force. There were no problems. The soldiers supplied manpower drained away by the Volksbund draft. They chopped wood, assisted with the harvest, and were treated like pets by the townspeople but not taken to bed— at least there were no babies. On Christmas Eve the German soldiers prepared a huge Christmas tree for the villagers, who reciprocated with a great feast. A soldier showed Erzsébet pictures of his family and wrote out his name for her—Adolf Hermann Rheinfluss. (She could never find out if Rheinfluss was his family name or his home village.) Another, who had been through Stalingrad and now was facing the prospect of the siege of Budapest, announced, "I seem always to spend Christmas in a ring." The next day both wound up among the dead when the Russians took the town. The Russians set up a "Stalin organ" (a twelve-missile rocket launcher) in the square and bombarded Várhegy (Castle Hill) in Budapest. Later, when the SS broke out of the castle and attempted to flee to the west, some of them came through Solymár and briefly drove the Russians out. The villagers fed them and gave them civilian clothes to assist in their escape. But most of the Germans were captured and killed on the roads. Those not dead when the Russians reoccupied the town were hustled into kitchen gardens and shot. They became local heroes, and the villagers buried them in the village graveyard. Once a year Erzsébet places flowers on a gravestone marked "Adolf Rheinfluss."

Erzsébet remembered the brief Russian occupation of Solymár as the most terrifying period of her life. They knocked at walls; if hollow, they tore them down, looking for valuables. (There was method in their destruction, for that is exactly where the villagers hid their silverware, clothes, and linen.) The Russians seemed to have a mania for collecting watches, which they exhibited on their arms like ticking bracelets. At night they prowled the village looking for women. They were loaded with lice and encrusted with scabies. On the day they arrived in the village, they carefully examined her father's inn, called her bourgeois, and left. That night they came back for her. Pursued by drunken soldiers, she fled to her aunt's house, where she joined a neighbor lady sitting in a cupboard with sacks of live chickens. The chickens were dazed and did not squawk as the Russians searched the house. As long as they were in Solymár, Erzsébet slept in her clothes and shoes, prepared to run off if any Russian invaded her house. In their cumbersome boots the Russians were slower than she was, an advantage that worked to her favor, provided she was not cornered. At night she could hear women screaming, "Captain! Captain!" because, officially, rape was a criminal offense in the Red Army and officers were supposed to protect women. Rape was so common that even while the Russians still occupied the region, doctors set up special clinics to inspect the women for disease and pregnancy. Months later there were sixty abortions performed on Solymár women at the Margit Hospital in Óbuda.[7]

A troop of Mongolian horsemen arrived in town one afternoon, got roaring drunk, and vowed they would ferret out every woman in the village. By the way they handled their horses Erzsébet knew these men were extremely dangerous. That night Erzsébet and six other girls hid in a cellar. They had heaped firewood in the doorway to hide themselves, but the troopers found them and exclaimed that if they did not come out, the troopers would burn down the house. Erzsébet had been resting her feet, but when she heard those voices, she made a panic-stricken escape out a back window. Barefoot, her feet sinking into deep drifts of snow, she was unable to run fast. The horsemen galloped all about her in the darkness, whooping and chopping with sabers, threatening to run her down. She crawled into another cellar and sat huddled and shaking till morning, when the Russians usually fell into a drunken stupor.

Women went to great lengths to appear repulsive to men. Cosmetology went into reverse. They dug into ragbags for their ugliest and dirtiest clothes.

---

7. Only one woman decided to keep her child. The father, a Ukrainian, promised to return after the war, but she never heard from him again. His son still lives in Solymár.

One woman stuffed her clothes with pillows to look like a hunchback. But all this dissimulation had little effect upon the Russians, whose taste in feminine pulchritude was primitive. Besides, after a whole day spent in drinking, they were rarely in a position to distinguish a hunchback from a homegrown Venus. Generally they did not disturb women in houses where they were billeted. Such places may have softened them because they seemed like home. They were uncomplicated people, capable of revealing a pathetic side. Erzsébet's friend, Teréz Gróf, remembered a Mongol billeted with her family who ranged miserably about the house, muttering, "Voina, voina, ne dobre" (The war, the war, no good).[8]

The villagers prayed for the Germans to return as they had promised, and in February there was a counteroffensive—the last gasp of German resistance in Hungary. For a short time the Russians billeted in Solymár seemed alarmed. They seized thirty-five villagers at random, both men and women, and locked them in the schoolhouse. The captives were certain they would be shot as hostages, but they were only put on a work detail. For eight days they dug trenches and tank traps. The Germans managed to crack the Russian line in several places near Veszprém, but they did not retake Solymár. An airborne attack failed; all the German parachutists were machine-gunned before they touched the ground. They drifted down in their harnesses, their heads slack, like hanged men.

As soon as the siege of Budapest was lifted, women from the city descended on Solymár eagerly seeking food. They came on the tops of trains, in trucks, and on foot, but only the women. The men would not dare because of the danger of being picked up at random by the Russians and sent to the Soviet Union as laborers. First they offered Red Army money, which the villagers refused, then pengős, which inflation had made worthless. They slept in barns and tried to exchange needles, thread, yeast, clothes, furs, jewelry—anything they had—for food. Magyars desperately needed the Swabians, and the Swabians drove hard bargains. In Solymár secondhand goods were already glutted the market, for the Russians had arrived with suitcases crammed with loot they had stolen in Budapest—clocks, watches, silverware, clothing. When they had moved out, their officers had made them leave their plunder behind, and the villagers inherited it.

The end of the war was not the end of Erzsébet Ökeli's troubles. In 1946 the Hungarian government resolved to eliminate forever the Volksbund movement and began deporting to Austria whole villages of Swabians. Since

8. Interview with Teréz Gróf (April 29, 1990).

the Volksbund leaders at Solymár, who had conspired to send the young men to their deaths as SS soldiers, had already skipped the country during the German retreat, those villagers who had stayed behind were made responsible for young men drafted into the Waffen SS.[9] Erzsébet meanwhile had married a Hungarian soldier. In April 1946 an order came for her deportation. She and her parents were forced into a freight car bound for Germany. In the nick of time her husband arrived to free her, but he had no claim on her parents, who were deported to Karlsruhe. Erzsébet returned home to find Magyar families installed in her home. She moved into the stable attached to the house. Here she had a baby and fought off attempts by the new owners to evict her.

When the Communists tightened their grip on Hungarian internal affairs in 1947, a party functionary named Kovács commanded her to move, invoking the name of Mátyás Rákosi, the feared party secretary. He was shocked and outraged when Erzsébet burst out with "Who the hell is interested in Rákosi?" For this blasphemy she was called before a people's court in Budapest and sentenced to twelve years for "antidemocratic attitudes." Because Hungarian law protected a mother with young child from being imprisoned, she obtained a two-year stay of execution while she filed appeals. At a second hearing at Solymár in 1949 there was a noisy outburst in her favor from the crowded courtroom, people shouting that the whole court should be impeached. Kovács was so rattled by the crowd that he forgot to take the oath before giving his testimony. A short time later he returned to Budapest. Kovács had done well at Solymár, having expropriated the house and land of a Swabian and sold it back to him at a handsome profit.

In November 1949, after leaving her two-year-old with her parents (who had defied the law by returning from Germany), Erzsébet began serving her sentence at the Márianosztra prison near Szob. This place separated the criminal from the political offenders, with the harshest treatment meted out to the latter. For six months she was in solitary confinement, able to talk only when carrying out slop buckets. The three daily meals never varied—a breakfast of tea and black bread, at midday vegetable sauce, at night bread and grease. Each month she was allowed one letter and one visitation from

---

9. The handful of Hungarian-born Waffen SS soldiers who managed to straggle back to Solymár after years in Siberian prisons had a particularly grim homecoming. Their families had been deported to Germany, but they were not allowed to follow them, because the border to the West was sealed. And, of course, the family house, land, and other property had been expropriated by legal process—or just stolen. A neighbor of Erzsébet Ökeli who had been drafted into the SS in 1944 was so badly beaten by Russian and Hungarian commissars that he never regained his physical strength or mental faculties. He was not given permission to visit his parents in Germany until 1970—some twenty-five years after the war.

her husband and son. Mingling with other prisoners was forbidden. When a cruel rumor swept the prison that political criminals would be sent to Siberia, she spent her days wailing and praying. She became hysterical at night each time guards came to take her on an exercise walk. In 1950, without any warning, she received a pardon on a technicality—Kovács's omission of the oath at her second trial. A policeman escorted her to Nyugati Station in Budapest and pointed out the Solymár train. Her troubles, however, were not yet ended; for months she kept indoors, terrified that someone would report her for some bogus crime. In her village she had been branded as a political "unreliable," and people were afraid to employ her.

Hungarian law works in mysterious ways. Long before the war, Erzsébet's father had bought a farm-sized lot in the village and deeded it to her and her brother. When the party council at Solymár tried to seize it, on grounds that the brother had been a member of the hated SS, Erzsébet fought back, claiming that according to the law only property belonging to deported people could be expropriated. Because her brother was deceased and she was his next of kin, full ownership of the property rightfully redounded to her; and since her brother had been killed in Belgium, but never deported, and since she could not be deported, because her husband was a Magyar, she retained that legal claim to the property. The law upheld her claim. The party functionaries were upset, but there was nothing they could do. Erzsébet and her husband accumulated bricks and pieces of lumber and built a solid house, which they diligently enlarged over the years to accommodate their family. There was a brief setback in 1962, when local commissars succeeded in collectivizing her animals, her bakery, her farm equipment, and her land. Not until the liberalization of the regime during the 1980s did she finally recover most of what the Communists had taken from her. She was given the privilege of buying it back from the people who had stolen it. Today she lives on Madách Street in a large house with connecting stables and shops. Solymár is a prosperous town, filling up with urbanites from Budapest and, in summer, with excursionists from Germany. Erzsébet Ökeli is thoroughly weary of both, but she says there are compensations. At least there are not, as yet, any Russians.

Aristocrat

When asked about his Germanic name, Arthur Sibelka von Perleberg (born 1901) bristled as he explained that his family has lived in Budapest ever since the removal of the Turks in 1686. When it became customary—as well as politically expedient—during the 1930s to magyarize foreign-sounding names (Schneiders becoming Szabós and Müllers becoming Molnárs), his family held on to part of their patronymic. After brief service in the First World War, Arthur returned to Budapest and watched in dismay as the country foundered during the short-lived regimes of Count Mihály Károlyi and Béla Kun. It was a time of chaos, when workers' committees broke into houses to make inventories of private property, when public services, including police protection, disappeared, when mobs roamed the streets, crying, "Death to the Bourgeoisie," when Romanian soldiers camped in Parliament Square. The family fortune disappeared under the tidal wave of inflation.

Sibelka had the landed aristocrat's belief that the wealth of a country lay in its soil. He studied geography at the university under Count Pál Teleki, who became his sponsor. After a year at Clark University in Massachusetts he took a post in the Office of Statistics, and in 1932 moved to the Ministry of Agriculture, where he worked on issues of land reform. "Despite our efforts it was largely a fake movement. On paper we arranged for large holdings to be broken up and the land to be distributed to the peasants, but the courts favored the larger owners."[10] He admired Admiral Horthy ("a gentleman influenced by his soldiers, who betrayed him") but made a personal enemy of Gyula Gömbös, the fascist-oriented prime minister during the early 1930s ("an ear puller and Napoleonic type"). Sibelka, in the years ahead, would often cross swords with major politicos whose mannerisms or policies he deplored. He was always more comfortable with gentlemen of the old school, like Count István Bethlen, the conservative leader of Parliament, and Teleki, who was slightly to the left of Bethlen.

Arthur Sibelka never doubted that Hitler's Vienna awards were only promissory notes that, when paid in full, would ruin the country. Like many of the older aristocracy of Hungary he admired Englishmen—"superb gardeners and fishermen." Germans were brash and noisy. He was aghast when Hungary committed itself to the war on the side of Germany, but took comfort with the consensus—that Russia was so hopelessly primitive and Communism so foolish as an economic theory that the war would last only a few weeks. After all, Russia had been nearly whipped by Finland. "I judged Russians from reading the novels of Dostoyevski. I failed to consider that Russia had eighty million bayonets."

When the German advance choked out in the Russian steppes in 1942. Sibelka shared the surprise of his seniors in the bureaucracy. "Something was

---

10. Interview with Arthur Sibelka von Perleberg (March 3, 1989).

terribly wrong. But we were already committed and had to pay for our error." Like Horthy or Bethlen he believed honor would be lost by backing out of the alliance. By this time he had charge of fourteen departments at the Ministry of Agriculture dealing with economics and foreign trade. He had an intimate understanding of how Hitler's "gift" to Hungary was largely bogus. For example, although the Voivodina region of Yugoslavia had been officially annexed to Hungary, Germany stipulated that its grain be set aside exclusively for German use. Moreover, in order to pay off mounting war loans to German banks, the Hungarian government had promised to supply Germany with a percentage of productive quotas in grain, oil, and other raw materials. Breaking these agreements by falsifying agricultural statistics became standard practice. "Poor harvest," "flood damage," and "drought" became, for German accountants, a maddening litany repeated by the Hungarians—and little could be done about it. Germany did not have the manpower to monitor every hayrick and cabbage field in Hungary. Sibelka sat on top of these statistics, and his essays on economic subjects in *Magyar Nemesség* often cast ironic barbs at the German alliance. Meanwhile he had married and moved into a family villa on fashionable Rózsadomb Hill, with a sweeping view of the Danube River and the spiky Parliament building on Kossuth Square.

With the German occupation the country changed radically. It was not so much what the Germans actually did as what they *could* do whenever they wanted. Persecution of Jews came into the open. The residence next door, owned by a Jew, became a yellow-star house for Jewish families in Rózsadomb, and Sibelka was appointed its Magyar *házmester*. Each day he visited the forty or fifty refugees, trying to give them hope, but he had to enforce the law, which restricted them to the house except for a single two-hour period each afternoon. In late November the Szálasi government closed the yellow-star houses and removed the occupants to a huge ghetto area in Pest.[11] Sibelka assisted his neighbors in moving to the ghetto and in sealing the house, which during the siege was damaged and looted. He had nothing to do with either, but accusation would surface later, at an inopportune time.

After the Arrow Cross took control of the government in mid-October, employees at the ministry had to line up and take an oath of allegiance to

---

11. The ghetto consisted of a sawtooth arrangement of about twenty city blocks in the Seventh District, and was surrounded by a tall wooden fence with four gates—built with Jewish labor and at their expense. Consolidation of the ghetto required the evacuation of 11,935 Christians from the area, most of whom appropriated Jewish houses outside. The ghetto was in existence only seven weeks, until the Russians liberated Pest. Randolph L. Braham, *The Politics of Genocide: The Holocaust in Hungary* (New York, 1981), 850–54.

Ferenc Szálasi. It was a ceremony in which the mockery was transparent, and afterward the personnel reported to work but did nothing. The only contribution of the new minister was a gratuitous exhortation to farmers not to neglect preparation for the next year's harvest.[12] Sibelka had a grudging respect for Szálasi, who had spent years in prison under brutal conditions for his extremist views. He regarded him as a "brave but half-crazy man who thought he was appointed by God to lead the nation," but the majority of his followers were "guttersnipes." In November, as the Red Army closed on Budapest, the Germans destroyed the Danube bridges, and ferries provided the only link between Buda and Pest. Stepping off the boat one morning near Parliament Square, he saw bodies and pools of blood scattered along the embankment. When he moved closer to inspect them, a policeman turned him back. This was a favorite spot for Nyilas executions of Jews. Usually they shot their victims so that the bodies fell into the Danube, but this gang had bungled their job. At one such massacre a friend of Sibelka's father managed to swim away in the darkness and escape, helped by people farther downriver.[13]

After the Red Army liberated Pest in mid-January, they carried the battle into Buda. House-to-house fighting was heaviest in the streets lying near Castle Hill, where General Pfeiffer-Wildenbruch prepared to hold out till the end. In the Sibelka household were eight residents including Sibelka's father, mother, and wife. On Christmas Day they went into the cellar and stayed down there until the morning of January 30, when the neighborhood suddenly became ominously quiet. Three Russians in white snow coats entered their garden and called them out. They emerged with hands up. After searching the house and finding no Germans hidden away, the Russians became very polite. "Compared with what the Germans and Hungarians did in the Soviet Union, the Russians behaved well. They had suffered from hunger and cold and fright and were in an enemy country. Hostility toward us was justified." For a brief time, Sibelka thought there might be some truth in the old shibboleth "liberation." But his euphoria quickly ebbed. Hungary fell squarely back into the tyranny of the Béla Kun regime.

On February 12 some Russian officers appeared at the villa with a Hungarian-speaking Yugoslav, who announced that Arthur Sibelka was assigned to a temporary work party in Óbuda. It was a trick. "The mother tongue of a Russian is the lie," Sibelka said bitterly. He was taken across the river to the big

---

12. Macartney, 2:449.

13. Based on his personal experience, Sibelka estimated that 40 percent of the Hungarians opposed Jewish persecution; 20 percent assisted in it; and 40 percent were indifferent.

prison at Vác. The Russians needed to fill a quota of seventy thousand POWs for labor in the Soviet Union. Probably his name had been picked because he had been an overseer of a Jewish house—but the "reason" was irrelevant, for if a prisoner escaped, some local man would be shanghaied off the street or pulled from his house to meet the quota. "Vác was the low point of my life— filth, lice, scabies, degradation." Standing out sharply from the Hungarian prisoners, who had lost all cohesion, were a few German soldiers. They were a miserable, half-frozen group whose boots had been stolen by Russians, yet they stood smartly at attention in the snow and behaved like parade-ground soldiers.

A report came that Hungarians less than forty years old could be released from prison if they joined a newly formed Hungarian (Red) army recruited to fight the Germans. Sibelka, who was forty-four, lied about his age and tried to enlist but was rejected. No one of German origin was accepted. He explained he was not a German, but no one who had a name ending in "ber" or "berg" was enlisted. (This army even rejected a man whose surname was "Ember"—the Magyar word for "human.") Instead, he was transferred to Hatvan and then Jászberény, major collection points for railways to Russia by way of Romania.

When Arthur failed to return at night from his "work party," his wife set out to find him. She had had her own problems during his absence. "Eight Russians raped a woman in our shelter while Arthur was away. I had rubbed coal dust all over me, and when a Russian flashed his torch on me I pointed to my belly and said I was sick. He then left me alone. My mother said that during this ordeal I looked like a sixty-year old."[14] It took weeks to collect documentation from the ministry that would allow her to move about and ask questions of the Russian agencies. Learning he was in prison, she went at once to Vác but arrived just after he had been transferred to Hatvan. She knew what this meant—he would be taken to the Soviet Union as a slave laborer. She boarded a train full carousing Russian soldiers and reached Hatvan at nine that evening. Since there was a curfew, the police ordered her off the street. So she wandered up and down the streets, knocking on doors and asking for a place to stay, but all doors were slammed in her face. A screaming girl ran down a street pursued by two laughing soldiers. Any female out of doors was prey for the Russians. Terrified, she climbed over a garden fence and spent the night in a shed, fortified against the cold by a flask of rum. The next morning she learned her husband had been taken to

14. Interview with the wife of Arthur Sibelka von Perleberg (March 3, 1989). She conveyed this information sub rosa, while her husband was briefly out of the room.

Jászberény. There were no trains for civilians. Though Jászberény was fifteen miles away, she set out on foot. A Russian soldier driving a horse cart offered her a ride. She was afraid to accept it but also afraid not to. During the siege she had studied a Russian phrase book and told him she had one child and, pointing to herself, another on the way. "It was a lie, but I feared he might attack me. But when I climbed down from the cart, the Russian reached in his bag and gave me a hare, saying, 'Give this to your children.'"

It was Easter Sunday when she found her husband, shabby and gray in a camp of over a thousand prisoners. They made their appeal. Arthur was overage, racked with scabies, and unfit for hard labor in Siberia. A Russian officer stamped his documents, and he was free. He returned to his duties at the ministry—all the more important now if Hungary were to avert a famine. After the Communists gained control of the government in 1948, the Ministry of Agriculture waged an ideological war against the technocrats, who argued that the hope for Hungary's future lay in heavy industry. Sibelka's newspaper articles questioning the efficacy of steel factories in a country without adequate iron or coal resources came under the gun of Ernő Gerő, a powerful commissar. On July 7, 1948, he was arrested with eighty-two others in the ministry and accused of spying for Tito. Even before the indictment he was told that Mátyás Rákosi, the party secretary, had predicted that he would be the first of that number hanged. He was imprisoned for five years and his wife evicted from the family villa, which was appropriated for use by party favorites. After his release from prison he was a pariah. The Ministry of Agriculture pretended that he had never existed. Sibelka and his wife moved into a small house in Buda, where she tended a goat, chickens, and rabbits in the garden. She has no feeling of vengeance. "I got my husband back." He is less mollified. "It is very ironic. The Germans always lied to us, and we knew that. So when they told us how bad the Russians were, we didn't believe them. That time they did not lie."

Today the city of Ózd, that bleak monument to heavy industry, the darling of the postwar breed of Communists, squats like the rusted hulk of a dead battleship along the Hangony River in eastern Hungary. As it falls to pieces, it is irrefutable evidence that Arthur Sibelka knew what he was talking about.

Arrow Cross

Attila Hunfalvy is not the name of this former member of the Arrow Cross Party, but his nom de guerre is of his choosing. Even after more than four decades he is troubled when he talks about his activities during the war, although some recrudescent alter ego makes him want to speak. He considers it still dangerous to open his past to scrutiny, and the danger is not imaginary. In 1990, when he consented to an interview, it was still illegal to wear, possess, sell, or buy paraphernalia pertaining to the infamous Nyilaskeresztes Party—the Arrow Cross.[15] Although the membership once counted several hundred thousand, few former members today wish to talk about their experiences, even though in most cases they may have done nothing more onerous than sign a membership card (in most cases torn up when the Russians came to town).

Although the Arrow Cross adhered to a grandiose scheme, based on high-sounding Magyar values, that promised to restore the country to what it had been in some woolly mythocentric past, the reality was that most of its adherents were little more than terrorists in shabby green uniforms who gratified their warlike proclivities not by joining the Honvédség and fighting real Bolsheviks but by waging guerrilla war upon unarmed and terrified non-combatants—Jews, for the most part. George Konrád, a Hungarian writer who studied them during the siege, characterized them as "the trash, the ones who flunk school, who are talented only at torturing cats."[16] Feared by civilians for their mercurial explosions of violence and brutality, they were despised by honest soldiers, Hungarians and Germans alike. The fact that the Germans had agreed (without enthusiasm, to be sure) to make Szálasi the puppet head of occupied Hungary speaks volumes about the ragged condition of German judgment and morale in October 1944, as the war entered its final stage.

Attila Hunfalvy (born 1911) came from Gyula, a small city in southeastern Hungary just a few kilometers from the Romanian frontier. One of his most vivid memories dealt with the brief war with Romania, when enemy soldiers, encouraged by the Allied powers that had foisted on Hungary the hated Trianon Treaty, swarmed across the frontier like hungry locusts and gorged on cabbages and wine.[17] Gyula was among the first Hungarian cities to rally behind the nationalist ideology of Admiral Miklós Horthy, who launched his anti-Bolshevik (and always anti-Romanian) crusade from nearby Szeged in 1919. By the early 1930s Hunfalvy was living in Budapest, where he studied law until his father's death cut off his income. Robbed of a law degree, he

---

15. The official name was the Party of National Will (*Nemzeti Akarat Pártja*). Suppressed several times during the 1930s, when Szálasi was jailed, the Arrow Cross came into its own only when Regent Horthy was removed by the Germans in October 1944.

16. "The High Priest of Frivolity," *New Yorker*, March 9, 1992, 32.

17. Interview with "Attila Hunfalvy" (March 30, 1989).

switched to education and began a long career as a physical education instructor in a succession of secondary schools. He became a fervent nationalist, eager to restore to Hungary its Magyar roots, without ever being quite clear what these were. Such amorphous values made him a natural candidate for the Arrow Cross Party, although he had no appetite for the rough stuff—physical assaults upon bands of Communists or Jews. At one point he joined a special unit of five hundred men training for some far-fetched plan to rescue Horthy from Hitler. He liked to hang about the main headquarters of the party at 60 Andrássy Boulevard. When the Arrow Cross Party was banned in the late thirties for seditious activity, Hunfalvy promptly went into political dormancy, but eagerly resurfaced again in 1944 when the German occupation began. By this time he had married and had two small children.

When yellow-star houses were set up, Hunfalvy became *házmester* of a building containing two hundred families. Warned that he would be held responsible if any of them disappeared, he enforced discipline carrying an iron rod—literal, not figurative—in his hand. (He explains that the truncheon was to prevent the Jews from panicking during air raids.) He obeyed the rules rigorously, which prescribed that Jews could leave the building only between two and three in the afternoon. (It was no fault of his that most shops were closed at that time.) "Most of the Jews would have starved if Christian people had not brought them food. All their money did them little good because few merchants would sell them anything."

Hunfalvy admitted that he often raged at his Jews as he led them through the streets on water details, but he says this was only playacting so that the authorities would not suspect how gentle he really was with them. Further, he admitted that he made them pile up bricks on one side of the courtyard and carry them back and forth for hours, but this was also because he feared that any sign of leniency would result in his removal and forfeit his capacity to protect them. He credited himself with establishing in his building equitable food distribution by confiscating all supplies and providing a kind of communal kitchen. After the war Hunfalvy was accused of assisting in the deportation of Jewish children and sentenced to eight months in prison, but he claimed this was a great mistake. Some Jewish youths had been seized by gangs of Nyilas. Hunfalvy examined their transfer orders and saw that the document was undated and unsigned. But he was not armed—what could he have done to stop them? On deportation of Jews in general, Hunfalvy had this to say: "Yes, I saw them taken away to the railway stations—mostly at Ferencváros Station, but I did not know where they were going, and I had nothing to do with it."

When the Red Army pushed into Pest, Hunfalvy slipped across the Danube to his aunt's flat on Krisztina Street in Buda. Food was in short supply, and he had no money. But for any ambitious entrepreneur the mounting numbers of civilians dead of starvation or killed by shellfire presented economic opportunities. Since no coffins were available, people were rolling bodies up in wooden shutters and burying them in the snow. Hunfalvy began breaking up wardrobes and cupboards and nailing together rude coffins, which were in great demand. He set up a coffin shop on his aunt's balcony and sold them for 1,500 pengős apiece. It was about this time that his wife left him permanently.

At some point in mid-January the Russians took control of the left bank of the Danube, and the shelling of Buda began in earnest. All who remained in the building removed to the cellar, where they remained until the city was "liberated." The first Russian breaking into their shelter was a Mongolian who threatened to blow up the building. Then began three days of looting and raping. Since all these females had draped themselves in rags and smeared soot on their faces to look as old and as unappealing as possible, the soldiers (whom Hunfalvy identified as Romanians) felt their upper arms to determine their age. If the soldiers felt firm flesh there, the women were taken out to "peel potatoes." Sometimes they ravished the women in front of the men. Four soldiers would hold the woman down while a fifth would rape her. Then the others each took a turn. One thirteen-year-old could not be penetrated, so the Russian—an officer—pistol-whipped her. Hunfalvy estimates that about thirty women in this cellar were sexually assaulted. In the cellar he began the courtship of his second wife. During one Russian incursion he had to watch while a drunken Russian, unsuccessful in his attempt to rape her, concluded his courtship by beating her with a pistol and breaking her collar bone. She managed to crawl away and hide in a pile of coats, while the Russian, who was nearly drunk on his feet, tried to find her. Another soldier, who had no stomach for such brutality, saved her by telling the drunk that she had left the cellar. One of Hunfalvy's stories is about a virgin in the cellar who, after being raped by eleven soldiers, committed suicide by hanging herself at Erzsébet Bridge. (An odd place for a distraught woman to kill herself. No other chronicler of the siege has alluded to this sight, which, if it had happened, would surely have been unforgettable.)

A few weeks after the siege ended, Hunfalvy watched as a Russian soldier at Kálvin Square tried to wrench a watch off the wrist of a young girl. When she fought back, he drew a pistol and shot her. A crowd of furious civilians buzzed about him and drove him back to a wall. At this point some Cossacks on horses galloped up and dispersed the crowd. Then, after learning what had happened, they seized the soldier, took him to the foot of Ferenc József Bridge, and put a bullet in his head.

With the Russians in command throughout the city, both men and women had to join work parties clearing debris from the city. In a nearby cinema on Krisztina Street one such work party found forty horses that had died for lack of fodder, and they had to pull the stinking carcasses to the river. Thereafter they used wheelbarrows and shovels to move rubble into the Vérmező, once the riding arena for Horthy's officers, now the graveyard of smashed German and Russian tanks. (After rubble from destroyed buildings had buried the tanks completely, the city authorities later brought in topsoil, planted trees, and converted the tank graveyard into the present-day park.)

Beginning in April Hunfalvy underwent months of investigation concerning his presumed connection with the Arrow Cross. During this period he worked a sixteen-hour shift, without food or drink, with a forced-labor gang reconstructing the Southern Railway bridge. The work was not as onerous as his trepidation about what might lie in the future. One day his gang was shaken when they learned that the shift preceding them had been shipped off to the USSR to meet some quota of Hungarian prisoners. Chance alone determined who went and who stayed. To the tribunal Hunfalvy repeatedly avowed his innocence of war crimes. Most certainly they had bigger fish to fry, and so they let him go with a warning. Later he successfully filed a claim for his salary as a teacher during the time when his school had canceled classes because of the siege. By this time inflation had virtually destroyed the value of the pengő, and he received only an amount sufficient to buy stew and beer.

Whether Hunfalvy joined the Communist Party, like so many other Arrow Cross activists, he refused to say. He resumed his teaching career and was never molested by the postwar regimes that watchdogged Hungarian education. Today he is an internationalist—of sorts. "I have visited Canada, where I gave lectures that earned $180 each." He does not explain what these lectures were about. Perhaps they develop more fully some thoughts he has about the future. "Unless the USA and the USSR agree to combine," he explains, "the white race will disappear. The yellow people will take over the whole world."

Gendarme

When Ruthenia passed into Hungary's control in 1939, Ilona Kriskó (born 1920) was vacationing with her parents at Verecke Pass, near the border.

There was great excitement as the Hungarian troops marched past her boarding house to seize Ruthenia. A few days later she met Lieutenant Tihamér Kállóy, who was posted to the region as a military lawyer for the Royal Hungarian Gendarmerie, the police organization charged with control of rural populations. Kállóy was already earmarked for distinction. He came from an aristocratic family of Nagykálló (named for the family) and was a recent graduate of the Faculty of Law in Budapest. Ilona, who had just graduated from a Catholic boarding school in Eger, where she had been sedulously protected from male society, fell headlong in love with this distinguished officer ten years her senior. Her father, a wealthy landowner and erstwhile Parliament candidate from Nyirmada, a village near the Soviet frontier, gave his blessing but withheld his financial support. And since the gendarmerie prohibited its officers from marrying poor, the couple had to wait until he was promoted to major in 1942 before they could marry. By this time Hungary was at war with the Soviet Union. If Hungary were ever invaded, their district would lie in the direct path of the invaders, but no one was alarmed. "We had no fear of the Russians. In fact, we never even thought of them."[18]

The newlyweds moved to Nyiregyháza, the district capital, where Major Kállóy handled cases in which gendarmes were charged with illegal activities—ration violations and black-marketing, for the most part. For Ilona the two years in Nyiregyháza were the best years of her life. "We had a small villa, and there was a constant round of parties and dances. Why, in one year we attended thirty name-day celebrations. It was not like war at all. Rationing was not yet severe. Besides, my parents had a farm and provided us with all the food we wanted. Packages of meat, poultry, fruit, and vegetables arrived by train and were delivered personally at our door by one of my husband's policemen."

All this began to change in 1944. In late spring Jews of the city were restricted to a ghetto area consisting of specific streets ringed with wire fences. The yellow star made its appearance. Jews were divided into two classes: those listed as "B" were banished from their houses, which were taken over by the government; those in "A" were also banished, but they still nominally retained their property. The gendarmerie supervised all anti-Jewish legislation coming from Budapest. According to Ilona, her husband disapproved of what was happening to Jews. He was an officer of the law, but his authority was restricted to internal affairs of the corps. Once he was reprimanded for shaking hands with his shoemaker, who was wearing a yellow star. In early

18. Interview with Ilona Kriskó (March 3, 1990).

summer orders came for the deportations. Gendarmes in their sporty rooster-tail caps cleared the streets of bystanders and led the Jews—men, women, and children—to the train station. They were allowed to take with them whatever they could carry. A few weeks before the deportations, Ilona had been visited by a Catholic schoolmate who had just had a baby. Her husband, a mechanic, was a Jew who had converted to Catholicism some years before. Ilona was distressed to hear that the father and daughter, who were legally Jews, had been relegated to the ghetto and were scheduled for deportation, while the mother, who was Catholic, had to stay behind. The woman begged Major Kállóy to help her. He got them all reclassified, although his intervention did not go down well with his superiors, who made the usual remark that if he liked the Jews so much, maybe he should go with them. Ilona and her husband watched the sad procession of Jews pass their window. According to Ilona, Tihamér had no idea where they were going, but he did say to her, "Some day we will have to pay a great price for this."[19]

The price came due almost immediately. In early September, as Ilona was making *gombóc* for a party, Russian airplanes flew over and bombed the railroad station a mile away. The house shook, and china fell out of cupboards. After the all-clear siren her husband reported for duty in a clean white uniform; he returned dirty, bloody, and nauseated. The Russians by this time were closing fast on the mountain passes just east of the city, and the family was evacuated to Kőszeg, a city near the Austrian border. Sharing their first-class compartment on the train was a German officer who kept saying that Hungary was kaput. Ilona refused to believe him. They had never conceived that the Russians might win, and could not now.

In Kőszeg the Kállóys, with their two daughters and a nurse, again settled into a villa provided by the gendarmerie. But not for long. In January they packed up again. At the train station in Wiener Neustadt they saw a long train on a siding filled with Jews begging for water. Ilona and other bystanders collected bread for them, but the guards kept them at a distance. They tried to pitch food through the barbed wire windows.

The Kállóys moved to Bavaria, this time billeted in a crowded *Gasthaus* outside Passau. The main activity of the gendarmerie at this period seemed to be destroying incriminating records. Major Kállóy was now working under a Colonel Imre Finta, whose zeal in ferreting out political dissidents and

19. Estimates of the number of Jews from Nyiregyháza deported to Auschwitz on May 17 range from 3,500 to 5,000. The chief rabbi and the president of the Orthodox Jewish Community of the city were murdered during interrogations by gendarme officers intent upon discovering where they had concealed their valuables. Braham, 548.

rounding up Jews in Szeged had won his rapid promotion from captain. Many gendarmes took the opportunity to melt into the German civilian population during the last weeks of the war, but the Kállóys waited at their *Gasthaus* for the end. It came in May, when American soldiers arrested the major and took him off to some unidentified collecting camp. For four months Ilona searched for him. Then came a postcard from a priest, indicating that he was at the Platling camp near Degensdorf. There was nothing she and her children could do except return to eastern Hungary.

The villa and its furnishings at Nyiregyháza had been gutted by looters. She moved in with her parents, who were harassed unceasingly by the village people. "They were the lowest class of humanity. We were reported daily for anything they could dream up—an unchained dog, an empty fire barrel, rubbish in the public street. It was not just us—all the middle classes were persecuted." It became much worse as the Communist regime gained control in the following years. Before the war her father had gained his livelihood from twenty-seven acres of orchards and forty-two acres of timber and a tree nursery. He was given the choice of donating his property for nationalization or having it taken from him by a lawsuit and possibly being imprisoned as a prewar "enemy of the people." He chose to give it up and moved Budapest, where he worked at odd jobs.

When Ilona heard that her husband's boss, Colonel Finta, had been tried in Budapest and hanged as a war criminal, she feared her husband would be next, but in the fall of 1945 the major turned up, stripped of his uniform, rank, pension rights, and perks. The American and Russo-Hungarian authorities had scrutinized his connection with Finta, but he had not been charged with any crime. "He had a terrible time in that American camp. The guards sometimes made him walk on all fours. Many of the prisoners starved to death. My husband had to dig for grass and dandelions to have something to eat." His land and his Vitéz title had been taken away. The only work he was allowed to do was physical labor. He rolled up his sleeves and took a job in Miskolc as a cement worker on a construction site, while Ilona plied her needle and thread for hire. In 1959, when the political harassment began to taper off, the Kállóys moved to Budapest, where Tihamér became a book-keeper and Ilona established herself as a society dressmaker for grand ladies eager to forget the sloughs from which they had so recently risen. It was easier for her, for she was armed with a sardonic sense of humor, but the life force drained from Tihamér.

Her husband's membership in the Vitéz Rend seemed always to spark some fiber of special hatred from officials in the postwar regime. No interrogation passed without some sneering illusion to it. Thus it was not unexpected that their two daughters failed to be admitted to public secondary schools. Hungary was a People's Republic, but the children of a former gendarme were not quite people.

Diplomat

Per Anger, a young official assigned to the Swedish legation in Budapest during the war, never doubted that there were deliberate attempts to liquidate the Jews in eastern Europe. Toward the end of 1942 a Hungarian journalist just returned from the eastern front told him that he had witnessed five thousand Jews digging a mass grave before being mowed down by two German soldiers. (Afterward, in a nearby Russian village, one of the soldiers played Beethoven on the house piano.)[20] Even allowing for possible exaggeration, this horrendous story squared with other reports intercepted by the Swedish government. Yet in Hungary the violent extremes of anti-Semitism lay dormant until April 1944, when, after the German occupation of the country, the first deportations of rural Jews began. Shortly thereafter Anger visited a brickyard in Óbuda where fifteen thousand Jews, guarded by gendarmes with submachine guns, endured a week without water, food, or shelter. While he watched, a train with empty cattle cars rattled in on a spur. The doors were opened, and Jews were forced in with kicks and blows— eighty in each car. One bucket of water was handed in, and the doors were nailed shut.[21] His and other reports to Stockholm moved King Gustav V to write a personal note of protest to Admiral Horthy. By early July Eichmann's plans for liquidating the Jews of Budapest en masse had been suspended— only temporarily, it was feared—and the diplomatic missions of Sweden, Switzerland, Spain, and Portugal began to improvise measures to forestall further deportations. The Swedish legation on Gellért Hill issued Hungarian Jews a variety of certificates authorizing travel to Sweden. Such journeys, which would have required visas to cross the Third Reich, were impossible to realize, of course, but the object was to fabricate protective documents that might be mistaken by ignorant functionaries for bona fide Swedish passports. Working day and night for several months, the whole Swedish mission, including the minister, was able to issue seven hundred of these certificates.

20. Per Anger, *With Raoul Wallenberg in Budapest* (New York, 1981), 25.
21. Ibid., 42.

This was a stopgap effort only, designed to gain time until the legation staff could be increased and more effective methods could be devised.

On July 9 Raoul Wallenberg arrived in Budapest as secretary of the Swedish legation, where Per Anger briefed him on the Jewish situation. For a diplomat his kit was unusual. In his rucksack he carried a revolver—"to give myself courage—I hope I never have to use it," he explained.[22] He plunged into his work at once. With funds filtered through the American legation in Stockholm and later supplemented with donations from within Hungary, the thirty-two-year-old Wallenberg began to recruit Hungarians, most of them Jews, for an enlarged staff that eventually numbered about four hundred. From the Hungarian authorities he obtained guarantees that his staff would not be molested, nor would they be required to wear the degrading cadmium yellow Star of David. Wallenberg stepped up production of the "protective passports," now impressively printed in the blue and yellow colors of Sweden and stamped with the triple crown. The Swedes rented buildings in Pest, hung their flags from the windows, and got the Hungarian authorities to agree that these would be protected houses, where passport holders could reside while awaiting their (mythical) "emigration" to Sweden. There was no problem in obtaining buildings, for owners, realizing that the flag of Sweden might discourage Arrow Cross vandalism and looting, eagerly loaned their properties. The Swiss and the International Red Cross quickly followed the Swedes' example. Even though the government passed a decree that no Hungarian could acquire foreign citizenship after March 19, 1944 (the date of the first German occupation), and Arrow Cross gangs often raided protected houses, these diplomatic shields were successful in saving an estimated fifty thousand Jews, of which about half have been linked to Wallenberg.[23]

One Jewish woman who benefited immediately from Wallenberg's arrival was Magda Simon (born 1913), who had spent two years in Sweden with an uncle following her graduation from high school but had returned to Budapest to care for her mother. Through her Swedish contacts she easily obtained *Schutzpässe* for herself and all members of her family (even for a brother-in-law serving in a labor battalion). Eagerly welcomed by Wallenberg because of her fluency in Swedish, she joined some thirty other Hungarian Jews working full time at the embassy on *Schutzpaß* production. Within a short time Wallenberg expanded his staff to more than fifty by renting an insurance office at Kálvin Square, where his operation worked round the

22. Interview with Per Anger (October 25, 1995).
23. Anger, 59–60.

clock. By this time anyone who applied for a pass got one—no questions asked or explanations required. No fee was charged. Magda and her mother moved into an unheated Swedish protected house on Jókai Street. Because the older woman suffered from the intense cold, Magda arranged for a transfer to another house on Révai Street that was equally crowded but at least warm.[24]

Raoul Wallenberg possessed an authoritarian personality, which he used to great advantage in his rescue missions. He could be ingratiating and courtly with Hungarian officials, many of whom foresaw that the Germans would lose the war and had their eye on Sweden as a place to flee, but when dealing with Germans he stormed and shouted, knowing that they pinned their hopes for personal survival in this dying war upon a peace treaty monitored by neutral powers. One ploy for getting a Hungarian official to acknowledge a Swedish *Schutzpaβ* was to assure him that Stockholm would shortly recognize the Arrow Cross regime or, in some cases, to tantalize him with Swedish protection after the war.[25] Many Jews were saved by the oldest of all stratagems— the outright bribe. And, of course, there were humane Hungarian policemen, outraged by the persecutions, who cooperated by ignoring the letter of the law at crucial moments.

Early in December Wallenberg and Anger, hearing that large numbers of Jews were being conducted in freezing weather on a forced march toward Austria, stocked an automobile with food and drove out the Vienna road. They passed long lines of men, women, and children in deplorable condition, more dead than alive, staggering along under blows from the gendarmes' rifle butts. The road was edged with bodies. At Hegyeshalom, the border station, German SS were taking over from the gendarmes, counting the victims like cattle, meticulously signing receipts for them, and pushing them into railroad cars. They refused to allow the Swedes to distribute their stock of food. Wallenberg saved about a hundred Jews by pretending he knew them and asking to see their Swedish passports. They were mystified until he hinted that the gendarmes must have confiscated them earlier in the march. When they caught on and agreed that this was what had happened, the guards

---

24. Magda Simon interview, in *The Wallenberg Project*, a Swedish Television series aired in Budapest during 1994.

25. Per Anger has argued that it was a grave mistake that the Swedish government stubbornly refused to recognize the Arrow Cross regime, because it undermined Swedish authority in Hungary. Spain and Switzerland, having succumbed to the dictates of realpolitik and received Szálasi representatives in Madrid and Berne, were therefore in stronger positions to assist the Budapest Jewish population. Anger, 112.

succumbed to Wallenberg's demands for their release. On their way back to Budapest the Swedish officials set up arbitrary checkpoints on the road. They knew they could not halt the death march. Their object was only to slow down the procession by breaking up its momentum and cadence. Anger estimated that by these delays they might have saved about 1,500 more.[26]

Just before Christmas, as the Russians tightened their noose around Budapest, the foreign ministries were ordered to evacuate the capital. Refusing to leave, the Swedes agreed to look after the affairs of seven foreign ministries, including the German, which fled west. What followed was a game of musical chairs played to a political tune. When Arrow Cross raiders broke into the legation, attempting to root out Jewish personnel, the Swedish officials notified the SS command charged with defending the city that hooligans were violating property "unter dem Schutze des großdeutschen Reiches."[27] In one of those ironies of history, the SS promptly chased out the Arrow Cross and placed a guard at the legation, thereby rescuing the Jewish staff.

As the Russians completed their encirclement of the city, the Arrow Cross gangs lost all central cohesion and ranged the streets like rabid animals. Conditions became so chaotic that even Wallenberg lost some of his élan. On December 24 he warned his staff at Kálvin Square that they must scatter, for he could no longer protect them. Magda Simon returned to the flat at Révai Street to hide and wait for the Russians. On New Year's Day a gang of Arrow Cross hammered at the big gate of the building. When her brother, on guard at the gate, refused to open it, they shot the lock and burst in. Her brother escaped to an upper story and crossed to an adjacent building, while the other Jews were herded downstairs with orders to pile up their jewelry and clothing in the courtyard. All this while a grinning gunman brandished a grenade and threatened to toss it among them. "At this state the only feeling I had was apathy," Magda remembered, "just indifference—it is very hard to explain this to anyone nowadays." Somehow her brother found Wallenberg, who dispatched his private gendarmes to expel the gang. Although the Arrow Cross looted everything of value, no Jew in the Révai Street building was physically harmed. It was a miraculous escape, for on the same day Jews sheltered in the Jókai Street house (where Magda and her mother had originally taken refuge) were massacred, with the exception of one man who escaped through an air vent to the roof.[28]

26. Ibid., 67–68, and Anger interview.
27. Anger, 81.
28. Simon interview.

When the city came under the Russian bombardment, members of the Swedish legation had to split up and seek private quarters. This was a particularly dangerous time because the Arrow Cross held the Swedes responsible for organizing opposition to their Jewish pogrom. Anger and a few companions, including Albert Szent-Györgyi, a Nobel laureate hunted by the Germans, found a place on Castle Hill in Uri Street, barricaded the door, and waited for whatever might happen. Here they extracted an old wood stove from the house and moved it to the yard, where the owner of the house, a Hungarian baroness, "with great contempt for death," took over the chore of preparing horse goulash, undaunted by nearby shell bursts.[29]

Anger last saw Wallenberg on January 10, when the fighting on the Pest side of the river was reaching its crescendo. Wallenberg had just come from SS headquarters on Castle Hill, where he was trying to obtain guarantees that Jews in protected houses in Pest would not be massacred at the last minute. Anger urged him to stay in Buda, where the presence of the Germans checked Arrow Cross raids, but Wallenberg insisted on returning to Pest, to look after his protected houses. His last words to Anger were, "I'd never be able to go back to Stockholm without knowing inside myself I'd done all a man could do to save as many Jews as possible." None of the Swedes ever saw him again. He called briefly on the fugitives at the Révai Street house to say good-bye. He said he was on his way to negotiations in Debrecen, where a provisional pro-Soviet Hungarian government was being cobbled together. After some cheerful words he left in his Studebaker, driven by his chauffeur Vilmos Langfelder, a Jew whom he had rescued from a labor battalion months earlier.

When Castle Hill took the main brunt of Russian bombardment in mid-January, Per Anger took refuge in the cellar of a house on Rózsadomb belonging to the legation. This sector shortly became a battle zone as Russians fought their way up from the river. When German soldiers began to dig trenches in the garden, Per Anger protested the violation of extraterritorial rights. The soldiers shrugged and retorted, "Krieg ist Krieg"—adding that they cared not a damn whose garden it was. On January 29 the inmates could hear machine-gun firing in the next block, and the Germans seemed to have melted away. The Swedes, who had not dared to fly their national flag for fear of attracting Arrow Cross bands, now ran it up a pole. They also had the good sense to replace the name plate of a former tenant, one Hauptmann Klinger, with a sign, in Russian, reading "Legation of Sweden."

29. Anger, 116.

On the following morning the Hungarian janitor awakened Anger. There were soldiers in the kitchen who spoke a queer language. Anger and his companion, Ekmark, found two Russians in white parkas and armed with machine guns looking around curiously. They politely examined the inmates' identification cards—written in Russian—and left. Soon there was hammering on the door, and a score of common soldiers stalked in. They had eyed the house as a likely billet but were daunted by the Swedish passports. Their leader led Ekmark away to speak with "the general," while Anger stayed behind to watch over the house. Soon Ekmark returned with a Russian noncom. He said, "The Russians want the house, and they want a watch. Since I haven't one, you'll have to give them yours." Anger pretended not to understand, until the Russian began shouting, "Davay! Davay!" (Let's go! Let's go!), slapping his pistol holster and making ticking sounds. When Anger handed him his watch, an expensive Swiss one, the soldier beamed like a child. He went out into the street, collected a patrol, and ordered them to guard the house and not let anyone in. One month later the patrol still remained on guard outside. Anger even persuaded them to extend their protection to the Swiss legation next door. Earlier a band of Cossacks had demanded gold from the Swiss cashier. He had none and offered them a bundle of Swiss francs instead. The Cossacks, having no notion of their value, contemptuously refused the bills and vented their anger by beating the cashier and looting the building. For Per Anger the loss of a watch was a small price to pay for protection during the weeks that followed, when drunken Russians turned Rózsadomb into a "ghastly cacophony" of women's screams, burning houses, and cries of dying men.[30] There was, however, some satisfaction when news arrived that during the looting of the Swedish legation on Gellért Hill the Russians carried off the silver table service left in their custody by a former Soviet mission.

After several months of confinement under armed guard, the Swedish mission was allowed to return to Stockholm by way of the Soviet Union. On their way they passed through Moscow, never suspecting that Raoul Wallenberg was there ahead of them, confined in Lubyanka Prison. What happened to him afterward is unknown.[31] In this clandestine operation the Russians were efficient—even Wallenberg's chauffeur, Langfelder, vanished into thin air.

30. Ibid., 122–28. Ignorance played a part in the thoroughness of the protective cordon, for the NKVD officer of the district apparently confused the title of "consul" with "commissar."

31. Ibid., 89. The supposition is that Wallenberg was arrested by the Russians as a spy because of his use of American funds in carrying out his rescue missions. Moreover, the Soviet Union regarded Sweden as little better than an Axis power for having supplied the Third Reich

DP

During the 1920s Magyars were a numerical majority in the Romanian village of Csikszentkirály, tucked away in the mountains of Transylvania, but one would not have guessed that after visiting the town hall or the public schools. The Romanian government, which had taken control of this ancient Hungarian province as a result of the Trianon Treaty, was systematically trying to root out—in violation of the treaty—the Magyar language, literature, history, and customs. Ferenc Gegsi (born 1926) knew only the hard life in this crabbed mountain village. His father, a railroad man, died in 1930 and left a wife with seven children. The family had a small piece of land, kept livestock and poultry, but the yield was poor. Ferenc attended the Hungarian school until the third grade, when it closed down and its students had the choice of transferring to the Romanian school or having none at all. He felt deeply alienated at the new school and did poorly—in part because he did not speak Romanian well. He was a double outcast—both poor and Hungarian. His teacher rubbed it in: "Your mother would be a beggar if it were not for the generosity of the Romanian state. You should be grateful for what we are giving you."[32] He stayed in school three more years, then quit to become a shoemaker's apprentice. During this time the Iron Guard, the Romanian Fascist Party, terrorized the Hungarians with raids, beatings, and murders.

When Transylvania became reattached to Hungary under the Second Vienna Award, there was great jubilation in the village. On September 11, 1940, the Hungarian army arrived, ripped down Romanian flags and obliterated street signs. Thereafter the Germans were regarded as saviors. The Hungarians set up a Levente school in the village, which was designed to give boys instruction in weaponry and military drill in order that they might be mobilized as militia as the need arose. Ferenc was pleased with the school, particularly with rifle practice, which was a novelty because the Romanians had prohibited Hungarians from owning or using firearms. Twice a week from 8 A.M. to 2 P.M. he attended the school, and by law his employer had to pay him for time lost from work.

Always there were disquieting rumors about the Russian menace, yet there were few hard facts about the progress of the war. News drifted into the

---

with iron ore during the war. Swedish efforts to locate Wallenberg were shunted aside by the Russians until 1974, when Kremlin resistance softened a bit. But further progress in enlisting international involvement in the case collapsed when Henry Kissinger protested against Sweden's anti-American attitude toward the Vietnam War. Ibid., 158.

32. Interview with Ferenc Gegsi (February 2, 1990).

village about a great battle at the Don Bend, but without specific details. A few commodities were in short supply, like sugar and cloth, but the lives of the townspeople were little affected by the war. They were mainly self-sufficient in food; gasoline shortages were crises only read about in newspapers, for no one in Csikszentkirály possessed an automobile. Sometime in the summer of 1944 gendarmes came to the village and rounded up the Jews and took them away. Ferenc never knew where they went and did not bother about it. There had been only a few Jews in Csikszentkirály, and he did not know any of them personally.

Late in the summer German and Hungarian troops arrived in the village. They rounded up the citizens and made them dig trenches and tank traps on the edge of the village. Along the whole valley they built four lines of concrete pyramids and strung barbed wire. Ferenc noticed that, on duty or off, the two armies did not fraternize. The Hungarians had few motorized vehicles. Horses pulled their cannon, while the Germans used trucks. The villagers enjoyed the presence of both armies, which bought eggs and milk from them and did not molest their women. At the end of August they learned that Romania had gone over to the Russian side, but nobody worried so long as the Germans held the Carpathian line. Besides, they always talked of their secret "wonder weapon," which they could use in an emergency. "We never worried, for we believed the Germans would save us." Many of the boys with whom Ferenc had trained as a Levente were conscripted into the crack Székely regiments and marched out of town for the front. (When they met the Red Army at the Carpathian passes some of the Székely troops were armed with nothing but swords.)

Thus it came as a shock in September when the villagers detected extreme agitation among the German soldiers, who began collecting their gear and rolling out of town. They stripped the shops and local factories but did not disturb the people's houses. In one frenzied night they packed and were gone. Members of the rearguard warned the villagers that a battle was looming and that they must hide in the forest until it was over. The Gegsi family collected their two cows and four pigs, and after loading carts with food and cookpots, they moved eight kilometers into the woods. On September 11, 1944 (a day always celebrated in the village because it commemorated the anniversary of the expulsion of the Romanians), they heard gunfire on a distant road, but Ferenc spent the day searching for a lost cow. At nightfall he figured that the cow must have wandered home, and set out for the village. At his married sister's house he heard voices inside, so he banged on the door. He was met by three Russian soldiers with pistols pointed at his head. In faltering Romanian he tried to explain who he was and what he was doing, but they scoffed at his cow story. He was afraid they would think he was a soldier and would shoot him. Finally a Russian laughed, put away his pistol, and said, "Don't be afraid. We won't shoot you." They said he must take them to his campsite in the morning. Ferenc had a troubled night. If the campsite had moved, he would be shot as a spy, but if the campsite were still in the same place, the Russians would steal their animals. As it happened, some Cossacks stumbled across the camp in the morning and told the family that they could go home. Except for swapping some horses, the Cossacks stole nothing from the villagers. Ferenc even found his cow. Nevertheless, the villagers took no chances. They did not trust words like "liberation." To be on the safe side they waited until the sound of gunfire had dissipated before venturing home. "The Russians did not seem like bad people. No women in our village were raped. Some who did it willingly. . . . Well, that is a different story."

Within a few months there were worse arrivals. The Romanians swarmed back into the valley, pushing the Hungarians off their land, appropriating their livestock, looting their houses. There was no recourse to the law. Ferenc lost his job at the shoe shop and had to become a farm laborer for a Romanian boss. "My greatest fear was being drafted into the Romanian army, because sometimes they beat Magyars to death." The Romanians did not even have to pretend that the Hungarians were human beings.

In April 1947 Ferenc and two other laborers decided to break out. Travel from one village to another without written authorization was absolutely forbidden, but as itinerant farm workers they carried permits valid for travel within their district. They climbed on top of a train bound for a village closer to the Hungarian frontier. Then on foot they cut cross-country to a hamlet within striking distance of Hungary. A guide pointed out a path, six hundred meters distant, that led over a hill to the border, and he also indicated where Romanian guards hid themselves along the path and shot refugees for sport. (Only later did Romania erect watchtowers and plant minefields to prevent such escapes.) They prayed for a dark night and a heavy rainstorm and got both. The mud was so heavy they could barely move through the field; their progress so slow they lost their sense of direction. Near daybreak, in a stable, they fell into a sleep of total exhaustion without being sure whether they had crossed into Hungary. In the morning the sun shone brightly, and a woman approached from a farmhouse. She was Hungarian and told them they were lucky: the commander of the border patrol lived only two farmhouses away, and if they had landed there, he would have been obliged to deport them to Romania in chains.

"This was the happiest day of my life," Ferenc said. The three refugees rode triumphantly to Budapest in the back of a potato truck, working for the driver to pay their way. On a bright Easter Sunday morning they reached Kispest. When Ferenc jumped off the truck, his ring caught on a nail and ripped his finger off. It did not matter—he had entered the promised land. A doctor gave him a tetanus shot, wrapped a bandage around the stump, and sent him on his way. But his problems were far from over. Apprehended by the police without papers, he was ordered to leave the country within fifteen days. He went underground and obtained a job in the shop of a carpenter, performing odd jobs for a pittance and sleeping on a bench. He became involved with a woman, and they saved their money for marriage. For two years he managed to avoid detection through sheer luck and a sixth sense for spotting plainclothes police. His luck ran out when he and his fiancée, returning from a Sunday outing in the country, were caught at Keleti Station in one of the random dragnet operations of the ÁVH, the Communist Party Police. They locked him up, and over a sixteen-day period they interrogated him four times, accused him of being a spy, and roughed him up, though they broke no teeth. In the end he was saved from deportation by his fiancée, who had hounded the officials, begging for his release so that they could get married.

Forty-five years later Ferenc Gegsi still lives in a village outside Budapest. He works as a machinist, owns a fine brick house, grows most of his vegetables, and shares his life with the woman who saved him from repatriation to the country he detests.

5 | Siege

Men

The bottom dropped out of Hungarian defensive morale on August 23, 1944, when Romania defected from the Axis and offered its armies to the Soviet Union. Within a week the much-vaunted Carpathian defensive line evaporated, sixteen German divisions were cut off, and Bulgaria surrendered to the Russians. With these satellite nations out of the war it might have appeared that Horthy's task in threading his way out of the Hitler alliance would be easier, but in fact it became more difficult. As the German army fell back into Hungary—and was reinforced from Austria—the numbers of Wehrmacht and SS increased steadily until they stood at half a million men. Further, Hitler had no intention of retreating farther west than Budapest. To this end, he sent General Guderian on August 31 to assure Horthy that Hungary would be defended with as much determination as the soil of the Reich itself. This sort of "good news" was the worst news for Horthy and the pro-Allied faction. From a transmitter in the royal palace Horthy's faction was begging the Allies for support and promising cooperation with the American and British armies if they moved on Hungary, but always the Allied command responded that if they truly wished an armistice, they must negotiate solely with the Soviet Union. Hitler was well informed of these overtures, which confirmed for him that Hungarians were treacherous and had to be held in the war by force.

On October 8 Horthy finally swallowed his pride and appealed to the Kremlin for an armistice. Once the Germans learned of this impending capitulation, Edmund Veesenmayer, Hitler's spokesman in Budapest, arranged for Ferenc Szálasi to take control of the government. While neither Veesenmayer nor Hitler had much faith in Szálasi as a man or a statesman, his Arrow Cross party alone seemed wholehearted in carrying on the war.

Thus on October 15 some forty new Tiger tanks rumbled through the streets of Pest as a show of German strength and as an intimation of what might happen if the peace-mumblers incited resistance. (Hungarians were not privy to the fact that the tanks had not yet been armed.) In early afternoon of the same day, Horthy delivered a radio speech that announced the war was over, but pro-German factions immediately seized the radio stations and declared over the air that the alliance with Germany still held and the war would continue. There was no armed rising. Only a few random shots protested the total loss of Hungarian sovereignty. The regent was taken into custody by the Germans (he survived the war as a prisoner in Bavaria), while Szálasi took over the government, selected a cabinet rubber-stamped by the Germans, and declared martial law. (An edict made defeatism punishable by death, a penalty that, had it been enforced, would have surely eliminated most Hungarians.) While there was little enthusiasm for Szálasi outside the ranks of his party, the Honvédség remained committed to the anti-Bolshevik crusade. (Only several hundred in the army went over to the Russians at this stage, although uncounted thousands deserted later.) Veesenmayer feared he might have to cope with armed resistance and acts of sabotage—particularly among the working-class population. He need not have worried, for nothing of the sort occurred. The working classes in Hungary were largely apathetic and apolitical.

During the weeks that followed many of the industrial and agricultural resources of the country were stripped and carried off to the West, always with assurances that they would be returned after the Germans drove the Russians out. The estimate is that from three to eight one-hundred-axle trains carrying this booty crossed the Austrian border daily, much of it at the request of Hungarian entrepreneurs wishing to save it from Russian expropriation.[1] Autonomy for the Honvédség disappeared altogether on October 21, when Hungarian units came directly under German command. Szálasi's promise to raise fourteen new divisions came to nothing, and there would have been no uniforms or arms for them even had he raised the manpower. Only one was formed; another was cobbled together during the last weeks of the war from refugee Hungarian troops in Germany. Meanwhile the Red Army steadily advanced. They overran the Tokaj-Kecskemét line on October 8, came within

---

1. C. A. Macartney, *October Fifteenth: A History of Modern Hungary* (Edinburgh, 1956), 2:453.

sight of Pest on November 2, and reached Lake Balaton by December 7. Even Szálasi could read the writing on the wall. Bearing the new title *Nemzetvezető* (National Leader), he visited Hitler and proposed to evacuate Budapest in order to save it from destruction. Hitler refused. He was tired of Hungarians backing out of his war. In effect he abandoned the city, with its eight hundred thousand civilians and its mixed army numbering about eighty thousand men, to its own devices. Budapest was shortly to become another Stalingrad— hopelessly cut off from escape and continuing the fight because there was no other choice.[2] On December 24 at the Ritz, in a dining room without heat or electricity and garnished with broken windows, waiters wearing white cotton gloves served split-pea soup on china plates with gold rims and blue crests to a full house. (The Ritz was one of the last places in the city to serve food.) In the evening, as people carried home small Christmas trees and packages, the BBC (not Radio Budapest) brought them news that the Russians had encircled the city.[3] On the following day it began to snow.

From his earliest years as a schoolboy in landlocked Eger, István Kós (born 1924) dreamed of entering the merchant navy of Hungary, which had a fleet serving the Danube River traffic from Austria to the Black Sea, as well as a collection of vessels in the Mediterranean. After graduating from the crack Calvinist school at Debrecen in 1942, he entered the merchant-marine program run by the Danube Marine Company and went to Siófok on Lake Balaton for training. This consisted of a six-week course in sailing craft, after which Kós and his class of sixteen cadets received training in motorized shipping in the Danube. With its barges of oil and bauxite being shipped upriver to Germany, the Danube traffic was heavy, but the war itself was far away—a remote event read about in newspapers. It never entered his head that as a seaman he would ever come under fire.

This halcyon period ended suddenly, during the summer of 1943, when the German and Hungarian armies retreated in full flight from the Stalingrad debacle. In September 1943 Kós was dispatched by rail to Constanza and went aboard the *Kassa*, which was rushing German army material to the Crimea. Ukrainian harbor workers at Odessa and Sebastopol regaled him with stories about Russians and Communism, which they hated in about equal portions. Kós spent the fall and winter rescuing Axis soldiers from the

2. Actually, Hitler planned to recapture the city. He moved in reinforcements from Poland in late December and gave the Russians a scare, but this counteroffensive shriveled by February.
3. John Lukács, *Confessions of an Original Sinner* (New York, 1990), 67.

Crimean trap in a Dunkirk-like operation. Small Russian bombers—converted fighters—attacked the convoys, which had no aerial support. The last crossing occurred on April 6, 1944, while the Red Army was investing Sebastopol. The *Kassa*, crammed with wounded German soldiers and personnel, was struck by an artillery shell, laying out Kós with a concussion. Of the eight ships in that last convoy, only four reached Constanza.

After release from a Budapest hospital Kós was ordered to Sailors Hall to await orders. The Danube, mined by British bombers in night raids, was increasingly useless as a commercial corridor to Germany. After the Arrow Cross came to power in October, the sailors were handed rifles and given a six-week infantry course by an amateur drillmaster at Ujpest, a northern suburb. The seamen, having witnessed the German collapse in the Crimea, had not the slightest intention of giving their lives for the Szálasi regime—or any other. In February they were hurriedly collected and thrown into a leaky front facing Vác, an upriver town. When they saw Russian soldiers advancing toward them through suburban gardens, they knew just what to do. They surrendered. "We knew we should surrender in a large group, for then we would be less likely to be shot as a nuisance."[4]

With a motley gang of other POWs, the sailors were locked in a hospital cellar. But the Russians had failed to secure the windows, so Kós and a companion slipped away at night and struck out for Debrecen, now well within the Russian zone of occupation, some 150 miles east. At dawn they were picked up again and forced to unload cases of artillery shells in an improvised military camp. They waited and watched, and when the lone Russian sentry vacated his post by the gate, they breezily walked out, each grimacing in anticipation of a shot in the back. In an abandoned house they found rags to wear and buried their Hungarian uniforms. The next night they reached the vicinity of the Budapest People's Stadium, in Zugló, where a family gave them some decent civilian clothes. Russian soldiers were everywhere, but they were not picked up. They reached a straggling agricultural village outside the city and had no sooner congratulated each other on their escape than a Cossack on horseback with a tommy gun took them prisoner again. He took them to a house and told them to wait in the hallway while he fetched his officer. It was dark. As soon as the Cossack had disappeared, Kós and his companion stepped out of a window and hid in a cornfield. There were shouts and curses and shots in the blackness but no pursuit.

4. Interview with István Kós (May 20, 1993).

For the next two weeks, fed by Hungarians, they walked steadily east, avoiding railroads and highways. From a distance they saw Russian soldiers and vehicles but were never pursued. Doubtless the fact that they were moving eastward, toward Russia—where no POW in his right mind would voluntarily go—dispelled suspicion. Eastbound trains were crammed with Hungarian and German POWs bound for labor camps in Russia. It took weeks of traveling by night, but they safely made Debrecen, which had become the seat of the new—Soviet-controlled—Hungarian government, which paradoxically made it a relatively safe place for Hungarian males. During the long Soviet occupation of Hungary, Kós divided his feelings about Russians between fear and rage. "My stomach churned whenever I saw one. They were a symbol of what had happened to Hungary. You never could count on what they might do. Few of them could even read. Hand them a valid pass, and they would arrest you and ship you off for slave labor. Give them an old bus ticket, and they would nod and let you pass." What he hoped for was that the Russians would eventually go away.

Kós found Debrecen safe, but he could not live happily without boats. In 1946 he moved to Budapest, where he salvaged an old skiff and an outboard motor and set up a ferry that could carry ten people over the river. Later, when the Danube bridges were reconstructed, he bought a larger boat and hauled firewood from upriver. When the 1956 revolution broke out, Kós seized his opportunity. He heard that after the Russian tanks had opened fire in Budapest, the Austrians had opened their frontier. He rushed onto a train bound for Sopron. He did not have a ticket or travel pass, but none were asked for. On the train was a former smuggler who was looking for customers. They sealed a bargain, and that night Kós joined a band who walked over to Austria. Consequent to his departure from Hungary he graduated from boats to ships. With seaman's papers he sailed all over the world, took Swedish citizenship, and settled in Göteborg. More than twenty years passed before he wanted to return to Hungary, even for a brief visit, even though he married a Hungarian woman whose family had remained in Budapest.

Many Budapest Jews avoided altogether both the yellow-star houses and the "protected" houses sponsored by neutral countries, preferring to take their chances hiding out in the city and moving from place to place as danger ebbed and flowed. István Körmendi (born 1923) was Jewish on four sides of his family. His was a family of means and expectations. During the First World War his father had served as a surgeon on the Russian front, and from his earliest years István planned to become a doctor. During his primary school years he encountered no anti-Semitism, but this changed radically on entering high school. Public schools had compulsory religion classes once each week, from which Jews were excused on grounds of respect for their religion, but the actual attitude of the other students was anything but respectful, and the excuse of Jews from the religion classes only helped in setting them apart. "This exemption branded us."[5] When he slapped a classmate who had insulted his father (even though the "filthy Jew" was the boy's own family doctor), he was punished by the principal, who boasted that he would personally prevent any Jew from enrolling at the university. The remark was gratuitous, because in 1941, the year of István's graduation, Jews were banned from the universities by edict of Parliament. Headmasters had nothing to do with it.

Refusing to accept this interruption of his plans, Körmendi decided to study medicine abroad. It was then that he encountered a maddening paradox. Although as a Jew he was no longer welcome in Hungary, the government refused to issue him a passport so that he could leave. For the next two years he worked as a laboratory assistant in a hospital, and became a "fugitive student" at the Medical Faculty of Pázmány Péter University, where in moiling crowds he passed unnoticed. He attended lectures, read all the books, but took no exams. Professors nodded to him in the hallways, recognizing his face but having no idea that he was a Jew. In September 1943 someone turned him in. The faculty took up his case and banished him from the university, although the dean, who admired his spunk, promised to assist him in getting academic credit for his work—provided that the barrier against Jews was ever lifted.

When the German army occupied Budapest in March 1944, two Swabians with pistols entered the Körmendi flat and ordered the family to clear out within twenty-four hours. István was drafted into a labor battalion and sent upriver to the camp at Vác, where he was employed in legitimate tasks, like unloading trains, and merely devilish ones, like moving building stones back and forth at the whim of a guard. Yet conditions were not unbearable. The camp was well run, the food was adequate, and he received overnight leaves for visits home. One bonus for Jews in labor battalions was that they were under the protection of the Honvédség, which meant that the Arrow Cross could seldom reach them.[6]

5. Interview with István Körmendi (February 16, 1990).

6. Jews in labor units had been exempt from the Auschwitz deportations because their labor was regarded as valuable. Ironically, they had a better chance of survival than Jewish civilians. See Randolph L. Braham, *The Politics of Genocide: The Holocaust in Hungary* (New York, 1981), 338.

After Szálasi came to power, conditions deteriorated for Jews everywhere in Budapest. Some labor battalions were ordered to Austria to work on the Hitler's West Wall. Through a Christian friend Körmendi arranged to be reassigned to a polyclinic in Pest as an orderly. He slept at the hospital to avoid an encounter with Nyilas gangs who roamed the streets looking for Jews and army deserters. When he heard that the gangs had begun to hunt their prey in hospitals, he slipped off to join his parents, who were hiding with twelve other Jews in a one-room flat on Váci Street just north of Nyugati Station. This building, owned by his uncle, had been abandoned because the station was a prime target for American bombers. The caretaker, a Christian, loyally supplied them with food and water every night, but he warned them that the Nyilas were "cleaning up" the neighborhood and shooting Jews at the Danube embankment. Since the building was supposed to be vacant, the fugitives dared not flush the toilet. A greater danger was a restless twelve-year-old boy who could not be restrained from making noise or looking out the window. Since this situation was becoming increasingly dangerous, they had to concoct another plan.

With them was István's aunt, a Christian woman who owned a large flat off Pasaréti Road at the foot of Rózsadomb Hill in Buda. She had every right to occupy her flat, but not with a collection of Jews. The greatest danger was that Pasaréti, a parklike avenue of trees and gardens, happened to be a favorite roosting neighborhood for both the SS and the Nyilas, who had stockpiled weapons there prior to the October coup. Despite the danger, it offered the best hope for the fugitives in the Váci flat. Early in December they crossed the river one at a time and settled into their new hiding place. They had to sneak into the new hospice without drawing notice from the other tenants. During the daytime they dared not shut the curtains, because this would arouse suspicion. They hid during daylight hours. István spent the day curled up in a wardrobe. The building across the street housed teams of black-uniformed Germans. One day a German rang their bell. They were terrified. The aunt answered the door. The German politely apologized for the disturbance. He had confused the address with the one across the street.

On December 24, as they peered through shutters, they saw that the Germans had become very agitated. They were packing up, moving their equipment onto lorries, and driving off in a hurry. That same evening artillery and rifle fire close at hand broke the glass in their windows. House leaders called for everyone to go down to the cellar, but they dared not go, fearing the other tenants would turn them in. István's grandmother, a seventy-year-old woman with heart disease, had a nervous attack and died. They concealed her body behind a heap of broken furniture on the balcony, where she lay for two weeks, until they could dig a grave in the garden. On the following day Russians, who had broken the German line near János Hospital and established a front three hundred yards away, set up trench mortars in the garden. István made friends with a young soldier from Odessa who had studied concert violin before the war. When he said how overjoyed they were, as Jews, to be liberated, the soldier looked around warily and whispered, "Don't ever talk like that to a Russian. I am a Jew, too. Russians hate Jews as much as Germans do." For István it was "a cold shower" to learn that anti-Semitism was not a monopoly of rightist fanatics.

For all that, the Russian soldiers were kind to them. A small group came regularly at dinnertime with a bucket of cabbage soup, which they shared with the fugitives. The first-line Red Army soldiers were disciplined men; the ones that came afterward—largely Mongols—were not. They began their routine of raping women in the area, taking them from cellars under torchlight "to peel potatoes." (István discovered that they avoided any woman suspected of gonorrhea or syphilis, so he taught the women in his cellar how to fake the symptoms.) The Russians could not resist stealing watches. Their ploy was to ask the time and then "liberate" the watches of all who checked. When István resumed his work at the hospital, he was warned not to use a watch in taking a pulse. He ignored the advice—and lost his watch.

One day he encountered the dean of the medical university standing in a long line at a water tap near the Russian military park. That once-distinguished man, now shabby and frightened, was hauling buckets of water on a child's sled. When István identified himself and reminded him of the promise to allow him credit for his two years of course work, the dean behaved as if he had found a long-lost friend. "He then said he had a small request: would I please write a note saying that he was not an anti-Semite and that I had been helped by *him*." This was the first sign for István that the worm had turned. (Subsequently he received his four semesters credit and a favorable report.)

The siege had not ended. Pockets of Germans held out, gerrymandered among the complex of streets and alleys. For two harrowing days beginning on February 13, 1945, the German and Hungarian garrison trapped in Castle Hill attempted to cut their way through the Russian ring. The Russians fought them from house to house in the Pasaréti district. A young German, about twenty years old, sought sanctuary in their house, which had a Red Cross flag on the door. He had no gun and had been shot in the lung. Dr. Körmendi treated him, but some hours later two Russians with machine guns found him. They shouted, "Stalingrad!" and shot him on his cot. The neighborhood was soon littered with German corpses, many of them resembling statues cast in outlandish positions, all completely frozen. They were buried where they fell. (Reburial took more than a year.) There was a massive slaughter farther west, where a number of Germans who had obtained maps of Buda drains attempted to escape by following sewers that embouched on Budakeszi Road. Unfortunately for them the Russians had the same maps and, waiting for them patiently, shot them as they popped out of their hole.[7] There were so many bodies that one could have used them as stepping stones.

A few months after the end of the siege, the family reoccupied their flat. Most of their furniture had been stolen or used as firewood, but in the years that followed Dr. Körmendi gradually located, among his patients, pieces that had been looted, including his largest prize, a grand piano. István's uncle, having survived the purge of Budapest Jewry, fared poorly in the new regime. Because he had been a man of wealth in the Horthy regime, he was always under suspicion by the ÁVH. In 1951 he was sentenced to three years imprisonment because the police claimed to have found ten kilos of flour and five kilos of sugar in his flat. Hoarding was a crime against the people. His wife was given half an hour to vacate her flat. She managed to retrieve an armchair, which was mounted in the rear of the lorry that carried her to a desolate hamlet in the Hortobágy, Hungary's rural wasteland. Her husband died within half a year after his release from prison.

Nor was István entirely happy with the liberation. He completed medical school with honors in 1950 and was immediately drafted for a five-year term as a surgeon in the army. One was always fearful. "This was the darkest period of our history. I knew a military doctor and a supply officer who were hanged because at a dinner celebrating the liberation of Hungary seventy guests contracted dysentery." Military hospitals were seedbeds of corruption and inefficiency, where peasants and workers after two-month courses in Marxism ruled on medical procedures as well as political behavior. Spies were everywhere. István himself underwent a criminal investigation because an anonymous letter to the Defense Ministry accused him of storing morphine and injecting it. "During the war there were many painful experiences to endure, but worse came after the war, when we had to undergo the new regime. We had looked forward to a true democracy—but look what we got."

By the middle of January 1945 the Red Army penetration of Pest had pushed the Axis defenders into the compound of the National Museum and into the

7. Interview with József Borus (April 5, 1990).

buildings along Museum Boulevard. Most of the Germans had withdrawn across the Danube to Castle Hill, but those left in Pest fought with the determination of trapped men who knew that, win or lose, they must die. The museum itself shook from the mortar shells exploding in the yard. Inside huddled a dozen historians from various institutes and museums in the city. They had already sent to hiding places the more valuable exhibits—especially those that were gold, or looked like gold. The scholars, along with half a dozen superannuated museum guards, none of them armed, had moved in earlier with a cache of food—mainly beans and meat fried in lard to preserve it.

On the main floor they built themselves a small cavelike enclosure with Roman statues and inscription stones pushed up against the shattered windows as a kind of palisade against enemy or friendly fire. From these same windows a month earlier they had watched Arrow Cross youngsters with rifles and machine pistols herding Jews to the Danube embankment beside Ferenc József Bridge for execution. Now this sector was defended by Hungarian SS, a convivial body of Volksdeutsche men who shared their cigarettes and warned the directors to keep out of sight because the Arrow Cross patrols still at large stupidly believed that all historians were Jews. The historians opposed an SS plan to fortify the museum, on grounds that fortification would merely attract an equal and opposite response from the attackers; the museum held national treasures that had to be safeguarded from damage or desecration. The soldiers agreed to keep the fight outside.[8]

On January 16 the museum occupants were startled by heavy pounding at the front door. They did nothing, hoping that whoever it was would go away. But the door was smashed open, and some Germans entered, seeking a place to hide. Domokos Kosáry, a director, protested, saying that the Russians would trap and kill them. An officer pushed him back: "What does it matter. We'll be killed anyway."[9] They pushed in and rushed upstairs.

The first Russians Kosáry saw, as he peered over the shoulder of a Roman statue, were at the museum gate firing at snipers in the upper rooms of buildings across the avenue. There was gunfire on all sides of the museum, with some Russians crouched behind trees in the garden. A Russian squad burst into the building through the back entrance and confronted the historians. The officer spoke French and asked if there were Germans in the building. One of the historians must have made a signal, because the Russians

    8. Interview with György Györffy (March 30, 1989).
    9. Interview with Domokos Kosáry (March 29, 1989). Kosáry calls these men Germans, but they may have been Volksdeutsche.

sprayed the ceiling and walls with machine gun fire. Others raced upstairs and cleared the building. By this time snipers in the buildings across the street had killed or wounded nine or ten Russians near the front gate. The Russian officer took charge. He ordered the museum guards, some of them so disabled they could barely walk, to retrieve the wounded. Two guards were killed in attempting the rescue.[10] No historians volunteered for this mission of mercy. After a brief firefight, the German snipers abandoned their posts or were killed.

Almost alone among these fugitive scholars Károly Vigh was a Russophile. A fellow of the Historical Institute, a translator of Russian texts, and a socialist sympathizer, he believed that to achieve radical reform Hungary would have to follow the path of the Soviet Union. For him it was an emotional moment when the Russian officer who had liberated the museum embraced each of them and began singing the "Marseillaise" (not the "Internationale"). It was as though two great revolutionary movements had been fused and reforged—one French, the other Russian. Later the other historians had a good laugh at Vigh's crestfallen face when he discovered that while the celebration was in full blast a Russian soldier had deftly gone through his pockets and stolen his watch. "They were very primitive people. I suppose they thought that anyone with a watch was bourgeois." But as soon as the Red Army officer learned who the scholars were and what the museum was, he provided them with a guard and urged them to continue their research as though nothing unusual had happened. On that day the Russians dislodged the last Germans from Pest, and the war moved across the river to Buda.

Other Hungarians greeting their "liberators" experienced similar surprises. Tamás Bárány, who had married on December 26 and spent his honeymoon in a cellar, eagerly approached the first Russians to arrive on his street. One soldier with slanted eyes and high cheekbones extended his arms wide to embrace him. "I was touched by this brotherly gesture until I felt him tapping my pockets." When he asked Bárány for his watch, which had been sewn into the lining of his greatcoat, Bárány waved to the west to indicate that the Germans had taken it. The soldier continued his tapping and found ten Mexican cigarettes bought before the siege. These he pocketed and rejoined his unit. Soon another soldier embraced him and felt his pockets for a watch. Bárány explained that the Germans had stolen it. The soldier was disappointed. "Papirousi?" (Cigarettes?), he asked. Again Bárány pointed to the west and alluded to the "Germanski." The Russian nodded in understanding

10. Györffy interview.

and, reaching into his own pocket, pulled out a whole packet of Extra (one hundred cigarettes), which he put into Bárány's hand and then ran after his comrades.

Bárány was left gaping. "At that moment I understood that the European norms were not valid any more. Something had ended completely."[11]

From first to last, Károly Orbán (born 1918) was an unwilling patriot in a war that pitted what he called unprincipled barbarians (i.e., Russians) against heel-clicking martinets (i.e., Germans). He had grown up in Pest near Népliget (People's Park), where his father owned a wholesale haberdashery. Having no appetite for the family business he went off to the teachers' college at Esztergom and acquired a primary school certificate. Family pressure, however, pulled him back into the haberdasher's trade until he was drafted in September 1940. He considered the next two years a terrible waste of time and government money, but dutifully went through officers' school and came out as a sublieutenant. He never expected to go to war. At this time Russia and Germany were professing great friendship, and Hungary, without firing a shot, was recovering territory lost at Trianon.[12]

When Hungary declared war on the Soviet Union in June 1941, Orbán was shocked. And it seemed like greater madness when his country declared war on the United States six months later. He never doubted that the Allies would win. Like other young subalterns of his class he was slated for duty on the Russian front; unlike most of them Orbán had vowed that he would not go. He arranged an interview with his commanding officer and told him that he would never fire a shot at a Russian. This was clearly a court-martial offense, but his bluff worked. Either the authorities thought he was demented, or they dreaded the kind of adverse publicity that would attend such a trial. In any case, he was dispatched to a boys' military school at Győr as teacher of "technical data" and as fencing coach (though he had never held an épée in his hand before). His stubbornness probably saved his life—the majority of the other lieutenants in his class were ground up in the Don Bend butchery.

Finally bored with his Győr assignment, Orbán in 1943 arranged for a transfer to Budapest, where he built concrete gun emplacements and bunkers. He now lived at home and had an easy commute to work. At the urging of his brother he paid five hundred pengős for a forged Swedish passport to head off trouble. Their father had been a foundling, and how could it be

---

11. Tamás Bárány, in *Élet és Irodalom*, February 3, 1995, 4.
12. Interview with Károly Orbán (January 6, 1988).

proved that a foundling was not a Jew? Orbán considered the money well spent, for he planned to slip into civilian clothes and vanish from the army when the Russians overwhelmed the Axis line. After Szálasi came to power in October 1944, Orbán joined swarms of Honvéd remnants madly digging trenches to form a line of last resistance between Kőszeg and Szombathely in western Hungary. "These trenches were never used. The Russians were moving so fast that not even our generals at headquarters knew where they were." When Budapest fell, in February 1945, and the remaining Hungarians still loyal to Hitler retreated to Austria, Orbán took advantage of the pandemonium by donning civilian clothes and deserting. On foot he struck out for home, protected by his magical amulet, the Swedish passport.

Russians near the town of Körmend picked him up, kicked him, and threatened to kill him. He was pitched into the cellar of a farmhouse with about a dozen civilian males, most of them covert deserters. Throughout the night four or five of the Hungarians at a time were pulled out for interrogation and failed to return to the cellar. Orbán demanded to see the officer in charge and flourished his Swedish document. The officer pocketed it and sent him back to the cellar. Orbán was now thoroughly alarmed. He heard women screaming elsewhere in the building and also shots fired into the walls. By morning only four of the prisoners were left in the cellar. He was convinced he would be killed. Two guards hustled him upstairs into the open air, kicked him, and let him loose. Behind a haystack were the corpses of the other prisoners. The Russians still had his passport, but Orbán did not tarry to ask for its return. He struck off toward Budapest, 120 miles east. On the road he saw Russian soldiers looting a German limousine. When they left, he crept over and found boxes of Hershey chocolate bars. He stuffed his pockets full. Chocolate was like gold in bartering for food and thus might sustain him on his trek home.

Russian patrols picked him up four more times on the road, penning him at night with similar fugitives and always threatening to send them to Russia as POWs. At one place he and three hundred others were crowded into a stable guarded at each end by Russians with tommy guns. When the guards fell asleep, some prisoners removed the grating from a window, and Orbán and about a hundred of his fellows climbed out in the dark. He was an easy mark on the road, and at Székesfehérvár he was impressed into latrine service at a Russian auto-park. The lorry traffic was heavy. Orbán and another fugitive decided to hide in an outgoing truck and pray that its destination was Budapest and not the front. At nightfall they hid under tarps and after some hours reached a checkpoint. Orbán peeped out and recognized Érd, an outlying suburb of the capital. When they climbed out, they raised the guards, who chased them into a cornfield firing a machine gun at them. After the guards gave up their search, they continued on foot to Budafok, successfully scrambling around Russian checkpoints along the road.

At the big market hall next to the skeletal ruins of Ferenc József Bridge another Russian patrol snared them. They were escorted into the cellar of the market, where two hundred male captives milled about, waiting to be sent to Russia as forced laborers. As this herd filed outside, Orbán jumped into a tank trap and somehow escaped detection. (His erstwhile companion failed to escape and spent three years in the Soviet Union as a slave laborer.)

He dared not go home—which was just as well, for a Russian general had installed himself and his entourage in the family flat. His mother and father had taken sanctuary at a nunnery. He sought refuge with his godmother, who, when she opened the door, failed at first to recognize the ragged scarecrow who spoke to her. For months he stayed tightly indoors, fearing a knock on the door that would signal his deportation to Siberia. Not until early summer did he command enough courage to join his parents at their flat. They were in the middle of a massive cleanup following the departure of the Russian general. It seemed that whenever his carpet had got dirty, his men had confiscated a fresh one from another flat and laid it on the old one. This accumulation continued until the doors could not be closed, at which point the general left and his men turned the room into a latrine. In these piles of feces Orbán's aversion to Russians was metastasized into loathing.

In the fall of 1945 Károly Orbán joined his father in the clothing business. In 1949 the firm was nationalized, an event that added fresh fuel to his smoldering hatred of Communism. Before he could return to teaching, he had to enroll at Karl Marx University and complete a ritualized list of courses leavened with Marxist-Leninist theory. Then, his mind properly certified, stamped, and sealed, he was permitted to begin his thirty-year teaching career in primary education. Today Károly Orbán does not trouble to use euphemism when he summarizes his impressions of four decades of Russian occupation. "Whenever I see one of those Russian soldiers at Déli Station, I feel sick. I just hate him."

Leányfalu, a riverside village twelve miles north of Budapest, became in early January 1945 a key command post for the Soviet artillery attacks on Budapest. Russians swept through the village with the sudden devastation of what novelist Sándor Márai called "an Arctic ice storm."[13] Thirty soldiers

13. Sándor Márai, *Memoir of Hungary, 1944–1948* (Budapest, 1996), 78.

occupied his house, which became a barracks as well as a military repair shop for overhauling broken equipment—everything from trucks to transmitters to tanks. (Almost all this military paraphernalia came from the United States.) They slept on the floor beside each other, arising at dawn—like lizards warmed by the sun—and working until midnight. Townspeople were forced to join work parties digging holes along the highway to lay mines against a rumored German counterattack from the capital, which never materialized. When invading a house Russians never bothered unlocking gates; they simply chopped down the gateposts or ran over the fences with a truck or tank. If they needed a small board they would saw up a bed and throw the rest of it out as trash. Within hours of their arrival in Leányfalu they had cut down every telephone pole and full-grown tree not used for supporting electric cables. They seemed to have no sense of failure. They spent hundreds of hours of forced labor, as well as their own, building a bridge to a Danube island without calculating that ice floes would quickly tear it loose. This failure did not matter to them: "they gave the impression of some instinctive biological power—human variants of ants or termites—that had assumed a military shape."[14]

Jews in the village rejoiced (at first) in being liberated by the Russians. A well-to-do pharmacist who had hidden during the Arrow Cross purge informed the first Russian to reach his house that he was a Jew. The soldier smiled, removed the machine gun from his neck, and kissed the old man on both cheeks, saying that he was a Jew too. Then he ordered the old man with his whole family to stand with raised hands while he robbed the house. He skillfully tapped the tile stove and walls until he found the hidden family jewels and all their cash—some forty thousand pengős.

The Russian soldiers behaved ruthlessly with the civilian population but just as ruthlessly with each other. Like Siberian dogs they lived on top of one another, growling and fighting over their precious bags of pilfered treasures, containing objects as useless as broken thermometers. The Márai house was always in an uproar of their singing, yelling, cursing, arguing. Only when one of the GPU officers entered were the workshops abruptly silent. None of the soldiers looked at him, and they worked with downcast eyes, trembling in his presence as though he were the master of life and death. These political officers, fur-capped and often with soft hands smelling of cologne, were the real power of the Red Army. Communists seemed to fear only other Communists.

14. Ibid., 80.

244   **Hungary at War**

A Russian lieutenant colonel, whom Márai's neighbor had invited to dinner, paid Márai a surprise visit. He had heard that a writer lived in the village, and wanted him to record that Hungarian soldiers had outrageously despoiled Tolstoy's residence in Yasnaya Polyana. After looking around for a while he saluted gravely, and left with his military escort. A short time later Márai learned that this same officer, who had kissed the hand of the lady of the house on his departure, sent back his chauffeur, armed with a machine gun, to demand that the master of the house hand over the gold wristwatch that the colonel had admired at dinner. The host was bewildered. Theft he understood, but this behavior from a guest who had kissed his wife's hand was beyond his experience. Márai had an explanation. The Russians had no sense of wanting to be "liked." Since their system cared not a whit about its own people's opinions, why should it care about the feelings of subjugated foreigners.[15] Only the peasants in the vicinity really understood the Russians. While the burgers of Leányfalu stayed and tried to reason with the Russians, and were rewarded for their visibility by being carried off in significant numbers as forced laborers, the peasants disappeared into the forests after storing food and valuables in pits. It was as if they had learned how to survive from tales handed down from the days of Turkish occupation. Moreover, they knew by instinct that the Russian soldiers not only plundered but were corrupt. They learned how to arrange deals with them, to become their middlemen. They would get a Russian to steal a horse or a piano in exchange for some hidden brandy.

The best that one could say about the Russians was that "they were childlike, sometimes wild, sometimes edgy and melancholy, always unpredictable." Their incessant looting resulted not from hatred of the fascist or bourgeois enemy but rather from an abject poverty so stripped of colorful objects that like children magnetized by baubles they carried off whatever they could. In Márai's library they came across an old copy of *Esquire*, which made the rounds, snatched from one pair to hands to another. They could not, of course, read anything in the magazine, and they were little interested in the pictures of Vargas or Petty girls. What fascinated them were advertisements displaying an array of Western luxuries—refrigerators, tennis rackets, men's shoes, belt buckles. Formerly they had boasted to Márai that Russia had everything a human being could want, and they had spoken of their bicycles and gramophones with great pride. Now, mesmerized by the array of exotic devices crowding every page of the magazine, they became subdued,

15. Ibid., 70.

then depressed, as though aware for the first time of nonbridgeable gaps in their expectations. Márai came to the conclusion that the appeal of Communism lay in taking, not sharing. Despite the high-flown polemics of the commissars, the average Russian soldier had little comprehension of ideals like equality and justice but only a desire to escape from poverty and drudgery.

When Budapest fell, the Russians disappeared from his house as though by magic. Only one of the thirty who had been billeted in the house said goodbye. A forty-year-old Ukrainian gave Márai a gilt-edged picture of Comrade Stalin before he left. The next morning Márai returned to his flat in Buda, where he found that his library had been hit three times during the siege and that the blasts had ground most of his books to powder. One undamaged title page lay on rubbish next to his top hat. It read: "On the Care of a Middle-Class Dog."[16]

Zoltán Falta (born 1938) grew up in a family of weavers of Spanish descent in Békéscsaba, a city in southeastern Hungary near the Romanian frontier. His father, who was sixty years old when Zoltán was born, had served as an interpreter on the Italian front during the First World War until shot in the lung and invalided home. He had gone into the war as an overaged patriot and had come out as a supernationalist who, during the dark days of post-Trianon, proclaimed his admiration for Miklós Horthy and Gyula Gömbös. He instilled in his progeny and in the five employees of his carpet factory the virtues of hard work and the values of "Hungarism," and for a time even echoed some of the shibboleths of the Arrow Cross Party. It was not that he was anti-Semitic—he had gone to the Jewish school in Békéscsaba and numbered Jews as his closest friends—rather, it was that his recollection of Hungary under the Béla Kun government supported an aversion to anything tinctured with Bolshevism. In his mind Jewry was inextricably implicated in both the Béla Kun government and Bolshevism.

For Zoltán the summer of 1944 was a watershed. As a boy of six he was bewildered when Hungarian gendarmes collected more than two thousand Jews of Békéscsaba, housed them in an abandoned tobacco warehouse, and carried them off somewhere in crowded freight cars. Then his older brother, Istvan, a lieutenant of artillery, returned on leave from the Russian front. Zoltán remembered him as a cheerful man who always whistled, but after the Don Bend battle the whistling quit. This was the summer when the Red Army was breaking the Carpathian line, and there were rumors that no schools would

16. Ibid., 113.

open in the fall. Zoltán's school became a military hospital, filled with German casualties from the front. With his best friend, the postman's son, he played soldier in the woods where garrison troops performed their drills. The boys became pets. "The Germans were always good to us. They showed us their guns, and in our town they were always clean and orderly."[17] On September 22, 1944, twenty-seven American bombers attacked the local railway yards. While others cowered in their cellars, Zoltán and his friend went outside to watch the excitement. The bombers made only one run and approached the station from the wrong direction. Their bombs missed the junction altogether but some fell in the town. After the raid Zoltán's friend went home and found his house destroyed and all members of his family killed.

A few weeks later, when the Russian advance reached Arad, only forty miles away, Zoltán and his sister, Mária, were packed off by train to Budapest to keep them out of harm's way when the Red Army invaded the town. In the capital they lived with two wealthy aunts on Naphegy Street, a few blocks west of Várhegy (Castle Hill). On Christmas night the Russians closed the ring around Budapest and intensified their shelling. As the family sat at table preparing for their Christmas dinner, shrapnel brought the chandelier down onto the table. For a few days afterward there was a lull in the shelling as the Russians consolidated their hold on the environs. It was so peaceful that the family joined a procession of strollers along the Danube embankment as though they had been warped back into prewar days.

In the weeks that followed, shelling and bombing resumed and increased. When bombs destroyed their house on Naphegy, they had to move into a cellar on Várfok Street, on the northern escarpment of Castle Hill. This was a badly exposed site overlooking the battle raging in Pest across the river. One night early in January, during a British air raid, a bomb hit their house, breaking a sewer main. The occupants were trapped underground while sewage flooded the cellar and reached the level of their necks. Not until noon on the following day did German soldiers hear their cries and dig them out. Zoltán was nearly frozen and unable to move or talk; others had drowned in the cellar. He and his sister then moved in with another relative, this one on Csörsz Street, south of the castle. In their pursuit of their father's idea of a safe place for a six-year-old boy and his sister, they were running short of obliging relatives.

In the middle of a bombardment one night in January a disheveled figure entered their cellar. It turned out to be Zoltán's brother, István, who had

17. Interview with Zoltán Falta (April 26, 1990).

followed a succession of notes pinned to doors and had found them. His artillery unit had dug in on Margit Island, but they had no equipment with which to defend themselves. The Germans had taken it all away from them. István had urged his men to desert, but they refused, saying that if caught, they were more afraid of what the Germans might do to them than the Russians. His aunt advised him to burn his uniform and remain with them, but he could not bring himself to abandon his men. For a time he visited them every other day, but in mid-January he no longer appeared, and they assumed he had been killed.

As the bombing intensified and the street fighting came nearer, they rarely left their cellar. A concrete stairway collapsed on a boyish-looking Hungarian deserter, and it took three days to dig out the body. Outside was a weird landscape of shattered buildings and piles of rubble where streets used to be. By the first week in February all their food and water was gone. Zoltán and his sister crawled out at night with a slop bucket and ladled water from a bomb crater in which lay a dead German soldier, whose ring finger had been cut off. They no longer bothered to boil the water. On returning to the cellar with his pail Zoltán seemed always to trip over the corpse on the stairwell and spill the water. He would then angrily slap the corpse in the face. For food they joined teams of survivors hacking pieces of meat from the cadavers of horses that lay in the streets. The young people still retained their sense of mischief. After a week of dining on horse meat they started neighing, startling the grown-ups, who thought the meat might be affecting their brains.

On February 12 they knew the end was near. Russian dive-bombers steadily attacked the Citadella on Gellért Hill and the old city on Castle Hill, where the SS defenders, under General Pfeiffer-Wildenbruch, were making their last stand. In their cellar on Csörsz Street they waited uneasily for the Russians. They hid Zoltán's sister under a pile of pillows and rags. In the evening Zoltán's brother, who had not been killed after all, joined them. He said the Germans planned a suicidal attempt to break the ring. He had had enough. He donned some civilian clothes and burned his uniform. Later a dozen German SS who had broken out of the castle slipped into the cellar and set up their machine gun at the cellar door. Fortunately for István they were too exhausted to look for deserters, their usual procedure. Zoltán's uncle begged them not to resist, for everyone in the cellar would be killed, and he promised to intercede on their behalf when the Russians arrived.

In the morning huge plumes of smoke hung over Castle Hill. At 10:30 A.M. the bombardment abruptly quit. People emerged from cellars into open air and met three bone weary Russian soldiers in the garden. Everyone wanted to try out his or her inventory of Russian words and phrases. The SS came out with hands over their heads and were herded to a garden wall. A young Russian with a tommy gun slung over his shoulder set up a telephone center in the cellar. Suddenly he began to dance, crying out, "Kaput voina!" (The war is over!). Other Russians swarmed into the garden shouting and laughing. "The horror came now," Zoltán remembered. Almost with one will they clipped on their bayonets and massacred and mutilated the SS at the wall. This butchery was barely over when a Russian officer, spick-and-span in new uniform, burst into the courtyard and, seizing six of the Russians, had his men push them against the same wall and shoot them. The Hungarians were stunned by this festival of crime and punishment. Far from being reassured by the fairness of their liberators, they were terrified by it, for it demonstrated too clearly that Russians regarded human life, whether of friend or foe, as a cheap commodity. For the next forty years these murders populated Zoltán's most recurrent nightmares. The butchery probably saved István's life, for when he was found hiding in the cellar, the Russians only took him prisoner.

In March Zoltán and his sister started home on foot. They dug carrots for food—when they could find them—and slept in the squalid hovels of Gypsies, whom they feared more than Russians. At the Tisza River his sister was seized for a work detail, but cannily she put her arm in a sling and was excused. From Szolnok they rode on top of a train, which stopped period- ically so that passengers could gather corn from the fields as fuel for the locomotive. Békéscsaba looked ravaged and forlorn. Their front door and most of the windows had been boarded up as though the house had been permanently abandoned. In the back they climbed through an open window. Their mother collapsed when she saw them. In the pantry Zoltán and his sister found a bucket of grease saved for making soap. Falling on their knees they gorged on handfuls of the muck as their mother wailed that it would kill them. "We swore that at least we would die with full bellies." On the next day his father, as autocratic as ever, packed him off to school.

The Falta family narrowly escaped expropriation and deportation. When the father tried to reopen his carpet factory, he was confronted with a membership list of the local Arrow Cross Party, which he had joined in 1935. He confessed that he had received a badge and card but explained that he had never attended a meeting or paid dues, and in proof of this he showed that his name on the list had never been officially stamped. There were affidavits alleging that when some Jews of Békéscsaba had been rounded up and sent to Auschwitz in 1944, he had bought valuable furnishings from them. He argued that these had been taken only for safekeeping, with the understanding that they would be returned. Where were these items? He regretted that some Russian "liberators" had confiscated them and shipped them back to Russia. He was also charged with having said when the Jews had been deported in 1944, "If they don't come back, it will be a good life here." He replied that he meant only that the city would be less crowded. Like everyone else in the city, including the Jews, he assumed they were being taken to Germany for resettlement, not extermination. The charges against him were eventually dropped, but all members of the family lived under a cloud for years.

In 1947 István turned up in Békéscsaba. He had been part of a "death march" to Mohács in southern Hungary, where Russian guards shot sick and disabled soldiers unable to keep up the pace. After a holding camp in Romania he was dispatched to Camp Chita, a forced labor camp in the Ukraine, where he kept alive by maintaining a strict regimen of hygiene and by volunteering for the hardest jobs, provided they put him into contact with the civilian population, who gave him extra food.

In time Zoltán went off to the University of Szeged, just renamed in honor of Attila József (1905–37), a newly canonized socialist poet.[18] Each month all students were required to write their autobiographies, which were scrutinized for discrepancies. He carefully avoided mentioning that his brother had been a Horthy officer, and he listed his mother as a textile worker and his father as a clerk. On one occasion he narrowly missed expulsion. He had told a fellow student that he had a pair of shoes being repaired at a shoemaker's. This was reported, and he was brought in for questioning: how was it possible that a comrade of working-class origins, at a difficult period of shortages, could possess a second pair of shoes?

Women

Until the American and British bombing raids in April 1944, the war was only a minor and temporary interruption for Eleonóra Majorosy (born 1921). Her family occupied a large flat under Gellért Hill, only a few steps from the Danube, and since her father was a director of the big market hall just over the Ferenc József Bridge in Pest, the family larder was full. The family had no quarrel with Admiral Horthy's regime—better by far than the rabble that had infested Béla Kun's short-lived Communist experiment of

18. Attila József had attended the university briefly before being expelled for writing a satirical poem about a professor.

1919. Her father, József Majorosy, had personal knowledge of Kun, for during the First World War he had spent three years as a Russian POW in camps at Minsk, Omsk, and Tomsk, where Kun, himself a POW and underground Communist, harangued disgruntled Hungarians about his plan to bring paradise to Hungary. When Majorosy finally returned to Budapest, he was so disgusted by his experiences as a POW that he refused to speak to anyone in his family about them.

By 1944 Eleonóra was teaching primary grades in a good school in Pest. When the air-raid sirens announced the approach of American bombers, she herded her children into the cellar, where they pretended to ignore the sounds and vibrations of the bombing. "Getting to the school was always worse. Each day I crossed the bridge, trembling with fear, not knowing when the alarm would go off, and in terror that I would be caught in the open."[19] She rarely saw German troops, and was only dimly aware of Jewish persecution. Twice she saw groups of Jews being herded toward the Pest ghetto, a sector of the city center where the streets were blocked off with wooden barricades. On another occasion she saw gendarmes leading another group out the Vienna road toward the Óbuda brick factory (the collection depot for concentration camps). But in general she was untroubled by the war. "I was young and was constantly with people I liked, even in the cellars."

One young man she liked was a young Honvéd named József Arató, the friend of her favorite cousin, Elemér Kiss (the brother of József Kiss, from Chapter 1)—nicknamed Csibi. She frequently visited them at their barracks, where Csibi regaled them with stories, some of them hilarious, about how much he detested army life. He could not abide cruelty and was physically sickened when his barracks lieutenant, knowing of his scruples, would beat one of the Jews in the labor battalion and force him to watch. He filed fruitless requests for release from the army. When the Russians closed the ring around the capital in December, Csibi's unit was ordered to join the last-ditch SS defense of Castle Hill, a military operation regarded as tantamount to a death sentence. Arató was able to escape the trap by attaching himself to a bicycle corps that was withdrawn to Veszprém. (Later, when the Red Army broke the Axis line in western Hungary, Arató's unit moved to Germany, where they were captured by the American army, then turned over to the French, who incarcerated them.)

Just before Christmas Day the *házmester* of Eleonóra's building convened the tenants, explained that the Russians had surrounded the capital, and

19. Interview with Eleonóra Majorosy (July 5, 1991).

made arrangements for them to occupy the cellars. The building was half-empty, for many Christian families had already fled to the West, while Jews had been moved to the ghetto in Pest or to so-called protected houses. (After the war the tenants learned that the owner of the building, a Jew named Gyula Finger, had made the mistake of fleeing to the country, where he was picked up and sent to Auschwitz. Had he gone into the ghetto, he probably would have survived.) In the cellar each family had a sofa, a few chairs, and a table. Moreover, each was allotted a room on the first floor for washing and cooking. Food was plentiful, but was not communally shared. On the day before the siege began, a peasant from József Majorosy's farm in western Hungary arrived with a truckload of vegetables and staples. (He was unable to leave, and joined the family for the duration of the siege.) Stored in cabinets of the Majorosy flat on the fourth floor were sacks of beans, poppy seed, almonds, and cigarettes. All the windows had been taken out and stored behind wardrobes to avoid breakage. The frozen carcass of a butchered horse hung in the parlor window. The greatest problem was securing an adequate supply of water after the municipal pipes were cut. They had to fetch it from an outside tap at the "Death House," a nearby military prison that in January came under fire from the Russians across the Danube. Washing was minimal and nearly useless in a cellar filled with coal dust. József Majorosy did not bother to wash at all, a subject that provoked disparaging comments from his wife, already incensed because he had invited his former mistress, Marika, to join them after her place had been gutted. Adding to the company was Eleonóra's maternal grandmother, who arrived from her village of Pécel, twenty miles east, muttering over and over, "Pécel is lost. The Russians have come. Pécel is lost." Even in a coal cellar the Majorosy family maintained a certain bourgeois veneer. Eleonóra had brought down from the flat her most beautiful dresses. Her mother conspicuously ignored Marika and spent the daylight hours reading *Gone with the Wind*.

One night in mid-February, when the Germans tried to break out from their isolated aeries on Castle Hill, Csibi Kiss turned up in their shelter with six peasant soldiers and a Lieutenant István Esküdt. They had picked their way through the Russian line and crawled over Gellért Hill on all fours. In the flat above them was an exhausted band of German soldiers. "A sorrowful people with fear on their faces, they lay on the floor like dead men." After a few days rest the Germans slipped out of the building in white gowns in an effort to infiltrate the Russian line and escape west. The Hungarian soldiers remained. Eleonóra became romantically involved with Lieutenant Esküdt.

She brought down a windup gramophone from upstairs, put on one of her best dresses, and they danced in the dim light of the cellar.

These romantic hijinks abruptly ended when Russians occupied their street and began hammering on doors. József Majorosy knew what Russians were like and had no illusions about being "liberated." He instructed everyone to drape themselves in the filthiest rags they could find, take a soot bath, and pretend they were half-dead of disease and starvation. On February 12 the first Russians entered the cellar, looking for Germans. They were fearsome-looking Tartars, evoking for Eleonóra the traditional bogeymen of Hungarian folktales. Csibi and his companions surrendered at once and were led away.[20] A Tartar looked Eleonóra square in the face and said, "Devoshka!" (Girl!). Eleonóra's grandmother, who spoke Slovakian, replied, "There are only old women here." The Russians looked them over briefly and left. In the next building, a seventeen-year-old girl was gang-raped by a band of Russians.[21] Elsewhere on the street there were women who put on their best clothes and waited for the Russians as though they were dates. This was a tactical error—for the Russians were nothing like German gentlemen. The wife of an opera singer drenched herself in Chat Noir cologne. A Russian sniffed her curiously, found and promptly drank the rest of the cologne, and dragged her off to his den. No females in the Majorosy cellar were assaulted, probably because the *házmester* had thoughtfully removed female names from the roster that he was required to hand over to the Russians.

Within the first twenty-four hours the Red Army established a head-quarters on the second floor of their building. This nearly guaranteed their safety from marauders, but every night they heard drunken Russians hammering at the doors of other buildings in the street. The Majorosys were allowed to return to their flat upstairs, where they pasted paper across the window frames and for warmth slept together in the big middle room. To sweeten relations with their new bosses, they would loan their dinnerware and their servant woman to the Russian staff whenever the latter threw a party. Below them lived a Russian lieutenant named Victor—"a very nice man"—who warned them that a captain was boasting that he would soon

20. Csibi made light of the capture, saying, "Don't worry, Nóri, we are going out to beat to death the fascist wild animals in their own lair." He survived by joining a supply unit of the newly formed Russo-Hungarian army. Lieutenant Esküdt, on the other hand, was swallowed up in the POW net and never seen again.

21. This outrage so incensed the girl that thereafter she became a rabid anti-Communist whose intemperate outbursts resulted in two separate prison terms in the 1950s and 1960s as an "enemy of the regime."

bed with Eleonóra. She had to be hidden. She spent one night cramped in a tiny pantry, and the next morning took the ferry over to Pest, where she stayed with a cousin. That same day the captain barged into the Majorosy flat, looking for her. He was impressed by their grand piano, said he was an avid lover of classical music, and demanded that the lady of the house play for him. Already sick with fear of what might befall her daughter on that dangerous trek to Pest, she now endured another worry. Having read how Yankee soldiers looted Tara in *Gone with the Wind*, she had taken the precaution of hiding the family silverware in the piano. Now, with shaking hands, she seated herself on the stool and prayed that no dissonant metallic notes would arouse his curiosity. Apologizing that the instrument was out of tune she played for what seemed like an eternity while the Russian captain leaned against the piano, raptly attentive. She was grateful for Victor's warning, and equally indebted to him for a more personal service, for he became enamored of Marika, who packed her bags and moved in with him.

József Majorosy quickly established a quid pro quo relationship with the Russians. While his family knew about his captivity in Russia during the war, they had no inkling that he was fluent in their language—so fluent that the soldiers made a kind of pet out him, calling him Papa-Papa and taking him along as an interpreter when they needed to "liberate" something. He found the Russians manageable, but he never liked them. They were abysmally ignorant and primitive. Few of them knew the name of the country they were in. Budapest might as well be have been Paris, so far as they were concerned. He noticed that the Russian military maps did not indicate national frontiers. His explanation was that the purpose of a Red Army map was to allow you to get from point A to point B, not to burden you with superfluous details like the names of countries beyond Mother Russia or to pique your curiosity about the Bourgeois West.

By the beginning of April conditions in Budapest began to stabilize. Eleonóra no longer had to fear gangs of drunken Russians bent upon rape or thievery. Ferenc József Bridge, like all the Danube bridges, had been destroyed, but ferries and a pontoon bridge connected the two cities. Trams were again running in Pest (but not yet in Buda). Eleonóra's grandmother insisted upon returning at once to Pécel, so the family escorted her to Keleti Station, where she boarded an "ox train" for the ride home. (She found her house completely looted of all valuables—stolen not by Russians but by fellow villagers.) In Budapest teachers were called back to clean debris from schools and public buildings, and classes resumed in May, even before windows could be reglazed. (Glass had nearly disappeared in Budapest.) On May 9 Eleonóra attended a monster rally commemorating the formal end of the war. "I went to this one happily and voluntarily. In years to come I went only because I *had* to."

Meanwhile her fiancé, József Arató, had been picked up by the French and thrown into a huge prison pen near Strasbourg. The French provided no shelter, no bedding, no food. For two weeks the prisoners lived in holes they grubbed in the ground, until local peasants contracted with the guards to hire able-bodied laborers in return for food. Like thousands of half-starved people in the Europe of 1945, he made the mistake of gorging on one huge meal, became deathly ill, and crawled back to camp. The Hungarians were never charged with anything, nor were they questioned about possible war crimes. The French explained that they were being held to save them from seizure as slave laborers by the Russians. Arató had managed to hold on to a gold ring, which he offered to a sergeant as a bribe for his release. The sergeant pocketed it and told him to come back in ten days. He gave no receipt, and there were no witnesses. Arató fell into despair: his ring was gone, and he had nothing to show for it. Three days later the sergeant handed him a pass for Budapest. At the Hungarian frontier border guards swarmed over the train, combing out suspected Arrow Cross. He was allowed to proceed, but someone warned him that Russian guards met every train at Keleti Station and drafted healthy males for forced labor. Whether war criminal or not—it made no difference as the Russians tallied their human quotas. He took the precaution of jumping off the train before it reached the station.[22]

Eleonóra's expectations that the old way of life would return were quickly dashed. "Our family thought that the old life would go on exactly as before; we had no notion of what was to come." By 1946 inflation wiped out their savings. Two years later the Communists nationalized her father's small farm in western Hungary—without compensation.

In 1946 Eleonóra Majorosy married József Arató. They rode the "ox train" to her grandmother's house at Pécel for a frugal honeymoon. (On their return they ran out of money and had to walk part of the way home.) Since József came from a working-class family, the Communist regime overlooked his service with Horthy's army. While other comrades-in-arms drove manure carts in obscure Hortobágy hamlets, he had a clear path leading to his doctorate in economics and a career in the tobacco and frozen-food industries. One of his major duties was to examine the books of factories that the government planned to nationalize. In private Arató was often demonstrative in his denunciation of Communism, but in public his lips were sealed.

22. Interview with József Arató (September 5, 1988).

Their friend Csibi Kiss fared less well, even though he had briefly served in the Hungarian army recruited by the Red Army. After the war he briefly became a rising star in the Ministry of Agriculture, until Stalin broke with Tito, an event that triggered a purge that reached into all branches of government. Csibi was charged with spying for Tito (and the FBI), and a kangaroo court sentenced him to life in prison. Released after serving eight years in the infamous prison at Vác, he was barred from engaging in any profession or white-collar activity. Thereafter he earned his living by chopping wood and hauling coal until his health, damaged during prison years, failed; he died in 1958. Eleonóra's father managed to hold on to his post as a director of the market hall until 1951, when he was denounced for the crime of having been prosperous during the Horthy era. He lost his pension credits and spent the remainder of his working life as a minor clerk in a garage.

Kató Borosnyay (born 1923) came from an old patrician Transylvania family exiled in 1919, when her father, a lawyer, refused to take a loyalty oath supporting the Romanian government. They moved to Sopron, a city next door to Austria and filled with a pro-German element. For a time the Borosnyays, having been uprooted by the territorial dislocations of the Trianon Treaty, shared some of this infatuation with Germany. While unhappy about the *Anschluβ*, which was received with jubilation among the German population of Sopron, they nevertheless were elated when Hitler partitioned Czechoslovakia in 1938 and gave back to Hungary a slice of Slovakia taken by Trianon. "Everyone burned with excitement. We expected Transylvania to be returned next."[23] Her older brother, a student at the local military school, joined others of his class when they broke into a military storehouse, seized arms, and cycled toward Kassa prepared to battle with the Czechs. It was an impromptu crusade that could have had dire international implications, but their officers jumped into cars and fetched them back. Punishment consisted in restriction to barracks for a few days along with much backslapping, winking, and other signs of unofficial endorsement of their patriotic fervor.

When the war broke out with Russia, the family was confident that the Germans would end it quickly. Kató's brother went to the front in 1943 as an officer, and in that year the family moved to Budapest, where her father became involved with legal issues bearing upon the restoration of Transylvania. They lived in a patrician house on Pasaréti Road, at the foot of Rózsadomb Hill, and from here Kató commuted to a gun factory in Zugló, a

23. Interview with Kató Borosnyay (April 18, 1989).

grim industrial area beyond City Park, where she was a social worker. Her agency provided advice and health services "patterned on the English settlement pattern." The idea was to intercept discontent among the workers before it took a radical political turn. When workers were bombed out, she assessed the damage and arranged for medical and financial aid. "I wanted to help poor people, through Christian charity, not through politics."

As the war wore down and degenerated into one dismal retreat after another, her brother lost his élan. Once she visited him at his base in the Carpathians, and together they listened to the distant rumble of artillery fire beyond the high mountains. Already the Russians were breaking through passes that the newspaper had classified as "impenetrable." He was gloomy and defeatist, not like his old self. He told her that the Russians could not be held back and that the promises of the Germans were all lies. A few weeks later Romania capitulated.

On October 15, 1944, Kató watched with sinking sense of hopelessness as monster tanks and columns of SS filed across Ferenc József Bridge. A day later Admiral Horthy was deposed and Ferenc Szálasi was head of state. At this time an officer friend of Kató's brother came with a message telling them that they should evacuate the city at once. He brought disturbing confirmation of the horrifying tales in circulation about what Russian soldiers did to women. Kató's mother wanted to leave for Austria at once, but her husband refused to go, saying that he had left his country once before and would not do so again. Already Kató's factory had packed up and moved to Austria with its entire workforce. She chose to remain behind with her family and wait for the whirlwind.

On Christmas Day they had a Nativity feast, inviting to their table two German officers who were quartered with them. They had plenty of food, shipped earlier from their country estate—smoked pork, flour, preserves, dried beans, crocks of sauerkraut. Toward evening, the shelling increased to a crescendo, and they spent their first full night in the cellar. A mortar round landed in the front garden, shattering the windows. They sat up, waiting for dawn, hoping that this underground existence would not be permanent. In the morning their German officers reported that Russians had fortified houses in Gábor Áron Street, just two streets away, and that the Borosnyay house had been designated a "hedgehog house"—a firing outpost to be defended until the very end. The family went upstairs briefly to collect food and supplies, and found the Germans had already set up machine guns in the windows to cover Pasaréti Road. The municipal power and water had been cut; drinking water now came from the furnace boiler. For eleven days their house was a strong point on the front line of the German defense, while they huddled in the cellar. There were fourteen of them down there.

On January 6 the Germans evacuated their house. A sergeant came downstairs, surrendered the key to the front door to the family, thanked them for the use of their house, and slipped away. His punctiliousness was unnecessary because the front door had been splintered by a mortar shell. Within hours the first Russians arrived. They were plainclothesmen who spoke Hungarian. Keeping their hands in their pockets, as though they had pistols there, they politely asked whether any Germans were in the building. This group was closely followed by Red Army officers, intelligent and good-looking men, who interviewed them through interpreters. However, the next batch were common soldiers in ill-fitting, stained uniforms who demanded pálinka, watches, canned food. They stripped the house of its bed sheets, which were in great demand because they provided camouflage coverings in the snow. After stuffing themselves with handfuls of sauerkraut, they poured the rest of it into a bed sheet and carried it away.

As the front moved westward toward St. John's Hospital, the parties of Russians became unruly. One night four of them burst into the cellar, crying, "Barishna! Barishna!" (Woman! Woman!). As they pulled Kató and her sister-in-law to their feet, her father got in front of them as a shield. A Russian aimed his machine pistol at his head, but at that moment there was a burst of gunfire out on the street, close at hand. The Russians streamed outside. Thoroughly intimidated, Kató decided to leave at once. She heard that nearby on Pasaréti Road there was a house under Swedish protection that might take her in. She packed a knapsack with food and, avoiding the street, from which there were volleys of fire, climbed over fences and crawled through gardens to the house, only to find it bombed out, deserted, and burning. She pushed on toward a cousin's house on Gábor Áron—crawling some of the way between the firing lines of the two armies. Here she found a refuge, except that they had little food. Several times in the following days Kató had to crawl back to her father's house for food. Shrapnel and bullets were not the only danger on such sorties. Once Russian soldiers spotted her and chased her in broad daylight—very unusual for their sexual sorties. She was saved only because of the chance appearance of a Red Army officer.

Since her cousin was a doctor who provided medical aid for the Russians, his house had a certain immunity during the daylight hours. Nighttime was a different story. Drunken Russians combed the house looking for women and plunder. For a few days her cousin's dog always gave them a few minutes' warning by his fit of barking, but then the Russians shot the dog. One evening Mongolian soldiers locked all the men of the house in the cellar. Knowing what was coming, the women fled upstairs, trying to hide in wardrobes or under beds. Their hope was that the Russians would be too drunk to make a careful search for them. Kató jumped into a bed and pulled eiderdowns over her. Russians began to ransack a bookcase for jewelry and gold, tossing piles of musty books on top of her. "I feared I might sneeze." They found her cousin's wife, who was eight months pregnant, and pulled her away, but after begging permission to go to the bathroom, she climbed out of a window and hid in a neighboring house.

After the German lines had either been destroyed or withdrawn to the high ground of Castle Hill, the Russian assaults diminished. They were unfailingly kind to children and old people—when not drunk. Kató found herself in an ticklish situation when a Russian officer gave her a bar of soap, declared his love for her, privately confessed that his family was bourgeois, and promised to return from Berlin after the war to marry her. She dared not show what she felt, because at least his amorous attention afforded her protection from cruder invitations.

The only available water supply was the outside tap in the courtyard of St. John's Hospital, where civilians queued up with jugs and pails. Kató, with her two ten-liter jugs seesawing on a stout stick, was bound for water the day the German garrison trapped on Castle Hill tried to break through the Russian ring. She fled back to her cousin's house as a furious firefight moiled through the Pasaréti quarter. From an upstairs window she watched a phalanx of SS dash across Gábor Áron, but they were soon surrounded. After a quarter of an hour the firing died away. Russians lined up the SS captives against a garden wall across the street from her window and machine-gunned them on the spot. "On that day, in the middle of Gábor Áron Street, there were so many Germans and horses killed, and so high, you could barely see over them. Russian tanks just ran over the bodies, turning them into jam." Only a few lone Germans escaped to the west.

When, a month later, the Germans launched their counteroffensive to retake Budapest, the Russians flew into a panic. Kató was waiting in a line for bread when guards forced everyone inside a courtyard and sorted out the healthy ones from the old and disabled. They said that the Germans were attacking down the Danube from Esztergom, and all of them had to dig trenches. Russian trucks took them north, past Szentendre, where they were ordered out and handed spades. Around them was a small army of Hungarian POWs, all of them digging. The newcomers were split into teams of ten, each with an armed guard. A woman next to Kató stumbled and fell. She had been giving her food allotment to her three children and was nearly starved. Kató stepped out of line to help her, but the others cried out, "Leave her alone! If we stop, the guard will shoot us!" Kató found a Russian captain and told him, "You cannot abandon a woman with three children." She offered to take the woman home and asked for a military pass and a chit for food. He wrote the paper, and she hoisted the woman on her back and walked across the fields to a Russian field kitchen. Fortified by soup they walked the ten miles back to Óbuda, where she met her father, who had come looking for her, sick with worry. Meanwhile the German offensive petered out on the edge of Szentendre. It had been a dying spasm. By the first of April the only Germans remaining in Hungary were POWs.

The warm weather brought an abrupt end to horse steak and horse stew. What with confiscation of foodstuffs by the Germans and thefts by the Russians, food supplies had all but disappeared. The national currency was worthless, although government agencies still paid employees in pengős at prewar rates. Kató and others scoured the Buda hillsides in search of thistle and other weeds that could be cooked into an edible sauce. Beans and lentils, a staple during the siege, now had to be hoarded as seed for spring planting. It was not uncommon to find on street corners ladies in prewar silk dresses hoping to trade a tray of gold collar buttons, scraps of lace, or antique stamps for food. The Borosnyay house had been nearly gutted by the battle. Furniture had been chopped up for firewood, and the place had been stripped of everything of value. "The Russians carried off most of it. Except for a valuable Brussels lace scarf. A German must have taken that, because no Russian would have known its value."

On Easter Sunday Kató's brother turned up. Shortly before the Esztergom offensive he had attended service and taken communion at the cathedral. A priest told him that if he ever needed any help, he should go to the Franciscan monastery. A few days later he was taken prisoner when the German-Hungarian army was cut to pieces. As the line of POWs wound through Esztergom at night, he ducked down an alley and was taken in at the monastery and hidden in the attic with some other Hungarian fugitives. After the Russians left, the brothers gave him civilian clothes, and he hiked back to Budapest. He had no papers. Billboard posters announced that all former Honvéd soldiers must report to their home barracks to receive official discharge and identity papers. Since his barracks was in Szeged and there was little to hold them in Budapest, the whole family decided to go with him. The train was packed, but they obtained space for their bundles and themselves in the baggage van next to cages crammed with unhappy dogs. "The trip took forever, and the dogs never stopped barking. In the end I thought I might be barking, too."

Conditions in Szeged proved to be better than in Budapest. There was a real market, and the population was "suffocated by food." Her brother was congratulated for reporting dutifully to his barracks (as many did not) and was issued his formal discharge from the army. It was a mistake, for the authorities had a record that he had survived the war. Three years later, when the Communists, under Rákosi, took over the government, he was hunted down, denounced as a Horthy fascist officer, and given a seven-year prison term.[24] Others in the family began a slow climb back. Kató never forgot being chased through the snow by brutalized Russians or shuddering under eider-downs as they ransacked the bedroom. "My attitude toward the Russians? I would like to go down to the train station and give the last Russian leaving Hungary a big bouquet of flowers."

Lily Muráti was one of the famous Hungarian actresses of her generation, and she feared that when the Russians took the city, she would be a special trophy for them, for an officer friend had spelled out to her in graphic detail what they did with women of a conquered country. Yet she had also heard stories about their queer gluttony for wrist watches, which they stacked up their forearms like the brass rings of primitive tribesmen. She had an idea. Before the shops closed down for good, she bought all the cheap wrist watches she could lay her hands on, planning to offer one to each potential attacker, to buy him off. She was in her shelter when her first Russian burst in. A common soldier with a tommy gun held at ready, he looked her over and ordered her to go out with him. Walking ahead, she reached into her purse for a watch. Probably thinking she was reaching for a pistol, the Russian raised his gun—she thought either to shoot her or to club her with it. He did neither. He had caught sight of the watches. He pushed her down, snatched her purse, and ran off in panic like a common street arab.

Her hoard of watches was gone, but she did not need them. A short time later, when she teamed with others and attempted to escape from the city, her group was captured by a Russian patrol. Suspected of being spies, they passed in and out of a series of interrogation rooms and prisons. Always she was well treated because, as she learned to her great surprise, Russians had a policy of raping women only *outside* prison walls. However, at one place she

---

24. During this interview her brother sat by her side. Even though more than forty years had passed, he would not consent to an interview.

shared a cell with a minister's daughter, who beckoned Russian guards into the cell and had sex with them. Unknown to the men, she had contracted syphilis from a Russian rapist, and this was her revenge. Lily Muráti escaped physical violation without having to go to the lengths of an actress friend of hers who smeared feces all over her body—even into her hair—in order to fend off amorous Russians.[25]

When war broke out in Poland, Mária Badal (born 1918) was on her way to Rome to begin a fellowship in classical archaeology. In Milano she was surprised at the urgency displayed by Italians, for young men being called up for the army crowded the train with their wooden boxes. When she heard that the German army had overrun Danzig, she started for home at once, only to find Budapest calm and detached from events in Poland. After the Germans overran Poland, she met many Polish officers who had crossed the eastern Kárpátalja region and taken refuge in Hungary, where they were interned comfortably at Lake Balaton or were assisted in making their way to France by way of Yugoslavia.[26]

Mária's father encouraged her to continue with her studies as though nothing had happened. In 1943 she was awarded a scholarship from the Italian government to work on her dissertation, "Christian Monuments in Ostia." Arriving at Rome in July, when the first Allied bombs fell on the city, she found herself in a country about to collapse. The people were living on starvation fare, for the Germans, retreating north, were stripping the country of its material and foodstuffs. Fearing they might carry off Roman antiquities, the Italian government sealed museums, and at Ostia constructed a corn-wire fence around the excavated sector. It was ironic that the closer the country came to total collapse, the more policemen guarded antiquities. Mária returned to her home on Zsámbéki Street in Buda and resumed her work at the university. She regularly commuted to the archaeology department until the Russians closed the ring around the city.

On Christmas Day Mária's family celebrated with a lavish meal, put the final touches on holiday decorations, and then went below, into the cellar, where they remained for forty-two days. With Mária were her mother and father, two sisters, each with small babies, and a brother-in-law. A few blocks away her brother János, an artillerist in the Honvédség, manned a piece that fired point-blank down Stromfeld Road, the principal artery for Zsámbéki.

25. Lili Muráti interview, aired on Hungarian Television, January 5, 1990.
26. Interview with Mária Badal (February 5, 1989).

The fighting soon raged around their house. The Russians used flame-throwers to root out the enemy from a house only four doors away, and the Badals were terrified that their house would become the next holocaust. Mária was particularly alarmed for her father's safety because the Russians were shanghaiing Hungarian men and forcing them to precede the Red Army storming parties on the theory that the Germans would either refrain from firing or would shoot the Hungarians and thus expose their hiding places. Mária was bitter about this: "Only the Russians would do such a thing. The Germans would not. They were human beings."

On February 2 the Russians broke into their cellar. An undetected sniper across the street had just killed a Russian soldier, and they assumed the shot had come from the Badal house. The Russians pulled the men outside, and everyone in the cellar thought their execution inevitable. Mária's brother-in-law kissed everyone good-bye, but her father, who, as a former submayor of his Buda district, was accustomed to command, maintained a stoical mask. It was Mária's mother who saved them. She was a native of Serbia and used her language to explain that the shot did not come from their house. There was just enough affinity between Serbian and Russian for the soldiers to understand. The family then got spades and buried the soldier in their garden, where he still lies.[27]

The Russians lodged with them for a month, stripping the house of everything valuable. The family saved a Persian rug by dragging it into the basement. Altogether three different Russian units were billeted in their house—one that camouflaged gas masks with white paint, another a medical unit, and the third a telephone exchange. The family was not molested physically, although women of all ages in the neighborhood were raped—even a fourteen-year-old neighbor. Her mother's Serbian seemed to reassure the Russians. She overheard one of them say, "These people are Slavs—they are good people." "Good people" became their litany. A Russian found an icon of the Virgin and showed it to the others, one of whom exclaimed, "These must be good people." But it did not prevent them from stealing whatever they wanted. Her father was seventy-nine and bedridden. When Russians demanded his watch, he refused to give it up. "This watch belongs to me." They took it. Her mother somehow possessed the authority to face them down. When a Russian demanded that she give him her ring, she refused. He reached in a china cupboard and seized a great stack of dinner plates and

27. Later the Badals planted a rosebush on the grave. "He now fertilizes a nice rose—a *white* rose."

said peevishly, "Unless you give it to me, I'll drop these." She looked him in the eye and said, "Then drop them. I won't give it to you." He put them back. When another one, brandishing his machine gun, pulled off his boots and ordered her to clean them, she said, "If you want them clean, you'd better lick them off with your tongue." He laughed and shouldered his gun.

The house-to-house fighting continued. The Russians bivouacked in their house and shared with the family their bread ration, which supplemented their basic food supply of boiled peas and beans. "Beans! After the siege we wanted to erect a statue to the bean!" The Russians had stabled horses on the first floor of a house across the street, while a school inspector, a fastidious and fussy man, occupied the cellar. (Years later, despite ingenious efforts at fumigation, the horse odor remained.) Bark stripped from trees was inadequate as fodder, and whenever a horse died, everyone in the street, Russian and Hungarian, descended upon the carcass with butcher knives. Electricity, gas, oil, and water had been cut off long ago. When Buda was liberated and the water was turned on again, the Russians quartered with them would wash their meat and store it in the toilet bowl. One of them accidentally pulled the flush chain and the meat disappeared. Assuming he was the victim of some Hungarian trick, he exclaimed, "You stole my meat!" Then he machine-gunned the toilet bowl.[28] When the Russians moved on at the end of March, the Badals again moved upstairs. Their house had been remodeled just before the siege. Now the roof was gutted, and there were gaping holes in the outer walls (from German, not Russian, cannon). In the upper rooms there were the telltale traces of recent Russian occupancy: every corner reeked of urine, books had been pulled from cases, ripped apart and urinated upon, while the carpets were rotten with feces.

News was not all bad. To their great surprise János appeared, now wearing a bloody hand-me-down Russian uniform. When captured he was given the choice of joining the new Russo-Hungarian army or going to Siberia as a POW. He chose the former. After a quick political indoctrination, he was issued the uniform of a newly dead Russian soldier and was soon blasting away at German checkpoints. In one attack he helped dislodge Germans holed up in his old high school, after which he knelt and kissed the floor to the astonishment of the porter, who failed to recognize him and was flabbergasted to see what he thought was a Russian soldier kissing that floor.

28. With such stories it is impossible to tell where historical fact ends and folklore begins. In the course of my interviews I heard at least three accounts of a Russian executing a toilet bowl. Another "repeater" has to do with a Russian soldier stealing a longcase clock. When it strikes the hour, he shoots it (or dashes it to the ground) in alarm.

Another brother, Edward, who was studying for the priesthood at Zirc Monastery, west of Budapest, also arrived with an account of his adventures. The seminarians had poured all alcohol down the drains before the Russians arrived. They had also filled aluminum boxes with silverware, which they sank into the fishpond. Accustomed to this dodge, the Russians confiscated a fire engine, drained the pond, and got the treasure. Some of these peasant soldiers had guilty consciences. A Russian coming out of the sacristy with a bag of booty met Edward. On seeing a priest, he colored, made the sign of the cross, and fled.

There remained a massive cleanup. Not one building on Zsámbéki Street escaped major damage. The residents were drafted at once to clear the streets of detritus, the first being the carcasses of thirty putrefying horses. Once these chores were done, Mária dusted off her books and resumed her research. Each day she passed through a landscape as ruinous as the Roman forum. In July, only five months after emerging from her cellar, Mária Badal received her doctorate from the University of Budapest, one of the first such degrees award after the siege.[29]

Growing up in Budapest during the 1930s, Gabriella Kornhauser never gave much thought to the fact that her mother was half-Jewish. On the other hand, she had many thoughts about her father, a voluble and headstrong man, who boasted that he was "a Saxon from Brasow," and went on to explain to anyone who would listen that he had been driven out of his native Transylvania when the Romanians took the country. In Budapest he made a good living as a lawyer for a steel corporation, and during the nationalistic fervor of the 1930s, when Germans flocked to registrars in order to magyarize their surnames, he refused to give his up. Gabriella (born 1924) grew up on Németvölgyi Street, in the leafy hills of Buda, where she followed her mother's footsteps in attending a rigorous Catholic school.[30]

Things began falling apart for the Kornhausers after the first German occupation, in March 1944. Although her father was an ardent Saxon, he had no use for Nazism and only contempt for the lumpen proletariat at his factory who rallied to the Arrow Cross banner. He seriously underestimated their capacity for mischief. His open expression of vaguely "liberal" ideas cost him his job and placed him under suspicion as a possible Communist

29. During the 1956 revolution her brother János escaped to the West, where he settled in Paris and became a successful film director. Her brother Edward completed his studies and entered the Roman Catholic priesthood.

30. Interview with Gabriella Kornhauser (January 4, 1990).

sympathizer—which in view of his conservatism was ludicrous. Alarmed by the mounting political hysteria, he took the precaution of obtaining a Swiss identity card for himself and his family.

When the siege of Buda commenced in earnest on December 25, the Kornhausers went into their cellar with fifteen other families of their building. Food was short—there were some potatoes and the usual dried beans. Their luckiest day came when an army horse fell down the cellar steps and had to be shot by a German soldier. They shared the meat—sweeter than beef or pork. The greatest problem was obtaining water. There was a deep snow, so the yard was divided into sixteen equal parts, each family having its own plot. Snow theft was commonplace, and they nearly came to blows over drifts. Inside they had a communal stove and broke up furniture or salvaged debris from houses and trees blown into kindling by the barrage.

The critical day was January 18. They had learned that Pest had capitulated to the Russians, and they knew that the German-Hungarian army was being steadily eroded in Buda. During a card game, when the subject came up, Gabriella's father made a sarcastic remark about the "German liberators." An informer in the cellar reported the remark to the local Nyilas headquarters down the road. Within hours a gang had seized the family and hauled them to their barracks. When her father protested that as good Hungarian citizens they could not be detained without due process, a Nyilas tough beat him up in front of his family. They suspected that Kornhauser was a Jewish name. Her father had the documents to refute it, but in her mother's purse was a birth certificate, which she had failed to destroy, revealing her as one-half Jewish. After the Nyilas went through her papers, the whole family was locked up in the basement with about eighty people accused of being either Jews or army deserters, all of them crammed shoulder to shoulder without space to sit or to lie down.

At dawn a guard read a list of names and took about a dozen people out, including Gabriella's mother and an eighty-year-old couple. They heard these people screaming; only later did they learn that guards had been breaking their fingers, making them admit they were "dirty Jews." Gabriella frantically wormed her way to a small basement window opening onto a dingy courtyard. As she watched, guards dragged out her mother, pushed her against a wall, and shot her. In all there were thirteen executions—all Jews.

In the morning Gabriella and her father were interrogated by a young Nyilas leader who looked at her in a puzzled way. Finally he introduced himself as Ferenc Megadja. Didn't she remember him? They were schoolmates together. Yes, even farther back he remembered her. At their first communion he climbed a fence and stole branches of lilacs, which he gave to her. His brother, the Nyilas who had beaten up her father the night before, became very apologetic. What had happened was regrettable. He said that if they had only known she was a friend of Ferenc's, the unfortunate affair would not have happened.

Gabriella and her father went home. On February 20, just two days after the "liberation" of Buda, two Russian soldiers broke into their cellar and raped Gabriella. A few nights later another Russian flashed a light in her eyes, pushed her upstairs, and raped her. (She thought he might have been a Mongol, but never saw his face.) Before he left, he said he liked her and gave her some advice: she ought to smear her face with red paint and say she was sick, so that no one would dare touch her. Thereafter she did this and wore her arm in a sling, pretending it was infected. It worked—the Russians left her alone. During the ensuing months she was tortured by the thought that she might be pregnant. Abortions were illegal in Hungary, but she swore she would not bear the monster's child. (As it happened, so many women were impregnated by Russians that during the summer a free abortion clinic opened in the sports hospital in Pest.)

When the siege was over, her father attended ten exhumations before finally recovering his wife's body from a mass grave. Gabriella later heard that the Megadja brothers had gotten off safely to the West—probably to America.

On March 19, 1944, Anna Tarr lost her best friend at the Foreign Trade High School. The girl, who was Jewish, simply vanished and was never seen again. She and her family had been on a Sunday excursion in the country, and when they returned to the city, they were caught in a police net at Keleti Station. On this same day Anna had seen a procession of Jews, led by gendarmes, on Grand Boulevard (soon to be renamed Lenin Boulevard), and had wondered where they were going. Someone said that they were being taken away for forced labor, but she knew nothing of death camps until after the war. She then had to conclude that her friend was among this or a like procession.[31]

Anna Tarr (born 1925) came from a working-class family that lived near Keleti Station. During the First World War her father had served on the Russian front until the last days, when he threw his rifle away, buried his uniform, and walked away from the Hungarian army. By this time he was in the middle of a revolution in which Whites and Reds were cutting one

31. Interview with Anna Tarr (March 4, 1989).

another's throats, but Russian peasants hid and fed him until he could make his way back to Budapest. Once back in Budapest, he, a blacksmith by trade, took a skilled job as designer at a fence factory, where he made a good living, regularly attended church, and, having seen at first hand Communism in all its convulsions, trusted in the political wisdom of Miklós Horthy. In the late 1930s he relocated to a food-processing factory and moved his family to a small house with garden on Üteg Street in Angyalföld, a working-class district in the northwest of Pest. They planted fruit trees, raised rabbits and chickens, and canned their own vegetables. For Anna they led the good life: "It is just not true that the Horthy period was miserable for working people. We were grateful to him. If he had not broken the revolution in 1919, Hungary would now be only a miserable province in the Soviet Union. Horthy supported the Germans only because they opposed the Russians, who were always worse."

After leaving school Anna took a clerical job in a cooperative. At seventeen she fell in love with a young forester, but he was drafted into the army and vanished in the slaughter pits of the Don Bend debacle. The war also encroached in other ways. Initially the American carpet bombings, which occurred during daylight hours, concentrated mainly on the Csepel Island factories far down the river, but beginning on July 2 they began to target the Angyalföld, in an attempt to take out a Mercedes airplane motor factory. At night it was the turn of the RAF, which was mining the Danube in order to cut river traffic to Germany. Since many of these mines dropped in the district, there was a blackout and curfew every night at ten o'clock. Sundays seemed to be the day favored by the British for their raids.

Anna felt humiliated and ashamed when she met former schoolmates wearing the telltale yellow stars. As an act of contrition she gave her birth certificate to a Jewish friend, and most certainly saved the life of an old Jewish man when she provided him with the birth certificate of one of her deceased uncles. When the Arrow Cross took control of the government, she and her father arranged for nineteen Jews to be sheltered and fed in an abandoned flat in their neighborhood. The Tarr family had plenty of basic foodstuffs. Her father collected from his factory such a quantity of dried lentils, beans, and peas that it lasted them for two years after the war.

When the ring around Budapest closed on December 25, the Germans converted the houses and garden plots of Angyalföld into a major defensive line. Two soldiers set up their machine gun in a window of the Tarr house. They were agreeable men who courted two local girls. There was no savage fighting in this district. The two armies on this front dueled with artillery pieces, their rounds whistling overhead harmlessly. Because the Hungarian word *üteg* means "artillery battery," the people on Üteg street made up jokes about it.

However, on January 11 the Germans began to pull back toward Buda. The two German soldiers, sensing that their defense was hopeless, burned their uniforms and hid in the houses of their girlfriends. (Although dozens of neighbors knew where these soldiers were, no one reported them to the Russians. They escaped the Russian dragnet and later married the girls.) The next morning Anna heard Russian voices outside. "We had heard stories about the Russians, and we had always feared Communism, but all this was nothing compared to what really came." The family huddled together in a corner of the basement and sang "Himnusz," the Hungarian national anthem, to keep their spirits up—"Isten áldd meg a magyart" (God bless the Hungarian). Some angry Russian privates came in. Her father had stabled twelve delivery horses from his factory in an outbuilding, and the Russians' discovery of these was clear proof that they were capitalists. When her father spoke to them in Russian, they showed great surprise and were instantly mollified. After shaking hands all round, they left the house alone and only stole the horses. A day later the family was ordered to evacuate the house, which became an officers' quarters. Her mother was ill and had to be carried to a neighboring house. Anna escaped assault by hiding in the rectory of her church, but at night, as the Russians made their rounds, she could hear doors being pounded and the protests, cries, and moans of women. One woman in the neighborhood was raped by twenty different Russians before her luck changed—she was appropriated by an officer for his own and exclusive use. Anna never recovered from the trauma of these first days of the Russian occupation. "Even now [forty-five years later], when I see a Russian soldier at the railway station, I quake with terror." After she returned to her job, she was attacked one night on the street by two drunken Russians bent on robbery, not rape. In high school Anna had earned medals as a discus thrower. She threw the Russian who had grabbed her over her shoulder and outran the other.

With the restoration of water, gas, and electricity by the end of May, Anna prepared to step back into the world she had known before the war. It was not to be. "Reconstruction began, and a real dangerous time began. People were denouncing one another." Moral values turned topsy-turvy. In her district she met a former Nyilas bravo who now wore a red star in his lapel. "Has my eyesight failed, or is that what I think it is?" she asked. He became very nervous. "Don't say anything about it;" then he whispered, "I have to hide somewhere." Inflation was out of control, encouraged by the Russians to destroy middle-class cohesion. They stamped "100 Pengő" on one-pengő notes to devalue the currency. Her job was phased out, and for seven years she was unable to find another one—probably because of some criticism she had leveled against the new regime, but in such cases it was never possible to discover reasons. She married, but the succeeding ten years were hard and bitter.

In 1956 she joined a hundred thousand shouting Hungarians near Heroes' Square and watched as the gigantic statue of Stalin toppled from its pedestal. "This was the biggest thrill of my life." All over the city crowds of demonstrators shouted, "Russians go home!" and "Strike tomorrow!" To control the crowds the government cut the electric power. Lights went off in the city, and torches came on. At military barracks soldiers broke into armories and passed weapons to young people. Anna was in the crowd demonstrating at Parliament Square when the ÁVH opened fire with machine guns from the rooftops. "I had a protecting angel on that day, because dead and wounded were falling around me." Later she gave blood at the Jewish hospital. News came that at Erkel Square the ÁVH had opened fire from their headquarters building and killed forty or fifty demonstrators. The citizens besieged the building. Anna was on hand when the ÁVH came out. Most of them surrendered as though on parade, but a few had put on regular police uniforms and tried to slip away. Nearly all of them were torn to pieces by the mob— kicked and beaten to death, shot, thrown from rooftops, or hung from lampposts with hundred-forint notes stuffed in their mouths. "We thought the Russian tyranny was over. The mood of the people was cleansed." Out on the Vienna road patriots assembled as they waited for American tanks to support them. Hopes rapidly faded. Tanks arrived, but they came from the opposite direction and had red stars on their turrets. Anna Tarr had to wait thirty-three more years before Hungary liberated itself from the "liberators." For Anna the cultural damage was beyond repair. "The whole Communist regime stank of corruption in every walk of life. It ruined the morals of our people as the Turks and the Hapsburgs failed to do. Its legacy? The Russians drove out the people with brains."

"When Russia and Germany chewed up Poland, we had no thought of Hungary ever entering the war. We were afraid of the Russians because they had destroyed their middle classes, and we disliked Germans as aggressive bullies, but when Hitler gave us back the lands lost by Trianon, we had to support him."[32] Ilona Almási Szabó (born 1917) had no illusions about an

---

32. Interview with Ilona Almási Szabó (February 2, 1989).

easy life. Her father died when she was ten, and she had to quit school to help support her family. She found a job as a bookkeeper at Ford Motor Company, where she met a young mechanical engineer who was trying to develop his own ball-bearing industry. Although his father had declared bankruptcy in 1929, the son had salvaged from the family estate a summer villa on the Danube above Vác and an empty factory building in Újpest. László and Ilona planned to marry, but always their finances were drained dry by the cost of machinery that he was buying for his factory. Then, in 1938, the couple suffered a worse setback. László was drafted as a reserve antiaircraft officer. He failed to obtain an exemption from military service because his ball-bearing factory, though counted as an essential industry, was not yet in production. All told they had to postpone their wedding six times.

The couple was on holiday at their Danube villa when news came that Hungary had declared war against the Soviet Union. Within a week László found himself on a six-week campaign march in the Ukraine. It was wholly superfluous, for the Wehrmacht had left the Honvédség far behind. In time he was assigned to an antiaircraft battery along the frontier, where he chipped away at occasional Russian planes but at least had the good fortune to miss the Don Bend fiasco.

Living conditions in Ilona's working-class district of Újpest took a downward turn in 1943. Her daughter was born in July and developed a vitamin-D deficiency because of a milk shortage. Bread lines stretched for blocks, and black-market prices soared. From time to time the Ford Company provided precious packets of meat. And after the German occupation she was able to trade household items for vitamins. By this time young males had nearly disappeared from the Újpest quarter, for after the Don Bend battle nearly every household hung out a black flag indicating the death of a father, son, husband, or brother. For eight months she fed her family on split peas cooked in salt water and then baked as a cake, or on pancakes composed of water, tallow, and flour. A major diversion was scanning the sky for the first signs of the American armada. "You could set your watch when the American bombers came over. It was always nine in the morning. Sometimes there were a thousand planes. It was a marvelous sight—but then we lived way upriver at Újpest, and they never bombed us."

After the second German occupation, in October, László's unit was ordered to evacuate their equipment to the west. Having no appetite for laying down his life in defense of the Reich, he and two other others of his unit deserted. He went underground, hiding out in his empty factory building and in his summer house, while Nyilas combed the district looking for deserters and

Jews. Ilona sneaked food to him. It was December, and the Russians had nearly reached Budapest, one army swooping down toward Vác from the north, and the other pressing up from Kecskemét and the *puszta*. It was an open question which adversary would capture László. If the Nyilas caught him, he would be killed; if the Russians got him, he would be imprisoned. One afternoon while she was returning from the cottage by rail, Russian planes swooped down and strafed the train. The car was so crowded that she had been standing on one foot. Now it was nearly impossible to push out through the mob, but somehow she squeezed out of a window and rushed into a cornfield while the Russian pilots took target practice on the crippled train.

Ilona first caught sight of Russian ground troops on January 10. Five or six of them in snow gowns broke into a pub cellar across the street, shot the head off a barrel and began to drink. They were soon too drunk to think of pillage or women. That would come later. Their search parties did what the Arrow Cross failed to do—they found László and put him in a labor battalion repairing a railway bridge northwest of the city. For a brief period some Russian soldiers were billeted in the house with Ilona and her daughter. "My teeth chattered so bad I had trouble closing my mouth that first day, but the fear of Russians was worse than what they did." Actually, Újpest fared better than other districts of Budapest because it was obviously a proletarian neighborhood. Still, the soldiers stole whatever they could carry off—cigarettes, cutlery, jewelry—even though they physically molested no one in that house. A soldier named Misha struck up a friendship. He seemed barely out of his teens but had been in the army for seven years. For him war was a simple matter. He had a dozen wrist watches on his arm and slept with a machine gun belt draped over his shoulder. When Russian officers commandeered the house for their own use, Ilona and her daughter moved into the unheated factory. After the siege ended, László escaped from the labor camp and returned to Újpest, where he went into hiding. He was not being paranoid; the Russians were filling trains with shipments of human cargo—Hungarian males bound for labor camps in Russia. Like many other men of his district, László stayed indoors, completely out of sight, until late autumn, when it became safe to venture outside.

At the first opportunity after the siege was lifted, Ilona went up to her summer cottage to collect items for sale or salvage. The place looked like it had been hit by a tornado. The Russians had kept horses in a bedroom and fueled the stove with books from her nine-hundred-volume library. The furniture not stolen was wrecked. Windows were gone; doors were smashed to kindling. Neighbors told her that her eighty-two-year-old caretaker had been raped. "They also said that some Russians had fucked a goat—but I could never decide whether that was true."

As soon as there was a semblance of order in Hungary, László returned to his factory. Russians had carried off some essential machine tools and wantonly wrecked tables, shelving, closets, but after two years of working late at night and on weekends, he began to produce ball bearings. He succeeded all too well, for in 1948, after the Communists took control of the government, his factory was nationalized. He was hired to teach the new manager his job—then fired. Thereafter he was a marked man, indelibly branded as an "ex–fascist army officer." Some weeks after being fired, a neighbor denounced him for listening to Radio Free Europe, and two policemen took him away. Ilona came home to find her husband gone and policemen with an order for her and her daughter to vacate the flat within two hours. When she asked what she could take with her, they said, "Only your ass." For three months László languished in the municipal prison near Chain Bridge, until released for lack of evidence. He found an assembly job in a metal factory, which during the Korean War manufactured land mines that were distributed to the Chinese and North Koreans through a Soviet Union network.

One day in 1951 Ilona Almási returned from work to find her flat illuminated. Agents of the ÁVH had ransacked the place looking for weapons, and had arrested her husband and charged him with sabotage. It seems that a government inspector had found some defective land mines. When Ilona went to the ÁVH headquarters and asked about her husband, they denied he had been arrested and laughed: "Look for him with his woman." She wandered from jail to jail, seeking some information about him, without success. Eighteen months passed, and then a stranger came to her flat. He had just been released from the military prison on Fő Street, where László occupied a sixteen square meter cell with thirty other prisoners. She petitioned the government for his release, and in 1953 Imre Nagy, who had succeeded Mátyás Rákosi as prime minister, released him.[33] When Ilona went to pick him up, she did not recognize him. He had to spend six weeks in a mental hospital, and after his release no employer dared to hire him. In order to clear his name, Ilona arranged for a hearing before the military court at the Fő Street prison. Yet when they reached the outer door, László burst into tears

---

33. Following the 1956 revolution, Imre Nagy was himself imprisoned and executed by the new regime installed by János Kádár. Buried in an unmarked grave, he was "rehabilitated" and reburied with honor in 1989.

and told his wife he could not enter that building again. She obtained an attorney and went before the court, where one of the judges told her that László had amnesty—but without the right to own property. "But he can now vote," the judge added brightly, "and he can file for a pardon." It was too much to endure. She lost control of herself, cursed the government and hurled obscenities at the judge. Her insolence cost her a four-thousand-forint fine (at a time when six hundred forints was her monthly salary as a factory worker).

Thereafter László was fit only for part-time jobs pushing a wheelbarrow at construction sites. During the 1956 revolution he fled to Austria permanently. Ilona remained in Hungary to care from her mother and to raise her daughter. The tragic events of her life had one more act. In 1959 her younger brother was beaten to death by ÁVH agents for taking part in the 1956 riots, and the beating was so severe that they insisted that his coffin remain sealed during his funeral.

For Ilona Almási the worst feature of the war was that it was a prelude to a forty-year period of Communist tyranny. "The Rákosi period was far worse than the war. During the war you knew, when you left the cellar, you were alive. In the Rákosi era any crazy man could denounce and destroy you." Speaking of the new wave of liberalization that swept the country in 1989, she muses, "Things are better now. At least I can attend all the demonstrations."

When Mariann Pertl (born 1906) moved into her husband's Budapest flat in 1930, she thought she had arrived in paradise. It was on Kavics Street in Buda, just one block from the Danube, and her sitting-room window overlooked the trees on Margit Island. The famous Lukács Baths lay only a few steps from her front door. It was like living in a beautiful park in the middle of a city.

Her former life had been harsh. She had grown up in Kolozsvár, the capital of Transylvania, where her father worked as a customs inspector and her mother as a postmaster. In 1919, when Romania took control of the city and changed its official name to Cluj, both parents lost their jobs—part of a policy that accelerated Hungarian emigration. Adding to their humiliation, a Romanian lieutenant was assigned quarters in their flat, which consisted of only two rooms, one of which had to be emptied for his use. He was not an offensive man, but her parents were pressed into service as caterers and servants at his frequent parties. When a prostitute moved in with him, an uncle complained to the Securitat that such flagrant immorality in proximity of a young girl was intolerable, and the woman was removed. Disgusted with treatment of the Hungarian minority in Romania, in 1922 they moved to Budapest, where Mariann dropped out of school to take a job as typist in order to add her mite to the family coffers. In 1924 she married, and after six years on a waiting list for council housing, she and her husband, Károly András, a customs officer, moved into the Kavics Street flat with a son and daughter.[34]

The war was at first only a minor inconvenience. Her husband's duties as an inspector of boats engaged in Danube traffic exempted him from military service. He was so convinced that Germany was invincible and such a stickler for rules that he refused to hoard food, even after the Red Army closed in on Budapest. He was jarred loose from his optimism only when Margit Bridge, just two blocks from their flat, was blown up on November 4. The family was sitting at their dining-room table when the whole building shook as if rocked by an earthquake. Without knowing what had happened, the whole family, led by the inspector, joined the human torrent flooding the staircase to the cellar.[35]

After the Arrow Cross rose to power in October 1944, civic order eroded. A Nyilas gang entered a yellow-star house across the street, pulled out the women, and marched them upriver. It was very cold. The women were wailing, and some collapsed in the road. Later Mariann learned that they had been held at the Óbuda brickyard for a few days before joining a group of several thousand Jews making a forced march toward Vienna. Many died on the road. (This was the last attempt by remnants of the Baky-Endre clique to deport Jews from Budapest.)

As the city prepared for the siege, food became scarce. The András family, which had nothing on hand except a few bags of dried beans, was saved by a woman on the ground floor who was supported, along with her two children, by a German soldier who had moved in with her while her husband was away in the army. She proved to be an angel of mercy, for she shared food brought by her German lover. By December 25 the noise of Russian bombardments seemed quite near. On this day they removed windows from their frames and stored them behind a wardrobe. Then they descended to the cellar to wait out the siege.

---

34. Interview with Mariann Pertl (June 4, 1989).

35. Three trams, along with automobiles and pedestrians, were on the bridge at the time, and the loss of life was estimated at three hundred. Although the Germans had laid explosive charges on all Budapest bridges and planned to demolish them if the Russian army reached the Danube embankment, only Margit Bridge was destroyed at this time. The explosion appears to have been accidental. The Russians had not yet reached the capital, and it was German policy to bar civilian traffic from bridges before destroying them.

When the Russians occupied Pest in mid-January, they took positions on Margit Island and dueled with German soldiers in the upper stories of the András building. To collect water from the Császár Baths nearby, Mariann had to run a gauntlet between the two firing lines. She also had to pass through a cross fire to reach the district school, where dried beans were being distributed. Inside the building were army horses dying of starvation, but no one had authority to butcher them for food.

The German defensive line went to pieces on February 12, and their soldier friends disappeared before the Russians arrived. On the following morning a young Russian officer, somewhat drunk, came into their cellar, shouting, "Kaput Magyar!" With him were two soldiers, who pointed their tommy guns at Károly and accused him of shooting one of their men. A young woman neighbor in the cellar jumped up and put her body in front of the guns. The Russians looked very surprised but put away their guns. Mariann had taken the precaution of burying her daughter, Kati, in a deep pile of bedcovers, but no women were raped in this cellar, almost certainly because the woman who had taken a German lover now attached herself to the Russian officer. Yet whenever Russians were around, Mariann kept Kati concealed. A good-natured soldier they called Rostov György once tried to lure Mariann into a warehouse. He held out a big slice of cheese as though she were a rat. She did not go, but he took no offense. Often he brought them tea and joined them at their table.

After they returned to their flat, Russians came in and went out as though it were a public corridor. They kicked out the glass windows of a case containing medals dating from the First World War. When they found out what they were, they became angry and scattered the medals, but did not steal them. From a neighboring flat came an offensive smell. Mariann investigated and found the floors ankle-deep in unwashed baby diapers. She offered to wash them, but the woman protested. She lived alone and was mortally afraid of the Russians. When they opened her door, the stench served as her protective shield against them. Knowing that Russians were kind to children, she had programmed her little girl to smile nicely and to say to anyone wearing a uniform, "Zdrastvui" (Hello). (After the Russians vacated the building, the child was taught to address any unfamiliar person with the singsong litany "I am Hungarian, not Russian.")

The fighting was still in progress when the Russians parked a long train on the embankment in front of their flat and collected labor from the nearby buildings in order to move boxes. Fearing that he would be picked up as a POW and sent to Russia, Károly hid while Mariann volunteered. She was terrified to discover the train was loaded with munitions. Remembering the Margit Bridge disaster, the women of the neighborhood crowded around the Russian transportation officer, wailing and begging him to move the train. Eventually they moved it farther south to Batthyány tér, where it did blow up, destroying an apartment building and burying residents in the cellar.

The Russians had liberated the population of Budapest but had no intention of feeding them. Mariann had to scavenge the surrounding countryside for food. Károly sneaked down to the custom house and obtained some fabric once used for making army uniforms. With great sacks of this cloth Mariann started westward on foot, accompanied by her young son, László, on the theory—hazardous at best—that Russians would be less likely to molest a woman with a child. For five days she tried to barter cloth for food among the country people. The pickings were poor. Too many other city scavengers had the same idea, and the peasants either had nothing to trade or put their prices out of sight. At Kaposvár, a hundred miles west, she fell ill and had to give up. They rode in an empty boxcar to Szekesfehérvár, and after two days camping in the ruins found space in the tool box of a train bound for Budapest. She was "black as dirt and nothing but a bag of bones" when she reached home.

All her family were in poor physical shape through fatigue, malnutrition, stress. Mariann fell ill and had to take to her bed. Her daughter, Kati, came down with tuberculosis, a major epidemic in the city at this time, said to be the result of inhaling pulverized glass and stucco dust. (One benefit of Kati's illness was that the Russians fled whenever she coughed.) Károly brushed off his uniform and hopefully reported for work, only to be fired on the spot. He protested that he was never pro-German, but that was beside the point—had he not once been the employee of the Horthy regime? Now over sixty, he drifted aimlessly through a succession of unskilled jobs for which contractors paid only a pittance because those on a political blacklist had no right to appeal and had to take whatever they were offered.

The good life promised by the Communists proved to be only empty words for the András family. Under the Horthy regime they had enjoyed only a marginal existence, but the new regime treated them as though they had been capitalist exploiters of the poor. "After the war life was very hard. Unemployment and illness seemed to have no end. What had happened to me as a young girl was now happening to my children; they had no time for play or education, only work. Always I have been an avid reader—of anything I can get my hands on. But since the war I have never been able to read one word of Tolstoy, Dostoyevsky, or any other Russian writer."

Tales told by Budapest women of daily life during the Russian occupation converge on one salient point: if the behavior of Russian soldiers was not always terrifying, it was nonetheless unpredictable and usually troublesome. During the war years Sára Szücs (born 1921) had come to the capital from Ibrány, a tiny village in eastern Hungary near the Russian frontier. Her husband, Miklós, had twice been drafted into the army, but when his unit returned from the Russian front in 1942, he vowed never again and took a porter's job at the Ministry of Defense on Castle Hill. When the Russians closed on the city late in 1944, Miklós and Sára had the option of being evacuated with the ministry personnel to Austria, but they chose to remain in order to watch over the modest contents of their little flat on Karolina Street. Since their apartment building had been taken as a protected house by the International Red Cross, they felt relatively safe. Just before the Russians broke into the neighborhood, the Jewish *házmester* assembled the tenants and instructed them on how they should behave toward their liberators. He emphasized that they did not need to hide anything, because, unlike the Germans, the cardinal policy of the Red Army was to bring, not *take*. A few hours later Sára heard pounding on their door. When she opened it, a Russian soldier rushed in, stripped Miklós's watch from his wrist, and emptied her jewel box. The *házmester* clucked with surprise to hear that thieves existed in the Soviet army, but he dared do nothing about it. Her dander up, Sára reported the theft to a Russian officer billeted in the building. He promptly found the thief and, after locking him in a toilet overnight, assured her that in the morning the culprit would be dispatched for hard duty at the front. (A few days later she encountered the soldier standing in line at the water hydrant and was terrified that he would remember her and take some kind of revenge, but he gave her no flash of recollection.)[36]

Because of the Red Army officers billeted in her building, no one suffered physical harm. But across the street a woman was forcibly taken away "to peel potatoes"—that is to say, to endure gang rape. After a week she returned. "There was no blame attached to her. It could have happened to any of us." Sometimes the Russians offered them food. The concierge of her building kept a white enamel bucket in the courtyard for emptying chamber pots. One day the Russians came into the courtyard and called out that everybody should come down for cabbage soup. The tenants trooped down the open stairways eagerly with their spoons and bowls. "Russians ladling the soup in that white bucket cried, 'Eat! Eat!' and beamed like happy children.

36. Interview with Sára Szücs (October 29, 1993).

They seemed very surprised that on that occasion no one in the building had any appetite."

They heard disquieting rumors that able-bodied males were being shipped to the USSR as laborers. Each time Miklós was picked up for neighborhood work details, Sára expected the worst, but always he returned home at nightfall. They now had an infant son, and because milk was impossible to obtain, Sára and the baby returned to Ibrány, her native village, where food was said to be abundant. Miklós followed later—a great mistake, for Russians picked him up and placed him among a draft of civilian males marching on foot to the Focsani prison pen in Romania. At night he slipped out of the line and hid in high canes while guards thrashed about in the undergrowth with their flashlights. One guard nearly stepped on his hand but missed him. On the next night he climbed aboard a flatcar loaded with rawhides for Budapest. He resolved to hide among the bundles. It was a poor plan, for from under nearly every bundle the head of a Hungarian fugitive peeped out. When the Russians searched the train, Miklós jumped off with all the others, damaged his leg, but managed to hide from the guards by climbing a tree. Then, remembering that bears foraged in the Carpathian Mountains, he decided that it was a poor policy to escape from Russians only to be devoured by bears, so he slept in the treetop until daybreak. Eventually, through the kindness of Romanian peasants who fed, lodged, and hid him, he was successful in threading his way past the Russian patrols in the region. These peasants were ignorant of the finer points of the hatefest fueled by politicians of the era. So when it came to deciding between a hunted man and an armed patrol, they had an instinct for knowing right from wrong. After reaching Budapest, Miklós laid low until the Russian slave hunts ended.

According to many reports, the first few days of the Russian scourge proved to be the most dangerous. Just ten minutes before the first Russian patrol entered the villa of Mária Schreiner (born 1912) on Törpe Street in Buda, a German soldier had come in and begged for civilian clothes so that he could escape. The Hungarians refused, terrified that the Russians on his heels would assume that they were collaborators. In the house were six children along with a large collection of relatives and family friends, including a Mr. Tóth, who had been a POW in Russia during the World War I. The Germans had turned the street into a string of "hedgehog houses" with connecting tunnels. Across the street the house of a neighbor had already been torched by the Russians because the Germans inside had refused to surrender.

"The first Russians to break in were animals."[37] They collected all the silverware, stuffed it into their big boots, and then ransacked the house for whiskey. The Schreiners had already poured it out, but the soldiers found half a liter of cologne and drank it with gusto. Her son had a toy train, and the Russians did not at first know what it was. When the boy showed them how it worked, they seated themselves and played with it happily, like tots at Christmas. The house had flush toilets, but the Russians did not use them. Instead, they took hats from racks, defecated in them, and left. Meanwhile, across the street a Communist neighbor was out in the street, protesting in Russian, "I am a Communist! I am a Communist!" as they slapped him back and forth and peeled a leather jacket off his back. For Mária's son of ten and daughter of eight "all this was a great adventure." They had no sense of danger but stayed glued to the front window, watching the drama unfold with a pair of binoculars.

Mr. Tóth prepared the women of the house for what he knew must come next. He showed them how to draw lines in their faces with charcoal and to flour their hair like a *stare mama* (old woman). He coached them on Russian equivalents for "I am sick" and "I am having my period." Some nights later a band of drunken soldiers burst into their house. Mária was spared because her husband lay on top of her, pretending he was asleep, and the soldiers were too drunk or lazy to drag him off. They turned their attention to easier prey, a sixty-year-old cook they found huddling in a corner and ganged-raped until they fell into a drunken sleep. On the next street the Russians took over a villa and set up a red-light house. They collected all the neighborhood women they could find, always with the phrase *malenkij robot* (a little work). At this house the soldiers had a free ride. Mária was spared through the efforts of Mr. Tóth, whom the Russians seemed to trust because he spoke their language.

Of much greater danger were the work details that followed. Mária was drafted to carry land mines and grenades from a warehouse and store them in her house. It was icy on the roads, and the streets were full of corpses, most of them naked and all of them stripped of their shoes and overcoats. It was frightening to pass through lines of dead people, with a bombardment in progress around her, carrying unfamiliar explosive devices in her hands. Once she slipped on the ice and fell, convinced she would be blown up, but a Russian soldier helped her up and reassured her. During one of these work details her husband vanished for several days—whether dead or shipped to

37. Interview with Mária Schreiner (April 6, 1989)

Siberia she had no idea. He turned up again on the day the SS command in the castle attempted to break the ring. In the middle of the furious firefight that raged across Castle Hill, the Russians decently released their civilian prisoners. Mária's husband got home safely after a harrowing trek between the front lines.

Judit Cser (born 1917) was in the kitchen of her flat in the Buda hills when she saw figures wearing dirty sheets sliding down a snowy embankment into the garden of her apartment house. Since she was a British citizen (though married to a Hungarian teacher and resident in the country since birth) and knew a little Slovakian, she had taken the precaution of pinning a note on her door: "YOUR FATHER IS STALIN—MY FATHER IS CHURCHILL." The first Russians to enter either did not know how to read or were little impressed with these credentials, for in a businesslike manner they set up a wheeled machine gun in the window and began firing at some Germans holed up in a house across the street. This exchange of fire continued all night, while the Cser family— mother, father, and two infant daughters—huddled together on the bed. For six weeks they had listened to the sounds of street fighting, encroaching ever nearer from the river, but this was very serious. Among other things, she worried about her goat, stabled in a shed in the garden. It provided the only milk available for her children, and fearing that it might become a casualty in the cross fire or butchered by the Russians, she brought it into the kitchen for the duration of the siege. Unnerved by the noise and change of habitat, the goat refused to eat anything and lost weight, but the milk held out until the end of the siege, when the animal served as a main course for a victory celebration.[38]

It was only after the sector had been cleared of Germans that the Russians took her by the hands and said she must go with them "to peel potatoes." Her fragments of Slovakian saved her. She told them, "If you take our food, then I will not have to peel potatoes." This retort surprised the Russians, but they accepted the offer and carried off her small trove of food. At this time there were seventeen Russians occupying her flat, including a Red Army major who openly and without guilt or apology stole her camera. Yet the Russians were kind to her children and to old people in the building. One of them used to take sugar lumps out of his filthy pocket and hand them to her babies. Then he would squat and watch them lovingly for hours. Sometimes the Russians would bring a pot of cabbage into the room, seat themselves at

---

38. Interview with Ilona Cser (January 27, 1989).

the table, and, sharing a single spoon, eat it. The leftovers they offered to the Cser family. "I ate it once, too hungry to resist, but came down with Ukrainian disease [dysentery]."

When the siege ended, the Russians packed up and moved out. But, for the Csers, troubles continued. The Russians began to collect civilian males to fill POW quotas. Twice they seized her husband, but he jumped into ditches and escaped. Finally they trapped him in the goat shed and hauled him away with other strays to Déli Station, where they locked up their charges in a beauty shop for the night. Cser gathered up her two babies and followed them. At the station a Hungarian Jew in Russian uniform told her the men were destined for a camp in Romania. She rushed home and fetched her husband a coat. It was a lucky impulse, for in the coat pocket he found an ID card issued to teachers for reduced railway fare. With this he somehow convinced the Russians that he had never been a soldier, and they agreed to release him, perhaps out of pity for his wife and wailing babies. Incensed because overruled, the Jewish soldier demanded that he be returned to the prison draft, but the Russians told him to shut up. Thereafter her husband remained out of sight in the family flat, while Judit used the railway pass to comb villages east of the city, bartering sheets and clothes for food.

6 | Liberation

Postmortem

At war's end Hungarians had cause for bitter reflections. Twenty-five years before, their leaders had fixed rigidly in place two cardinal principles of foreign policy: (1) restoration of territories and population lost by the Trianon Treaty, and (2) extirpation of Bolshevism in all of its guises. Both had completely failed. In 1945 the frontiers of Hungary were exactly what they had been in 1920. (The population had actually decreased because of deaths in the war and expatriations afterward.) And far from having eliminated Bolshevism, Hungary found itself occupied by the army of the most powerful Communist state in the world, an army that gave no clear signal that it ever intended to leave. Although the Germans had come, seen, and conquered, their tenure had lasted only twelve months. By contrast, the Russians were planting and nurturing a regime that would endure for nearly half a century. Back in 1919 Hungarians had been victimized and terrorized by the Béla Kun dictatorship, with its martial law, its sentences without right of appeal, its gangs of executioners in armored trains. Yet within 133 days Kun and his henchmen had been toppled by a coalition directed by the Allies. In 1945, however, the case was otherwise. Already the first chilling blasts of the Cold War were being felt, and no force on Earth was prepared to save Hungary from the Soviet Union. For the second time in half a century Hungary had to play the victim's role in a geopolitical drama that was written and directed by foreign hands.

The agreement drawn up at Yalta in February 1945 by Roosevelt, Churchill, and Stalin had called for the occupation of Hungary only until a peace treaty was signed, at which time there would be free elections and the establishment of a permanent government. However, at Potsdam in July the Soviet Union insisted on an extension of its military presence in Hungary in order to "protect supply lines" to Austria, where its occupation army numbered half a million. During this period supreme authority was nominally vested in an Allied Control Committee consisting of representatives from the four Allied powers, but in actuality the Soviet member in Hungary, Marshal Kliment Voroshilov, had virtual dictatorial powers until a treaty was signed in Paris on February 10, 1947. At that time there was not the slightest possibility that Hungary posed a danger to the Soviet Union, but more than a hundred thousand soldiers remained in the country to guarantee that Hungary would remain an obliging vassal state. A major task for Voroshilov and the Soviet military mission had been constructing from scratch a Communist Party that could eventually take the reins of power. The future party secretary, Mátyás Rákosi, who had once served with Béla Kun, was heard to complain that he could find only 110 Hungarian party members when he first arrived under Red Army protection.[1]

At the end of the fifty-one-day siege, much of Budapest lay in ruins. All highway bridges over the Danube had been destroyed. Of the 35,677 buildings in the capital, 29,987 had been destroyed or damaged.[2] Of this latter number an estimated 1,500 had been totally destroyed, while 9,140 were classified as "gravely damaged." The physical destruction was greatest in the Castle Hill district of Buda, where the German-Hungarian forces had made their final desperate stand. Up there only 4 houses out of 789 survived intact, and eight of twelve ministries had been completely gutted. Major portions of the castle, once the residence of kings and regents, had been reduced to rubble. The prospects for rebuilding were daunting. An enterprising statistician estimated that just to replace windows Budapest would require five million square meters of glass. Water mains in the city had been broken in 611 places (usually in Buda, where the defenders had exploded street crossings as temporary barricades).[3] Put in purely fiscal terms, one-quarter of the capital investment of Budapest real estate had been eradicated.[4] Among European capitals Budapest had suffered less damage than Berlin or Warsaw, but considerably more than Vienna, Paris, or London.

A census for Budapest taken immediately after the siege counted 832,800 inhabitants—approximately half a million less than in 1943—this despite the

---

1. Nicholas [Miklós] Kállay, *Hungarian Premier* (New York, 1954), 3.

2. Ferenc Nagy, *The Struggle Behind the Iron Curtain* (New York, 1948), 128. Nagy was the first postwar minister of reconstruction.

3. *Heti világgazdaság* (HVG), February 18, 1995.

4. *Források Budapest multjából* (Sources on the past of Budapest) (Budapest, 1985) 4:248ff.

fact that, during the weeks immediately preceding the siege, the city had been flooded with 300,000 refugees from the east. Many had fled to the west to escape the Russians; others, who had taken refuge in Budapest temporarily, had returned to their home villages and towns. During the siege there were only 19,718 civilian deaths—one-third of these younger than fourteen. No accurate figures exist for the number of combatants killed in the siege. The usual number given for the German-Hungarians is 35,000 dead, wounded, and captured. Because a high proportion of these were in SS divisions, few of the wounded or captured would have survived. The Russian losses are estimated at 75,000, but this figure is rejected by the USSR. At the close of the siege the Soviets claimed they took 110,000 prisoners (30,000 of them on the last two days from the castle district).[5]

The most pressing task was burial of the dead, which had begun even before the siege had ended. While the Russians glorified heroes in the abstract, they paid little attention to their fallen comrades, most of whom were buried by Hungarian work parties, often close to where they had been killed. (In present-day Buda countless families tell tales about individual Russian soldiers fertilizing rose bushes and fruit trees in their gardens.) Travelers arriving by train were shocked by the cadavers of nameless victims—whether purged by Arrow Cross or Russians, none could say—imbedded in the timbers of the Danube railway bridge, ghastly creatures with arms swaying in the current as if yet alive. Local citizens wished to remove them, but the Russian regulations were unbending: it was forbidden for any civilian to set foot on the bridge.[6] Elsewhere in the city heaps of civilians were buried temporarily in mass graves to await exhumation and identification later. Jews who died in the ghetto were piled to the ceiling in a corner of the café on Klauzál Square until the firefights ended, when they were placed in mass graves dug with great trouble in icy ground.[7] The German dead (along with unidentified Hungarian soldiers) were hauled to the huge Rákoskeresztúr cemetery and dumped into mass graves. (After three decades of collecting rubbish and growing monumental weeds, the site was cleaned up in preparation for the arrival of Chancellor Helmut Schmidt

---

5. C. A. Macartney, *October Fifteenth: A History of Modern Hungary* (Edinburgh, 1956), 2:467. On the other hand, József Borus, a contemporary historian of the war, estimates that the number of POWs taken by the Russians may have been as high as 180,000. This would have included an uncalculated number of civilians picked up by the Russians on a random basis. Interview with József Borus (January 8, 1990).

6. Interview with Béla Király (July 19, 1996).

7. George Konrád, "The High Priest of Frivolity," *New Yorker*, March 9, 1992, 37.

in 1978, who laid a wreath. Thereafter the West German government funded maintenance crews.)[8]

Yet the city moved rapidly to restore its infrastructure. Water mains in Pest were repaired within ten days of the siege; electricity returned by early summer to most districts of the city. Within weeks government ministries had taken over commercial banks of the inner city and opened for business with hand-written notes marked "Prime Minister" or "Undersecretary" hung on the doors. As the citizens dug themselves out of the rubble, pushcarts became the vehicle most in demand, even for transporting large timbers. Injured army horses brought high prices. Although the Russians had confiscated all auto-mobiles and they alone dispensed gasoline, a few luxury American cars wended through rubble, sufficient cause for newspapers in the fall of 1945 to announce, perhaps ironically, that the time had arrived for a Budapest car show. All highway bridges had been tumbled into the Danube, but by late March two pontoon bridges linked Buda and Pest, and by the following January Kossuth Bridge, a temporary structure, had been erected just south of Parliament, and it served the city until torn down in 1961. Although the Comedy Theater lay gutted, the National Theater staged the old standby opera *Bánk Bán*, which harbored a covert swipe at the Russians that few Hungar-ians could have missed. (Viceroy Bánk, a twelfth-century patriot, struggles to rid his country of a depraved band of foreign thieves and rapists—in his day, Germans.) The new regime also staged its own stark dramas—harbingers of others to follow. At the Academy of Music the people's tribunals were in full operation, where, in the words of Sándor Márai, "political executions afforded daily entertainment as in the time of Caligula."[9] By winter the city swarmed with belted policemen. At times it seemed that uniforms—rare in prewar Budapest—were standard attire. At a meeting in the Parliament building to discuss ways that the wounds of Hungarian Jews could be healed, the chief rabbi of the Reformed Israelite Congregation attended, grotesquely decked out in a general's uniform. (After one session, in which extremists called for hanging every suspected anti-Semite, the movement dissolved.)[10] Public schools reopened in March, with Jews and non-Jews attending the same classes.[11] (The

---

8. Borus interview. Ironically the German graves are close to those of the so-called renegade Communists, including Imre Nagy, who were executed in 1958.

9. Sándor Márai, *Memoir of Hungary, 1944–1948* (Budapest, 1996), 188.

10. Ibid., 207.

11. Interview with Andrew Nagy (August 10, 1995). Jewish students had attended public schools until the first German occupation (March 19, 1944) but in classes separate from Gentiles.

Communists did not succeed in shutting down church-run schools—some of them the most outstanding in Europe—until 1948, the year they were also successful in eliminating other subversive organizations, like the Boy Scouts and Rotary Club.)

Visitors to Budapest found the population grim. Part of the grimness was intentional. Among men, beards and stooped shoulders were fashionable because, the older and frailer they looked, the less the chance of being shanghaied to Russia as forced laborers. Among women lipstick had all but disappeared, and they fancied trousers—the baggier the better—in order to avoid attracting the attention of Russian soldiers. A comic skit of the time featured a lovesick swain speaking of his dream girl: "Her father's baggy pants, back bent under heavy rucksack, and under her arm a stovepipe."[12] Food was scarce, particularly dairy products, and doctors warned that the shortage of milk would result in a generation of children with bone problems. Only black bread could be found in the markets. Meat and staples could be obtained only by bartering clothes and valuables, for the pengő was worthless. Peasants knew their time in history had come; in the markets of Budapest a fattened pig was worth more than a grand piano. Inflation was like hemophilia, Sándor Márai remembered. "The peasants and sharks and Party parasites became fat. Everyone else lost blood." Few even knew how to calculate the number of zeros on a banknote. "Just give me two blues with a yellow," bargained the woman at the market stand, "and you can have the chicken."[13] The writer George Faludy was paid 300 billion pengős for a new edition of a book he had written before the war. He collected the money and raced to the market, knowing that, by the time he got there, the sum would have been devalued by at least 90 percent, and had the good fortune of purchasing one chicken, two liters of olive oil, and a handful of vegetables. Although the American dollar was illegal, it served as the lodestone currency. With $1,500 cash one could have purchased a five-storied building in the center of Budapest.[14]

The Soviet Union had "liberated" Budapest and did not allow the city to forget it. Renaming streets became *de rigueur* for the new regime. In Pest, Andrássy Boulevard, under which ran Europe's first subway, became Népköztársaság útja, or Avenue of the People's Republic (in which at least the "útja" was accurate). Surely Marshal Voroshilov must have had a hand in choosing

---

12. Nagy, 123.
13. Márai, 193.
14. George Faludy, *My Happy Days in Hell* (New York, 1962), 206.

the name Szabadság tér (Freedom Square), the site of a marble monument commemorating the Red Army, for it sits almost in the front door of the American embassy. *Szabadság* apparently was a word much appreciated by Soviet abstractionists, for it also figured as the new name for Ferenc József Bridge. The Franciscan's Square in the pulse of Pest was renamed Felszabadulás tér (Liberation Square). Over in Buda, the hub of the bus, tram, and subway system became Moszkva tér. Nor were the Communist heroes of yesteryear wholly forgotten. It was predictable that the principal "ring" boulevard of Pest would take Lenin's name, but something of a surprise that Béla Kun would have his own square (albeit very small and inconspicuous) and that even his despised and feared executioner, Tibor Szamuely, would be remembered in a Pest street name.[15] Russian efforts to impose socialist realism in art, theater, and literature failed. Their plays were staged in nearly empty theaters; their novels gathered dust in bookstores.

Yet the crown of Soviet memorials in Budapest is the mastodontic Liberation Monument on Gellért Hill. The forty-foot female figure standing on a forty-foot base and holding a palm branch (peace? victory? both?) is visible from nearly any location in Budapest, day or night. Originally planned by Regent Horthy as a monument to his son István, who was killed in a flying accident on the eastern front in 1942, the Russians substituted a palm for the propeller and unveiled their masterwork in 1947. The monument was further embellished with a statue depicting a Communist youth strangling a fascist monster-man, along with other testimonials and icons of Russian heroism and salvation. This reminder of Hungary's "debt" to Mother Russia sticks in the craw of many Hungarians, and for one Hungarian the monument has a meaning entirely other than that intended. A relative of this Hungarian was working on the foundation when his family cat died. He wrapped the animal carefully and buried it in a pier of wet cement. For the politically correct in postwar Budapest the monument might symbolize Soviet omnipotence, but for the family of the worker it was nothing more grandiose than the tombstone of a favorite pussy cat.[16] Because the Liberation Monument was closely guarded day and night by Hungarian policemen, it was defiled by neither vandals nor art critics—at least not publicly—during the whole period of Russian occupation.

Perhaps the most permanent contribution of the Soviet Union to the new Hungary was an infamous and complex network of police systems. As early

15. In line with the liberalization movement of 1989, most streets and squares have recently been renamed, many acquiring their pre-1945 names.

16. Interview. Name and date withheld by request.

as January 1945, even before the fighting had ended in Buda, the Soviet authorities sponsored Gábor Péter, a faithful party man, as head of the Budapest police. He proved to be no laggard at his job, which he characterized as "clearing the capital of elements who hinder democratic development." By the end of the year he had ordered 14,114 persons arrested, of whom 3,372 had been dispatched to "internment camps." Among this number was his former rival for the job, a wanna-be commissar who rusticated in jail for the next ten years but somehow escaped execution. (To be sure, Péter's efforts were little more than scarification compared with the massive political surgery of 1951, when in a two-month period some 13,670 Budapest citizens were deported to the Hortobagy and their property sequestered.) Péter convened his first people's tribunal—of many—on January 27, 1945, which tried, sentenced, and hanged three war criminals in a public square, all within ten days. Peter's precipitate rush to justice was not lost upon non-Communist municipal officials. Little wonder, then, that the mayor, even before the public avenues had been cleared of human corpses and equine cadavers, ordered his staff to comb the city and remove all Arrow Cross placards and to scrub their inscriptions off walls.[17]

In this same year the Communists set up the Katonai Politikai Osztály (Army Political Department), or KATPOL. This agency of the Ministry of Defense, headed by a former factory worker, scrutinized the dossiers of all returning Horthy soldiers, trying and sentencing suspected ones, and screened out political undesirables from the people's army. At about the same time the KGB infiltrated the country and organized the Államvédelmi Osztály (State Security Agency), or ÁVO, whose principal mission was to weed out all opposition to the Communist Party. Originally consisting of about one hundred agents under László Rajk, the minister of interior, it grew to more than eighty thousand by the end of the decade.[18] Along the way it absorbed KATPOL and the Border Guards (which numbered forty thousand men). It was a case of old wine in new bottles, but the agency attempted to upgrade its public image with a fresh name, the Államvédelmi Hatóság (State Security Authority), or ÁVH, although this taxonomical nuance was ignored by most Hungarians, who continued to call it the ÁVO.

---

17. László Varga, "The Devastation of Budapest in the War and Its Role in the Revolution, 1945–56," in *Budapest: A History from Its Beginnings to 1997*, ed. András Gerô and János Poór (in press).

18. In 1949 both László Rajk and György Pálffy-Osterreicher, the head of KATPOL, were caught in their own traps and executed for conspiracy, only to be "rehabilitated" posthumously in 1956.

Communist justice worked in inscrutable ways. The case of Major General Béla Király was typical of countless others. In 1950 he was serving as superintendent of the General Staff College in Budapest, at a time when hysteria about Yugoslavia's "defection" from Stalin's bloc was reaching epidemic proportions. With mounting concern he noted the erosion in quality among the new candidates—proletarian origin and party loyalty were fast becoming more important criteria for admission to the college than intellect and character. The arrival of Colonel Voloshin, a Russian overseer, marked the end of Hungarian autonomy, even though the Russians always maintained the fiction that they were only "advisers." The colonel, who proudly wore on his breast the golden star of "Hero of the Soviet Union" and liked to boast that he had personally shot five Red Army soldiers during the war for "cowardice and treason," began to monitor all aspects of personnel and curriculum. The Hungarian staff had to report directly to him, and he seeded informers throughout the college. Esprit de corps in the college all but disappeared. By 1951 it was clear to General Király that the Hungarian army was fast becoming no more than "a satellite armed horde for the USSR."[19]

One day Voloshin burst into Király's office and, in a passionate rage, accused him of planting anti-Soviet propaganda in the school. He laid out his evidence on a table. An informer had brought him a worksheet from the military-geography class depicting a minor tactical problem in an offensive formation. Attacking units were on the left side of the page, defenders on the right. When Király failed to understand what was treasonous about these scribblings, the colonel explained, with mounting heat: Everyone knew that on a map left is west and right is east, and since Russia was to the east of Hungary, the exercise concealed a cryptic attack upon the USSR. Nor was this all. In the same class students were using maps of the Ruthenian region as they worked on problems of attack. Since this region bordered the USSR, the instructor was implanting in the subconscious minds of his students bellicose attitudes toward the Soviet Union, whereas, if he were truly loyal, he would be using maps of Yugoslavia. A short time later General Király was brought before a court-martial, his record as a member of the general staff in the Horthy government was aired, and he received a death sentence for conspiracy. The Russians had simplified their judicial system by consolidating the roles of prosecutor, judge, jury, and executioner in the same tribunal. He spent five years in Gyüjtő Prison, at Kőbánya, where he waited daily for the

19. Béla Király memoir (unpublished manuscript).

hangman (who had previously examined his neck for a proper fit) without being told that his death sentence had been commuted to a life term. He was released in 1956, a few weeks before the October revolution, in which he took part as commander of the National Guard. When Russian tanks broke the revolt in November, Király joined the hundreds of thousands of fellow Hungarians who fled the country.[20]

In 1952, the peak year for ideological persecution, there were two hundred thousand Hungarians who had served some time in prison for putative political crimes.[21] Changes had been made in penology, but usually for the worst. Until 1950 physical beatings for prisoners had been legally forbidden (which is not to say they did not occur); after that they were routine and even encouraged by wardens. At the guard barracks of one ÁVH prison in Budapest a printed sign read, "RUTHLESSNESS TOWARD ENEMIES OF THE PEOPLE STRENGTHENS CLASS CONSCIOUSNESS."[22] At this place prisoners had to face the wall whenever a guard came near. To look a guard directly in the face was to run the risk of being beaten to death and buried in an unmarked grave. Guards in the ÁVH developed their own specialties—for example, forcing a prisoner to lie on his back and breaking his vocal chords with a boot or inserting glass tubes in a woman's vagina and kicking her in the stomach. During interrogations in jails run entirely by the Soviet KGB in Hungary, prisoners were sometimes threatened, with telling effect, with transfer to the ÁVH unless they cooperated.[23]

In November 1944, while the war was still in progress, the Soviets had set up a puppet government in Debrecen, which was nominally in control of the country. Ferenc Nagy, a prominent leader in the Smallholder's Party, was invited to join the new administration as minister of reconstruction. The whole operation was, in his words, "a travesty," for the Soviets had no intention of relinquishing their hold on the country. Each cabinet minister was assigned one room and anteroom to house himself and his staff. Serving one's constituents was impossible because no cabinet minister had access to an automobile, although the Hungarian Communist Party had unlimited

20. Király interview. He settled in the United States, earned a Ph.D. in history from Columbia, and taught for many years at Brooklyn College. For an account of General Király's wartime experience, see "Collapse" in Chapter 1.

21. István Fehérváry, *The Long Road to Revolution: The Hungarian Gulag, 1945–1956* (Santa Fe, 1989), 16, 24.

22. Ibid., 112.

23. Ibid., 87.

transportation. The new government had no money or presses to print money. It had to borrow Red Army scrip. The wealth was rapidly being drained from the country. Every day Nagy saw trainloads of machinery stripped from Hungarian factories passing en route to the Soviet Union. Even larger quantities sat on open flatcars along railroad sidings, where through Soviet ignorance or inefficiency it rusted and became scrap.[24]

The Russian soldiers were now out of control. Even Debrecen, head-quarters of the Red Army, had become so dangerous after the 7 P.M. curfew that chauffeurs of the Russian mission insisted on getting home before the deadline. Occasional show trials at the Debrecen Theater sentenced soldiers to be shot for looting and rape, but these were no real deterrent. Officers with loaded pistols who attempted to prevent assaults, vandalism, or thefts were often ignored or laughed at by their men. Conditions were even worse in the countryside, where Russians with machine guns on slings scourged the countryside like locusts, shooting cattle and pigs, ransacking cellars, stealing the last ounce of flour from the poorest peasants. In traveling about, Nagy saw more Red soldiers than male civilians, and with good reason—male Hungarians were either hiding or had been carried off to Russia as forced laborers. It was ever the same. A band of Russian soldiers would arrive at a household and borrow the male member for *malenkij robot* (a little work), the catchphrase for a journey to the USSR. Often after soldiers had gorged on meat seized from the country people, they engaged in "hunts" for cattle and pigs hidden in the woods, shooting them wantonly with their machine guns. In another version of this sport they set fire to barns and ricks and burned the animals alive. Peasants abandoned efforts to raise livestock, switching to chickens and ducks because they matured faster and could be hidden more easily than cows or pigs.[25] Venereal disease was pandemic in the country, and peasant girls were often too ashamed to seek treatment. Nor were Russian males the only sexual aggressors. At a recreational camp near Kecskemét were three thousand Russian women connected with the army or the police. At night they banded together and kidnapped men for sex. Hungarian women, who had been hiding in attics and haystacks, now concealed their men in those choice spots.[26] Nothing like this mayhem had been experienced in Hungarian history since the Mongol invasion that scourged the country in the thirteenth century.

24. Nagy, 66ff.
25. Ibid., 104ff.
26. Ibid., 63.

When the provisional government moved to Budapest during the summer of 1945, Nagy expected some improvement. What he had not foreseen was that the Western powers had washed their hands of Hungarian affairs, which were totally within the Soviet sphere. Originally, formal occupation was planned only for Germany, but at Stalin's insistence his satellite countries were included. Hungarian reparations were set at $200 million due Russia and $100 million due Yugoslavia and Czechoslovakia. To pay these exorbitant amounts power plants were dismantled and expropriated, mines were sold outright (at a discount), and consumer goods crated away. These reparations absorbed more than 60 percent of projected Hungarian industrial production, and if the payments fell in arrears, the penalty was a 60 percent fine. Perhaps the oddest wrinkle in the Potsdam agreements was that the Soviet Union was entitled to all German property that was in any way connected with Hungary. Debts that Hungary owed to the now defunct Third Reich had to be paid to the Soviets. If a Russian accountant found in some ancient invoice evidence that a German machine gun issued to the Honvédség had never been paid for, the Soviets had the authority to collect. When Hungarian ministers complained about the impossibility of fulfilling these terms and explained that their country lacked even the basic raw materials to reactivate their industry, the Soviets offered to help out. They proposed a trade agreement according to which the USSR would supply Hungary with the needed raw materials in return for subsuming nearly all industries, shipping, mining, aviation, and agriculture under newly constituted Soviet-Hungarian monopolies. In effect, this meant that capitalism was virtually eliminated in one stroke of the pen, and that in the future most working Hungarians would be state employees.[27]

Early in 1946 Hungary officially became a republic, with Ferenc Nagy of the Smallholders Party as its prime minister. In the elections the Communist Party had garnered less than 10 percent of the votes, but it demanded, and got, the Ministry of Interior, which controlled the police force, border guards, and two agencies whose methods and purpose were borrowed from the NKVD—the ÁVH and the KATPOL, security forces for civilian and military populations, respectively. For Nagy to have denied the Communists the Interior portfolio would have been folly, for the Red Army occupied the country. The interior minister launched a program in which billions of scarce forints were expended for construction of barbed-wire fences, minefields, and watchtowers along all Hungarian borders, thereby converting Hungary itself

27. Ibid., 138.

a vast prison cage. Another priority was expulsion of the Volksdeutsche. An order came from Russia that 500,000 German-speaking Hungarians had to be expelled, even though the 1940 census total was only 477,000. Nagy fought the order, arguing that expulsion should be based upon just cause, but he lost. In the end, about 300,000 Volksdeutsche were seized at random, their property was expropriated, and they were transported to Austria and Germany.

It took no extraordinary powers of clairvoyance for Ferenc Nagy to see that his country would shortly lose all vestiges of its sovereignty. In 1946 he joined an economic mission to Moscow. When he told Stalin how the Germans and Arrow Cross had plundered Hungary, Stalin laughed and said, "Our soldiers carried away quite a lot from there, too—even if you do not talk about that now."[28] At one session Stalin astonished everyone present by telling the Hungarians not to condemn Horthy, for Horthy was an old man and did try to arrange an armistice in 1944. The mission resulted in nothing conclusive. Nagy's hope that Hungary would participate in the Marshall Plan was vetoed by Marshal Voroshilov. The Russians did not wish one of their vassal states to become self-sufficient.

Early in 1947 Nagy carried his economic concerns to Washington. The United States granted $10 million credit to buy surplus army materials left in Europe. This, the first postwar loan by any country to Hungary, infuriated the Russians. While out of the country, Nagy was denounced as a conspirator by Rákosi, the Communist Party chief, and Nagy's son was seized as a hostage. In return for delivery of his son to Switzerland, Nagy consented to resign as prime minister and not to return to Hungary. No one saw more clearly what the Russians were doing or knew better the hopelessness of resistance without outside aid, which clearly was not coming. He collected his family and joined the swelling company of Hungarian refugees in the West. He had come from a family of small farmers in southern Hungary, and he wanted to grow things again. Within a year of his expatriation he was settled in Fairfax County, Virginia, where he rented a small farm, bought a tractor, and began growing corn, wheat, and alfalfa.

Nagy was well out of it, for nationalization, designed to wipe out the bourgeoisie as a class, proved to be an unmitigated economic disaster. First to be swallowed were mines and power stations (1946), then banks and the largest industrial firms (1947), then wholesalers (1949), and finally came an onslaught against retailers that nearly eliminated bakers, greengrocers, and

28. Ibid., 310.

egg-and-fowl peddlers (1952). In the workforce absenteeism was soon out of control, especially during the autumn months, when city workers, lured by promises of extra food, joined harvesters in the countryside. By 1956 inefficiency threatened to swallow the country. The cost of raw materials in many industries exceeded the price of the manufactured product. In the same year six hundred trains suspended service for three weeks because of coal shortages caused by disgruntled miners, many of whom had deserted the mines for higher-paying jobs in construction (where a black-market economy reigned beyond bureaucratic control). In desperation the government placed the blame for economic chaos on saboteurs and counterrevolutionaries. A new political crime was trotted out—"offenses against a planned economy"— the purpose of which was to compel workers to remain at one workplace no matter how little it paid. The fruits of this Mad Hatter economic policy were finally plucked during the aborted revolution in late autumn of 1956.[29]

Tibor Zinner calls himself "the urologist of modern Hungarian history."[30] He is referring to his position in the Ministry of Justice as archivist responsible for collecting all materials bearing upon human rights violations between 1945 and 1962. For the moment, his focus is centered upon legal abuses of the postwar Communist regime, but by way of background he has become an authority on indictments, trials, and sentences of those persons charged with war crimes during the Horthy and Szálasi regimes.[31]

Even before the official end of the war a chain of people's courts was organized to investigate charges of what were called "crimes against the Hungarian people." These tribunals were independent of the Nuremberg trials, which they preceded by eight months. Because so many public buildings in Budapest had been destroyed, the major trials were held in the auditorium of the Academy of Music. Their political coloration was obvious: no indictments were ever brought against criminal behavior committed by Communists or Russian sympathizers. Between February of 1945 and April of 1950 a total of 26,997 Hungarians were sentenced to some form of punishment, of which 477 received death penalties (although only 189 were

---

29. Varga, "Devastation of Budapest."

30. Interview with Tibor Zinner (February 26, 1990). See also Tibor Zinner and Péter Róna, *Szálasiék bilincsben* (Budapest, 1986).

31. During the period of Communist domination, between 1948 and 1989, Zinner estimates that 40,000 Hungarians were persecuted for political reasons and 500 were executed. Approximately 400,000 others, out of a population of about 10,000,000, were regarded as sufficiently "dangerous" to warrant building files on them in the Ministry of Interior.

actually carried out).[32] Punishment consisted of imprisonment (from one year to life), expropriation of property, deportation from the country or to remote regions, or forced labor (one year to life). Slightly more than 500 received life sentences, but all of these were eventually released through amnesty or pardon, except for those who died in camp—particularly in 1946, when a food shortage in Hungary killed 1,000 prisoners of all categories. No war criminal is currently in prison for crimes connected with the 1941–45 war, according to Zinner. While it is still legally possible in Hungary to be tried and sentenced as a war criminal, no such trial has taken place in more than twenty-five years, and Zinner believes that the public would not countenance another one now. "Whether they would tolerate a trial of Communist Party crimes against humanity—that is a wholly different question. There are ample grounds for as many as a hundred thousand such trials."

The centerpiece among the trials of war criminals was, of course, that of Ferenc Szálasi, who had been captured in Germany and flown to Budapest. Prosecutors had access to his voluminous diaries, which reflected wide reading in Western history, especially Spengler and Toynbee. In the courtroom he behaved with dignity and spoke of his political ideals openly and logically. Those anticipating a craven performance were disappointed. "It is a myth that Szálasi was crazy. That is mere demagoguery. To the Stalinists anybody is crazy if he doesn't toe the line." Zinner sees Bárdossy as the major villain because he was directly responsible for Hungary's entering the war against the Soviet Union and misrepresented the facts to the regent. His trial and execution were followed closely by the international press, but thereafter public interest in Hungarian war crimes began to dry up. Zinner believes that all who were executed deserved it, with the exception of General Gusztáv Jány, a convenient scapegoat for the Don Bend disaster. All the virulent Jew haters like László Baky, László Endre, and Andor Jaross were either hanged or shot. Prime Minister Sztójay and General Iván Hindy, who commanded the Hungarian units defending Castle Hill, were also executed. (Hindy's superior, SS general Karl Pfeiffer-Wildenbruch, got off with a prison term in Russia.) Further, he adds that many who deserved hanging got off with prison terms or deportation, including such rabid anti-Semites in the Horthy ministries as István Antal. As the trials continued with mind-numbing monotony,

---

32. Executions took two forms—firing squad and hanging. Hanging was particularly painful because the victim was not dropped from a trap but dangled from a pole. In effect, he died from strangulation. Randolph Braham's statistics differ from Zinner's. He reports only 146 executions. Further, he records that there was one trial and execution as late as 1970. See his *Politics of Genocide: The Holocaust in Hungary* (New York, 1981), 1163–69.

they became counterproductive and even farcical. During their fourth year war criminals were being released faster than new ones could be incarcerated. By this time courtrooms would usually be empty except for those actively engaged in the case and a handful of strays who had come in to get out of the cold.

Regent Miklós Horthy and his prime minister Miklós Kállay, both of whom had tried to carry Hungary out of the war before the German occupation, survived the war. The Germans had kept Horthy under house arrest at Schloss Hirschberg in Bavaria, where he lived in comfort, guarded by a hundred Waffen SS, twelve Gestapo officers, and three police dogs. His guards were supposed to execute him before the Americans arrived, but they disobeyed the order and slipped away into the countryside. The American army took him in custody as a witness and interrogated him many times but never put him on trial as a war criminal. In 1948 he was allowed to retire to a modest villa at Estoril in Portugal, where he was supported largely by gifts from many European friends.[33] Throughout his ordeal Horthy behaved with dignity and had that kind of demeanor that elicited respect from his captors. He had taken nothing from the Hungarian treasury.

Kállay had a more difficult time. When the Germans occupied Hungary in March 1944, he took refuge in the Turkish legation and remained there until November, when he voluntarily surrendered. Hitler seemed unsure what to do with him. He was transported to the concentration camp at Mauthausen and housed in the warden's section of the prison, where he caught only distant glimpses of the brutal persecution of prisoners in the infamous quarry. At Mauthausen Kállay had access to the library and enjoyed creature comforts like a steam-heated room and hot showers (fueled by the corpses in the crematorium located elsewhere in the camp). When the Russian advance reached Austria, he was transferred to Dachau and housed with other important political figures, like Leon Bloom of France and Kurt von Schuschnigg of Austria, along with no less than two minor Churchills. Just before the Americans liberated the camp, all these dignitaries formed into a caravan—which included a portable gas chamber—that wended south into the Tyrol. Their SS guards had been ordered to execute them in the event that there were any attempts at a rescue. Beyond the Brenner Pass, when news came that Hitler was dead, the SS turned their charges over to the Wehrmacht, which obligingly lodged them in a resort hotel to await the arrival of the American army. The American authorities had no idea whether to consider a former Hungarian premier as friend or enemy, so after brief interrogations

33. Nicolas [Miklós] Horthy, *Memoirs* (New York, 1957), 238.

they passed him south to Caserta for more definitive investigation. When the Allied authorities concluded that he was not a war criminal (but might somehow be valuable to them), they escorted him to the Eden Paradise Hotel on the island of Capri with other unclassifiables. It was there that Kállay learned that during the siege his wife had been killed in the Turkish legation by shellfire. Thereafter he was a man without a country, for the Soviets and their Communist Party underlings would never have allowed someone of his political stature to return to Hungary.

The task of hunting down Arrow Cross party members, eagerly undertaken in 1945, quickly petered out. Most were never arrested. The Communists recruited great numbers of them because the Communist Party, whose membership in 1945 numbered considerably less than five hundred, badly needed a mass following. It was easy to rationalize that those recruited from proletarian ranks had only been "misled," and had all along been nascent Communists in wolf's clothing. Many of them had records as anti-Semites that would not bear looking into, but since they were experienced in intimidation, they were valuable recruits for the Communist Party. In such cases they merely exchanged green membership cards for red ones. Their visible presence in the ranks of the Communist Party was all the more ironic when one considers that even today it is illegal in Hungary to own, display, or traffic in Arrow Cross literature or regalia. There were other convenient arrangements between the old adversaries. Ironically—or perhaps perceptively—the ÁVH took over the former headquarters of the Arrow Cross at 60 Andrássy Avenue. They kept the same exterior but had to enlarge the cellars to house greater traffic in political prisoners. Passing the building in the spring of 1946, Sándor Márai looked up at grinning policemen on the balconies and had a flash of déjà vu: "They were the very same faces seen on the very same balcony the year before, when the Arrow Cross was quartered there; only their names had changed. Brother Szappanos changed his clothes and became Comrade Dögei or someone like that."[34]

The frenetic haste with which the Arrow Cross turned their coats provided a rich vein of humor for Hungarians. Irén Gercser, a high school teacher of Hungarian literature, had a memorable encounter with a former Nyilas officer. She despised socialist realism as the worst sort of transparent hogwash and refused to teach it, even though it was part of the required curriculum. When complaints that she was politically unreliable reached the district board of education, a state inspector came down to observe her lesson. She recog-

34. Márai, 213.

nized him at once, but evidently he did not recognize her. After the lesson, he explained that she knew nothing about the correct way to inculcate literary values in young minds, and he told her that unless she reformed, he would recommend that she be dismissed from her job. She listened patiently to his denunciation of her political crimes, and when he had finished, she said, "All right, now talk to me about your Arrow Cross membership during the war." His face turned white as a turnip. He was too stunned to reply. His official report about her class was glowing.[35]

Yet there were others who never lost the faith. During the late 1940s a young writer named Nicolas Nagy-Talavera visited a displaced-persons camp near Passau in Bavaria. To his great surprise he found in one barracks a large gathering of Hungarians holding a religious ceremony that commemorated the anniversary of Ferenc Szálasi's execution—or "martyrdom," as they called it. The writer, who had been persecuted by the Arrow Cross during the war, was incensed that such a service in the so-called American occupational zone would be tolerated. But as the ill-fed and ragged crowd dispersed after the service, and he heard them speculating about the possibility that Szálasi's son would grow up and carry out his reforms for the poor people of Hungary and muttering about how Szálasi had saved the ungrateful West from Communism, his anger gave way to compassion. These were the faces not of bullies and cruel aryanizers but of the poorest, lowest, and most miserable peasants and factory workers of Hungary. They truly believed that Szálasi would have brought them the good life; now they were truly prisoners of starvation, unwelcome abroad yet afraid to go home. They had been exploited and lied to, but they held on to the shards of a dream. "The longer I looked at these simple folk and heard their impotent protests, their inane hopes, and their impossible loyalties, the more my irony dissolved in pity."[36]

Compatriots

József Borus and György Zsohár are compatriots who share a country but not comrades who share an ideology. They are anticomrades from opposing ends of the Hungarian political spectrum. They are as antithetical as feline and canine. József's father was a partisan of Béla Kun and was frequently

---

35. Interview with Irén Gercser (April 7, 1990).

36. Nicholas Nagy-Talavera, *The Green Shirts and the Others: A History of Fascism in Hungary and Rumania* (Stanford, 1970), 113–14.

jailed during the Horthy period for suspected Communist activity. György's father, who had been roughly handled for "reactionary attitudes" by Kun's terrorist squads, became a rural police constable during the Horthy regime. Borus senior, a highly skilled ironworker of Kisujszállás, a small city between Budapest and Debrecen, was proletarian to the core and fiercely proud of it. Zsohár senior was an unapologetic kulak who had a small vineyard on a hillside above the village of Alcsútdoboz, a predominantly Swabian enclave twenty miles west of Budapest. An amicable meeting between the two parents would have been inconceivable. Both were hardheaded and forceful men eager to express what they believed, and prepared to back it up with fists or pistols. It would have been the age-old, classic enmity between the industrial worker and the peasant, between the maker and the grower. Both were resolute patresfamilias whose ideas their male children took as their own.

Although almost the same age, József Borus (born 1926) and György Zsohár (born 1927) progressed along antithetical tracks during the war years and after. József, at age seventeen, although not Jewish, was drafted into a labor battalion during the final months of the war. Later, when the Communists took control of the government, he fell into a preferential category because of his father's working-class credentials and anti-Horthy activities. Before the war he would have been relegated to a trade school and forgotten, but the new regime encouraged the sons of working-class people to enter professions formerly out of reach. In 1945 he was recruited by the university under a special program seeking children of peasant and working-class origins. (He was the only suitable candidate the admissions committee could find that year.) While a student he was commissioned in the army, and after earning his bachelor's degree, he was posted to Vienna with captain's rank to work in the Hapsburg military archives. Then, after taking a doctorate in history at Budapest, he began a distinguished career as research fellow of the Institute of History, specializing in World War II.

While József was working at airfields with his labor battalion, György was a very proud seventeen-year-old volunteer in a Hungarian Waffen SS division. When his unit was cut to pieces in the early spring of 1945, the Russians took him prisoner and shipped him to a POW camp in the Ural Mountains. Returning to Hungary, he finished his high school course and took a job as a clerk. About the time that József was completing his graduate work at the university, György was serving two separate prison terms for political deviation. After he was released, he took over his father's small farm and supplemented his income as a stonecutter. At this late stage of his life he became consumed with a passion for piecing together what had happened to him and to his generation. An autodidact, he crammed the workroom above his wine cellar with books of history, literature, political science. He began to read.

József Borus is a Marxist without apology. While conceding there have been mistakes, particularly in the Mátyás Rákosi era, he nevertheless believes that the thrust of Communism in Hungary has been constructive and that it has improved the lot of most people. György Zsohár vehemently disagrees. Persecution is the only modus operandi of Communism—without intimidation, it dries up and dies. If the Soviet Union had not intervened in the internal affairs of the country, Hungary would be as healthy today as Austria or Germany. These two men personify the two antagonistic ideologies that have racked Hungary during most of this century. For the past quarter century, in György Zsohár's study above his wine cellar in the little house at Alcsútdoboz, the two men have debated endlessly and monotonously, seeming to agree upon nothing. Any auditor, listening to each man give his canonical litany about Hungarian history and personalities, would have to conclude that these two men are as hopelessly incompatible as oil and water.

SS

After Béla Kun's terrorist gang, known as "the Lenin Boys," swept through the Bicske region in 1919 on their armored train, the father of György Zsohár became a bitter, unrelenting foe of anything remotely smelling like Marxism-Leninism. He was a simple man of natural intelligence who worked his few acres, raised his family of two boys, and eked out a marginal existence during the depression years. Of Slovenian origin and with a wife who traced her descent to the Kuns or Cumans (a once fierce Turkish tribe proud of their military prowess), he felt comfortable among the Volksdeutsche minority of the neighborhood even though he spoke only a pickup German. His older son, János, joined the Honvédség during the 1930s and eventually acquired a commission. At the local school his younger son, György, fraternized with the Swabian youths and soon shared their enthusiasm for the astonishing recovery of the Third Reich. While Zsohár senior did not welcome the war, he expressed satisfaction that Hungary had allied itself with Hitler, whom he admired as a self-made man. Always he remained a rabid anti-Bolshevik. Once, when his older son came home on a furlough sporting a shirt open at the neck, he exclaimed, "Button it up. You look like one of those damned Communists of 1919."[37]

---

37. Interview with György Zsohár (March 3, 1990).

In October 1944, when the Axis armies were in full retreat upon Budapest, György Zsohár enlisted in the Twenty-Second (the Maria Theresia) Cavalry Division of the Waffen SS at nearby Bicske.[38] It was like a reunion with boys he had known at school. Morale was very high, and the soldiers, nearly all of them Volksdeutsche, were in high spirits. Like them, György assumed the unit was top of the line. He was too green to detect what the officers saw— that there were only a few tanks in a so-called armored division and that horses, not trucks, carried soldiers up to the front. Nominally the Twenty-Second Division was at full strength, but in late 1944 this meant that it had marshaled only 50 percent of its men and equipment. A picture taken of György just before his induction reveals a curly-haired smiling youngster who looks more like a choirboy than a storm trooper. He was his mother's pride. As an eight-month-old baby he had won a beauty contest in Budapest, and she kept the newspaper story and photograph prominently displayed in her kitchen.[39]

Because of his youth György was assigned to telephone duty at divisional headquarters—called by the veterans *Etappenschwein* (rear-echelon swine). The new recruits received no combat training, and within three weeks they went into battle southwest of Budapest in a counterattack to prevent the Red Army from encircling the city. This blocking action caught the Russians by surprise, forcing them to fortify a line and temporarily halting their advance toward Vienna. The performance of the Maria Theresia in this attack confirmed György's conviction that Bolsheviks were no match for the SS. Yet by the end of December Russian attacks began to come from the west as well as the east. The Red Army had gotten around Budapest to the north and was seeping into the Axis defensive positions from the rear.

Since the German synthetic gasoline factories had been badly mauled by Allied bombing in recent months, Hitler was adamant that Budapest be held so that Hungarian wells would continue to pump for the Reich. To this end he transferred two elite Panzer SS divisions, the Totenkopf and the Wiking, from the defense of Warsaw to Hungary, but they failed to crack the siege ring of the Soviets.[40] In the melee the Twenty-Second Waffen SS Division found itself cut off and on February 11 attempted to break out to

---

38. Originally the Waffen SS recruited exclusively among the Reichsdeutsche, but their ranks had become so decimated by 1943 that foreigners were sought. By the end of 1944 only half of the Waffen SS were native Germans. George H. Stein, *The Waffen SS: Hitler's Elite Guard* (Ithaca, 1966), xxxi.

39. Interview with György Zsohár (November 24, 1995).

40. Stein, 236.

the west.[41] Officers told them they must fall back five kilometers to get clear (actually, their estimate fell thirty-five kilometers short because of a rapid Soviet advance). György found himself in a group of several hundred SS and Honvédség captured after tramping through icy mud for twenty kilometers to Perbál, almost within sight of his home. Russians roughed them up and marched them to the village of Érd, south of Budapest. Men unable to keep up the pace were pulled out of the line, pushed into a ditch, and shot. Those in the Waffen SS were singled out for brutal treatment, and in some cases for torture. Along the road lay bodies of SS soldiers with bloody trousers at the crotch, where they had been castrated (or amputated) before being shot. In some places the stacks of bodies were a meter high. As they passed through Zsámbék, György saw the bodies of hundreds of slain Hungarians—not SS— slaughtered because a divisional emblem on their sleeves had been mistaken for an SS insignia. There seemed to be no system or consistency in these executions, and it was the erratic behavior of the Russians that so unsettled the prisoners. In recounting his story nearly half a century later, György broke down. He could not explain why he had been spared—unless it was his youthful appearance, or perhaps because he was a Scorpio.

Then began a 170-kilometer march to Baja, a market town far to the southwest, near the Yugoslav border. They had been joined by prisoners taken from Budapest hospitals. A German lieutenant later told him that when the Russians arrived at his hospital ward, they ordered everyone out into the courtyard. His leg had been amputated, and so he could not move. He survived, while the others were lined up against a wall and machine-gunned. In his ward another soldier—a Hungarian—with an amputated leg was unexpectedly released when his uncle arrived with a wheelbarrow and got permission to wheel him to his village outside of the city. There was no accounting for the behavior of these Russians. On the six-day march to Baja thousands of prisoners flooded the roads as far as the eye could see. At the village of Solt, György's section of about four hundred men got a one-day rest, and here the guards gave villagers permission to feed and water them. This was the only food distributed on the march. At Baja a companion showed György his wound. Shot in the stomach, his intestines protruded, yet he walked six days. He had no other recourse—except to be shot again, this time for good.

---

41. At approximately the same time, the force in the Budapest castle area attempted to infiltrate or to pierce the Russian lines. Only 780 succeeded in escaping to the West. See François Duprat, *Les campagnes de la Waffen SS* (Paris, 1973), 1:185, and Stein, 236.

The camp at Baja held Hungarians, Germans, and Romanians without regard to national distinctions and was administered by Russians. Their food was just enough to sustain life—half a kilo of bread and ten grams of beet-root sugar per day. In March a rumor swept through the camp that the Russians were going to give them documents and discharge them. György believed this; after all, wasn't Hungary now officially an ally of the Soviet Union? But there were also floating about camp disquieting rumors that they would be shipped off to Siberia as slave laborers.

A short time later they were locked into freight cars and shipped into Romania through Temesvár to a huge holding camp outside Brasow. (En route György wrote his name and address on a slip of paper and dropped it onto the railway tracks, which, when delivered, gave his parents their first intimation that he was still alive.) The prisoners were interrogated and separated. György joined three thousand other young captives sent for a few months to a special reeducation camp for soldiers aged eighteen or less. (Some were only fourteen—many of them civilians dragged from their homes to fill quotas.) Although forced to perform rigorous work in a forest, they were well treated and adequately fed.

During the early summer of 1945 they boarded freight cars with crude bunks and bumped slowly eastward. It was very hot, but once in the Ural Mountains they were permitted to open the doors and to bathe in mountain streams. No one died on this trip, for they had been strengthened in the youth camp. Near Sverdlovsk they disembarked at a brick factory and went to work in twelve-hour shifts at the furnaces. In this remote place, Russian supply services had completely broken down. One time they had nothing to eat but a spoonful of some American tinned meat paste; another time they had no bread issue for three days, and when their three-day ration (2.4 kilos) finally arrived, they devoured it all at once. Later, when György developed infected blisters, he was reassigned to a potato field. "It was paradise! We could steal potatoes. At one sitting I ate five kilos of potatoes."[42] Soon great numbers of prisoners were too ill to be useful as workers.

Because of their youth and debility, many prisoners were sent home in February 1946, after only a year of captivity. Another source of anxiety lay ahead—their reception by Hungarian police. The night György arrived home, his parents warned him that Hungarian police were methodically combing the Volksdeutsche villages and jailing former members of the SS. They had heard that his brother, a Honvédség officer, had been captured at Prague, but

---

42. Interview with György Zsohár (March 24, 1990).

he was now reported missing. Earlier the police had appeared at the home and demanded of the parents, "Where are your fascist sons?"[43] The hope was that György's dossier might be overlooked or lost in the bureaucratic nightmare of postwar Hungary. For the first month he stayed indoors, venturing out only after nightfall. A classmate working at the Bicske police headquarters obtained a new ID for him and destroyed the original file forwarded by the Russians. Confident that no record existed of his SS service, but wary about informers among prying neighbors, he moved away and worked as a day laborer. He took a night course to obtain a high school diploma and was hired as a clerk in a factory near Budapest.

His world came crashing down in 1953. On the eve of his marriage, as he was leaving work, he was intercepted by some men in black leather coats, shoved into an automobile, and taken to a police station. "There were three or four plainclothesmen in the room. One of them greeted me mockingly with a 'Heil Hitler!' and at once I knew the war was not yet over for me." He learned that they had searched his flat and claimed to have found some anti-Communist circulars. When he denied knowledge of a conspiracy and refused to finger other "conspirators," the beatings began. Four or five men held him while another beat him with a truncheon and kicked him in the kidneys. "My only defense was to pass out—to hold out or to struggle only provoked them." At the Justice building on Markó Street, he was charged with having voluntarily joined the SS and with making notes about departments and personnel at the factory—presumably to sell to a foreign power. The trial took less than ten minutes. His prison term—hard labor in a lignite mine at Várpalota—lasted three years and six months.

The Várpalota labor camp completed his political education. He established friendships with former members of the Arrow Cross, renegade Communists, Zionists, and other "enemies of the people." The camp attempted no political indoctrination because the prisoners there were said to be incorrigibles. "It was a good place to work if one was ready to work. The warden knew that his job depended on monthly production figures, and he would not meet these if he abused his prisoners," György recalled. "We captives organized the place, asking newcomers, 'Do you want to work your ass for money or get a comfortable place?' I chose the former. They paid us well. I was in excellent

43. A year later, the Zsohárs received a postcard from their older son, confirming that he was alive in a Russian prison. On it he had written, "Vote for the Communists." His father thought he had lost his mind, because the family had been disenfranchised for "fascist attitudes," but his mother realized that without that political plug he would not have been allowed to send the letter.

physical condition and could carry the world on my shoulders. I sent home over six thousand forints each month. We even had a football team, like a seminary." Each New Year's Eve the inmates routinely beat up the stool pigeons, but never killed them. It was like a ritual, and the warden did not intervene.

György's brother, János, had been a model prisoner in a Russian POW camp. Cleansed of fascist contamination, he remained in the army when he came back to Hungary, and became a professor at the artillery school, where he specialized in antiaircraft weaponry. In 1954 he visited György in prison. When this was reported to his superiors, he was discharged from the army. It was customary for discharged officers to receive six months' mustering-out pay. János received nothing. An intelligence officer told him, "Now you can visit your brother."[44]

Released just before the 1956 revolution against the Soviets, György joined a committee of former political prisoners that had seized control of the Ministry of Interior on Andrássy Street. They held the building until the arrival of Russian tanks. Then they scattered. Most of his companions fled to Austria, but György remained in Hungary because his parents stubbornly refused to accept exile, and he knew that if he went, he would never see them again. Earlier his mother had narrowly escaped a prison term when an informer reported she had once declared, "I wish the Germans had won, not these barbarians." (At her trial, to the consternation of the judge, she did not deny the accusation.)

Because of the logjam in the courts following the 1956 revolt, two years passed before the police hammered at his door. He was charged with complicity in the counterrevolution and held for investigation for five months in the Fő Street prison. In itemizing his political crimes, a prosecutor included his incarceration at Várpalota—"that breeding ground for dedicated fascists." (György said he took this as a compliment.) Since it was impossible to jail every Hungarian who had taken part in the 1956 rising, he was released in 1959. After this he was an untouchable so far as clerical or factory work was concerned. His marriage fell apart. Eventually he found a job as a stone-worker near Tök and spent his weekends cultivating the family vineyard. In Hungary, as elsewhere, death pays a good wage, so he specialized in cutting tombstones, which involved large tips—money not recorded and therefore not taxed. By this time his health had broken down: the mine had ruined his

---

44. Some years later, János entered the technical university, received a degree, and became a professor of engineering.

lungs, as well as his legs, which, after long years in the mine shoveling dirt on his knees, he could barely bend.

In the 1980s György established contact with the Waffen SS veterans' organization, and he now attends their reunion each year near Klagenfurt in Austria. He explains, "I live for irony, humor, and once a year to see my German friends." What were the Waffen SS? "We were soldiers, not murderers." He tells me that the Bonn government now pays a pension of 160 deutsche marks per month to Hungarians who had been drafted into the SS. Dozens of these veterans live in the nearby villages. He shrugs and laughs as he says, "I volunteered. I get nothing. It's not important. In 1944 the Hungarian government promised a land grant of five *holds* [about seven acres] for each soldier destroying a Russian tank. A friend of mine destroyed two tanks, and he is still waiting for the land."

György's study is crammed with books written in German and Hungarian—much of it military history but also translations of modern American writers, like John Updike and Ernest Hemingway. In his bookcase there are two pictures of himself. One is a framed picture of a curly-haired smiling youth of seventeen wearing a wing collar; the other is a recent photograph of himself, an adult with a broken face kissing the door of the inn at Braunau-am-Inn where Adolf Hitler was born. He keeps this picture prominently displayed to goad police when they periodically arrive to search his house. "I am partly to blame for being persecuted by the regime. I always have said what I thought." Nothing better measures the bitter distortions that have characterized the past half century of Hungarian history than this picture. For György its display has less to do with glorifying Hitler than with demonstrating his contempt for the Communists.

In 1989 György escorted me on a tour of his hillside vineyard and pointed out a mature fir tree, somehow out of place among the network of vines. After a firefight in February 1945 a Soviet soldier crawled to the vineyard to die. His parents buried the man and erected a wooden cross over the grave, but some Russians came along, kicked over the cross, and chopped it up for firewood. On the site the Zsohárs planted the fir tree. While we talked, György's wife drove in. She had been shopping at the market in Zsámbék, and she said that Russian soldiers who were evacuating an army base nearby were selling automatic pistols, rifles, machine guns, and even small missiles to Hungarian civilians in the square. She said this trafficking had been going on for several weeks. It was illegal, but the Russians would do anything for money. From a lorry privates in ill-fitting yellowish uniforms were handing out the weapons, while their officers collected the money, waving off photographers with a menacing "Nyet!" Forty-five years after coming into Hungary, the Russians were at long last taking their departure, not as liberators and conquerors, but as seedy hucksters peddling junk iron from a cart.

CP

From his earliest years József Borus had been taught that inherited rank and social privilege were intolerable in any decent civilized society. He grew up in Kisújszállás, a small town in eastern Hungary, where his father, a smith by trade, was a voluble and fearless spokesman for rights of the working class. The local gendarmerie had collected a thick dossier on József senior, but neither threats nor jail cells ever silenced this man, whom, despite their different political orientation, they could not help admiring. He was no screeching ideologue. Although he had put his life on the line many times for ideas he served, he worked steadily at his trade and never neglected the needs of his wife and five children.

At the age of twenty-one József senior had rallied to Béla Kun's call for a Hungarian soviet republic in 1919. For him it was axiomatic that Marxism was the only feasible way to reform a system that had pauperized the working classes and treated its farm laborers as little better than serfs. He served as an engineer aboard one of the armored trains that ranged the countryside, but he had no hand in the murders by the Red terrorists. Led by a gaggle of self-appointed martinets, the Red Army was easily routed by the Romanians. (Kun's minister of war was a former typewriter agent.) Borus was taken prisoner and held in a vast open-air pen in southern Hungary. When a typhoid epidemic raged through the camp, Borus decided he would rather be shot in the back than die of strangulation. He waited for a moonless night to walk out of camp, still in uniform, and then steered for Kisújszállás. On reaching home, he barely had time to grab a handful of food and shed his Red Army uniform (which his mother immediately buried) before a mounted patrol of Whites ranged through the village shanghaiing men for their army. Borus was drafted on the spot, but he refused to serve. He was jailed and could have been shot, but was instead expatriated to Vienna. He moved on—first to Bavaria, where he lived with a German sailor, and finally to Lyon, where he learned French and took a job in a foundry. He married and started a family.[45]

Unwilling to raise his children as French citizens, he returned to Hungary in 1928. He was arrested immediately for his part in the Béla Kun affair and

---

45. Borus interview.

spent half a year in the military prison at Martinka in eastern Hungary. Much to his amusement there was a rider tacked on to his sentence that stipulated that under no circumstances would be ever be permitted to serve in the Hungarian army. After his release he settled in his home village and opened a blacksmith shop. He raised chickens and hogs, grew great quantities of vegetables, and carefully supervised the education of his children. Several times he was arrested and held briefly on suspicion of being a Communist, but nothing was ever proved.

In 1938, when the army was reorganized, József senior, despite the proscription ten years earlier, was drafted into a battalion of ironworkers who were expanding the railways east of Budapest. (Many of these lines had been restricted to single tracks by terms of the Trianon Treaty, now ignored.) Discharged after one year, he went to work as one of the thirty thousand laborers at the Manfred Weiss factory on Csepel Island, where they produced every sort of metal object, from razor blades to Messerschmitt 109s. For the next four years he worked a ten- to twelve-hour shift, seven days a week. It was hard work, but the pay was good. He kept his family at Kisújszállás, where they were almost self-sufficient in food. Every second weekend he returned for a visit, pedaling three hundred kilometers by bicycle to save train fare.

When the Americans and British began bombing Hungarian targets on April 3, 1944, József senior took a week off from work to build a bomb shelter for his family. He warned them to stash away as much food as possible because he knew that the authorities would try to draft him again. In mid-April, after the first German occupation of Hungary, he went on record against further support of Nazi Germany. He was seized and taken up Sváb Mountain to the Majestic Hotel, the headquarters of a magyarized offshoot of the Gestapo, where he refused to retract his remarks or to serve in the army. For several weeks he was held in the cellar of the hotel and roughed up by guards. With him—although treated with velvet gloves—was Baron Móric Kornfeld, who was negotiating the contract that surrendered the Manfred Weiss factory complex to the SS in return for allowing the owners and other important Jewish families to escape to Portugal. For Borus this was just further evidence of how capitalism trafficked in human lives. When the Gestapo turned him over to local authorities at the Mosonyi Street prison, downtown, he was able to smuggle a note to his family. József junior at once cycled to Budapest but was not able to get past the guards and visit his father. "I was very naive. No one had ever told me that you were supposed to tip a jailer."

Along with other leftist prisoners József was taken to a huge concentration camp outside Nagykanizsa, near the Yugoslav border. He knew the Red Army was breaking through the Carpathians, and he wanted to be at home when the first Russians arrived to liberate his village. With his basic knowledge of Russian he knew that he could assist his townspeople in the transition to a democratic society. Undeterred by the smashed faces of prisoners who had tried to escape but had been caught by gendarmes, he planned to break out. Hoarding his small daily ration of food, he volunteered for harvest work at a nearby village, and marched off with thirty other prisoners and one armed guard. No one honed and swung a scythe more skillfully than József Borus, and he soon left the other harvesters far behind. Once out of sight he moved rapidly cross-country, holding onto his scythe so that, if detected, he could pass as a local worker. There was one bad moment at the Dunaújváros bridge, which was crawling with gendarmes, but he meandered south and found a fisherman who ferried him across the Danube and asked no questions. By landmarks he recognized this spot as the same place where he had crossed the river after escaping from the Romanians twenty-five years before. It was a good omen. He covered the three hundred kilometers to Kisújszállás in ten days. In his stable he built a false wall as a hiding place but never had to use it. On one occasion the gendarmes came to his house for water and a smoke, but news of his escape apparently never reached them. The Hungarian gendarmerie wore jaunty cockades in their caps but were never celebrated for efficiency. Soon József was able to join other villagers in gathering the harvest.

Meanwhile his son József, just turned sixteen, had been called up for service in a labor battalion. With a local landowner's son he was trucked to Szolnok where he received an object lesson in social discrimination. After feeling calluses on his hands, the recruiting officer inducted him. But when the mother of a companion arrived and passed some jewelry to the officer, her son was dismissed because of "jaundice," or such was entered in the record book. For two months József cooked and poured asphalt at an airport under construction outside Szolnok. On September 5 a fleet of 150 Flying Fortresses caused great excitement when they tried to knock out the local railroad bridge, a major artery for the German retreat. "It was a thrilling spectacle, but when it was over, we found only one bomb had hit a trestle, and this was quickly repaired." On September 20 the Russian advance came so near that work on the airport was abandoned and the labor camp dissolved. József junior went home to witness, with his father, the long-awaited liberation of his town by the Russians.

Kisújszállás was liberated not once but several times because of a seesaw battle that raged through the town. The Borus family cottage lay on the Debrecen road and for a time was at the center of the fighting. The Russian First Army Group pushed out the Germans on October 8, but a fierce Axis panzer attack drove the Reds back. Looking out, József saw the road in front of their house flooded with Russians fleeing eastward on foot, on bicycles, and on all fours. Reinforcements then shoved the Germans back and blew up a Panther tank near their house. Only one German tanker survived. He climbed out, blackened by soot and with a shredded uniform. He hid in a wood until rooted out two days later by a Russian search party that flailed the undergrowth as though driving hogs. When asked whether he was Hungarian or German, he admitted the latter and was shot. (The tank remained where it was for many years, a favorite plaything for village children until finally broken up for scrap.) The Second Army Group, which finally occupied Kisújszállás, included natives of many Soviet republics, but they were kept under control by their officers. József senior was pleased with postwar developments, although he was too much his own man to cotton to the commissars. He had lived to see his political ideals vindicated, and he never doubted that the new regime, for all its flaws, was superior to what it replaced. His children were educated at levels formerly available only to the aristocracy or the bourgeoisie. He was especially proud when his son earned a doctoral degree in history and joined the staff of the National Historical Institute.

In 1990 József Borus junior took me on a tour of Kisújszállás. We drank coffee in the town hall with the mayor, and visited with a genial collection of aunts and cousins in long-galleried houses. We walked over to the Borus homestead, recently sold. Near the front gate his grandfather had stood next to a tin pail when the Russians opened their rocket attack on the town. A shell blew the pail to smithereens, but the old man was untouched. József pointed out the ditch where the tank exploded and the road used by the Russians and Germans in their attacks and counterattacks. His thoughts drifted to his father's experiences. In many ways he had led a charmed life. He had been captured by Romanians, exiled by the Whites, arrested more times than he could remember, and finally imprisoned for refusing military service—yet always he pulled through. The charm drained out in 1989. At the age of ninety he was living alone in his cottage when a Gypsy vagrant broke in, tied him to a chair, and cut his throat.

József Borus and György Zsohár first met in 1971 through a mutual friend, a teacher in Bicske who knew that both shared a consuming interest in the war years. At first, they circled one another warily, György bristling in the presence of any party functionary and trying to figure out this rare bird in his blue suit with his academic degrees, and József confronting in the flesh not only a self-proclaimed former fascist but one who had served in the SS and was proud of it. In 1971 there were thousands of former fascists in Hungary, but he had never met one brash enough to proclaim it eagerly. Yet their shared passion for all periods of Hungarian history provided the cement that bonded their friendship. When the police from the Ministry of Interior raided György's house and carried off his books and papers, József used his party connections to have them returned. Since György was forbidden to receive books from abroad, József received them through his channels at the institute and passed them on to his friend. At this time József was a reserve officer (a major) in the Hungarian army, and informers were legion. A general summoned him and warned that his career in the army and at the institute could be terminated if he consorted with the likes of such an incorrigible "enemy of the people." The general went on to ask what Zsohár had done during the 1956 revolution. Having scoured the military archives of that period, József knew all too well about the general's dubious equivocation during that epoch of Russian tanks and street fighting. "We'd better not speak of what Zsohár did in 1956 unless we speak of what you did." This shut down the general permanently.

In the late 1970s József needed 20,000 forints to negotiate the purchase of a Budapest flat. A rich aunt, who had squirreled away 100,000 forints in books and crannies of her home, had just died. He approached the heirs for a loan, and they offered him 500 forints. Disgusted by the stinginess of these relatives, he blurted out the story to György. The next day György took the train to Budapest, knocked unannounced on József's door, and handed him a packet containing 20,000 forints in cash. He said tips had been good in the gravestone trade that year. He refused a promissory note, and later, when József returned the money to him, he absolutely refused to accept interest. It was an altogether curious financial transaction, mirroring the chaotic social and economic ruptures of that period—the son of a kulak, himself reduced to manual labor, on his own volition turning over his money (much of it from an underground economy) to a white-collar party bureaucrat, whose father was working-class to the bone.

What is so striking about these two men is that although they can agree on practically nothing theoretical, they are the best of friends. Their debates, always held in the room above György's wine cellar, are interminable. György has a knack for cutting through professorial pontification, while József's forte is marshaling facts and figures that are irrefutable. The friction of their relationship is an object lesson in symbiosis: two dissimilar organisms in close association mutually nourishing each other. And one senses that if another hardheaded debater dared to intrude in their disputatious arena, he or she would be set upon by József and György in aggressive harmony, no matter what the outsider's political orientation might be.

Half a century ago millions of Józsefs and Györgys were toeing their respective lines in Hungary and throughout the world, devising ways of killing one another in the name of a "higher ideology." Better this sort of confrontation—two old men in an upper room breaking bread and drinking wine.

Fable

A favorite Hungarian story dating from the First World War was conveniently revised and edited for the Second. It seems there was a lonely Hungarian in a Russian POW camp deep in Siberia. Call him István. Out of desperation some men periodically escaped, knowing that they would be recaptured, but preferring the chase—no matter how dangerous—to the nothingness of camp nonexistence. Even in his deepest self István had not the slightest inclination for adventure. He wanted only to go back to his village, a place on the Great Hungarian Plain too small to attract the attention of mapmakers. Before being drafted into the Honvédség, he had grown peppers and tomatoes on a tiny plot of land. His worldly ambition was to grow tomatoes and peppers on the same small plot.

One day, while on a wood cutting detail in the forest, the Russian guard handed István a bucket and told him to fetch some water from a stream some kilometers away. He collected the water, but before he had traveled halfway back, he found the bucket empty. He examined it and found it had a tiny hole in the bottom. He filled the bucket again and this time walked as fast as he could on the trail leading back to the work party. Again the bucket was empty. Clearly, unless the bucket was repaired, he could not return with the water. He set out in the opposite direction. After a few kilometers he came to a small camp of Russian soldiers. They asked him what he wanted. He could see that they had no patches or solder with which he could repair the bucket, so he asked them for permission to fill his bucket from their tank. The soldiers gave István some bread, cheese, and cigarettes. The food and the cigarettes were better than anything he received at the camp. He continued walking, and when the sun set, it was in his face.

As the days, weeks, and months passed, István continued walking. Whenever stopped by policemen or soldiers, he showed them the empty bucket and told them he was carrying water to his work party. Nearly everywhere he stopped, people gave him food and cigarettes, and sometimes even vodka. The bucket was his passport. Without it he would have been picked up, jailed, maybe beaten. With it he could go anywhere and live off the fat of the land. No one cared where a man went who was carrying water to a work party. And the fact that the water soon drained out made his walking that much easier.

In the morning the sun was at his back. In the late afternoon it was in his face. He walked through Kharkov and Kiev, and then turned south toward Hungary. He walked past both sets of border guards and no one yelled or fired a shot. When he arrived home, the villagers were overjoyed to see him. Of all the men taken off by the Germans as conscripts or by the Russians as prisoners, István was the first to return home. Afraid of being rearrested, he never told anyone about his escape and always spoke kindly about the Russians. When the villagers saw the bucket with the hole in it, they could not understand why he carried such a useless object. The bucket leaked very slowly, and he used it when he watered his tomatoes and peppers. The villagers thought he was a little crazy—but perfectly harmless.

Index

Also by Cecil D. Eby

The Road to Armageddon: The Martial Spirit in English Popular Literature, 1870–1914

"That Disgraceful Affair": The Black Hawk War

Between the Bullet and the Lie: American Volunteers in the Spanish Civil War

The Siege of the Alcazar

A Virginia Yankee in the Civil War: The Diaries of David H. Strother

"Porte Crayon": The Life of David H. Strother

Printed in the United States
71950LV00004B/113

9 780271 032443